"Nothing Without Labour"

Northampton Saints-
the first 125 years

by Brian Barron

Acknowledgments

SOME time in 1990 I had the bright idea to write the history of Northampton Saints. I was at the time only a recent convert to watching rugby on a regular basis.

I found it incredibly rewarding. The Saints seemed to be a club going places and it was exciting.

In 1993 *Oh When the Saints* was published and as far as I was concerned that was it. The next history would not be written until well into the 21st Century.

Then alomg came professional rugby union and with it a whole new army of fans, not just for the Saints but to the entire game in Britain.

So much had happened since the 1993 publication that the decision to publish the history again 12 years later to mark 125 years since the club was formed was more than justified.

Researching those latter years was infinitely easier with extensive coverage in the media and, of course, the advent of the internet.

My thanks to all those who helped with the first book – they were acknowledged then, most notably Bob Taylor and Ian Watson, who had spent considerable time putting together the players' statistics and the club-by-club record, and Roy Gordon, who had been compiling Saints statistics for his personal satisfaction.

This time around the list is shorter. Stuart Farmer, the Premiership's official statistician, who I first met when he was press officer at Leicester Tigers, provided details of international careers and league records. He gave his time freely and willingly.

Keith Barwell enlightened me as to his reasons for investing so heavily in the Saints.

Roger Horwood was again my link with the 'Gang of Seven' that took control of the club in 1988 and gave birth to the vibrant Saints of the past 17 years.

Thanks to Nick Beal for writing the foreword. Nick was an ideal choice as he caught the tail-end of the amateur game and reaped the benefits of the professional era.

Caroline Moore, a far more efficient Saints press officer than I ever was, was able to shed light on the lifestyle of a professional player.

I spent many months delving through the pages of the *Chronicle & Echo* and two people especially were of great help – editor Mark Edwards, whose love of sport is reflected in the paper's excellent coverage, and librarian Jan Warren, who trawled the database for photographic images.

There were still many pictures to be scanned and that task was undertaken by my work colleague Louise Fry. My wife Julia, a passionate, utterly biased supporter, has been an invaluable proof reader as has Radio Northampton Saints commentator James Knight.

Sadly several giants of Northampton rugby have died since the first history was published, the likes of Jeff Butterfield, Ron Jacobs, Lewis Cannell, Roger Hosen, Ian Wright, George Adkins, Tommy Gray, Spriggs Baillon, Hector Woolnough and Peter Sweet.

They provided great memories for generations of Saints supporters. I hope this book helps to capture some of those moments.

This is definitely the last Saints history that I will be writing. I hope you enjoy it.

Brian Barron, June 2005

ISBN-10: 0-9551699-0-9

ISBN-13: 978-0-9551699-0-8

First published in Great Britain by: Northampton Saints

Designed by: Brian Barron
Pictures courtesy of: Chronicle & Echo, Tony Hardacre, Martin Lovatt, Louise Fry, Getty Images, Mark Thompson

Printed by: Avalon Print, Heathfield Way, Kings Heath, Northampton NN5 7QP

Contents

**Above: Founder
Rev Samuel Wathen Wigg
Below: Owner Keith Barwell**

Foreword

by Nick Beal
Northampton Saints, England, British Lions

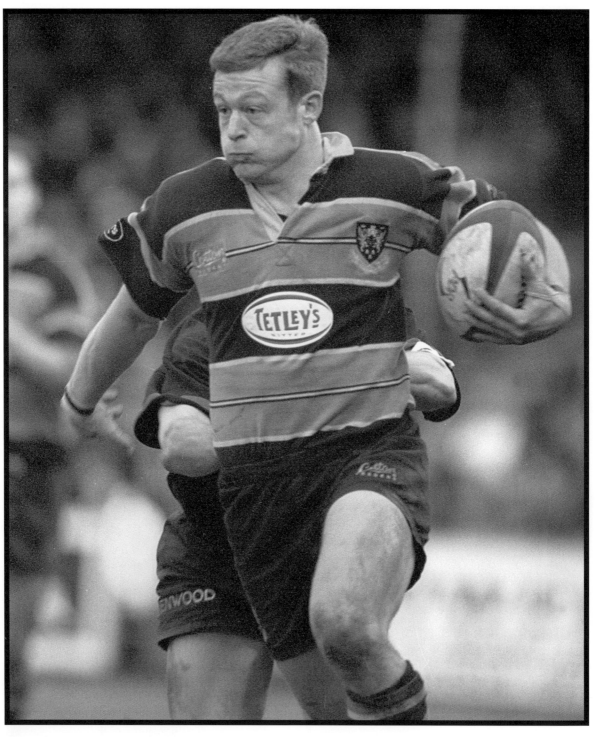

I N the words of Wayne Smith – your time in a Saints jersey is just a snapshot of history. It is not yours to own but merely to borrow and while you wear it you need to respect those who have worn it before you and enhance it while it is yours.

I have been lucky enough to wear the Saints jersey for 12 seasons and hope that during my tenure I have added to it and passed it on to the next bearer to wear with pride and add to the history of the famous black, green and gold.

There have been more changes in the last 12 years than the club has seen in its previous 112. We have experienced relegation, promotion, the introduction of professionalism, several near misses, a Heineken Cup win, a ground development and a whole host of English and international stars and world class coaches.

The stress and pain that went with relegation in 1995 was eased by the appointment of Ian McGeechan OBE who literally rebuilt the style and patterns of play during his five years at the club and it was a pity that he left the club a season too early to see the reward for all of those years of planning come to fruition in our Heineken Cup victory.

It was fairly inevitable that during Geech's time the club moved from the amateur to the professional era. It was not for everyone's taste but as a player it meant that you were able to fully prepare yourself and this change was crucial in the development of English rugby and its ability to compete with the Southern Hemisphere sides. I was thrilled to become a full-time sportsman and not have to try and juggle rugby with a career outside the game.

I did however benefit from my amateur days. With an alternative career to rugby already under my belt I was able to make the smooth transition back into financial services once my playing days ended.

I feel the Rugby Union and the clubs have a responsibility to the new generation of rugby player to make sure they are provided with the time and advice to prepare themselves for life beyond rugby as, with all good things, a professional rugby career doesn't last forever.

Professional rugby, although providing an unbelievable opportunity, also had it downsides. Having Tim Rodber shouting in your ear in the gym that you really can do another five reps and pain is only a figment of your imagination or Phil Pask announcing that that wasn't really the last two-minute run and we still had four more to do. Great fun!

Players have become quicker, fitter, bigger and stronger due to professionalism and I personally think this has improved the game from a players' and spectators' point of view. There is still the camaraderie that was always there and although the rewards are greater so is the pressure to perform both on and off the field.

No mention of professionalism can go by without mentioning Keith and Maggie Barwell. Without KB's generosity the club would undoubtedly not be in the strong position we see it today – a fantastic new stadium regularly being filled by 12,500 enthusiastic Saints fans who have continued to cheer on their team home and away through all the ups and downs.

In my early playing days I was lucky enough to play with Buck Shelford, one of the world's greatest players, and at that time probably the only overseas player to be found in the league.

How things have changed. I have played alongside great players from virtually every rugby playing nation including the likes of Pearce, Pagel, Lam, Mendez, Bateman, Blowers and Reihana and not forgetting my old mates Rodders, Hunts, Daws, Grase and, of course, Harvey.

Along with all the famous names who have come and gone, the club are lucky enough to have a wealth of individuals who provide the continuity needed to make sure the history and tradition associated with the jersey carries on with each new season.

I can honestly say that I have had a fantastic 12 years at the club and wouldn't change a thing (apart from a broken leg and smashed up face!) and look forward to bringing my family down to the Gardens to cheer on the future Saints.

Bealer

NICK BEAL
Northampton Saints
1992-2004
Appearances: 268
Tries: 74
Points: 482
England caps: 15
British Lions tourist
(to South Africa) 1997

Chapter One
Sporting vicar sets the ball rolling

THE birth of Northampton Saints in 1880 is credited to a former curate of St James Church, the Reverend Samuel Wathen Wigg, father of nine children. Originally called Northampton St James, the club was formed out of an improvement class, a latter-day youth club.

Rugby was still in its infancy as a sport, having originated at Rugby School 40 years earlier and for only 17 years had there been a distinction between Association football and Rugby football.

Long before Reverend Wigg's death, he was to see his idea grow into one of the foremost rugby clubs in the country. From that early team emerged men of vision and ambition, most notably the first long-serving secretary, Albert E Orton. The boys played wherever they could find a field, and that added up to quite a few in the early years.

Much the same thing was happening in other parts of the town, including the pleasure gardens in St James, part zoo, part recreation ground and a social focal point for families at the weekend with its herbaceous borders, bandstand and lake. In the centre of the gardens was a football pitch. A team called Unity played at the Gardens, containing several members of the Kingston family, a splendid Victorian sporting dynasty.

The gardens, originally known as Melbourne Gardens, were created by John Collier, and after his death in 1886 they were bought by John Franklin, a successful hotelier. The following year he renamed them, Franklin's Gardens. Two years later, in 1888, they were put up for auction but were sold privately for £17,000 to the Northampton Brewery Company.

The company started making extensive improvements. New features included a running track, bicycle track, cricket ground, swimming pool, bear pit, a large ornamental lake, an improved monkey house and a larger zoological garden.

The Gardens were especially popular on bank holidays. An advertisement in a Theatre Royal programme dated 1888, announced that entertainment planned for Whitsun was high trapeze and horizontal bar acts, dancing on the lawn, brass band concerts in the Jubilee Hall, an "Ascent of monster Fire Balloons", firework displays and illumination of the lake with "Prismatic fires". Admission

The Reverend Samuel Wathen Wigg, a sporting clergyman and father of nine children, who is credited with the birth of the Saints during his time at St James Church

was 6d (two and a half pence).

Franklin's Gardens was described as the "Champs Elysees of Northampton", trams ran from the town centre every few minutes for a penny.

Before Franklin arrived on the scene, the trams ran only as far as what was then known as Cafe Square, the intersection of Harlestone Road and Weedon Road. He soon realised that more people would frequent the pleasure gardens if trams ran right to the entrance and he paid for the lines to be extended.

Details of the earliest years of the St James rugby team are only sketchy. No records exist between 1880 and 1894. Archive material from that period was apparently lost in a fire at the Black Lion pub in St Giles Street in 1931, then run by Edward Shadrach Dunkley, one of the original members of the team.

Informed history on the club starts from 1895 thanks

The earliest team pictures still in existence. The one above is from 1884. Back row (left to right): A Orton, H Dunkley, A Timms, G Bradbury, Herbert Dunkley, T Griffiths, F Goodson, A Williams, G Stanley, W Blackwell, J Facer (E Bradbury is pictured extreme right back row but has not stood the test of time). Front row: T Facer, C Parr, A Fitch, C Stanley, F Stanley, T Stanley, F Timms.

The picture (right) was taken in 1886. Back row (left to right): C Stanley, T Stanley, T Griffiths, C Parr, J Barker. Middle row: A Orton, F Timms, E Jesson, E Bradbury, A Timms, H Dunkley. Front row: E S Dunkley, A York

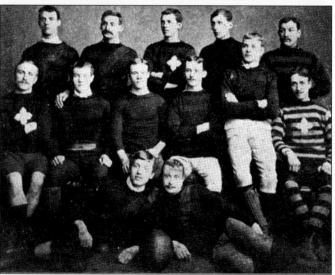

to scrapbooks kept by Tommy Mitton, who covered the team from that year until his death in 1943 for the local press. Details of the early days come from various accounts in later years by men such as Wigg himself, who played for 18 months during his time as curate from 1878 to 1880, and some of those early pioneers like Orton and Dunkley.

Wigg was described as "having a broad frame, which enshrined a character full of broad sympathies, which never harboured any narrowness or pettiness in his public or private life amid which he lived like some modern vicar of Wakefield, beloved by all for the transparent sincerity with which he could share the sorrows and joys of others."

He died in August, 1934, and a three-column obituary in the *Northampton & County Independent*, said: "To those who were familiar with his ruddy, bearded face and burly form, appearing all the bigger in his flowing clerical cloak, it is difficult to realise when he first came to Northampton he was, to use his own typically candid confession, a pale, callow curate."

His contribution was never forgotten and in 1927 he was invited back to Northampton as guest speaker at the club's dinner along with Adrian Stoop, the former England player and then secretary of Harlequins.

He recalled to an audience of around 100: "I put up a notice that I would meet them and try to form an

improvement class. After a time there came a great bang at the door and eight or 10 boys tumbled into the room.

"I sat quite still and that put them about. I said to them: 'Go out and come in as you should do' and they did. I never had the slightest trouble about discipline afterwards. We began the class with 10 boys and in less than two years we had over 100."

They came up with a motto: *'Nil sine labore – Nothing Without Labour'*.

Wigg continued: "The energy of this class was remarkable – we held a general weekly meeting which initiated and controlled all the branches which grew out of it. The class was arranged on Masonic lines, each officer had his fixed place and in the opening ceremony gave an account of his duties.

"It was from this central body that the branches were formed and to which they had to report – perhaps this class will best be remembered by one of its branches – the football club, still going strong under its old name, The Saints Football Club."

Not surprisingly those knockabout matches went unreported in the Northampton media even though the town had two daily newspapers and two weeklies.

They were not so obsessed with sports coverage, save for horse racing (the Derby was by then already 100 years old and the Grand National 40 years old).

A fascinating glimpse of a bygone era. The pleasure gardens, known as Melbourne Gardens, before they were bought by John Franklin. The drawing is from 1867 and (below) families enjoying the gardens

Football – of both codes – merited only the odd paragraph.

Wigg described those early matches: "The one rule we had was to kick the ball whenever we could. We put our pennies together and bought goalposts and little flags for the corners of the field.

"If there was a dispute we talked things over on the field and settled the matter. We had no gate money and the only spectators were four or five cows, who did not take much interest in the game."

By the time Wigg gave his 1927 speech, the Saints had produced six internationals, but the clergyman was alarmed by the influence of commercialism creeping into the game, a comment greeted with loud applause.

"The playing of the game," said Wigg, "was far more important than money. When there was too much emphasis placed on the money side crowds lost their heads, referees nearly lost their lives, and an excitement prevailed which was unnatural."

His summed up his philosophy with a poem.

"Play the game as a sportsman should
Remember that life is but a span
It's up to us all to be cheerful and good;
And make life as bright as we can"

The first man to 'coach' the team was a currier by the name of Jimmy Rosedale, who also refereed a lot of those early matches, regularly interrupted by peacocks strutting across the pitch. The first 'proper' match is generally accepted to be against a team known as the Star, made up of boys from the rough Bailiff Street area. It was played on Northampton Racecourse on a snow-covered pitch but no record exists of the score. One Jim Barker was the first captain of St James.

Home matches began in Abbey Fields, next door to

3

Impressive Saints programmes from 1895/96 (top) and 1900/01 (above). Llwynypia Football Club toured the Midlands in 1898 to play Leicester on Boxing Day and the Saints the following day. The side from Tonypandy drew 0-0 at Leicester and lost 5-0 to the Saints. Left: A Bedford programme from 1898, the return fixture that season in which the Saints did the double over their old rivals, 19-0 and 12-3.

Franklin's Gardens where houses now stand on the old Express Lifts site.

Among the local opposition were Anchor, All Saints and St Michael's and by far the strongest of all, Unity, an amalgamation of several teams, the Scorpions, Northampton Rugby Club (not to be confused with the Saints) and the Wanderers. While Northampton St James had been formed for ruffians, Unity had its roots in a much higher social strata. Players included James Manfield, the mayor, whose brother Harry was a Member of Parliament, and solicitor T H 'Tubby' Vials, who was later secretary of Northamptonshire County Cricket Club.

Unity and St James, known from the outset as the Jimmies, held a meeting on September 9, 1887, to consider the possibility of creating a "thoroughly representative town club."

Unity brought a four-strong deputation to a packed meeting and pointed out all the advantages such a merger would create. The idea carried little weight at the time with the James boys, perhaps fearing they would be smothered by their social superiors, and it took four more years before the clubs did join forces under the banner of Northampton St James Football Club.

On November 22, 1890, St James played St Michael's, described as the town's two principal clubs, attracting an estimated 2,000 spectators, "whose conduct was most objectionable."

Two months earlier the club had held a trial game "between the first fifteen and the next twenty". The game introduced another member of the famous Kingston family to the Northampton sporting public, W H 'Billy' Kingston.

A newspaper described the young Kingston as "likely to prove as good a player as his brothers. He runs fast and dodges well, whilst once or twice he passed the ball very well indeed."

Kingston was to become captain in 1895 and continued until 1904 except for one season. From the 1895/96 season until the Second World War, Thomas Wrighton Mitton, of Garrick Road, Northampton, covered virtually every match, and glued each report into a scrapbook.

Mitton covered the Saints right up until his death, despite a series of heart attacks, for many years under the pseudonym of 'Reynard'.

His only child was christened with the initials NFC, Norah Frances Charlotte. Miss Mitton used to sit next to the press box at Franklin's Gardens for many years, while Tommy's younger brother Frank took handwritten copy to the Echo offices on his bicycle, the deadline being whatever time he got there.

Altogether Mitton spent 57 years in journalism and wrote every word in long hand. The reports were prodigious in length. In the early years Mitton's opinion piece at the end of a match report ran almost to the same length as the reports. Mitton became a father figure to many of the players and was sympathetic towards them and the club but he was never afraid to criticise.

Mitton played a large part in the formation of the *Football Echo*, which lasted as a Saturday sports paper until 1992. The club's history up until the Second World War is almost exclusively based on Mitton's scrapbooks.

The most significant piece of Mitton's first season's journalism appeared on October 12, 1895, originally a blank date in the fixture list. The committee arranged a match with newly-formed Bedford Wanderers and used the opportunity to blood some youngsters, among them Henry Thomas Franklin Weston, who would go on to become the first Saint to play for England. Saints lost 7-5, and Weston, a farmer from Yardley Gobion, did not receive a single mention.

The Northampton men were " disappointing in the

Twenty years into existence and the Saints are beginning to look like forerunners of today's superstars. This is the 1900/01 side that included W G Grace Jnr (fifth left back row), son of the great England cricketer. The others are (back row, left to right): C J Stanley (treasurer), A E Orton (secretary), W Patrick, H T Weston, W Brown, W West, E S Dunkley (financial secretary). Front row: C Naylor, C Leigh, H Atterbury, W H Kingston, J M West, A Chalmers, H E Kingston. On ground: F Simmonds, G Burke

Pillars of the establishment, photographed in Swansea in 1909 in the picture (left) are star players Edgar Mobbs (front left) and Joe Beasley (standing behind him) with Albert Orton (centre), A Dunham (behind), whose company built the first stand at the Gardens for £45 and another player R Harrison. In the other picture is Tommy Mitton, who covered the Saints for over 40 years in the local press

extreme. Had a racehorse exhibited such a reversal of form in so short a period (they had been to Leicester the previous week and lost narrowly 3-0), there would have been a jockey club enquiry, and perhaps a warning off."

In another game with Bedford, the official, Mr Geoffrey Marks, of the London Association, came in for a lot of criticism. There were no holds barred – "Mr Marks allowed Bedford a try, which was scored from a palpable knock on…it was not surprising that the seven hundred Northampton supporters were thoroughly disgusted with the performance…it is doubtful whether anyone, beside himself, was satisfied with the manner with which he performed his duties…it is rare that an official so thoroughly succeeds in giving offence. There was a strong and regrettable demonstration of feeling against him at the close of play."

The following week the paper asked: "…is it true that Mr Marks went to Bedford under the impression that he was to be referee in an Association match, and that when he found the game was under rugby rules he said he thought he could manage to referee, as he had seen one rugby match previously." Caustic comment or fact?

All that was forgotten four days before Christmas on a dank, foggy afternoon with the return visit of Leicester. It was described as "the most anticipated game in the history of local football." Some 7,000 shivering fans, who were hardly able to see a thing in the last 20 minutes, witnessed a Saints win, 11-8.

It was suggested that there had rarely been a more enthusiastic crowd and "had the day only been clear, so that play could have been followed more closely, the shouting would have been heard for miles around."

In March there was a deciding rubber. Leicester, having been knocked out of the Midland Counties Cup by Moseley, had a free date as did the Saints. The Saints won 5-4. There were around 5,000 fans inside Franklin's Gardens, who were kept hanging around until 4pm as two of the Leicester players were late turning up. The ground was wet and a gale blowing, so the delay caused considerable annoyance. The fans were appeased by the arrival of the Temperance Silver Band, who stepped in at the last minute to provide some pre-match entertainment.

The following season it was planned to strengthen the fixture list and Mitton warned: "…seeing the way in which some of the larger clubs sap the strength of smaller ones by obtaining the services of the best men they can find in them, it behoves the officials of the smaller organisations to stop this as much as possible."

The 1896/97 season was remarkable as in 17 of the last 22 games, the opposition failed to score and only 93 points were conceded in the entire campaign.

A new stand was built by Mr A Dunham's building company, 45 feet long and costing £45 5s. It was carpeted and reserved for members paying 10s 6d (52p) for season tickets – ladies five shillings (25p).

A member was defined as: "a past player, a present player, or a present official, whose subscription is not in arrears, and who has been proposed, seconded and carried at a committee meeting."

Over the Christmas period the side played four times, from Boxing Day to December 31. Against Buckinghamshire on the 28th, P H Cave suddenly departed the field with 20 minutes to go. It transpired he had a train to catch to London, which begs the question why he was picked in the first place, although resources must have been stretched pretty thin. The club would also have been saving its best players for the match on the following day, the first ever against Harlequins. The crowd was estimated at an unlikely 10,000.

Quins were on the third leg of a Midlands tour, having beaten Coventry and drawing with Leicester. The Saints also looked set for defeat, trailing 3-0 at half-time. But they took a 6-3 lead in the second half only for Quins to draw level near the end. Saints won eight of the next nine meetings – the other being drawn – until Quins got off the mark in 1909/10.

This was a time when certain clubs were elitist in the extreme. Northampton St James were striving for recognition nationwide and the game with Quins was part of that process. In March 1897 came another breakthrough. Coventry finally agreed to give Northampton a game on condition that they received half the gate money. The sides had, in fact, met before, in 1893, Coventry winning easily and remaining somewhat aloof after that.

Saints took their revenge by winning 3-0 and continued to do so for the next five seasons, home and away. The Saints strung together 10 victories until an 8-3 reverse in 1903.

Before the game a cocky set of Coventry players were heard to remark "that they would show Northampton how to play." On losing, they contented themselves with remarking "that Northampton would stand no chance if they entered the Midland Cup competition."

Just over a month later, Leicester were beaten 15-11 and the passions which have been such a feature of this local derby over the years were very much to the fore. The Leicester press took defeat badly. In the *Leicester Daily Post*, the rugby writer commented bitterly: "Football enthusiasm in Northampton runs at white heat, and if the Saints had not won on Saturday, the weeping and wailing of their supporters would have been deep and long. This is but natural, seeing that they are but young at football. The enthusiasm of youth is always strong, often headstrong, but age and experience beget wisdom, and there is yet hope for Northampton. A halo always surrounds a young and rising team, but sooner or later the brightness will be eclipsed, and then bitter will be the disappointment."

In April 1897 it was unanimously decided at a meeting at the Grand Hotel to ask the Rugby Union to sanction the formation of the East Midlands Rugby Union to comprise Northamptonshire, Bedfordshire, Buckinghamshire and Leicestershire. Alan Ingram, secretary of Bedford, said it was certain the new district would contain the first three counties but was not sure about Leicester. He was right.

Saints officials were not only progressive, they were generous. Following the win over Leicester, the Saints entertained Portsmouth with all proceeds going to Northamptonshire County Cricket Club.

Saints skipper Billy Kingston and his brother H E (Tim) were key players in the county's struggle for first class cricket status. Three thousand fans paid to see the match, forgoing their normal privileges, and saw the Saints win 3-0.

The 1897/98 season was only two weeks old when controversy flared as the Welsh Rugby Union declined to sanction the transfer to the Saints of Frank Simmonds and S Catley from Abercarn.

It was decided not to play them because to defy the Welsh was to risk losing the forthcoming fixtures against Abercarn, Swansea and Mountain Ash. The Welsh eventually climbed down in time for the men to play against Olney on October 16.

Catley had just the one season, making 29 appearances, but Simmonds became a star of the side, playing 166 times and scoring 107 tries, amassing 581 points in all.

The intense rivalry between the Saints and Leicester made for a 12,000 gate at Welford Road on November 6 and Northampton's 10-0 defeat led to the production of a mourning card which read:

IN MEMORY OF THE
NORTHAMPTON F.C.
Who perished after a 'Severe Mauling'
by
THE "LEICESTER TIGERS",
SATURDAY, OCT. 6th, 1897.
GAME TO THE "LAST".

The fans got so carried away with victory, they

Mourning cards produced by Leicester and Saints fans in the 1897/98 season underlining the intense, but good natured rivalry that quickly developed between the clubs

managed to put the wrong date, October 6 instead of November 6, on the card.

Revenge came just two weeks later, the Saints winning the return 16-8. More guesswork put the Gardens crowd as high as 15,000, and such was the confidence of winning that retaliatory mourning cards were prepared in advance and sold to fans even as they left the ground.

The two Saints heroes were Billy Kingston, who had missed the match at Leicester through injury, and Simmonds. Kingston scored three of four tries, while Simmonds cut through the Leicester defence time and again with surging runs.

The after-match scenes were euphoric – and chaotic. "Never has such a scene been witnessed in St James' End as that which was witnessed at the conclusion of the game. Right from Franklin's Gardens to the clubhouse, the Green Man, there was a dense crowd of enthusiasts, who cheered heartily the Northampton men as they proceeded to the dressing room, and a section of whom gave a childish exhibition by hooting the Leicester players. Outside the clubhouse there was a struggling mass of humanity, swaying to and fro, and vehicular traffic was carried on with only the greatest difficulty. On all hands congratulations were showered on the Northampton men on their achievements."

The mourning card produced in Northampton was of an infinitely superior design.

Secretary Orton sent out a novel 1897 Christmas card, the Saints fixture list for the following season, bound in black and green ribbon, all part of the flair that stamped him as the first real driving force behind the Saints. Born in 1864, he was 14 when Wigg started the club. A fine all-round sportsman, Orton captained the side for three seasons between 1889 and 1903. He started his first stint as secretary in 1886 and for 40 years held an official position at the club.

Albert's dad, Alfred, a dairy farmer and a leading member of the Conservative Party in the St James area, was one of the first to help the newly-formed rugby club by loaning them the use of a field. Orton's background suggests he was a cut above the ordinary working class lads and he was also above the ordinary as a sportsman. He was one of the top sprinters in the town and used that speed to be a prolific try-scorer in those early years.

NUNN, BROWNE & CO
For COALS,
21, ABINGTON STREET.
—SEASON 1897-8.—
East Midlands Football Union.
Official Match Card, 1d

Published by Authority of the Northampton Rugby F.C. by W. BILLINGHAM & SON,
THE BRIDGE STREET PRINTING WORKS, NORTHAMPTON.

THE GROSE GEAR CASE, Ltd.
63, GOLD STREET, NORTHAMPTON.
THE LARGEST STOCK OF CYCLES
IN THE MIDLAND COUNTIES.
ACCESSORIES OF EVERY DESCRIPTION IN STOCK
REPAIRS Executed on the Premises by Skilled Workmen.

The stylish programme for the first ever East Midlands game against Kent on November 3, 1897

In 1899 Orton proposed at the club's annual meeting that the words 'St James' be removed from Rule 1, so making the club's name: Northampton Football Club.

Orton argued that 'St James' smacked of a junior club and he was also anxious that no other club adopted the name Northampton. He pointed out that the soccer team, formed on March 6, 1897, at a meeting in the Princess Royal pub on Wellingborough Road, were already called Northampton, and it appears from newspaper reports that English RFU secretary Rowland Hill played some part in getting the Cobblers to add the word 'Town' to their name.

Orton finished playing in 1896, by which time he had already been secretary for eight of the previous 10 years. He continued as secretary, match secretary or both until the outbreak of the First World War, and in 1919 he thought he had done enough. However, he was coaxed into giving two more years' service and retired in 1922, having been involved in arranging every Saints fixture since the start.

He was asked to accept a testimonial in recognition of his services but flatly refused, remarking that all the work had been a pleasure and that the position the club held in the rugby world was ample reward. He was made a life member in 1905.

Orton was one of those who realised early on that if the Saints were to be one of the top clubs in the country, they could not simply rely on local talent.

In business, Orton worked for Northampton Brewery Ltd, starting as a clerk and ending as manager for the Stony Stratford area. Gardening was his hobby with a passion for spring onions, which regularly took top honours at the Stony Working Men's Club annual shows. He died of pneumonia on February 15, 1924, at the age of 60.

If the Leicester fixtures were grudge matches, the trip to Harlequins, whose ground in those days was in Catford, was the social trip of the season. An estimated 2,000 made the journey in a fleet of trains laid on from Castle Station. Fans were intent on enjoying themselves in the traditional manner, being well armed with jugs of beer and bottles of whisky – all of which was needed in celebration of an 18-3 victory.

The season ended with another win over Leicester and a final points record of 653-73, an all-time high for any club in England.

The Saints again showed their generosity towards the cricket club by donating all the proceeds from the Bedford match. Unfortunately, it was a gesture that often seemed to be dogged by bad weather.

A snowstorm the previous year had restricted the crowd against Burton Albion to under 1,000, and after expenses just £6 was paid over to the county. In the circumstances, the Saints gave the cricketers a choice: a guaranteed £10 or the proceeds from the Bedford game. They chose the latter and they struck lucky. The weather was beautiful and the match was watched by 3,000 spectators.

Problems with the Welsh Rugby Union arose for the second successive season – this time over a T Barnfield from Crumlin. The Saints defied the Welsh and played Barnfield, although to preserve their fixtures with the Principality he was left out of the Welsh games.

A 3-0 victory over Richmond was another feather in the club's cap. Richmond belonged to the snobby London set and had previously wanted nothing to do with Midland upstarts like Northampton. Now with Harlequins and Richmond on board that left only Blackheath and London Scottish to be won over.

On the first-ever Easter tour in 1899, 18 players, including three guests, made the trip. Although beaten in both games, at Gloucester and Swansea, the Saints won new friends. Swamped 34-3 at Swansea, the Saints were nevertheless loudly cheered and apparently responded in song:

'Then what care I, let the world go by
'Tis better far to laugh than cry'

At the end of the season the players were urged to devote more time to training, "a feature which has been sadly neglected. Men ought to have sufficient pride in their own reputation and the reputation of the club to keep themselves in condition, and that is more than some have done."

The Saints saw in the 20th century with a mundane game against Old Merchant Taylors. Celebrations were muted as the newspapers were full of reports from South Africa, where the Boers were being fought. Interest in rugby was lukewarm and some clubs went to the wall. At Northampton attendances slumped but good housekeeping meant the club had built up a healthy balance to keep them ticking over.

Dwindling support may possibly explain the decision to put up the admission price for the Leicester game from threepence to sixpence, a 100 per cent rise that understandably caused anger from the Gardens faithful. The game ended 3-3 and not only did the fans have to pay double they were short-changed, the game ending early because darkness was rapidly descending.

The Saints were winning their prestige battle, and another barrier was broken down with the first match against 'formidable' Cambridge University. It was seen as a shop-window game: do well against the Light Blues and maybe "Blackheath and London Scottish would descend from the high pinnacle on which they have placed themselves." The students, having won six games in a row without conceding a single point, were 15-0 too good for the Saints.

In the summer of 1899, a 21-strong touring Great Britain rugby party included Blair Inskip Swannell from Northampton. Under the captaincy and management of the Reverend Matthew Mullineux, the party played four tests against Australia, losing the first but winning the next three. Swannell, born in 1875, was a Saints forward and described as being of independent means, which went a long way towards being selected. He missed the first test but played in all the victories as a second row forward.

Five years later Swannell returned with the 'Darkie' Bedell-Sivright side, which played 'internationals' in Australia and New Zealand. Swannell, now listed in the back row, played in all four matches. The three in Australia were won, the one in New Zealand lost. In a 16-0 win in Sydney, Swannell scored one of the two tries.

Described as a tough, courageous forward with outspoken opinions, he had formed friendships with some of the Australian players and settled in New South Wales, joining a club in Sydney. On September 2, 1905, Swannell played for Australia against the All Blacks in Dunedin. The All Blacks won 14-3.

Known as 'Blair I', he was not everyone's cup of tea. His rugged tackling did not go down well with the New Zealanders, who criticised his over-vigorous play. Apparently he disarmed them by replying in verse.

Schoolboys used to be in awe of him as he ran out to referee their games wearing his British Isles blazer.

Some of his playing contemporaries, among them Dr Herbert Moran, the first Wallabies captain, despised him. Moran said of him: "Swannell was for a number of years a bad influence in Sydney football. His conception of football was one of trained violence. He kept himself in perfect condition, and this alone enabled him to conceal his slowness on the field. He used to teach schoolboys all sorts of tricks and tactics that were highly objectionable. In appearance he was extremely ugly, but he could talk his face away in half an hour."

In 1906, after a punch-up in a match between NSW and Queensland, the referee sent off Swannell. The NSW players knew the referee had dismissed the wrong man but nobody came forward on his behalf at an inquiry held in Sydney, and he was suspended for a month. When Swannell went to New Zealand with the Australians, none of his team-mates reacted when he was kicked in the face by a New Zealander in retaliation to Swannell's rough-house tactics.

At the outbreak of First World War, Swannell joined the AIF, and became a major in command of a battalion that landed at Gallipoli. He was killed leading a charge on Anzac Day, April 25, 1915.

There was a rumour that he was shot by one of his own men, but Moran dismissed that as a canard. "It was always expected of a Roman Emperor that he should die on his feet," Moran wrote. "Swannell, no doubt, thought a footballer should die following on."

These are the Weston Turks made up of Saints players from the 1897/98 season. The origins of the side are not known but perhaps it was a Saints Fun XV. The players are (back row left to right): L Taylor, A Smith, W Patrick, F Simmonds, J F Stops, H E Kingston, A Baxter. Front row: E S Dunkley, R P Swannell, B I Swannell, A E Orton, H Soames. On ground: S Catley, A Hannen

Chapter Two
Harry Weston – first of many

WITH the Saints now meeting and beating some of the best in the country, it was no surprise when a player was picked to don the white shirt of England.

Harry Weston played just one international – against Scotland at Blackheath (an 18-3 defeat) on March 9, 1901 – but it was to be the start of a long and illustrious list, all honoured on the walls of the Sturtridge Pavilion. Weston, a home grown player, would later captain the side, serve on the committee and become president. His son Billy went on to even greater heights, playing 16 times for England at blindside wing forward and regarded as one of the club's pre-war greats.

The Weston family have a superb collection of memorabilia: pictures, caps and jerseys. The only thing missing is Harry's England cap.

It would be eight years before Edgar Mobbs became the club's second international.

By now Northampton's success had made them a target for rugby league clubs. A promising centre, C Civil was lured to Oldham, the first recorded defection to the paid ranks seven years after the League broke away.

The club hit a player crisis towards the end of the season and a couple of Coventry men were drafted in. It was lamented that no-one from the club's A team, made up of local talent, was considered good enough to step up.

A famous name made 18 appearances in three seasons between 1900 and 1903, that of W G Grace, eldest son of *the* W G. To avoid confusion he carried *Jnr.* after his name.

He made his debut for the Saints against his old university, Cambridge on November 10, 1900, which the Light Blues won 10-8. A second row forward in the same burly build as his legendary cricketing father, Grace scored two tries during his brief spell. An assistant master at Oundle School, he played for the East Midlands and for the school (against the Saints). Two years after playing his last game for the Saints, he died, following an operation for appendicitis. He was buried at Elmers End Road cemetery and was followed there 10 years later by the great man himself. Grace Junior was just 30 years old.

Grace Senior was a great friend of the Kingston family and stayed at Abington House School whenever Gloucestershire CCC were in town. Grace offered a shilling for any boy who could bowl him out in the school playground and George Herbert Kingston, one of nine nine brothers and three sisters, whipped one through W G's defences. In later years Kingston modestly claimed that the ball had probably pitched on a pebble. Other Kingstons, apart from Billy and Tim, also played rugby, but this would almost certainly have been with Unity before the almalgamation

Billy's son, John, said of his father. "He enjoyed cricket more but reckoned he was a better rugby player. He was very quick off the mark and knew when to retire when he was was tackled from behind – it had never happened before."

A sports outfitter in the town, who used to advertise on the front of Saints fixture cards, Billy was not the greatest businessman, according to his son. He was far more interested in sport.

Said John: "My father was a very kind man. Kids would run up to him when he turned up for a game. He would let one lad hold his bag and another his

Harry Weston, fifth from the left back row, in the England line-up, the first Saint to be picked for his country. The cap he won is missing from the family collection

boots so they could get in for nothing."

Billy was named after his father, who had been a farmer in his native Lincolnshire. The story goes that he taught himself Greek and Latin, while ploughing the fields. William Senior was founder and principal of Abington House School and eight of the sons played for Northamptonshire County Cricket Club, notably Billy and Tim, the two youngest.

Billy was at the non-striker's end when Northamptonshire made their debut in the County Championship on May 18, 1905, partnering George Thompson, who had virtually batted and bowled the county into first class cricket.

After Abington School closed down the family moved to Guilsborough and Billy and Tim would run the 10 miles back home, after matches or training at Franklin's Gardens.

At a dinner to honour the brothers in Northampton Town Hall in 1907, county cricket captain Tom Horton paid this tribute: "Gloucester had her Graces, Middlesex the Studds and Lytteltons. Lancashire the Steels and Worcester the Fosters. Why not then Northants of the Kingstons? Able and devoted exponents of outdoor sports, both cricket and football, they have helped the sport that was pure and manly, and strengthened the body and elevated mankind, and they have left behind them a great tradition for young Northants to follow."

The 1901/02 season saw the loss of star scrum-half Billy Patrick, condemned by his own folly. He signed for Bradford Rugby League side but never played a single game for them. Bradford had tracked him for 12 months, watching him at several games and contacting him by letter. It appears he probably signed to get them off his back, unaware that new, tougher regulations had been brought into effect. The new law meant that a player was a professional as soon as he put pen to paper.

News of his signing broke on November 23, the day the team lost 11-6 to Leicester at Franklin's Gardens. In apparent ignorance of the rule, Dallington-born Patrick played a couple of Saints games and for the East Midlands in their first ever match, against Kent.

A correspondent wrote to the press: "Patrick has not only professionalised the members of the Northampton team but also members of the Lennox team, members of the Leicester team and the

Scrum-half Billy Patrick signed to play rugby league and although he never took up the offer he was never allowed to play union again

members of the East Midlands and Kent teams, for no amateur rugby footballer is supposed to be capable of playing by the side of a professional without becoming tinged with professionalism."

Saints officials were furious about the activities of rugby league agents. Skipper Trevor Phillips wrote:

"In these days of competition, it is, perhaps, but natural that the Northampton club should not have escaped the notice of the eager agent of the Northern Union. Up to date, however, he has had, from his own point of view, extremely barren soil upon which to work. The executive of the club,

The Kingston clan gathered for their father's funeral in 1900 and (right) the menu from the dinner held in honour of Billy and Tim Kingston at the Town Hall on April 5, 1907, for their services to sport

indeed, have treated his efforts in drastic fashion. They have exposed to view on the football ground the following rather grim notice: **'The committee do not hold themselves responsible for the personal safety of Northern Union agents'**. Lynch law, as I have remarked elsewhere, has its advantages."

Patrick had been unlucky not to win an England cap and in some quarters it was suggested he had been overlooked because he was an ordinary working bloke. A person, describing himself 'A lover of Rugby Football' sent this letter to a London newspaper: "If working men cannot get even the reward of an international cap when their abilities deserve recognition, there can be small wonder that they yield to the tempting bribes held out by northern union emissaries who, I may add, have followed Patrick from place to place this year as well as approaching him by letter."

It was the end of Patrick's union career. He was barred from playing for the Saints. Patrick never took up the offer even though a newspaper report said he was set to make his debut against Hull Kingston Rovers.

Patrick played his earliest football with Dallington in the 1890s. In one junior game, he scored seven tries and converted them all. Most of his football at Northampton was played alongside Tim Kingston as a half-back pairing, including an England trial game for Rest of the South v London.

One of seven players to receive his club cap in the 1897/98 season, Patrick, father of nine children, died of pneumonia at the age of 56 in 1934.

After his controversial ban, he remained a passionate supporter of the Saints, who tried to get him reinstated, although they must have known in the prevailing climate of snobbery towards rugby league that there was no chance of success.

Patrick was just 22 when the life ban was imposed. It is quite possible that he would have gone on to win an England cap, time was certainly on his side if not the attitude towards the working classes. He took his three sons, Edgar (named after Edgar Mobbs), Len and Tom to the Gardens, and they became well known around the ground, operating the scoreboard, while their father was always ready with a razor sharp assessment of a player – not always complimentary.

Charles 'Cock' Leigh, who created a sensation by scoring a try from full-back, was another target for the northern boys but the story handed down in the family goes that an agent trying to tap him up was chased out of the ground.

Patrick's rugby demise was permanent, while Weston, the new skipper, did his chances of further international recognition no good at all by falling off a horse. The beast then rolled over him, putting him out of action for several weeks early in the season.

It was ironic that Saints should improve their fixture list still further in 1902/03 with games against Blackheath, at last, Llanelli and Oxford University at a time when the club was enduring all sorts of on-field problems.

All three new fixtures ended in defeat but maybe the playing problems were exaggerated as Quins were beaten 23-5 and Gloucester defeated for the first time, 8-3 at Franklin's Gardens.

By now the Saints fame was spreading and on Boxing Day, in front of 8,000 spectators, the club entertained Racing Club France, although at one stage the game was in danger of being called off. Three days before the game Saints received a telegram saying it would have to be scratched as the French government, somewhat unsportingly, had decreed the country's universities, from where the players were drawn, would have to stay open on Boxing Day.

The All Blacks pictured with the Saints players and officials before their game in 1905 - The first time Saints wore Black, Green & Gold

Monsieur Reicke, the French vice-consul, was already in Northampton. He wired the club describing how a cancellation would be a huge disappointment for the people of Northampton. That did the trick and at 7am on Thursday a telegram arrived confirming the fixture.

The French set off that night and arrived at The Plough Hotel at 10am on Friday with a Scotsman at full back, W H Crichton, and an English captain, C Rutherford. Saints won 10-0.

After drifting into decline, the Saints were rejuvenated in 1904/05 by the introduction of some new faces.

In November, Jack Miles, who had played three times for the Saints before joining Leicester, agreed to rejoin from Leicester Stoneygate. This was quite a coup as Miles had become the first Leicester player to be capped by England, two seasons after Weston.

He made another 49 appearances over the next two seasons and chalked up 46 more tries, an incredible 73 in all in 68 games. With a record like that it is surprising that he didn't add to the one appearance for England against Wales in 1903.

He later became an international referee, taking charge of Ireland v France and France v Wales in 1913 and Wales v France a year later.

The side had its customary warm-up game with Olney at the start of the 1905/06 season and a young player on the wing for the opposition gave, according to the *Football Echo*, a "brainy exhibition". He was Edgar Robert Mobbs. That was on September 9 – two weeks later he was at scrum-half for the Saints against Bedford.

Five days after that the Saints played the touring New Zealand side. It is a measure of the club's ambition that they clinched a fixture with a national touring side, the only such game in the club's history. With rugby so passionately supported in the town, club officials had no fears about meeting the financial guarantees, £35 and 70 per cent of the gate.

The Saints lost 32-0 but there must have been immense pride on that Thursday afternoon – September 28, 1905. The civic dignitaries made full use of the trip to show off what Northampton had to offer.

The Saints side, including a few guests, had the satisfaction of restricting the All Blacks to fewer points than in any previous match. The manner of victory created a big impression on the Saints' thinking in subsequent seasons. There is evidence they tried to copy the All Blacks, who had the revolutionary idea of planning moves in advance and using specialist positions. Even then they were using the hooker to throw-in at a lineout.

The All Blacks later played Bedford, a game that stirred considerable controversy. Mobbs, not risked by the Saints so soon in his career, played for Bedford, who brought in several other outsiders, among them the Northampton half-back pairing of Tommy Preston and Claude Palmer, which infuriated the New Zealand management.

The All Blacks manager protested to the Rugby Union, who pointed out it was purely a friendly game, and so would not interfere. Another appeal was made before kick-off to play only Bedford men. Getting no encouragement, the manager jumped up and with his clenched fist struck the table, said angrily: "Play who you like. Search all England for your stars. We will

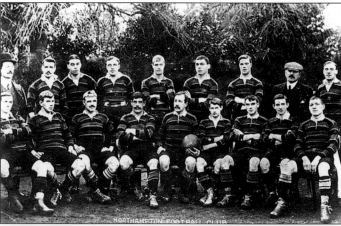

Top: The side of 1904/05. Back row (left to right): E S Dunkley (secretary), F G Nurser, H B Follitt, H E Kingston, G Burke, J Hobbs, J H Miles, A E Orton (match secretary), W H Kingston. Front row: H Palmer, L Johnson, J Mason, R West, T H Preston, F Coles, H C Palmer, C Leigh.
Bottom picture: The 1906/07 side featuring skipper Jack Miles (holding ball) who was the first Leicester player to be capped by England before joining the Saints

show you how to play football." Suitably motivated, the All Blacks won handsomely 41-0. A blinkered Bedford press had suggested the All Blacks were in for a good hiding.

The visit of the All Blacks and the emergence of Mobbs made 1905/06 a landmark season. There was also another reason. For the first time the players wore the now famous, black, green and gold jerseys. The new colours were proposed at a general committee meeting on May 1, 1905, as an amendment to Rule 3. Sadly, there is not a single comment to indicate why they added the gold to the black and green.

From the promise of 1905/06, the Saints plunged into a season of disarray. On the field results were poor and internal bickering among officials took the club to a low ebb. Tommy Mitton wrote: "It is an open secret that there are dissensions in the management of the club. In the interests of the game these differences should be healed. A house divided against itself cannot stand; a football club with its management at sixes and sevens cannot succeed. The Saints are in a more serious position than some of those connected with the management perhaps realise, and a strong, united effort must be made to raise the club to the old standard."

Chapter Three
Edgar Mobbs –
Boys' Own Hero

I N 1907/08 Mobbs began his reign as captain and after a sticky start, he presided over a much improved campaign. The verdict on his captaincy was favourable from the outset: "Mobbs, on whom devolved the onerous duties of the captaincy, set his men a capital example. A born optimist, he never despaired, however strong the opposition, and his enthusiasm counted for much in the success attained."

In June, 1907, having just been appointed, Mobbs gave an illuminating insight into crowds of the day in a newspaper interview – comments not entirely out of place today: "Well, what amuses me most and amuses most of the team as well, is to hear the criticisms from the members' stand and from those who stand behind the press box," said Mobbs.

"One minute they are praising a man as if the least he ought to be is an international, and the next minute their remarks indicate that they do not consider him fit for the village team. If some of the people on that stand knew what fools they made of themselves by their shouting and talking that day, they would never express an opinion on football again."

Trouble was looming when allegations of professionalism were levelled at the Saints, Leicester and Coventry, leading to an inquiry by the Rugby Union. The claims were made by Percy Adams, of the Old Edwardians club, based in Romford, Essex, a club the Saints started fixtures against in 1897 and which continued until 1929.

At the Grand Hotel, Leicester, on Tuesday December 17, 1907, Saints representatives appeared before the professional inquiry committee of the English Rugby Union to answer 'general charges'.

The Saints officials were Edgar Mobbs, Albert Orton, Teddy Dunkley, a member of the committee; and E F Goulding, the secretary.

Adams had created a sensation in the rugby world 12 months earlier, claiming that veiled professionalism was rampant at many of the leading clubs, particularly in the Midlands.

Goulding was called before the inquiry and questions were asked about two players, Hube Harding, who played a few games the previous season after joining from Cardiff and Frank Coles, who had left Northampton to join Leicester only to return to

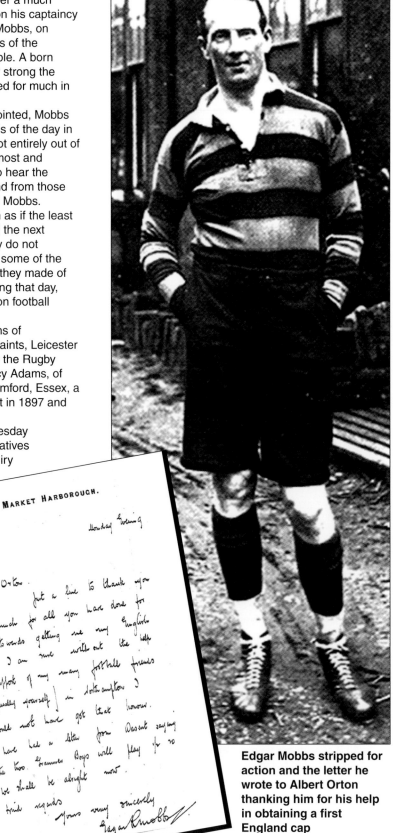

Edgar Mobbs stripped for action and the letter he wrote to Albert Orton thanking him for his help in obtaining a first England cap

Goulding told them that unemployed Harding found a job at Northampton and being a footballer sought a game with the Saints. Coles moved to Leicester because of work but returned to Northampton to get married. His bride then refused "to leave the home where all her friends resided."

The club's accounts covering the past 18 years were scrutinised and the inquiry declared "the books were splendidly kept and that everything was very clear."

It was pointed out that players were provided with tea and cigarettes in the dressing room at Franklin's Gardens after the matches. This created a slight ripple and the dishing out of cigarettes was to be discouraged – more to avoid accusations of providing perks than for any health reasons.

One of the committee held the view that there was a tendency to make money out of football. Orton was asked whether there were any indications of players walking to the railway station, carrying their bag, and having a sandwich, and then charging the club with cab fares and dinner.

Orton replied that if Northampton found a man doing as was suggested the committee would demand an explanation and the player would have to refund the money. "We should drop him," added Orton. "We would not for a moment countenance anything of that sort."

Mobbs asked the committee to issue a statement exonerating the Saints and all connected with the club from the charge of professionalism. He had been called a professional in the street and strongly objected. Mobbs received an assurance that such a statement would be made "at the earliest possible moment."

In 1908/09 Mobbs was picked for England. The selectors could hardly ignore him after he had led a combined Midlands side to a 16-5 victory over the touring Australians at Leicester on December 2, their only defeat to an English side.

Mobbs was showered with praise by the Aussies, and he followed that up with a North v South trial game at Franklin's Gardens, the first time the ground had been selected for such a prestigious fixture.

It was assumed the trial would be the last such fixture at a provincial ground as 10 and a half acres of land at Twickenham had just been acquired for £5,572 12s. 6d. and a national rugby stadium was to be developed, eventually stretching over a far wider area.

Mobbs went on to score the only try, after just two minutes, in a 9-3 defeat by the Aussies. He played in every international that season, scoring three more times. On hearing of his selection, Mobbs immediately wrote to Albert Orton: "Just a line to thank you very much for all you have done for me towards getting me my English cap. I am sure without the help & support of my many football friends (especially yourself) in Northampton I should not have got that honour."

Orton, a spectator at Blackheath for the international, wrote in the *Football Echo* that it was only the desperate tackling of Mobbs that kept them out, and that he was the best back on the English

Wonder winger Teddy Cook

side. "His defence and attack were perfect alike. The Australians did not seem to relish the attention he gave to them, and they avoided him as much as possible by kicking instead of attempting to run by him."

Straight-talking Mobbs was critical of the England tactics. "The whole idea of our side was wrong. We ought to have gone into it with the intention of attacking instead of which we defended. I suppose most of us will be kicked out of the team for the next match."

He was right. Only eight survived for the game the following Saturday against Wales in Cardiff. It would have been seven but Mobbs, dropped in favour of Tom Simpson from Northumberland, got back when Simpson dropped out.

England were beaten again, 8-0, but after the game, Rowland Hill, secretary of the Rugby Union, said to Orton: "We are very proud of Mobbs. He played a magnificent game, and he is our best three-quarter."

They didn't drop him again and at the end of the season the Saints held a dinner in his honour at The Plough Hotel in Bridge Street, a night of revelry which had an extraordinary ending – a roller skating football match between Evening Dress versus The Rest. A few years later these pillars of the Establishment would gather again in much more sombre circumstances to honour the same man.

The Saints made a scorching start to the season winning their first eight games, the most notable at Portsmouth, where the United Services side had not been beaten for three seasons.

The Saints had acquired the services of Bristolian, E C (Teddy) Cook, who was to prove a prolific scorer in the seasons immediately before the First World War and into the Twenties.

Such was the impact of Cook's debut at Birkenhead Park, that Mobbs sent the sports paper a telegram after the game, printed underneath the match report:

CAPTAIN MOBBS ON THE GAME
COOK PLAYED WELL
Hardly had the ball, but Cook made the most of his opportunities. It was a grand win. A very hot game in very hot weather. The Park are a fine side. Curly Denton, who used to play half back for Olney and Northampton was a spectator – Mobbs.

Gloucester ended the triumphant march, winning 11-3 at Franklin's Gardens before the Saints bounced back with a 29-0 thumping of Harlequins and a 10-3 success at The Reddings, which ended Moseley's unbeaten home run.

Mobbs celebrated his England debut with a stunning performance against Birkenhead Park at Franklin's Gardens, scoring six tries.

Arthur Gilbert Bull, like Mobbs recruited from Olney, made his debut as did J W (Ranji) Ward in the 1909/10 season. Bull, a front row forward, went on to win a solitary England cap against Wales in 1914. He was to have a long association with the club and the area, starting a doctor's practice in Kingsthorpe in 1923. Originally he studied law but the Great War

had such a profound effect on him that he switched careers. One of many Olney men to join the Saints he was the son of the preacher and hymn writer, the Rev Charles Bull.

After his success with England the previous season, Mobbs was a marked man and a report of the Bedford match at Franklin's Gardens read: "Mobbs was receiving as much attention from Bedfordians as the Prime Minister is receiving from the Suffragettes…"

The Saints won their first eight games of the season. With Cook on one wing, Mobbs on the other and Joe Beasley in the centre, the Saints had a formidable back line. That was never more true than in the game at Leicester on October 16, which Mobbs later recalled was his most cherished memory from his club career.

In 16 previous meetings at Welford Road, the Saints had only won once and Mobbs sent a letter to all his men starting with the words: "We must win". The Saints did, 11-3, with two tries from Cook and the other from Mobbs, but the real star was guest full back Douglas Schulze, who played 13 times for Scotland between 1905 and 1911. The euphoric post-match comments said: "I don't think Schulze will be in a losing Saints side this season." He was right, he didn't play another game for the club.

It was predicted this would be the start of a long, winning streak at Welford Road, a touch wide of the mark as it was another 13 games stretching to the 1928/29 season before Saints tasted victory over their great rivals on their own patch again.

On February 26 the Saints travelled by train to meet Devonport Albion, accompanied for the most of the journey by the Cobblers, who got off at Exeter for a Southern League game. Relationships between the two sides were then very friendly. At the 1909 annual meeting Mobbs made a point of congratulating the Cobblers on winning the Southern League championship: "Many men liked to see League football, and he had nothing to say against it. He tendered his congratulations to the Association club on their success. There was a time when the Association team was last, and that was not creditable to Northampton, but they had brought fame to the town by finishing at the head of the table and every true sportsman must honour them for it."

The season wound up with Mobbs and Cook equal top try scorers with 29 apiece. It was a vintage year for English rugby as they regained the Home International championship for the first time in 18 years, helped in part by Mobbs.

Players are just about discernible in these pictures from games at Franklin's Gardens in 1910 against Gloucester (top) and Bridgewater

Press reaction to to the Saints' 18-3 win over Swansea in 1911 with the Swansea captain in the role of Napoleon retreating from Northampton and the inevitable shoe-town metaphor

On March 3, another milestone in the club's history was created when Mobbs captained a successful England side in France. The 11-3 win was to be his last international – and he knew it.

He told Tommy Mitton: "My international career is finished. They made me captain against France, and you'll find the England selectors will not choose me again."

Mitton doubted the logic but Mobbs was right. Percy Lawrie was on the wing and John Birkett was captain for the last game at Inverleith against Scotland. Mobbs was on the international scrapheap, the captaincy some sort of final accolade from the selectors.

The 1910/11 season was only weeks old when rumours started that Teddy Cook was about to defect to Leicester. These were quickly scotched and Cook went on to score 51 tries for the season, a record never equalled and never likely to be. Far from moving, Cook would replace Mobbs as captain two seasons later.

What had been fierce rivalry between the Saints and Leicester spilled over into controversy in 1910, following a 0-0 draw in the game at Welford Road.

This was the story in full that broke in the *Echo* of Friday, December 16:

RUGBY SENSATION
TIGERS' EXTRAORDINARY ACTION
FIXTURES CANCELLED WITH THE SAINTS

The decision to break off relationships between the clubs was taken by Leicester's committee because of "certain questionable tactics by certain members of the visiting team". Two forwards and one of the three-quarters on the Northampton side are mentioned as the chief offenders.

The Northampton press described the reaction as "amazing." Mitton wrote: "Rugby football is no child's game, and it is nothing unusual to see vigorous bouts in contests between Leicester and Northampton. There were vigorous bouts on Saturday but to suggest that vigour was shown by Northampton alone is absurd. The Tigers were just as keen as the Saints and if blame is to be apportioned it must be evenly distributed. One side was no better than the other – and no worse, and one is astounded that Leicester should desire to scratch the fixtures on so flimsy a pretext."

Mobbs, who ran touch for the game because of an injured thumb, dismissed the Tigers' action as "absolutely childish".

"It was a vigorous game," said Mobbs, "but by no means the roughest I have seen, and I cannot understand why Leicester have taken such a step. There is no ground for the complaints that are made."

The Saints received a letter cancelling the fixtures for next season three days after the game. The Tigers tried to insist that certain players would not be picked against them, a suggestion totally rejected by the Saints.

"For any club to stipulate – or to attempt to stipulate – as to how the side opposed to it shall be built up is ludicrous in the extreme," said Orton.

The *Leicester Post* correspondent wrote: "Providing an apology be received, and that Northampton punish the offending players in some way, this would possibly open a channel to reconciliation. It is to be hoped that something of this sort may be done, for the matches between the clubs, if sometimes unduly vigorous, have always proved a great attraction in either town. and amongst the most interesting on each club's fixture list."

This was ridiculed in Northampton. "Really, the more these Leicester folk say, the more ridiculous does their action appear. The precipitate scratching of the fixtures was silly enough in all conscience, but to ask for an apology is only adding to the absurdity of the position. The Northampton Club will laugh at the suggestion of bended knees and a white sheet," wrote Mitton.

Needless to say there was no cancellation of fixtures – normal hostilities were resumed with relish the following season, both games won by Leicester.

On February 13 came what was described as "the finest win the Saints have ever accomplished." Swansea, considered the best side in Wales, were beaten 18-3, the first over the Welshmen and their biggest defeat for 22 years. It was missed by the team's greatest supporter, Albert Orton, who was at home unwell. Orton had supposed to be touch judge, and the referee, F W Nicholls somehow managed to start the game without noticing he was an official short.

Saints roared to victory with tries from Mobbs, Cook and Frank Coles. Mitton used the victory to have a swipe at the England selectors: "Such a victory as this is the best comment on the mistaken tactics of the Rugby Union executive, who so persistently ignore the

East Midlands players…"

The 1911/12 season was one of turmoil for the Saints. The problems started in the summer as a great side was about to break up. Joe Beasley emigrated to Australia; pack leader W W Hoskin left the area; Coles took a season off; and A V Manton switched allegiance to Bedford.

Beasley was given a farewell dinner given in his honour at The Plough Hotel in August 1911 before he set sail for farm life in Queensland at the age of 30. Mobbs described Beasley as "the best three-quarter in England." Here was yet another case, the audience agreed, of the selectors snubbing Northampton players.

At the end of the season, Mobbs also announced his retirement but was talked into leading the side for one more campaign. He scored 16 tries in the first month but it was Boxing Day before he added to his tally.

The 1912/13 season was definitely to be Mobbs's swansong, the sixth in a row as captain. Now an 'elder' statesmen of the game at 30, he continued to be outspoken against authority. He gave the RFU a double-barrelled verbal assault for their treatment of the touring South Africans. It was reported in an organ called *Truth*: "Betwixt mob oratory and Mobbs oratory there is no great gulf fixed. He roundly attacked the Rugby Union for the miserable, miserly manner in which it was treating the visitors. Tea or coffee after dinner forbidden; the team brought up from Portsmouth by the midnight train and landed in London at 3am."

The paper gave its whole-hearted support for Mobbs: "I had already referred to the symptoms of this penurious disease, when, on the South Africans leaving the hotel at Southampton after landing, taxis were dismissed and the visitors put on trams. But I had not the least idea they were being treated like naughty schoolboys, everything being made as an unpleasant as possible by reason of petty meanness simply because some infatuated noodles on the Rugby Union were afraid that the amateur status of the visitors might be imperilled. Wherefore it was mighty plucky of Mobbs to give tongue at the dinner. It is a great pity that Mobbs did not have a chance of speaking weeks ago. A strong line was needed, and he took it."

A grateful touring party sent Mobbs a team picture, signed by every member, which hung in the window of the *Echo* offices for many years. The speech was

enthusiastically reported in South Africa, and for his boldness the *Kimberley Evening Star* awarded Mobbs, 'The Star Cake'.

On May 29, 1913, at Northampton Town Hall, sportsmen and leading Northampton citizens held a dinner in Mobbs's honour, presenting him with a silver tray, tankard and beakers. The warmest tribute came from his great friend, Orton: "Wherever he led, everyone would follow. Rugby football tended to bring to the surface all that was good in a man – courage, resolution, sacrifice, unselfishness and forbearance."

Prophetic words for 18 months later hundreds would indeed follow him. For most of them, to an early grave in the Great War.

The club had an horrendous 1913/14 season prior to the outbreak of war, when rugby ceased for five years. Rugby was of only minor importance as the country braced itself for war. Mitton wrote in his scrapbooks, filled with hundreds of match reports: **'No games – War'**.

It was now time for the Boys' Own hero Mobbs to lead from the front again. Mobbs was a man of enormous stature in Northampton and far beyond, when he finally hung up his boots on April 5, 1913, a 17-11 win over Old Edwardians.

In his tribute to Mobbs, Mitton described his career as one of the most remarkable stories in modern football.

"Standing well over six feet, with great pace and immense strength, Mobbs is undoubtedly the finest footballer Northampton has produced," Mitton wrote.

"The Saints have had men who in some directions have shown greater skill; they have never possessed a player who equalled Mobbs in all-round ability. His pace, his strength, and his terrific hand-off made him one of the most dangerous attacking three-quarters of his period.

"His right arm would shoot out, and men fell like ninepins to his powerful thrust until he had carved his way to points.

"He went to Bedford Modern School and there was never any suggestion of the coming international in his schooldays, and getting no further than the school Second XV, he left without obtaining his colours.

"At that time, in fact, Mobbs was so little enamoured of the game that for some four or five seasons he forsook football – except as a spectator – for hockey.

The parental home had some years previously been

Mobbs (centre) put on an air show in Market Harborough in 1911, having developed a passion for flying

Mobbs with his volunteers lined up at the Racecourse and (below) at the home of Claude Palmer. He told his old friend he did not expect to be coming home

removed to Olney, and there Mobbs became known as a good centre forward in a mixed hockey eleven.

"In 1903, the Olney Rugby Club pressed Mobbs into service; but he was not keen, and played in only three or four matches. In the following season he played for Olney, the Weston Turks, and the Northampton Heathens.

"Mobbs has held as many captaincies as are possible to one man. Starting with Northampton, he became skipper of the East Midlands, led the Midlands and East Midlands against the Australians, London and the Midlands against the West at Richmond, the South against the North at Twickenham, England against France at Paris, and this season he is captain of the Barbarians. This is a record that can hardly be beaten.

"Mobbs has several times played in France. He is a great favourite at Toulouse, the home of the Stade Toulousian, the champion club of France. And there a curious custom prevails. The man who plays opposite to Mobbs always wears a cap, the reason being that the Frenchmen have the idea that Mobbs hands off on the top of the head, and the cap is therefore worn as a protector. As a matter of fact, Mobbs always tries to place his hand under the opponent's jaw."

When war broke out in August, 1914, Mobbs was running the Market Harborough branch of the Pytchley Auto Car Company, and was, apparently, contemplating emigration to Canada, according to an army friend, Major Henry Grierson.

Cambridge Blue Grierson, who rallied to Mobbs's call for the 7th Northamptons, wrote of Mobbs: "The most extraordinary thing about Edgar was his personality. He could walk into an hotel, for example, and in a few minutes would be master of the whole show."

War with Germany was announced on August 4, and by September 12, the remarkable Mobbs had 400 men had volunteered to serve with him in his own special corps.

The Mobbs corps was his personal answer to the Army, following his failure to get a commission on the grounds of being too old at 32.

Under a Northants Rugby Union banner, a committee was formed to provide essentials and comforts for the men. Decked out in straw boater, Mobbs assembled the 264 men, who were passed fit to fight, at Northampton Barracks (now the site of the

Vision of E. R. Mobbs and his Corps at the Front.

War and peace: A Mobbs-inspired cartoon and the programme for an England-Scotland friendly international at the County Ground, Northampton, the last game of rugby that Mobbs played

Post Office sorting department) for an historic picture for the *Independent*, who listed the name of every man serving in the Mobbs division. They became known as the Sportsman's Battalion, and formed a large part of the 7th Battalion, the Northamptonshire Regiment. Many were personal friends who refused commissions, preferring to line up with Mobbs as a private. Within 18 months he would be battalion commander, a testimony not only to his courage but also the enormity of the death toll.

He was as formidable in battle as he had been on the rugby field; stories abounded about the man, who is said to have gone over the top punting a rugby ball.

No lover of authority, when a clerk in London sent him forms to be filled in in red ink, he replied: "No red ink, but there's plenty of blood. Will that do?"

Mobbs was wounded three times and while recovering from one injury played his last game of rugby, not at Franklin's Gardens but at the County Ground in 1915, an England-Scotland international.

He spent one of his last days in England at the home of old friend, Claude Palmer, in Church Brampton. He shook Palmer's hand and told him he didn't expect to see him again. Nor did he. Soon after he was

confirmed as a colonel and returned to the Battalion just in time for the Third Battle of Ypres – the one that would go down in history as Passchendale, claiming 420,000 lives. The preliminary bombardment could be heard in England, blasting craters big enough to hold All Saints' Church. Then the infantry went in. They were battling to capture key machine-gun nests and one of these was holding up the 7th. So Mobbs charged it. Lieutenant Spencer, his old Bedford school friend, said later: "I saw the old three-quarter in his own 25, get the ball from a scrum and go. Thank God for such men." Mobbs died as he lived, leading from the front. War historians say his actions would have appalled his senior army officers but Mobbs would not have given that a second thought.

He was only 30 yards from the guns when he was hit. As he lay on the ground dying, the story goes that he scribbled the gun's map reference for his Brigadier and gave it to his runner. He was 35 and his body was never found in the mud and the blood.

There was no wife to mourn Mobbs. On July 31, 1917, Edgar's father, Oliver, received the DSO on behalf of his son at a special military parade on the Racecourse.

Chapter Four
The Roaring Twenties

Thousands turned out to see the unveiling of the Mobbs Memorial in the Market Square in July 1921, including the 85 survivors of the Sportsman's Battalion (above left) marching to the Square

FOLLOWING the trauma of war, the Saints got back on their feet with a record-breaking season. Under the chairmanship of Claude Palmer, the committee worked like fury to re-establish rugby in Northampton.

Franklin's Gardens was in a sorry state after the Army left. The club appealed for financial support and fund-raising events were organised. In a short space of time his team had raised £3,000. A new stand was built on the east side of the ground and a team was pieced together. It consisted of a handful of old players, including Cook, Beasley (back from Australia), and the new skipper Bull, some pre-war juniors and newcomers to the town.

The Saints announced they were back with an astonishing 685-point season.

The first serious game of 1919, against Bedford, could not be played at Goldington Road as it was still in military occupation, so it was switched to Bedford School. It was the first meeting between the sides since February 1914. Two of the more colourful Saints characters of the period made their debuts in the next game against Coventry at the Gardens, forward A F (Freddie) Blakiston, a master at Northampton and County School (later Northampton Grammar School and now Northampton School for Boys), and New Zealander, W H Udy, an outside-half with a big reputation.

Blakiston, later Sir Arthur Frederick after inheriting his uncle's baronetcy in 1941, had a bubbly wife, May, who grabbed hold of the nearest piece of headgear and hurled it into the air every time her husband contributed something of note to a game. He married her in 1915 and they were divorced when he was 62 in 1954. He remarried in May of that year.

Blakiston, educated at Bedford School and Cambridge University, was a war hero in the King Edward's Horse Artillery and later, as a captain in the Royal Field Artillery, he was wounded and won the Military Cross.

A larger-than-life character, Blakiston was to find himself in court after one bout of horseplay and was also sent off during his on-off career with the Saints. He also played 17 times for England, scoring against Ireland and France in 1921.

In his book *The History of the Rugby Football Union*, O L Owen, the leading sportswriter of his period, says of Blakiston: "…he played his rugby like some Elizabethan adventurer, reckless, without ruth or fear. Facing a back row made up of Blakiston, Wakefield and Voyce, opponents had to take the rough with the smooth and know their game well."

He apparently continued with that rumbustious attitude throughout his life. The story goes that when he was Master of the Hounds at Seavington in Somerset, the noble Lord went to blow his hunting horn only to discover his teeth missing. A younger rider was despatched to retrace the hunt's tracks, and found the missing set lying on the ground, covered in mud. Blakiston promptly pushed them back into place and blasted away on his horn.

Described as a perfect gentleman on foot, he changed into the reckless cavalier of his rugby days once astride his horse.

In his working days as a teacher, he moved across the country, playing rugby for Liverpool and Blackheath. But he made his name at Northampton, winning England recognition as a front row forward in the last match of 1920 against Scotland.

In 1921 Blakiston was part of a surprisingly stable England team that carried off the Grand Slam.

The first time he was moved into the back row coincided with a 28-6 defeat at Cardiff and he was out in the cold for five games before returning in 1923 for the final two internationals.

As a back row forward, Blakiston took part in the 1924 Grand Slam campaign before England's run of success came to an end at the hands of the 1925

All Blacks, who won 17-11 at Twickenham. He fluctuated between second row and back row for the rest of 1925.

The Saints won at Bedford 21-13 in front of 2,000 no doubt relieved spectators, thankful that normality had returned to their lives, but domestic problems almost caused a false start to the post-war period at Franklin's Gardens. The country was in the middle of a rail strike, so Coventry tried to get here by 'motor charabanc' but one could not be obtained; a cancellation looked inevitable. The Saints were desperate to play and Coventry eventually got to Northampton in taxis.

Hundreds of fans, eager to see rugby again, queued outside the ground long before the gates were open, and were rewarded with an 8-6 win. In both games, the Saints trailed at half-time, but each time the revival was started by that ace pre-war try scorer Teddy Cook.

The fixture list reflected the war years with several games against Army and Air Force sides.

On Boxing Day, 1919, the first playing tribute to Mobbs was played between Saints and the East Midlands. It would be another year before it became East Midlands versus the Barbarians.

For many years the Mobbs match was virtually an England trial with selectors turning up in force, and players anxious to impress. Six thousand fans saw Saints scrape home 11-10.

Despite the need to build up their own cash reserves, the club still found time to play Leicester for a third time, the proceeds going to the county cricket club.

New Zealander Udy, who was renowned for coming off the field with his shirt in tatters, proved to be the best half-back since the days of Tim Kingston, and Cook was as elusive as ever with a superb total of 42 tries.

On October 9, 1920, a two-page advertisement appeared in the *Independent* offering 15,000 shares in a new company, Franklin's Gardens Sports & Pleasure Co Ltd. Six directors were named: Major James Charles Lewis, Claude Palmer, Ernest Travis, William Pepper Cross, William Barratt and Teddy Cook. In the company prospectus it was proposed to turn the site into a latter-day sports complex for rugby football, cricket, tennis, bowls, badminton, athletics, Fives and gymnastics. They also intended to refurbish and extend the Jubilee Hall. The cost of

Swashbuckling Sir Freddie Blakiston, who figured in two England Grand Slams

this work, they envisaged, would be £10,000. The new company would allow the Saints to play at the Gardens in return for a percentage of the gate money.

Even before this advertisement appeared, modernisation work had started at the Gardens. Under the heading 'Northampton Zoo Disappearing', the *Independent* showed the monkey house at the Gardens being knocked down. The animal cages had long since fallen into decay.

In 1920/21 the Saints had such a desperate season, they called on the unlikeliest of players – such as Frank Coles, a dashing centre of the Mobbs era, who had made his debut in 1902 and had not played for 12 years.

On October 23, the Saints paid their first visit to Bristol, and got a 25-3 hammering. Bristolian Cook had asked to be excused from playing because of the death of his sister but the club had no replacement and so Cook turned out.

The Saints then left their ragged form behind to inflict an 11-5 scoreline on Gloucester and in the return with Bristol conjured up a 6-0 win.

But the most notable success was a 12-0 win over Leicester, the first at Franklin's Gardens since October, 1908, and then the widest margin of victory for the Saints. Tigers took ample revenge in the return, winning 30-0.

In July 1921 came the year's most important event, the unveiling of the Mobbs memorial on the Market Square on a sweltering Sunday afternoon by the club president Lord Lilford in front of a crowd of thousands, including the 85 survivors of the 7th Battalion of the Northamptonshire Regiment, who the night before had dined in Mobbs's honour.

The scene was described in the *Independent*: "Never has Northampton witnessed a more impressive ceremony than the unveiling and dedication of the beautiful memorial to the late Lieut. Colonel Edgar R Mobbs, DSO. The heat was tropical and thousands thronged the square bearing the rays of a burning sun, but everyone was happy in the knowledge that they were able to pay homage to one

Claude Palmer (left) and Jimmy Minihan at the unveiling of the War Memorial at Franklin's Gardens

Easter tour 1922

Images of the Easter tour to Wales in 1922. Top left: A gloomy looking Aberavon. Top right: New Zealander W H Udy coming off with ripped shirt in the same game. Middle left: The finish of the Aberavon game. Middle right: A lineout against Pontypool. Above: Several players have the use of a car. Right: G J Piper, Gilbert Bull, Eric Coley and committee man Eddy Page, who four years later blew his brains out on the verge of being exposed as an embezzler, on Swansea Pier

of our noblest sons. There was no mournfulness about the service, save in the poignant notes of the 'Last Post', the requiem sounded over so many thousands of our best and bravest. The gallant hero's father, Mr Oliver Mobbs, and the family desired the service to reflect the spirit of thankfulness for such a life and inspiring example. "My Edgar is not dead", said his father to the writer the other day. "He still lives in the hearts of us all and his memorial will now, I hope, serve to stimulate the present and future generations to remember that the path of duty is the path of glory."

Within a few weeks of his death in 1917, the Mobbs Fund committee had raised £2,000, including £100 from his battalion on the Front. The committee, headed by Lord Lilford, voted £500 to the East Midlands to encourage rugby among junior clubs, a cause still supported today. A cup was presented to Bedford Modern School, which is still played for, and a presentation album, containing the names of 500 subscribers, was given to Mobbs's father Oliver.

The remainder was paid to sculptor Alfred Turner to pay for the bust of Mobbs. The bronze figure stood on a 20-foot high Portland stone pedestal. The pedestal is on three steps, and the front panel of bronze with the victor's laurel wreath forms a backdrop to a life-size bronze bust of Mobbs in uniform. There are bronze panels on either side, one a high-stepping Mobbs in sporting action, the other representing war with Mobbs falling on the battlefield surrounded by his comrades.

The inscription on the front of the pedestal reads:
'Lieut. Colonel EDGAR R. MOBBS, D.S.O.
Commanding Officer
7th Battalion Northamptonshire Regiment
Killed in Action July 31st, 1917
O valiant hearts who to your glory came
Through dust of conflict and through battle-flame
Tranquil you lie, your knightly virtue proved
Your memory hallowed in the land you loved'
Erected by Subscriptions of admirers the world over to the memory of a great and gallant sportsman. When the Great War broke out he founded Mobbs Company, joined as a Private, and rose to command the Battalion to which it belonged. He did his duty even unto death'

Lord Lilford said: "I sincerely hope that every man, woman and child, who passes this memorial will remember what it stands for, and as they walk along they will ask themselves seriously what they are doing to follow the example of Colonel Mobbs. We all know well what he stood for – patriotism, devotion to duty, and above all, self-sacrifice – and I fear that we know only too well that England stands in greater need today of his noble qualities than even at the direct period of the war."

The Saints, Cobblers and county cricket club joined in the wreath-laying ceremony, the inscription from the Saints reading: 'In loving memory of our old skipper. We dinna forget'.

In 1939, the memorial was moved to the Garden of Rest in Abington Square, where a service is held every year before the Mobbs game.

Saints failed to draw inspiration from all this.They plumbed the depths in 1921/22 – the worst season in the club's history up until then.

Blakiston did not appear in a single game that season, having moved to teach in Brighton, while Udy was available for only a handful of games. Cook had retired and G E Kilbey, top scorer the previous season, turned professional.

A promising young winger Jerry Gordon began his association with the club. He would not achieve much on the field but off it was a different matter.

A new and abiding fixture was made with Aberavon, who had shown their mettle already that season with a draw at Swansea and victory over Llanelli. From Castle Station the Welshmen made straight to the Market Square, where the secretary W J Rees placed a wreath on the Mobbs Memorial before the party sang a hymn in Welsh in front of a large crowd. This was a gesture greatly appreciated by the club. The game itself was spoiled by thick fog but it was completed and the Saints won 7-0.

The team opened with four defeats and ended with seven, failing to score a point in the last month but the fortunes were turned round in spectacular fashion in the next campaign, albeit with the aid of a weakened fixture list. Sides like Burton-on-Trent and the Household Brigade were introduced and given a sound thumping. Cinderford were another also newcomers but that backfired as the Saints lost 15-13.

The Saints turned to Welshmen for the players they needed to lift them out of the depression. They acquired Ivor Davies, a winger who had played three internationals in 1914, Richmond fly-half Bobby Jones, destined to play for Wales, and full-back Bob Vaughan from Pontypool. The squad was stronger with the

Famous four: England internationals Bob Webb, Eric Coley, Tom Harris and Billy Weston

new arrivals along with the return of Blakiston and the veteran Cook.

In March, against Bridgwater, American Fred Layman made his Saints debut. A law student at Oxford University he had been a sensation on the left wing in the East Midlands-Barbarians game.

He was a bundle of power on the wing, scoring 12 times in 10 games, including four in the win over London Scottish. Weaned on American Football, Layman quickly became a cult figure for the way he bulldozed his way past opponents.

Vaughan, who later captained the side, was in the top flight of full-backs, comparing favourably with the internationals of the day. Mitton, who had proved a shrewd judge of ability over the years, reckoned he lost out on a Welsh cap by moving to Northampton.

He was a product of the Welsh coal mines and recruited for Northampton by one of the town's top industrialists, Billy Wren, the man who took shoe cleaning out of the spit and soot age and made a fortune to boot. Wren visited Vaughan to make the offer in Newbridge, where he lived with his new bride. Before that Vaughan had lived in a small mining cottage in Abercarn with his father and five brothers – his mother had died giving birth. Within a 10-mile radius five major rugby clubs played – Newport, Cross Keys, Abercarn, Newbridge and Pontypool.

Vaughan had graduated to the Pontypool side that won the Welsh championship in 1920/21, and was already creating a big reputation for himself. Wren offered him a job and a house next to the factory. Vaughan jumped at the chance of leaving the pits.

Vaughan was immensely proud of his physique and good looks. He was an outstanding sportsman and when a travelling fair visited the area he went into the boxing ring determined to win 10 shillings by lasting three rounds.

He knocked his opponent out with his first punch, prompting thoughts among his brothers that he could be another Jimmy Wilde. It was a short-lived notion, after being told by a promoter in Newport that the first thing he must do was have his nose broken to give him a more rugged appearance. For handsome Bob this was too much of a sacrifice.

Instead he worked in Wren's factory and in 1939 he went into partnership to form the Tate Chemical Company at Wellingborough. He was managing director of the firm until his retirement in 1959. He died three years later at the age of 62 from Hodgkinson's Disease. Right up to his death he was a dedicated follower of the Saints and served on the committee.

The club was also starting to develop useful home-grown talent. Two youngsters tipped for bright futures were Eric Coley, a flanker or No 8, and centre Billy Weston. Both went on to gain England honours, Weston, emulating his father, Harry.

Coley was one of the founder members of Old Northamptonians along with Harry Crask and Jack Bass, both going on to play for the Saints, although with nothing like the same success.

Coley's career spanned 14 years from 1920 to 1934. He played only a handful of games in his first two seasons but began to make his mark in the 1922/23 season. He went on to make 292 appearances and got two England caps at No 8 against France in 1929 and Wales three years later, scoring in a 12-5 defeat at Swansea.

Unknown Saints players in a match at Bristol in 1920 (Saints lost 25-3). A year later Bristol moved to their current site, the Memorial Ground

In 1927 he toured Argentina with a British side designed to sow the seeds of the game in South America. The discrepancy in ability was underlined by the fact that in nine games no Argentinian or exiled Briton crossed the team's line. It took the party, led by old England international, James Baxter, three weeks to reach Buenos Aires and Coley missed the first four games, a problem occurring with a vaccinated arm.

Clearly revelling in the lifestyle of playing golf, tennis, squash and riding polo ponies, Coley remarked: "We stayed at the Hurlingham Club in Buenos Aires, a palatial place, which seemed like living on £20,000 a year." Coley returned a stone overweight.

Ten years later Coley became the first Northampton man to be made an England selector, a post he held for 11 years. Coley had risen through the administrative ranks as secretary to the East Midlands and was described as a man of "charming personality and unfailing good humour."

Those qualities explain how, in 1932, he was chosen from 200 applicants for the £250-a-year secretary's job of Northamptonshire CCC. He stayed for five of the leanest years in the county's history, the side finishing bottom seven times between 1930 and 1939.

In 1936 he had the most appalling duty to perform, when it was believed that Jack Timms, scorer of over 20,000 runs for Northamptonshire, had been killed in a car crash on the A50 in Leicestershire at around midnight. A passenger in the car, A H Bakewell, who had just scored a masterly 241no against Derbyshire lay in a hospital bed crying out, in his delirium, for 'Timmy'. It was the start of a harrowing night for Coley, who drove to Timms's parents house in Whitfield near Brackley to prepare them for the worst. They went round to Timms's house to see his wife and found him safe in bed. The dead man lying in the ditch turned out to be another county player, Reggie Northway.

Coley resigned his cricket post to become assistant secretary for Northamptonshire, Leicestershire and Rutland area under the Physical Training and

BEFORE AND AFTER THE FOOTBALL CALL AT THE

PEACOCK HOTEL,

MARKET SQUARE.

Best of everything to EAT and DRINK.

E. INGMAN, Proprietor.   Grill Room. :: Billiards.

County Ground   Northampton.

SOLE OFFICIAL

Souvenir Programme 2d.

FOR THE MATCH

NEW ZEALAND v. EAST MIDLANDS.

ON SATURDAY, DECEMBER 6th, 1924,

Kick-off at 2.30 p.m.

Published by authority of the East Midlands R.U. by Billingham & Son, 38, Bridge Street, Northampton.

AFTER THE MATCH YOU ARE INVITED TO

Visit Jeffery's Model House

Showing the latest ideas in home furnishings at

The programme for the East Midlands-New Zealand game at the County Ground on December 6, 1924

Recreation Act the Second World War intervened and gave him the chance to show his real leadership qualities.

For years he had been in the Territorial Army and was always trying to persuade his friends to join. He rose to brigadier during the war, and was attached to the Canadian army in North West Europe, winning the OBE (military division) in 1943.

In 1949 he returned to Northampton to take over the Franklin's Gardens hotel from his old pal Jerry Gordon, who, fairly late in life, thought he'd have a go at farming.

Coley died young in 1957 just 53 old but at least he had seen his eldest son David make his debut for the Saints in his old back row position.

If Coley's route to the top was swift, his contemporary Billy Weston's was long and slow. But when he did reach the heights of England, he stayed there, having been transformed from ordinary centre into a brilliant wing forward.

Born on December 12, 1905, almost five years after his father had become the first Saint to play for England, Weston made his international debut on February 11 against Ireland at the age of 27, almost 10 years after his Saints debut. He would make 15 more appearances, stretching to 1938.

Weston was taught both codes of football at Oakham School, where he excelled at athletics. In 1922 he won five events – high jump, long jump, 100

yards, hurdles and football place-kicking.

He made his first appearance for the Saints against London Welsh in November, 1923, but could never command a regular place. By this time his father was a prominent committee man with the Saints, becoming president in 1925-26. Both were farmers at Yardley Gobion and Billy's sons carry on the tradition.

Weston played against the All Blacks twice, for the East Midlands at the County Ground in 1924 and for England in the famous 13-0 on January 4, 1936.

In his twilight years, Weston met his old Thirties team mates at a reunion in 1983 brought about by former BBC broadcaster, Peter West.

Weston met up with the likes of prop Joe Kendrew, who won four DSOs in North Africa, Italy and Korea and became Governor General of Western Australia on retiring from the Army, Bernard Gadney, scrum-half and captain, who had many battles against the Saints for Leicester, and Peter Cranmer, the centre who had a long and distinguished career in broadcasting.

Gadney recalled the brilliance of England's defence against the All Blacks. "No-one was better than Bill Weston. No-one ever got past him on the blind side."

Weston captained the Saints in 1928/29, 1929/30, 1932/33, 1933/34 and 1937/38. In 1936 Weston was a member of a British team that toured Argentina, playing in 11 of the 12 games.

He died in 1987 at the age of 81, having never lost his affection for the Saints nor for the game.

Before one international, Bill could not find his white shorts and borrowed a pair of his father's baggy turn-of-the-century style. On the train to London for the international Weston told this story to a fellow passenger, who turned out to be a reporter. To his amazement the story appeared in print, allegedly under the headline: 'Willie in long shorts'.

While Coley and Weston became part of the fabric at Franklin's Gardens, Layman played only 39 times for the Saints but he was given an emotional farewell in 1924.

He gave the fans plenty to remember him by – a first half hat-trick of tries against Wakefield, and afterwards the players lifted him shoulder high, while the band played *Auld Lang Syne* and *For He's A Jolly Good Fellow*. He was carried around the ground as thousands sang themselves hoarse.

In 1926 Layman returned to marry Miss Brenda Wright, described as being from a well known Higham Ferrers family. Eric Coley was best man.

With more schools now playing rugby, the trend of emerging local talent continued, and at 17 lock Tom Harris was being tipped as a future international, which he was to become in 1929. He announced his arrival on March 8, 1924, with two tries against Leicester.

The highlight of the 1924/25 season was the game against the all-conquering All Blacks, who faced the East Midlands at the County Ground on Saturday, December 6, 1924. For once the match had been wooed away from Welford Road and some 15,000 responded, paying receipts of £1,100. All seats were sold well in advance of the match.

Nine Saints men lined up against the team known as The Invincibles – Dodgson, Williams, Jones and Weston in the backs; Luck, Harris, Coley, Webb and Binyon in the forwards. Weston and Coley were late replacements for Massey, of Leicester, and Blakiston, who was now playing for Liverpool.

The All Blacks came to Northampton with a magnificent unbeaten record: played 22, won 22, scoring 511 points and conceding just 74. They did not concede a point in the first four games. They were to go through the tour winning every game with a final record of: P38 W38 F981 A180.

On the County Ground that day were some of the greatest players ever to play international rugby. Maori full-back George Nepia played in all 38 matches on the tour that took in France and Canada. Born in 1905, Nepia was still giving exhibitions of bare-foot kicking almost up until his death in 1981. During the Depression of the 1930s he turned to rugby league and played for Streatham and Halifax before returning to New Zealand, where he was reinstated as an amateur. He became the oldest man to play in a first class match, when he skippered Olympian at the age of 50. His son, also George, was captain of the opposition, Poverty Bay.

Also in the side was Cyril Brownlie, who was to gain considerable notoriety later on the tour by becoming the first man to be sent off in an international, against England, but the All Blacks still won 17-11. The powerful Brownlie scored two tries against the East.

Against all the odds, the East Midlands side had the audacity to take the lead. And it was a Saints player, fly-half Jones, who collected a kick forward to score out wide after just eight minutes. It only delayed the inevitable but a scoreline of 31-7 meant the East players could hold their heads high, especially Jones as he also scored a drop-goal in the second half.

The All Blacks wore town-made boots, the Hotspur, provided by Read, Myall & Read, of Billington Street. On arriving in England, the squad was supplied with two pairs for each of the 29 players.

Before leaving for Coventry, the entire squad paid a visit to the Edgar Mobbs memorial, and skipper Clifford Porter laid a wreath.

There was a delightful sequel to the All Blacks trip when East Midlands secretary Jimmy Minahan took his annual party to France. Before a game in Lyons, Minahan led the side in an imitation Haka which went something like:

Leader (fiercely):
    Favilo
Chorus (fiercely):
      Les Anglais
      Favilo
      Les Anglais
Chorus (fiercely):
      Ick nicki dimi imi imi
      Ick nicki dimi imi Oh!
      Ick nicki dimi imi imi
      Ick nicki dimi imi Oh!
      Oh! Oh! Oh! Oh! Oh! Oh! Oh!
      Vive la France

On January 3, New Zealand defeated an England side containing the old Saints, Blakiston, and with his uncanny knack for controversy found himself in magistrates court the next day. On Saturday night, when mistakenly identified as the first English try scorer, he was part of rowdy behaviour in Regent Street. He was given a ticking-off and a fine.

Vaughan found the burden of captaincy weighing on his shoulders and at the end of the season the returning Blakiston took over the reins unopposed.

Since before the turn of the century, Saints had

On a tour of France Jimmy Minihan (below) led a group of players in an English version of the Haka

complained that their men did not receive the recognition their talents warranted. It was a charge they could not lay at the door of the authorities in 1925/26.

Hooker Bob Webb played for England and Jones for Wales. Coley and Harris were England reserves. Webb was an unlikely international. Born on October 17, 1900, James William George Webb, was, for some inexplicable reason, known as Bob. He had not played any rugby before joining the A side in 1919 but rose to become the regular first team hooker by the 1924/25 season. His wife, Gladys, was sister-in-law to Tottenham Hotspurs and England footballer, Northants cricketer and Test match umpire, Frederick (Fanny) Walden from Wellingborough.

In 1926 Webb, robust and powerful, played against Scotland and France but then fell foul of the selectors until 1929 when he was recalled to face Scotland at Murrayfield along with Harris.

He was not a man to be trifled with, Mitton once writing of him that he was not a man to turn the other cheek. But there was one famous occasion when he came off second best. Before a Leicester game, the captain insisted that the ball should stay in the scrum from the first whistle to the last, and the opposition ground down.

The first scrum was a Saints put-in, yet Webb made no attempt to hook the ball. A strike against the head, and when the scrum broke up Webb crumpled to the floor. Fists were flying all over the place, suggesting the Leicester team talk had been on the same lines as Northampton's.

Webb first came to the fore in the East Midlands-All Blacks game, and his recall in 1929 owed a lot to a tremendous performance for the East Midlands against the Barbarians in the Mobbs Memorial Match. The Baa-Baas scraped a draw in what was a semi-official England trial game. When the team for Murrayfield was announced, the selectors had axed six men. Webb and Harris, seven years younger than his team mate, were brought in and Coley missed out by a whisker.

Although born in the tiny village of Upton, Webb, was raised in Fife Street in the shadow of Franklin's Gardens and after leaving Dallington School was apprenticed to a Kingsthorpe nursery. He later became head gardener at Upton Hall, now Quinton House school.

The selection of Jones, born in Shanghai of a Welsh father and Chinese mother, for the internationals against England, Scotland and France caused a furore in the media. Former Welsh international, Clem Lewis, writing in the *London Chronicle*, laid into Jones: "I have one grouse, and that concerns Jones, of Northampton. Last week I wrote that Jones had only to make any sort of show to walk into the Welsh team and, to my regret, my words have proved to be true. I have nothing to say against Jones personally. My grievance is that it was possible to give him a Welsh cap, for no amount of argument will convince me that he is a Welsh footballer.

"Many people during these past few days have pooh-poohed my scruples, and said that since the laws stand as they do we are justly entitled to be ruled by them. I suppose there is sense in that, yet the thought will persist that Jones is not a Welsh footballer. It is rumoured that there may be trouble over his selection; that England may make it a test case. I hope it is true."

Jones may have upset Mr Lewis but the Welsh crowd loved him. They carried him shoulder high off the pitch, after a draw with England, although he played only twice more. His brother Richard, known as 'Chink' in those less politically correct days, made one appearance for Wales three years later.

Saints, meanwhile, had three skippers in the season. Blakiston found it a handicap living in Liverpool and along with a couple of injuries he only played 15 times, and when his deputy, Jones, was on Welsh duty, seasoned campaigner Harry Griffin was left in charge. Griffin had the rare distinction of playing in every game.

Of all the 27 victories, two, achieved within the space of 10 days in the last month of the season, stood out. On April 6, the first visit to Cardiff, the Saints, led by Griffin, won 8-0, after Neath and Llanelli had posted big scores against Saints. Then came a record margin of victory over Leicester, 18-0, five tries without reply.

On a more unsavoury note, Blakiston, was sent off for an incident against St Bart's Hospital before a shocked Franklin's Gardens audience. Sendings-off were a rarity, but for a man who had played 17 times for his country it was little short of a national disgrace.

The *Tatler* pleaded on his behalf: "Quite an unnecessary amount of publicity was given to his case, all the stunt merchants of the yellow press making the most of their opportunity.

"Doubtless the East Midlands committee, who had to deal with the affair, acted to their best judgment and ability, and there is no fault to be found with their decision. But it seems only just in a case of this kind the accused player should be given a chance of appearing before the committee; he might, and in this instance he certainly would, have something to say on his own behalf. It is true that Blakiston tried to appeal, but the Rugby Union very properly decided that there was no ground on which an appeal could be based, and so the matter was at an end."

Publicity raged for weeks in the national and local press, and Blakiston did not play again for the Saints for eight matches.

Blakiston had been idolised by the boys at his old school, Northampton Grammar, but this incident tarnished his reputation.

If the Blakiston affair was a sporting scandal of national proportions, the Saints were rocked even more in February, 1926, by the suicide of committee man, Ebenezer Coles (Eddy) Page.

Page had left work one Tuesday, driven to a field at Sapcote near Hinckley in Leicestershire and shot himself through the head with a Webley and Scott

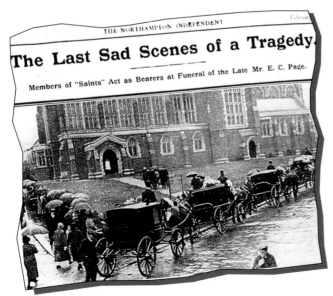

THE NORTHAMPTON INDEPENDENT Februar

The Last Sad Scenes of a Tragedy.

Members of "Saints" Act as Bearers at Funeral of the Late Mr. E. C. Page.

Saints committee man Eddy Page, who blew his brains out, fearing exposure of embezzlement. His funeral was extensively covered in the press

revolver. It was found tightly grasped in his left hand with the fatal wound through his temple and a hole on the far side of the car. It was not until Friday that his boss, Billy Wren contacted Northampton police. He was at the police station, when news of the discovery came through from Leicester.

The report of the inquest in the *Independent* of February 27 indicates that Page, was about to be found out of embezzling money from his employer, Wren & Co, where he had been company secretary for 16 years.

Two letters were found on the body – both to his wife. Despite the odour of scandal, the Saints turned out in force for the funeral at Holy Trinity Church, and the pall bearers included Eric Coley, Jerry Gordon and Welsh international Edgar Morgan. Saints representatives included Harry Weston, Gilbert Bull, Bobby Jones, Bob Webb, Jimmy Minahan, Leslie Barnes, Edwin Barnes and former skipper Billy Kingston.

Wren's factory closed down for the afternoon and 50 employees attended. Also represented were Wellingborough Rugby Club, Kingsthorpe Golf Club, Northampton Hockey Club and Kingsthorpe Bowls Club. The Saints dinner was postponed for five weeks.

The following year another Saints man committed suicide; Harry Burke, one of five brothers to play for the club, cut his neck and throat in May of 1927, shortly after taking over as landlord of the Crown Inn in Luton.

Burke, who had been in Mobbs' XV that defeated the Aussies in 1908 and was one of the survivors from Mobbs Sportsman's regiment, was found lying in a pool of blood by his sister in the pub cellar.

A notebook in the cellar contained the message: **'Dear Clara, You have everything. Forgive me – H'**. Unlike Page, there had been no money troubles. An Army boxer, champion sprinter and excellent cricketer, he had taken a keen interest in developing rugby in the Luton area.

To lift the gloom Saints secretary Leslie Barnes, a captain in the Territorials, had been made an MBE in the King's Birthday Honours List. In the summer of 1926, the idea for a new stand gathered momentum. The initiative came from Teddy Dunkley, captain in 1888 and secretary from 1903 to 1907, but out of office for almost 20 years, before being elected back on to the committee.

A steel stand, which would accommodate 1,300 people, would cost £2,350 exclusive of seating and glass panelling at either end. That would cost another £50.

The final cost of the stand, with seating for 2,138, was just over £4,474, and a major form of fund raising was two raffles with a car as the prize. Harry Crask recalls the scene for the first draw with 17,247 tickets piled high into one of the dressing room baths; dressing room attendant Dan Lyons stirring the pot and the Mayor of Northampton drawing out the winning ticket.

A chap from Bedford won the car and was killed in a crash two days later, this being before driving tests. The second competition sold 4,000 less tickets with the prize a £175 two-seater Morris Cowley. The winner was a Mr J H Crutch, who was just about to get married.

There was also a jumble sale at the Guildhall, with

Drawing the winning raffle ticket for a car, part of the fund raising efforts towards the cost of the main stand that was opened in 1927

queues stretching for miles. When the doors opened, the scenes were chaotic, and although £182 was made, loads of people made off with unpaid garments in the confusion. These events raised just under £1,000, almost a quarter the cost of the entire project.

A Stand Appeal realised over £1,406 and a £500 donation came from William Barratt followed by £200 from Phipps brewery and two donations of £100 from Ernest Travis and R Barratt.

The Stand and Improvements Committee secured a longer lease on the Gardens. The percentage of gate takings was cancelled in favour of a fixed rent of £250, out of which the Sports & Pleasure company allocated £50 for maintenance, over a 36-year period.

The stand was designed by Archibald Leitch, and the scheme was given the go-ahead on May 16, 1927. In their final report, the committee declared: "The stand is a magnificent asset and represents the largest undertaking in the whole history of the club."

The stand was used for the first time for the visit of Torquay Athletic on September 24, 1927, although at this stage it had no roof on it and, of course, it rained. With the addition shortly after of new dressing rooms the final cost was £6,000.

Back on the field, Vaughan, in his fourth season with the club, set a record in 1926/27 that stood for 65 years – 61 conversions in a campaign that brought him 163 points. It was over 60 years, in 1991/92, before John Steele, improved that conversion record and indeed every other kicking record.

Saints again featured in England trials without one of a quartet of players getting the nod from the selectors. Three of the names were familiar to fans of the day – Webb, Coley and Harris – but a fourth, F N Birch was called up, having played first-class football for just two months. From Long Buckby, he made his debut on October 23 against UCS Old Boys and on December 18 accompanied his more famous colleagues to Exeter for the second England trial. Ironically it was against UCS in 1928 that Birch sustained an injury and never played for the Saints again.

29

Long-serving secretary Jerry Gordon and the man he replaced, Leslie Barnes (top inset) and Barnes' father Edwin who followed shortly after

This was the season Weston made the switch to wing forward. Coley suggested he tried his luck in the pack. Weston had not made the team in any position by the end of November. He came into the back row against King's College Hospital, but had to make way when the England trialists returned.

Northamptonshire cricketer Austin Matthews made his first appearance for the Saints in 1927. He was to play 94 games in nine seasons before he angrily left Northampton to play cricket for Glamorgan. A former Penarth and Welsh trialist forward, Matthews moved here to teach and play cricket. Born in Penarth in 1905, Matthews had an outstanding career as a fast bowler. He took 567 wickets at an average of 26.45.

He joined Glamorgan midway through the 1937 season, leaving without the approval of Northamptonshire, after a row over a benefit year. He wanted one in 1938 but that was granted to Jack Timms, and when the county said he would have to wait until 1939, he returned to Wales.

Matthews was also a Welsh table tennis player, coached cricket at Cambridge University between 1935 and 1950 and went on the combined Oxford and Cambridge rugby tour to Argentina in 1948 as referee.

Among the highs of the 1926/27 season were an amazing 45-15 win over Moseley, the Saints coming back from a 15-14 half-time deficit, yet another victory in Cardiff at the end of the Easter tour by a staggering 18-6 margin and an 18-9 victory over Leicester.

Such was the interest in the Tigers game that portable stands, owned by Northamptonshire County Cricket Club, were used to accommodate overspill fans, among them Mr Justice Sankey, who discharged the jury at Northampton Assizes and advised them to be at Franklin's Gardens the next day. He told them they would see a fine game.

Saints added another French side to their fixture list, Lyon, and found themselves on the wrong end of a 3-0 scoreline. The Town Band gave it an

international flavour by playing the Marseillaise as the Frenchmen ran on to the pitch followed by the National Anthem.

Off the field and on, Franklin's Gardens was booming. In September, 1927, the final touches were being given to the neighbouring Salon-de-Danse, the transformation of the bleak Jubilee Hall into a social high-spot with Chinese pagoda decor and hanging lanterns. It underwent several name changes and refurbishments until bought by the club and demolished as the Gardens expanded into the magnificent present-day stadium.

On Saturdays, the Saints and their opponents would sit in one corner of the Salon, enjoying post-match refreshments, while the dance fans of Northampton would indulge in tea and sandwiches interspersed with a waltz or a quickstep at the popular tea-dances.

In the 1927/28 season, the Saints lost just four games with a side containing two internationals in Jones and Webb and four who were to join them – Coley, Harris, Weston and prop Ray Longland, who was to become a rock of the England front row.

Longland, a future captain and president of the Saints, was born in Lavendon in 1908. He started off as a soccer player for Olney and only gave it up when the club folded. He switched to rugby and after starting with Olney A made the first team the following season.

Bedford offered him a game towards the end of the 1926/27 season and he started off the next campaign still at Goldington Road, but after an injury lay-off he joined the Saints, causing some friction between the clubs at the time.

His widow, Greta, who he married the day before the Second World War broke out, has no idea why he switched clubs, but suggests that it was probably due to the fact that he was working in Northampton as a carpenter.

"He was a dedicated trainer and it would have been so much easier to leave work and be at Franklin's Gardens for Tuesday and Thursday night training sessions."

Longland, who died of leukemia in 1975, was the son of a gamekeeper. He had a superb physique and kept in trim as a youngster by walking three miles to school. He was naturally bursting with pride at being picked for England even though it regularly cost him a day and a half's pay for being off work.

Said Greta: "If the train fare was 12s 11d, that's what Ray got from the Rugby Union. There was no rounding up. He once took a taxi to the hotel and was ticked off because it was on a bus route."

Greta's courtship with Ray converted her from Cobblers season ticket holder to Saints fan, after meeting at the Salon. "I was there for the dance. Ray was looking for something to eat in the kitchen after training on a Thursday night. We literally bumped into each other."

Fiercely patriotic, Longland volunteered when war broke out but was told to go home and wait for his call-up. He was made a PTI in the RAF with the rank of corporal and was one of the lucky ones, spending the war in Skegness. He spent much of the time playing rugby including a host of war-time internationals, used as morale boosters for the troops.

An intimidating opponent on the rugby field, he was

the original gentle giant off it.

His Saints career began at Beeston against Nottingham on December 3, 1926, for the start of a long and wonderful association with the club. He kept his place and made his home debut a week later against Devonport Services.

For much of the 1926/27 season the Saints had to play without scrum-half Johnny Millward, while he nursed his sick wife who sadly did not recover.

A prankster by nature Millward amused and bewildered a French audience in Bordeaux by swinging from the top of a lamp post. A distinctly unamused French gendarme came to arrest him, at which point his team-mates broke into an impromptu Hornpipe, so distracting the policeman that Millward was able to disappear into the crowd.

Those elusive England caps finally came the way of Coley and Harris in 1928/29. On March 16, 1929, Harris and Webb, winning his third cap, faced Scotland at Murrayfield, the first time the club had been represented by two players in the same international. England were beaten 12-6 and both were dropped for the French game. Consolation for Saints fans came with the inclusion of Coley, the perennial reserve (17 times, 10 as a travelling reserve). Coley helped England to a 16-6 win at Stade Colombes, the last game for full back Tom Brown, of Bristol, who signed for Broughton Park Rugby League side, instantly regretted it and returned the cheque. The RFU refused to re-instate him.

Local bragging rights were secured as Saints beat Tigers at Welford Road for the first time since 1909 (10-8) and completed the double, a feat not achieved since 1905/06. Many of the 3,000 Northampton contingent stayed behind to cheer the players as they left the ground. At a cinema opposite, *Tarzan of the Apes* was showing. Longland picked up a plywood tiger advertising board and held it aloft like a prize fighter with the crowd roaring their approval.

Cardiff were swamped at the Gardens 29-0 but far from deriving any pleasure Saints officials were so annoyed by the poor side the Welshmen turned out that they axed the fixture for a season.

The letter cancelling the following season's fixtures was one of the last acts by Saints secretary Les Barnes. Five months later he was ousted from the post at the June 24 annual meeting at the Peacock Hotel.

It made front page news in the *Echo*. Former skipper Tim Kingston set the ball rolling by suggesting that a paid secretary be appointed

He proposed that club rules be changed to allow for a third of the committee to have to seek re-election every year.

Barnes, one of Edgar Mobbs' Sportsman's Battalion heroes from the Great War, subsequently found himself in a three-way battle for his job with Jerry Gordon and A G Hoste, a player between 1900 and 1906.

After the first ballot, Barnes had 11 votes, Gordon, who was assistant secretary, six and Hoste one. Hoste then withdrew and in the second round Gordon was voted in.

Gordon, who had worked for the club accountants, A C Palmer & Co – his boss being former skipper Claude Palmer – was at the time secretary of the Franklin's Gardens Sports & Pleasure Company, who

Top class full-back Bob Vaughan, recruited from Wales who became a successful businessman

rented the ground from the owners. Palmer was a director of that company as well.

Over 60 years later, Harry Crask, later to be elected on to the new-look committee, revealed that Les Barnes lost his position at the Saints because of his unpopularity.

"He had been a player before the war, but had lost an eye and took over as secretary. He seemed to carry a chip on his shoulder, probably due to the eye wound," said Crask.

"I remember intercepting a pass virtually on my own line and running the length of the field to score against Neath. When we got back to the dressing room I didn't get any praise. I was told by Barnes to go for the man next time and not the interception. He was that sort of bloke and it came as no surprise when he was voted out of office."

Instead of the full-time administrator that Kingston spoke of, the club got instead Ernest James (Jerry) Gordon. He started in office in 1929, the same year that Wall Street crashed, Prime Minister Ramsay MacDonald presided over Parliament and Zeppelins made successful inter-continental flights.

Gordon's reign ended in 1966 with his death, when the Beatles and Rolling Stones were making music, Bobby Moore was lifting the soccer World Cup for England and astronauts orbited the earth.

Gordon proved an inspired and inspiring choice. Not one person had an unkind word about him. For years he ran the Franklin's Gardens hotel before handing over to Coley, while he went into farming at Rothersthorpe. He may have got the idea during the Second World War, when the Franklin's Gardens pitch was turned over to livestock.

Former *Chronicle & Echo* chief photographer, Alan Burman, an apprentice electrician just after the war, was one of a number of youngsters who used to do maintenance work at the hotel. "The vivid thing I remember is how immaculately dressed he always was, his clothes were very stylish and fashionable.

But there not a trace of arrogance. He never talked down to any of the kids."

His daughter Jennifer Dickens remembers her father constantly on the telephone to irate hotel proprietors after many an Easter tour. "He was often negotiating the cost of some mishap or other. 'Does £50 sound okay', he would say, followed by: 'The boys *did* so enjoy themselves'."

After taking over the farm, Easter tours would always start with a trip to Rothersthorpe to pick up a giant hamper of food to be consumed on the way down.

An extraordinary total of 23 men were tried at either centre or wing in the 1929/30 season, and the *Echo* dryly observed that Saints had probably created a rugby record. The problems did not end there. Thirteen men had varying lengths of incumbency at half-back and four men occupied the full-back spot. All this while there was comparative harmony in the forwards.

Not surprisingly a forward, lock Tom Harris was top scorer with 17 tries, one more than veteran winger Teddy Haselmere, who also had a panache for dropping goals – nine in all that season.

Harris was a well known figure around the county, running a mobile fishmongery and fruit and vegetable business with his father. Like Coley he died young, at the age of 50, in 1958.

He played for 14 years, making 426 appearances and ending up with two England caps, against Scotland (1929) and Ireland (1932). Educated at Barry Road School, he first played for a junior club, Alexandra Park.

A new name was added to the fixture list in 1929, Bath, who marked their arrival by completing the double over Saints.

The new-look Franklin's Gardens, with its £6,000 Members' Stand, staged an England trial in November 1929, featuring Longland and Millward as reserves.

The 1930/31 season was the Saints Jubilee Year, and they tried to win back spectators by providing more spectacular back play. Attendances were on the slide as fans were fed up with the lack of excitement behind the scrum.

The management of the club set its stall out to play a more attractive style and were helped by the discovery of Charlie Slow, an odd-ball character, but the best fly-half since Bobby Jones.

He went on to make one England international appearance in the victory over Scotland in 1934, but by then Northampton-born Slow had changed his allegiance to Leicester.

In 1930 he made his debut in the centre against St Bartholomew's Hospital, having been spotted as a player of promise playing for Unitarians and Crusaders in junior football. Two games later, on Boxing Day, against Penarth, Slow was introduced – unsuccessfully – at fly-half. He was promptly put back to centre for the next two games and in the second, at Guy's Hospital, he scored his debut try, a great solo effort.

He was tried again at fly-half for the next game against the RAF and made the headlines for an outstanding display. The performance cemented his place alongside brilliant scrum-half Millward, who was often touted as a player of England calibre.

Slow, most inappropriately named, continued to catch the eye with a series of dazzling tries, including one at Welford Road two minutes from time, which earned the Saints a 10-10 draw.

Born in 1911, he lived only until 1939, killed in a motor accident while serving with the RAFVR. In 1930 he was all the rage and his attributes were a "quick brain, safe hands, speed and unlimited pluck." He learned his rugby at Kettering Road Intermediate School and spent two seasons with Unitarians before joining the Crusaders. His partner, Millward, was described as "one of the smartest scrum-halves in the kingdom."

Vaughan hung up his boots after an illustrious career spanning nine years and 255 games in which he amassed 667 points. Mitton wrote: "He goes down in history as the finest back the club has possessed. The man who succeeds him has a formidable task."

Webb also retired, having made 201 appearances and scoring 20 tries.

Mitton's remarkable judgment on new players was spot on again in predicting a big future for prop-cum-lock John Dicks, born in Mears Ashby and a pupil of Northampton Grammar School.

He made just two spaced out appearances in 1931/32 yet in his summary of the season he forecast that Dicks "seems likely to advance rapidly."

England colours: Eric Coley shaking hands with King Edward VIII and Bob Webb in a watching role in the 1926 international against France. England won 11-0.

Chapter Five
Saints men help fulfill Jimmy's dream

JOHN DICKS did indeed improve rapidly. By 1934 he was in the England side in a golden era for Saints internationals. The England pack of the Thirties was dominated by three Northampton men: Longland, Weston and Dicks, who was in his sixth international before tasting defeat, on March 23, 1935, to Scotland at Murrayfield.

All three would have gained more caps but for the home unions pompously telling the French to clean up their act, refusing to play them until they did so. In January, 1931, 10 leading French clubs broke away from the FFR to form their own union with the intention of competing for a separate club championship. Disturbed by these events and rumours of professionalism, the four home unions met in February and passed a resolution that relations with France would not be resumed until the "control and conduct of the game had been placed on a satisfactory footing."

From 1931 until 1946 the French did not appear in the Five Nations. They played Germany, Italy and Romania instead. Relations were eventually patched up and but for an even bigger argument with Germany, France would have been back in the fold at the end of the Thirties.

Longland reached the international arena first, against Scotland on March 19, 1932, a 16-3 win at Twickenham; next came Weston on February 11, 1933, against Ireland at Twickenham, a 17-6 victory (the only international Longland missed for six successive years); and finally Dicks, on January 20, 1934, at Cardiff Arms Park against Wales, a 9-0 win.

All three Saints men appeared together in seven internationals, and in two of the seasons, 1934 and 1937 England won the Triple Crown. In 1934 against Scotland at Twickenham, the Saints trio were joined by their ex-team mate Charlie Slow for his one and only England appearance, alongside East Midlands skipper Bernard Gadney at half-back.

A year later at Twickenham, and the three Saints were in opposition to another team-mate, Welshman Wickham Charles Powell, who went on to play in all three internationals in 1935.

Years earlier Mitton had suggested that Welshmen playing for English clubs had little or no chance of recognition. The Powell story contradicts that theory. 'Wick' Powell first played for Wales in 1926 and was seldom out of the side up to and including the 1932 season. He was the last Welshman – in 1931 against England – to score a goal from a mark.

He joined the Saints in October, 1934, when he could no longer command a place in the London Welsh side, and within three months was recalled to the international fray. He went on to make 30 appearances for the Saints, but was not the long-term solution to the scrum-half position, which had not been adequately

Putting on the style: John Dicks (left) and Billy Weston at the post-match dinner between England and Ireland at the Metropole Hotel in London in 1933

33

Ray Longland (left) makes for a Scottish opponent at Twickenham in 1932

Springboks, the only defeat of the tour, at Welford Road on November 14, 1931. The South Africans entered the game with 11 victories and a 0-0 draw against South of Scotland behind them. The points tally was 222-49.

Interest was intense with 30,000 said to be packed into the ground. Trains were laid on from Northampton and buses from Kettering, Olney and Bedford. A third of the side were Saints men. Slow, originally picked for the centre, replaced Leicester's Greenless at stand-off, while the rest of the Northampton contingent came from the pack – Coley and Weston were the wing forwards, Harris in the second row; and Longland in the front row.

The tourists were beaten 30-21 and two Northampton men dominated the scoring: Slow, who opened the match with a drop-goal and went on to score two tries, and Weston, who kicked four conversions and a crucial penalty when the Springboks had clawed their way back to within three points.

It was an extraordinary result and comparisons were made with the Mobbs-inspired Combined Counties victory over the Australians on the same ground 23 years earlier.

At half-time the score stood at a staggering 19-6 and despite a hat-trick of tries from Zimmerman the Counties held their nerve, particularly Weston.

Strangely, he was the only Northampton forward not rewarded with an England cap that season. Coley (Wales), Harris (Ireland) and Longland (Scotland) all made it into the side, although none of them got the chance to play against the Springboks again.

Harris would have played against Scotland but was injured in Dublin and although he had recovered by the time of the Calcutta Cup match the selectors decided not to risk him. Slow got only as far as the England reserve bench.

filled since Millward had returned to junior rugby with Olney.

Powell, whose forté was the reverse pass, qualified to be an architect in 1933 and 13 years later he emigrated to South Africa to set up in private practice. He died there in 1973.

Never in the club's 53-year history had so many Northampton men graced the international stage. The club forged a reputation, not always flattering, for hard, uncompromising forwards. Their performances demanded that England could not afford to ignore them, the most significant was a magnificent East Midlands/Leicestershire victory over the touring

Skipper Bernard Gadney's England side of 1936 to face Scotland included John Dicks (next to referee), Ray Longland (front row second left) and Billy Weston (front row extreme right). Prince Obolensky is standing three away from Dicks.

The 1931/32 Springboks lost their unbeaten record to an East Midlands side including Billy Weston and Charlie Slow

Longland picked up a knee injury in the opening minutes of the Springbok game. He gamely carried on and was singled out as one of the stars of a stunning victory.

Several careers came to an end in 1932/33 through a mixture of retirement, injury and disloyalty.

Coley, after 11 brilliant seasons, called it a day. Millward was injured early in the season in an evening knockabout at Olney and shortly after

announced his retirement. The quicksilver Slow sustained a cartilage injury on Christmas Eve in the home defeat by Gloucester and was not seen in a Saints jersey again. Having played 61 games in a short but brilliant career he left for Leicester for reasons not made clear at the time.

It was a season noted for away wins, nine from 13 matches, including first time successes at Bath and Bridgend.

The financial picture was gloomy despite the efforts of rookie secretary Jerry Gordon. The Saints were not helped by East Midland matches being switched to Saturdays. The switch to Saturday matches proved the making of East Midlands. Saints provided 10 of the East side and one Northampton-born ex-Saint, which lifted the county championship for the first time, thus realising the ambition of secretary, Jimmy Minahan, who would retire at the end of the season after 30 years in office.

The championship success was the crowning glory for Minahan, who seems to have been years ahead of his time as an administrator. Always resplendent in bowler hat and spats, James Bernard Minahan was a genial, lovable Irishman, who had a passion for rugby.

Victory in the final came against his first adopted English county, Gloucestershire, who were going for a ninth success to equal that of Yorkshire. Minahan moved jobs with the post office from Gloucester to Northampton 1901 and took over as East Midlands secretary two years later.

It became his burning ambition to see the East win the county championship, then a prestigious and meaningful competition. Before the final on March 10, 1934, at Franklin's Gardens, Minahan sent a letter to every player urging them to give off their best. This is the one sent to Spriggs Baillon, then a 22-year-old full-back of great potential.

'Dear Baillon,

'As your Hon. Secretary for nearly 30 years and your proud President of the above Union, we wish

County champions of 1934, the East Midlands pictured at Franklin's Gardens before the final with Gloucestershire. Back row (left to right): T D Thevenard, J A Tallent, J Dicks, R T Perkins, C Slow. Middle row: R A Palmer, R J Longland, F Garratt, A D Matthews, A R Chorlton, N A York, J G Bott (referee). Front row: R G Baillion, J H Treen, T Harris, H C Palmer (president), B C Gadney (captain), J B Minahan (secretary), W H Weston

Fun and games: Jerry Gordon astride something called a pushball, a novelty game sponsored by the *Daily Mail* nationwide. The Saints players are on the right.

Eric Coley (back left) with a motley crew of England selectors. Coley was a selector from 1937 to 1948.

every East Midland player to know they carry our full confidence in Saturday's Battle for the Championship, and given immunity from casualties we feel assured the splendid fighting spirit that has achieved so much, will carry us to a final and glorious victory.

'We know every man has kept fit and will key himself up for a special effort for the honour of the East Midlands in anticipation of the hardest and most vital game of the season.

'We look to you boys confidently to play your own game, not Gloucestershire's game, as their tactics have no doubt been determined upon.

With best wishes and all Good Luck'

His highly personal and fascinating notes for the match day programme still make entertaining reading today.

'For many years now I have penned a few notes…as an introduction to the County games played at Franklin's Gardens, but never before have I found such difficulty in preparing a short story as to-day. Here I am an old Gloucestrian, yet 30 years Honorary Secretary to the East Midlands, endeavouring to keep an open mind on today's issue. My old friends, Archie Hudson, Tom Voyce, Sam Tucker, Kit Tanner, and others, say it's impossible and I shall cheer for my home county.

'Thirty-three years ago I came from the County that our visitors have made famous in the Rugger world…I determined as far as in me lay to build up my adopted county on the lines of Gloucestershire.

'I found myself with a choice of three Counties, Northamptonshire, Bedfordshire and Buckinghamshire, with only two premier Clubs as a sheet anchor, Northampton and Bedford, and for years an insuperable barrier to success – mid-week fixtures. My first season was a disastrous one, for all matches were lost, but the next season was more successful…This was the year that the late Lt. Colonel Edgar Mobbs made his debut and began a brilliant Rugger career…We made steady progress, always striving to get to the top but the mid-week fixtures…was always too heavy a handicap.

'This season we have won all our group fixtures, defeated Lancashire at Blundellsands by 19 points to 18 points after being down at half-time by 15 points, in a match that surpasses anything I have seen in my 45 years of first-class football. We followed this up by defeating a powerful Barbarians XV in the Mobbs memorial match last week and so we take the field to-day with a feeling it is high time the Midlands won the Championship, and we incline to the hope it is ourselves who will take the honours.

'I have dreamed long of this day. Dreamed that we should get into the final, that it be played at Northampton and that our opponents should be my home County. My dreams have at long last been realised. Will my ambition, the winning of the Championship, be fulfilled today or will Gloucestershire equal Yorkshire's record of nine times Champion County?'

The East rose magnificently to the occasion to win 10-0. The Saints men on display were Baillon, Chorlton and Treen in the backs, while the pack was entirely Northampton save for hooker Perkins. They were: Longland, York, Harris, Dicks, Garratt, Matthews and Weston.

Six of the East side, Longland, Harris, Dicks and Weston from Northampton, Gadney (Leicester), the England captain, and Tallent from Blackheath were internationals to Gloucestershire's three: Carpenter (prop), Burland (centre) and winger Champain Tanner, who died seven years later in the Second World War, posthumously awarded the Albert Medal (later replaced by the George Cross).

The Championship final was watched by an estimated 12,000, including all three England selectors, Bob Oakes (president of the Rugby Union), John Daniell and Harry Coverdale.

A Slow drop-goal gave East an interval lead in a dour forward battle and in the second half Matthews and Tallent scored tries to give East a comfortable margin of victory.

The championship won, Minahan retired as secretary but in 1936 was elected president.

County success came at a price for the Saints. With trials, internationals and county games, a host of players were lost for a third of the Saints season – and it showed in the revenue. The fans would not watch weakened sides in the same number. The *Echo* described it as 'The Penalties of Greatness'.

Jerry Gordon wrote in the last programme of the season: "It is this inability to raise representative teams that accounts for the very disappointing attendances and loss of membership."

The Saints did at least receive a donation from the East Midlands.

The international honours fell to Weston and Dicks for the first time and to Longland again. Weston's

international bow had come 12 years after his club debut, while Dicks had shot to prominence in just two years. In 1932 he had been playing for Wellingborough. Now he was picked for the first international of the season against Wales at Cardiff Arms Park alongside Longland. Dicks was picked for England in the second row, but it could have been up front or even in the back row. He had played all three positions for the Saints in less than two seasons.

Dicks went on to make 124 appearances for the Saints from 1931 to 1937 and played eight times for England. Yet he dropped out of the limelight quicker than he zoomed into it. At the age of 25 he was finished, and was never seen at Franklin's Gardens again even though he farmed most of his life in Great Doddington.

Married life put a stop to Dicks's career. His wife Freda, an extremely attractive woman, hated the game. She also disliked farming.

Dicks, outside of farming, had only one interest – horse racing, and was a frequent racegoer around the Midland tracks. Among his group of friends was Frank Gilman, owner and trainer of Grand National winner, Grittar.

In complete contrast was Gordon Sturtridge, an outside-half who made his debut in the penultimate game of the 1933/34 season against Old Alleynians, just a week after he had played against the Saints for Rosslyn Park.

Dicks was born in Northamptonshire but took no part in the club once his playing days had prematurely ended, while Sturtridge, born on the other side of the world on his father's farm in Queensland, went on to dedicate his life to the club.

The house surgeon at Northampton General Hospital was quickly deemed a 'splendid' player.

The 1934/35 season brought the best playing record since 1928/29 with doubles over Gloucester and Bath for the first time.

A controversial win at Rugby when touch-judge Gordon was almost lynched by the crowd kicked off a 13-match winning run.

The winning sequence was broken by Coventry at Coundon Road, a game which finished 3-3. The run of unbeaten games stretched to 17 before the Tigers had the satisfaction of lowering the Saints colours at Welford Road, 13-8.

The 1935/36 season went into May to make up for a severe winter that cost four fixtures between December and February. The extension allowed the home game with Coventry to be played but did little to retrieve the worsening cash situation.

The club owed around £850 and had only £20 in hand, so in a bid to improve finances a fete was organised for Whit Monday at the Gardens.

The touring All Blacks were the main attraction of the winter, and before their game with the combined Leicestershire and East Midlands side at Welford Road, they watched the Saints beat Rugby at Bilton Road 19-5 the previous night.

Longland, Dicks and Weston represented the Counties and Longland scored the only try in a 16-3 defeat.

If the Midlands men were not up to beating the New Zealand giants, England were, thanks to Prince Alexander Obolensky, scorer of two tries, one that is part of Twickenham folklore. On January 4 in front of the Prince of Wales, within weeks to become King

Edward VIII following the death of George V on January 30, England, with Longland and Weston in the pack, won 13-0.

Longland, a humble carpenter, propped alongside Douglas (later Sir Douglas) Kendrew, known to his team mates as 'Joe'. Kendrew won four DSOs in North Africa, Italy and Korea, and on retiring from the Army he was made Governor General of Western Australia.

The critics, naturally, were euphoric, and Longland was singled out for particular praise. "Longland was the greatest forward on the field…always on the ball and tackling like a demon. Hamilton-Hill, Dunkley and Weston made swift raids…that caused the opposition endless annoyance" – *News Chronicle*

"Longland played the game of his life…In defence, nothing could have been finer than the endless spoiling work of Gadney and the ever vigilant Weston" – *Morning Post*

Meanwhile, the club had a miserable time with injuries, the most serious to Baillon, who broke his leg in the Boxing Day match with Moseley. Richard Obre (known to everyone by his family nickname of Spriggs) Baillon got an England trial in 1934 but never made it into the national side. He was one of four sons of Louis Baillon, managing director of Northampton Brewery Company, who was a member of the 1908 Great Britain hockey team to triumph at the White City Olympics.

Spriggs Baillon became equally well known in Northampton for playing tennis. Much of what is now the Beacon Bingo hall car park was United Tennis Club. For many years Spriggs played for Northamptonshire and was part of the team that got to Group One of the county championships in 1952, having been promoted each season since 1947.

In the Fifties Baillon used to practise with a promising teenager once a week on Abington Park's public courts. Billy Knight, son of the late Alf Knight, a tireless worker on the Saints committee and a former president, went on to become British No 1 and a Wimbledon quarter-finalist.

In April, Saints fans were, for a second time, denied the pleasure of seeing Prince Obolensky. He had been announced as a Barbarian to face East Midlands but dropped out and he did so again when Rosslyn Park were visitors to the Gardens.

The best result of the season came in almost the last match, a 6-6 draw at Llanelli after 13 visits to Stradey Park and 13 defeats. It would have been an 8-6 victory, but captain Tom Harris, from in front of the posts with virtually the last kick of the game, screwed a conversion wide.

The Saints would have to wait until 1949/50, nearly 50 years after the first attempt, to taste victory at Stradey Park.

Sturtridge, by now a staunch Saints man, was made captain for the 1938/39 season, but it was a disappointing campaign and for the first time since

War was shortly to break up this side of 1938/39. Insets: R O Baillion, D King. A E Brookes. Back row: F Jeffcoate, J Smith. Middle row: E J Gordon (secretary), A Wood, W Fallowfield, R G BUrrell, W Gascoigne, J P Stevens. Front row: J T Bradley, R C Powell, G S Sturtridge (captain), R J Longland (vice captain), E C M Palmer, S F Petts. On ground: J E Bailey, D W A Vann. (Powell was one of five Saints killed in the Second World War)

1932 the club failed to produce an England international. Longland appeared in the trials but lost his place in the national side, after winning 19 caps. Only eight men at that time had won more in the history of the England team.

On April 30, 1938, the club held a dinner for Longland and Weston to mark their careers. Longland was 30, Weston 32 – considered past their sell-by date in international terms.

Longland was also to get an unofficial accolade when Vivian Jenkins, the Welsh full-back who went on to be a colossus of the press box, chose the Saints prop in his all-time British team. Weston also got a mention but did not make the final line-up.

Of Longland, Jenkins said: "I will only repeat the remark once made to me by a famous hooker who said: 'Packing with Ray is so comfortable; it's like getting into bed'."

As Europe lurched towards war, attendances fell away and it required some individual generosity for the club to show a £71 19s 7d profit on the season despite the gate receipts falling from £723 to £497.

In the summer of 1939 Sturtridge was re-elected captain and the Saints published a strong fixture list, including one against Combined Services, which was to act as a trial game for the Services in preparation for a match with the touring Wallabies. They never arrived. War was declared on September 3.

The Saints decided to suspend fixtures, but the dynamic Sturtridge organised his own XV, taking over the fixtures as from Boxing Day.

Gordon Short Sturtridge arrived in England in October, 1939, courtesy of the Australian Rugby Union. Sturtridge had played nine times for his country, when he set sail for South Africa never to return to his homeland, leaving behind his bride of one day.

The Sturtridges were married in secret in Melbourne. No-one, not even the couple's parents, knew of the marriage and the next day Sturtridge left with the Australian rugby team for a Test series against the Springboks.

Born in 1907, the son of a Queensland farmer he went to a Brisbane boarding school and then on to Queensland University, but there was no medical faculty so he switched to Melbourne University, where he met his bride-to-be.

He was one of 12 children, and his father gave him a choice: a piece of land to farm or a proper education. He chose education, the only son to do so. His father paid for him to go through university but gave him nothing else.

He was a natural sportsman, almost reaching Olympic standard as a hurdler. He made his international debut against New Zealand on July 20, 1929, the first member of the Victorian RU to be recognised at that level. He didn't play again until 1932, in a three-Test series against the All Blacks.

When he left for South Africa his new bride had no idea he would not be returning. The players had a choice – the Board would either pay for the return trip or pay a fare on to England. The first Mrs Sturtridge knew of his decision was via a cable: 'Sailing for England'. So his wife, who had played in an Australian hockey team that lost 14-1 to England, forked out £35 for a boat to England and set sail on the six-week journey. The couple were still not reunited when Mrs

Sturtridge arrived in England. She lived at the Ladies National Club in London, while 'Sturt', as she called him, lived in at a London hospital.

He joined Rosslyn Park and then the Saints at the back end of the 1933/34 season. He made 118 appearances for Northampton.

In 1934/35 Sturt played eight games and then returned to Park. "Northampton told him he was no good so he went back to Rosslyn Park," said Mrs Sturtridge. The real story was that Sturtridge did not like the team's forward-dominated style, and always being told to kick. That was to have a profound effect on him when he set about rebuilding the Saints after the war. He was determined to mould the Saints into a great side that would be famous for its backs.

At Northampton General Hospital, he soon rose to superintendent and then specialised in gynaecology.

By now the couple were firmly entrenched in Northampton life, and after the war Sturtridge came into his own as an administrator. While the players went off to fight Hitler, Sturtridge was asserting himself at Franklin's Gardens and in 1950 became the most powerful president the club had ever known, staying in office for 14 years. Indeed Sturtridge was not so much a president, more a soccer-style manager with an encyclopaedic memory of opponents. Before a game, Sturtridge would go through the opposition virtually man for man, elaborating on strengths and weaknesses, bringing a touch of Aussie professionalism to the dressing room. It was an attention to detail picked up by post-war skipper, Don White.

Lock forward Bob Hamp, one of the early post-war characters, was one of Sturtridge's early proteges, making his debut in 1939.

In an end-of-season report, the *Chronicle & Echo* was fretting over the merits of the youngsters who Dr Sturtridge had unearthed. "Whether the war be long or of short duration the Saints will need some new men."

In a masterpiece of understatement skipper Sturtridge said that fixtures would be hard to arrange. In the event 25 games were played, the last of which, against an RAF XV, was Sturtridge's farewell. His commitment to the club was by now total, and he carried with him a precious 'little black book' containing the name of players, who he saw as the future of the club – providing the war did not drag on too long. Sturtridge kept fixtures going until April, 1943. It was more than two years, September, 1945, before rugby returned to the Gardens .

On February 28, 1942, Corporal Longland, of the RAF, appeared in the first war-time international against Wales at the St Helen's ground, Swansea, in front of 20,359 fans, who raised £2,000 for the British Red Cross and the three Services' charities. Old differences between Union and League were forgotten as Longland played for Combined Services Rugby Union against Rugby League at the huge Odsal Stadium in Bradford. Programmes were even produced with a useful piece of information inside – 'AIR RAID SHELTERS just outside the ground behind the grandstand'.

Five Saints players, who lost their lives in the Second World War, J T Goosey, W M Jackson, R C Powell, R Solomon and G Parker, are commemorated on the war memorial at Franklin's Gardens.

Chapter Six
Backs to the future

THE Saints restarted after the war with £62 in the bank. By December that had risen to £615, "a remarkable recovery from a precarious position", treasurer A J Penn told a special general meeting.

Sturtridge and Gordon were geared up to pick up the pieces on the playing side, and for two decades they worked in harmony with a youngster, who began his Saints career on February 27, 1943. Donald Frederick White made his debut as a 16-year-old schoolboy as a prop against Coventry in a 17-3 defeat. He was pencilled into Sturtridge's black book as a player of potential.

White was to be the most influential figure at the Gardens for the next 40 years.

With war in Europe over, the players ran out again at Franklin's Gardens to face the Royal Australian Air Force on September 29. A crowd of around 1,500 welcomed rugby back to Franklin's Gardens, and a minute's silence was held for those who had made the supreme sacrifice.

The person who claims to be first in the queue when rugby resumed is Ron Slinn, later to become club president but then a little lad of 14. Being a Jimmies End boy he was first to arrive at the old turnstiles that faced out on to Weedon Road.

Such enthusiasm was instantly rewarded, when Bert Lawrence, secretary of the Supporters' Club, collared him to sell programmes. He did it for the next 20 years.

Fresh-faced international, Don White

"That was one of the key moments of my life. Who knows? I might have watched a couple of games and never gone again," said Slinn, who rose from humble

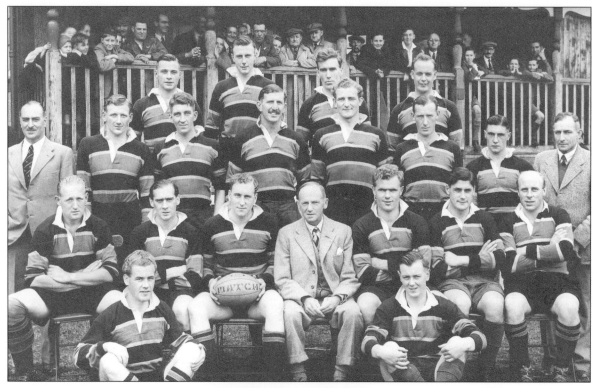

The Saints glory boys of 1949/50 with admiring fans behind. Back row (left to right): J M Pell, N Bailey, P J Langley, G Adkins. Middle row (standing): E J Gordon (Hon Sec), T Barker, T Smith, W R Hamp, R C Hawkes, J E Lomas, J P Hyde, G S Sturtridge. Seated: J Whiting, T Gray, D F White (capt), Dr A G Bull (President), M J Berridge (vice captain), L B Cannell, R O Pell. Front: J W Smith, G R Desborough

Three great internationals from the early post-war period (from left to right) Lewis Cannell, Ron Jacobs and Tommy Gray. All three have died within the last six years

programme seller to be president of the Saints from 1991 to 1993 even though he never played a single game of rugby in his life.

On October 27, the Saints and Tigers met at the Gardens for the first time since the war with only six players from the previous encounter, three from each side. After a pointless first half, a try from Alec Bell, converted by White, secured a 5-0 home win to the delight of 3,000 spectators.

A young Northampton Grammar School boy made his debut on the opening day of the season, even though he had only reluctantly wandered down to the Gardens for pre-season trials. Lewis Cannell would go on to play 19 times for England between 1948 and 1957. It would have been more, but twice he wrote to the selectors asking not to be considered for the season as he was taking medical exams. He also turned down the British Lions tour to New Zealand and Australia in 1950 because he could not spare six months from his studies.

The post-war years were ultimately run by the triumvirate of Sturtridge, Gordon and White, but the recruitment of Cannell owed an awful lot to chance – even Adolf Hitler played a part.

The Cannell home in Coventry was one of the thousands to be hit by Nazi bombers, and Cannell's father, a post office employee, was moved to Northampton.

Cannell, who died a couple of years ago, had played soccer at Droitwich College, but he turned to rugby on joining Northampton Grammar. A schoolmaster recommended him to the Saints, and the assiduous Gordon sent him several invitations to pre-season training, all of which were ignored except the last.

"Then on one particular Saturday I had nothing else to do, so I picked up my boots and went down to the Gardens. Jerry Gordon scolded me for not replying to his other invitations but he still put me in the team," said Cannell, who soon got a reputation for being a bit

of a swot.

White describes a game at Bath, when the rest of the team indulged in the usual post-match revelry, while teenager Cannell sat on the team coach studying his text books. It soon got so dark, Cannell could not carry on reading, but the drinking continued in earnest. A thoroughly miserable Cannell told the Hon Sec: "Mr Gordon, I'll play for you at home but I don't want to play away again."

Cannell played between 1945 and 1960 but made only 138 appearances. After National Service in the RAF, Cannell studied at Oxford University and then had a career in medicine starting at St Mary's Hospital.

"We had a very fine side at St Mary's, all the players drawn from the hospital, and at Oxford the team contained around 13 internationals from all over the world, the likes of C B Van Ryneveld. He was a brilliant centre and I think we learned a lot from each other.

"I always retained a strong affinity for the Saints. I think that was mainly due to people like Doc Sturtridge. He took a great interest in me because of his medical background and encouraged me a great deal."

Cannell agreed he had a reputation at Northampton for being a greedy player. "I used to get ticked off a lot by Ray Longland, when he was skipper, for not passing the ball more. But that wasn't for me, I loved to run with it. I just loved running.

"I was indifferent towards rugby. I enjoyed flying and soccer and was very intent on my medical career. I had no aspirations towards an England cap. When I won my first cap my father told me: 'you're in'. I had no idea what he was talking about."

He made his England debut against France in Paris on March 29, 1948, and played his last game – against Ireland – in 1957 with fellow Saints Jeff Butterfield, Dickie Jeeps and Ron Jacobs also in the side. After nine successive games for England,

Cannell dropped out of the 1951 season because of studies, but was immediately reinstated in 1952. He did not play in 1954 or 1955 but came back to partner Jeff Butterfield in 1956 and they stayed together for another five internationals. He became a radiologist in Durban and later Stoke Mandeville. His wife became director of radiology at St Bartholomew's hospital.

Rugby had taken its toll in later life with degenerative muscle problems affecting his lower back and knees, leaving his mobility seriously impaired, a sad irony for a man who just 'loved to run'.

Proof that the Saints had recovered quickly from the trauma of the war years came in 1946/47 as the side finished just four points short of 400. It was the best haul since 1934/35, although the club itself in later annual reports admitted the standard of rugby was not the highest. But the formidable side of the Fifties was beginning to take shape.

There was White and Cannell. Scotsman Tommy Gray moved into the area, and despite having part of his right foot blown away in the war, was a brilliant runner and hugely successful kicker.

Welsh Services international Ronnie Knapp was another to move into Northampton to work for British Timken. Knapp was an opportunist try scorer and powerful defensive kicker, and at full-back was the fearless, George Adkins, who had spent most of the war as a prisoner in Italy and Germany.

In the pack, apart from White, there was Mike Berridge, who had three England trials at prop without getting a cap that season, although he would eventually. Berridge was another to die young – of

One of the many brilliant cartoons of the period by Pat Adams

Trio of internationals (from left to right): Jeff Butterfield, John Hyde and Mike Berridge

throat cancer at the age of 50 in 1973. Joe Lomas made the unusual transition from winger to wing forward with great success. White reckoned him unlucky not to win a cap. Lomas died young, committing suicide. Longland played out the twilight of his career, while Fred Jeffcoate, Hamp and prop Jack Whiting were useful performers.

Jeffcoate suffered horrific facial burns in the war, trapped in a tank when it exploded. He got out alive but needed massive skin grafts on his face. He soldiered on for a couple of seasons after the war. It has always been assumed that he was the inspiration for the caricature of a smiling Saints player, drawn by Pat Adams, that adorned the cover of many club publications. Adams was the brilliant cartoonist 'discovered' by Adkins, the two of them working together for LMS Railway.

Adams was invited to a Saints training session, and for a couple of seasons his cartoon strips appeared in the Saturday night *Green 'Un*. They were brilliant, but not instantly appreciated. After the first one appeared, following the Metropolitan Police game, Adams was greeted by a growling Longland: "So you're the •••••• who did those •••••• pictures, are you?"

Adams went on to draw many inspired cartoon strips, the most famous possibly being Macnamara's Band, featuring the Saints as a male voice choir.

Adams also composed two verses to go with it:

'Our name's Northampton Football Club, the Midlands pride and fame,
We've beaten teams from far and near and never lost a game.
Though county cricketers and Cobblers cause the crowd's complaints
A credit to Northampton are the boys they call THE SAINTS

O'Mullane puts the ball in and Ray Longland hooks it out
It's well away to Tommy Gray, and then without a doubt
There's Cannell or Knapp going slap through a gap

and travelling like a train
And on to Snell who runs like – well – and THE SAINTS have scored again!'

The club was keen to promote junior football for players between 16 and 18, but no such thing as sponsorship existed, so Gordon put this appeal in the programme for the first game of the season against Metropolitan Police:

"…playing kit is proving a very serious handicap and all old players are earnestly requested to sort out any old jerseys, shorts and boots that they doubtless have put by. Those who have any spare kit please send a post card to the undersigned, who will arrange for its collection, or deliver it to Franklin's Gardens Hotel. Any kit, whatever the condition, will be gratefully received, for it will contribute towards the success of this new venture."

International rugby, after a series of Victory games, resumed normal service resumed in 1947, at Cardiff on January 18, with White a member of the England side.

For 46 years of his life, from a 16-year-old trembling schoolboy until the upheaval of 1988 that ousted him from office, the Saints were a way of life for the shoe boss from Earls Barton. He was bitter at being kicked off the committee.

He was recommended to the Saints by R V S Ward, a formidable history teacher at Wellingborough Grammar School, and the two of them were props on his debut against Coventry.

"I was scared stiff," admitted White. "I was a strong lad for 16 as I used to spend my holidays on a farm at Mears Ashby but that didn't stop me from being scared. I thought I'd get a fearful hiding but I came out of it unscathed."

By the time White was 18 the war was virtually over and he joined the Army at the suggestion of Eric Coley. Within weeks he had a rugby trial for the Army and was pitched in to face the Navy. He left the forces in 1948 and was by then an integral part of the Saints and England back row.

White took over as captain from Knapp for the 1949/50 season and was encouraged, particularly by Sturtridge, to develop a more expansive game.

He was enormously helped by having Cannell and John Hyde, also from Wellingborough Grammar School, turn up on the doorstep.

White also got a helping hand from his old headmaster at Wellingborough, Dick Wrenn. "He had two rugby players vying for a post as PE teacher, and said to me: "If they are equal as teachers, what do you want, a forward or a back?" I told him I'd prefer a back." And so Jeff Butterfield got his first job on leaving Loughborough College and another piece of the jigsaw slotted into place.

The Gardens in the Fifties became a breeding ground for internationals. The club was described as "the best in England" and White's initial season as captain brought the first-ever victory at Stradey Park over Llanelli.

White relished playing the Welsh as the challenge was at its fiercest. His international debut as a flanker was against Wales, on January 18, 1947, as a 20-year-old. Not even Cardiff Arms Park held any fears for the youngster and with the game just eight minutes old, he collected a crossfield kick and scored to set England on the way to a surprise 9-6 win. He was to play 13 more times but surprisingly never made a Lions tour.

His record for the Saints is immense. He made 448 appearances, scored 116 tries, 71 penalties, 183 conversions and a drop-goal (a match-winner) for a total of 930 points.

The one blemish in White's playing career came in December, 1947, when he was ordered off in an East Midlands match with Notts, Lincs and Derby. It caused him to miss England trial games and, he believes, subsequent selection for two internationals

Fond tribute: Author Michael Green wrote an intimate sporting epitaph to Don White

that season. It doesn't explain why he was totally overlooked in 1949 and 1950 before being brought back against Scotland in 1951, a recall marked with a try.

White was unrepentant about his fiery reputation. "If a wing forward does not get some stick from an away crowd, he is not doing his job. You have to upset them."

A fond farewell to White, written by former *Chronicle & Echo* rugby correspondent Michael Green, appeared in the *Sunday Times* in 1961:

"So Don White is retiring. And more than one referee, I fancy, will sleep more peacefully of a Friday night next season, in the knowledge that the old fox of rugby has decided, at 35, to blow his own 'no-side'.

"For White's reputation doesn't rest simply on his record: open side wing forward for England 14 times between 1947 and 1953, a captain of East Midlands and the Barbarians, skipper of Northampton seven times. Without a cap to his name he would still be famous.

"His knowledge of the laws is a by-word in the game. Frequently senior referees have been known to ask White's advice on some knotty points (after the match, of course, although White would be happy to advise during the game). Minor referees, called upon to control a match in which he is taking part, have been known to go pale and grab the Rugby Union handbook. And not without reason. For White takes advantage of every sub-clause.

"In one England trial, he baulked a player running back to attempt a snap drop-out, claiming that as the ball was not in play he could not be obstructing the man. The referee penalised him, but, as White says: 'He was wrong and I was right. Later they had to change the laws to cope with the situation'.

"Side by side with this phenomenal knowledge of the laws, goes a card index mind. Remorselessly, White dockets all the weaknesses of every first-class player, and then shares his knowledge for the benefit of Northampton.

"A pre-match talk from White would go something like this: 'Now you don't have to worry about the stand-off, he can only side-step off the right foot so he'll only jink one way. The left winger's a bit windy – if you go in hard he'll try and get rid of it in a hurry and make a mess of things. But watch Jack in the centre – he's got a habit of shaping to kick and then straightening up and running like hell.

"Fortified by the cough sweets he always carries, White calls out further advice throughout the game, especially at half-time when he has added more information to his filing system.

"Although his detractors say he always plays six inches off-side, White is one of the greatest constructive players of the day.

"So much for the player; the man is burly, outrageously cheerful, outspoken and with a heart of gold. He fusses over young players like a father, advising and protecting them even to telling the press not to be unkind.

"The Northampton crowd adore White, for he has served the club heart and soul since 1945. His relations with spectators at Leicester and Coventry, Northampton's traditional rivals, are more on a love-hate basis.

"The verdict at Leicester is best summed up by the

bus conductor (not entirely sober) who, throughout the game, had been gibbering for White to be sent off. "Eh Whitey," he said at length in reluctant admiration, 'you ain't half a crafty b-----d'."

This was the era of the prank – and the biggest joker of all in the Saints dressing room was George Adkins, glad and perhaps a little surprised to have survived the previous five years.

The life and times of Adkins, a full-back between 1946 and 1951 who made 149 appearances, epitomised the immediate post-war years – a period of catching up on lost youth.

The Second World War robbed him of priceless years, and he was determined to make up for lost time. He was 27 before pulling on a Saints jersey after twice being a prisoner-of-war in Italy and Germany.

When he returned to England in January, 1946, he was immediately offered a contract with the Cobblers, but the maximum wage was a pittance and Adkins preferred the security of his old job at British Rail.

If he needed any further convincing, a Saints representative saw him the very next day and suggested he try his luck at the Gardens. Adkins went on to become a pillar of the Establishment at the Saints: player, touch judge, team secretary and president.

Adkins was at the centre of all sorts of mischief for which rugby clubs became notorious. He was associated with two of the more outrageous episodes of that era – the lassoing of a cardboard cut-out figure of an actress, Jean Kent, from the Gaumont cinema, Monmouth, on the Easter tour of 1946, using a piece of electric flex, and a motor bike ride on the polished floor of the Salon ballroom.

The players decided that Ms Kent, a big box office star of the day, would make an ideal team mascot. An unamused cinema manager called in the local constabulary and a constable was despatched on his bike to investigate.

It was April 19, just three months after Adkins had been demobbed. In his scrapbook, the details are all there including the police report under the heading: Larceny of a cardboard fixture. It reads:

"I beg to report that a telephone message was received at this station (Newbridge) from Pc Allen, Monmouth, respecting the theft of a cardboard fixture from a cinema (The Gaumont) at Monmouth at about 1.30pm on Friday 19th of April 1946, and that a member of the Northampton Rugby team was suspected of the offence. It was requested that the team be interviewed upon their arrival at Newbridge.

"At 4.30pm I made certain enquiries and as a result I searched the omnibus that conveyed Northampton rugby team to Newbridge. On the rear seat I found the cardboard fixture that was reported stolen from the station at Monmouth. I then interviewed the players in the dressing room. I told them the nature of my enquiries and after some questioning GEORGE ADKINS, 27 years, of Great Houghton, Northampton, stepped out of the group of players and said 'I am the one that took it'.

"I then told him that he would be reported for stealing the fixture valued at 10/- (50p), the property of the Gaumont British Film Ltd. I cautioned him, and he replied, 'I only took it as a joke'.

Signed David Lloyd P.C.No 304"

The magistrates dismissed the charge on payment of costs. Adkins told the *Chronicle & Echo* after the hearing.

"Jean Kent is the team's most popular film star. We thought she would make a good mascot for the tour. We intended to return 'her' when we had finished.

"Some of us think the team's heavy losses were due to the loss of our newly-appointed mascot before the first match."

A second, even more bizarre incident, took place on the doorstep of Franklin's Gardens, when, after the usual post-match celebrations in the hotel, Adkins was dared to ride his old Enfield Army motor-bike around the Salon dance floor.

The bike had cost George just under £100 of his demob money, and the fearless full-back, who never shirked a challenge on the field, took up the gauntlet.

"Ronnie Knapp bet me half a crown I wouldn't do it. It was around 11.30pm, I suppose, and Fred Jeffcoate, another Saints player, was on the door of the Salon," recalled George.

"I said I'd do it if it could be squared with Fred. He entered into the spirit and to the amazement, and probable fear of hundreds of dancers, I took the motor-bike on to the dance floor. I was scared stiff, the floor was very shiny and I was frightened of coming off.

"There was never anything malicious in what we did. It was just a group of young blokes, relieved at

George Adkins, always in trouble (from the left), for a prank on his motorbike, with the Nazis and with the police for his part in acquiring a life-size cardboard cut-out of a film actress during an Easter tour

getting through the war, doing the odd daft thing now and again. It was a form of escapism."

Escapism had been the key-word of George's war, which started for real in Tobruk, where he was captured in 1942. He was imprisoned at Fara-Sabina, near Rome. A year later he was on the run.

Said Adkins: "When the Italians capitulated to the Germans, our guards thought the war was over for them and they got blind drunk. We just strolled through the gates.

"I had some Italian clothes from somewhere. We kept clear of the roads, walking across the hills eating grapes and figs. We would also meet old goat herders, who let us have some goat's cheese."

He was recaptured on November 29, 1943, a date he remembers because his on-the-run exploits are recorded in a diary given to him by an Italian priest. He was one of thousands of prisoners in Stalag IVB from December 1943 to April 1945.

They kept themselves sane by playing football and rugby in various leagues, all recorded on the camp noticeboards and later reproduced in book form by a South African prisoner.

They were set free by Cossacks on horseback, who rode round the perimeter of the camp shooting the German guards as they went; after 18 months of incarceration Adkins felt no compassion, just relief.

The Russian prisoners, he recalled, made straight for the potato fields, digging the soil with bare hands and eating the potatoes raw.

Adkins took to the

Bill Fallowfield, the Saint who ran rugby league for two decades

road, walking 120 miles due west towards American troops. He knew where they were because a radio was hidden in a piano accordion. The Americans flew him to Rheims and then on to Wing. He caught a bus to Derngate, where he thought he would buy some chocolate. No such luck, he did not have any coupons and three years in POW camps did not cut any ice with the shopkeeper.

At the same time that Adkins was joining the club, a player departing was Bill Fallowfield, a Cambridge University graduate, who was picked from hundreds of applicants to fill the post of rugby league secretary.

Originally from Barrow, the Fallowfields were a rugby league family but Bill was a union man and attempted to re-shape the league along union lines. One of his great wishes was that there should be greater affinity between the two codes. "If the Rugby Union had been more tolerant when the 'split' came in 1895, I think there could have been professionalism accepted in both games," he told a reporter in 1952.

Only the third secretary in league history, staying in office from 1946 to 1974, he was a great experimenter with the rules. He was awarded the OBE for services to the game, and died in 1985, aged 71.

So thrilled were the club by the 1947/48 season that the Supporters' Club published a 54 page booklet, tracing the club's history from 1880 to 1948.

Entitled 'The Story of a great club – The Record of a great season', it contained articles by president, Gilbert Bull, past president, J W Langley and David Reid, the *Chronicle & Echo's* rugby correspondent.

Bull wrote: "The brilliance of our present team may have been equalled but I feel certain that it has never been excelled. There has been a wonderful team spirit, and as long as the game is played with the same keenness, so characteristic of rugby football, Northampton will retain the high place that it

The success of the 1947/48 side prompted the club to bring out a 54-page booklet

W. R. Hamp

J. E. Lomas

D. F. White

Bob Hamp, Joe Lomas and Don White – all gave young reporter Michael Green a baptism of fire

holds in the rugby world to-day."

The *Chronicle & Echo* correspondent, then under the famous *nom de plume*, The Scout, called the Saints the outstanding English club of 1947/48:

"A fighting pack was admirably supported by a talented, often brilliant set of backs, and the team-work of the Saints at their best was a delight to watch. The Saints played fine rugger in the best traditions of the game; rarely have their haloes shone so bright."

Over 30 years later Reid, by then a Reuters correspondent in Lisbon, wrote in another Saints publication. "It was a privilege to know them and a pleasure to write about them (and sometimes share) in their exploits at a time when it was so very good to be young and alive despite rationing, weak beer and other hardships of those post-war years.

"I can still feel the tingle in my bones when I recall the electric atmosphere at Franklin's Gardens during a needle match with Coventry or the Leicester Tigers. Still smell the liniment in the dressing room. Still taste that first pint in the bar after another exhilarating game."

The man to follow was the most famous 'Scout' of them all, author Michael Green, with several best sellers to his name in the *Art of Coarse...* series, starting with *The Art of Coarse Rugby*, first published in November 1960 and reprinted twice within two months.

Green covered the Saints for just two seasons but they made a lasting impression on him, and provided him with endless book material, not that he was aware of it at the time.

"The first time I reported the Saints, I finished up playing for them instead. I was sent to Franklin's Gardens to cover the Wanderers against Bedford Swifts, and just before kick-off the Wanderers captain came into the stand and asked if anyone would like to play, as they were one short. 'Go on, Mike' said Harold Hollowell, a popular freelance reporter, who covered the Saints for so many years that they made him a presentation when he retired, 'I'll phone in a report for you.' So I volunteered and duly played on the wing. The Saints lent me an old jersey which had been used

to lag a boiler pipe and was still warm. In my book *The Art of Coarse Rugby* I've described how I kept it and wore it to frighten the opposition when I played for Ealing Extra B years later.

"Soon afterwards I became the Scout and discovered how close is the relationship between Scout and Club. Some teams butter up the press, others give it the cold shoulder, but Northampton looked upon the Scout as their own personal property. He was expected to look after valuables, play pontoon on the coach, buy his round, sing his song and join in the fun along with the rest. In return he was accorded privileges few pressmen receive, being treated with total confidence by officials and players. As when I drunkenly lurched against a valuable vase at Cardiff Athletic Club and broke it. 'Don't worry,' said the ever-kindly Jerry Gordon, 'we'll pay for it. You're one of us'.

"But there were drawbacks. Because a Scout was one of the lads he could not expect any preferential treatment. I discovered this early on when I strolled into the dressing-room full of self-confidence and was pulled into the bath by Don White and Joe Lomas as a retaliation for 'some rubbish' I'd written. I always say Don White was the best journalism instructor I ever had.

"The Scout was expected to put up with endless practical jokes. During an Easter tour we went down to the beach near Porthcawl and I decided to have a bathe. When I got back my clothes had disappeared. So had the Saints.

"My most extraordinary experience was in the dining car of a train to Liverpool, when Bob Hamp and others seized me, tore off my trousers, and hurled them out of the window, where they were last seen decorating the front of a train going in the opposite direction.

"I walked out of Liverpool station in my overcoat, bare from the knees down. That evening at the hotel, I came down to dinner in my pyjama trousers. Don White told the head waiter I was some sort of nut who kept following the team about and asked him to remove me, which he promptly did. However, they took pity on me and Jerry Gordon delivered a new pair of trousers to my room in the morning.

"The exploits of George Adkins in those days have become legendary. George always brought a touch of wit to his post-match misdeeds that marked them as different. For instance, at Coventry where we visited a pub kept by Harry Walker, the famous Coventry forward, George announced to customers that Harry would give a set of golden darts to anyone who scored a sealed number. A huge queue formed at the dartboard, with George announcing, 'Bad luck, sir, but that was not the secret number, next please' until time came to go, when George announced a winner and told him to collect the Golden Arrows from Harry. He then left hurriedly.

"The secret of Northampton's greatness lies in the loyalty it seems to attract. I reported Bob Leslie's first game for the Saints (against London Welsh at Herne Hill in 1950) and I reported his last, nearly 20 years later against Blackheath when I was on the *Sunday Times* and he was club secretary. There are not many clubs where that could happen. Players who never knew me as Scout, such as Dickie Jeeps and David Powell, have always greeted me as old friends. Returning after years away one finds the same faces, but in the committee box instead of on the field. Something happens to people who put on a Saints jersey. We Scouts are proud that even if we haven't got the jersey (except for my charred relic) we are still part of the club."

In the annual report it was announced that caps could not be presented as they were unobtainable. The club named the players who had earned them in 1946/47 and 1947/48 – even if they had to wait until a supplier could be found until they actually got the cap.

In 1947 the list was: Hamp, Whiting, White, Berridge, Lomas, L Longland, Adkins, Bob Pell, Birch, Cannell, Hazel and Knapp. A year later they were awarded to: Gray, O'Mullane and Bailey, two Irishman and a Scotsman.

Gray, who died five years after the original history was published, was particularly deserving of his Saints cap, and later three Scottish ones, for the bravery in overcoming adversity.

Gray, who was living in a flat in St Andrew's, Fife, Scotland, where he is a member of the Royal and Ancient Club, the most famous

N. Bailey

Dr. E. J. O'Mullane

E. Birch

company of golfers in the world, when I interviewed him in 1992, had his career resurrected when his insurance company moved him from Scotland to Northampton.

In Northampton – the heart of the footwear industry – he was able to have a boot specially made to protect his left foot that had been blown to bits in 1945, at Gunnep on the Dutch-German border.

An officer in the King's Own Scottish Borderers, Gray was leading a dawn attack, when several of his men sheltered behind a tank as they came under attack. An anti-tank shell exploded near him and his little toe and part of the next two were amputated. For six months he hobbled around on crutches. His left leg shrank and was never as muscular as the right again. It took Gray a long time before he could even walk properly and he was told he would never play rugby again.

But he got a new lease of life at Northampton and his form at 33 years old that was a called up to the Scottish side – not in his Northampton position of fly-half but at full-back.

The Scottish selectors paid an unexpected visit to Northampton and Adkins stood down to allow Gray to play at full-back.

In 1950 he kicked two conversions against England in a Scottish victory and a season later played against France and England again, both defeats.

The wound still troubled him when I spoke to him and he never got further than playing 10 holes of the old course before the pain got too great.

At his golfing peak he played off a two-handicap at Northants County and played for Northamptonshire.

The annual report said his brilliant kicking, sure handling, opportunist and constructive play were of the highest class and contributed in no small measure to the success of the side.

In Northampton he met and married, Pat Cook, daughter of Saints record try-scoring winger, Teddy Cook, by then a successful businessman, servicing the footwear industry. Gray joined his father-in-law in business, before moving back to Scotland in 1961.

He was unimpressed by the rugby of the 1990s. "I have been watching the Lions in New Zealand and I couldn't believe how both fly-halves would just kick and kick. My old schoolmaster used to tell us to kick

Gordon Sturtridge: An Australian who became a dedicated Saint

at fly-half as a last resort. Now it is a first resort.

"The fun has gone out of the game. I am sure the players do not have the fun that we did. There was no pressure on us. It was just marvellous to play rugby, and there was nowhere better than Northampton. I have wonderful memories of my time there."

Another player to get glowing reports from this period is Eddie Birch, who formed part of an outstanding back row with White and Lomas. Birch's father Jim has an unusual place in Saints history – a Northampton man, born and bred, who played two internationals…for Wales.

He played for the Saints between 1906 and 1913, but in 1911, while playing for Neath, the Welsh selectors picked him to face Scotland and France. Wales that season won the Grand Slam, but Jim did not play in either of the home fixtures.

Birch was invited to join the Glamorgan police force by Cardiff captain Billy Spiller, a policeman and a Welsh international.

Birch won his caps in his first full season with Neath, and a report of the time commented: "The Welsh authorities have quickly found merit where the English selectors failed to discern anything out of the ordinary. England did not pay 'Jim' even the compliment of an invitation to a trial game."

The finds of the 1947/48 were Hyde and Yeovil-born lock Dick Hawkes. Hyde is spoken of in almost reverential terms, but his career, which lasted until November, 1962, was dogged by injury.

Pupils from Wellingborough Grammar School would go to the Mobbs match hoping to see their sportsmaster play against the Barbarians and every

year he dropped out through injury.

Hyde's problems started with a broken leg sustained at a Loughborough College trial game just days after he had been demobbed in 1951.

Hyde's career was still outstanding, but he never added to the caps won as a 19-year-old in 1950 against France and Scotland, both times with Cannell inside him.

Hyde's international debut was in the 6-3 defeat at Stade Colombes on February 25, 1950. He had already been chosen for a schools international against Scotland on January 2 at Richmond, when he was called up for the first senior trial at Gloucester. Five days after the schoolboy match he played in the final senior trial at Twickenham. He was totally unflappable, and when an eager reporter called at his home on the verge of his Twickenham trial date, Hyde's only comment was: "I always look forward to a Rugger match." His father, Philip, had been at the first trial at Kingsholm, the report continued, but his opinion could not be obtained. "He doesn't say much," explained John. Of his younger brother, James, also at WGS, John said: "I don't know if he is any good or not. I haven't actually seen him play."

Thought to be a confirmed bachelor, Hyde stunned everyone by getting married. They first they knew was when they received a postcard from the honeymooning couple.

Hyde had a steel plate inserted in his leg following the injury at Loughborough. He lost some pace as a result and developed more of a jinking style. A physics teacher at WGS, George Sharp, wrote to two internationals renowned for their sidestep, England's Dickie Guest and Welsh star Bleddyn Williams. The reply from Williams was short and to the point: "forget it, the sidestep cannot be taught, it is God given talent."

Guest, on the other hand, took the trouble to send a whole series of diagrams, and Hyde did indeed become a master of the sidestep.

In his first full season, 1948/49, Hyde collected 15 tries from 30 games and formed a lethal wing duo with Irishman Niall Bailey, who collected a lone cap against England in 1952. Dubliner Bailey, nephew of Aidan Bailey, a star of the Thirties, stayed for seven years, and with Hyde formed the first pair of international wingers for the Saints.

Among the victories in 1948/49 was a 15-8 success at Cardiff, achieved on the fourth leg of the Easter tour and described in the annual report as "the highlight of our season, and indeed also one for English rugby."

A season later White embarked on his record breaking spell as captain in tandem with Doc Sturtridge as president. Sturtridge went about the presidency with a passion, and White said of him.

"He was undoubtedly the father of the great side that we put together in the Forties and Fifties. He was a marvellous leader and a great enthusiast.

"He used to say: 'When I'm pushing up the daisies I want you young fellows to develop a 15-man rugby game'.

"He was always conscious of the fact that the only international back the club had ever produced was Edgar Mobbs and he wanted to change all that. We started to acquire and develop great backs. In fact, we had the best in the country for 20 years.

The 1950/51 East Midlands county championship winning squad. Back row (left to right): N Bailey, C R Jacobs, G Jenkins. Middle row: A Marshall (Hon Sec), D MacNally, W R Hamp, J F Bance, R C Hawkes, J H Whiting, R A Palmer (Hon Treasurer). Front row: F M Fletcher, R H Haynes, L F Oakley, L A R Fensome (President), D F White, A C Towell, T Gray, T Smith

"He was a great judge of a player and was very much involved in team selection. He was like a father figure to the players; everyone liked and respected him."

Sturtridge's judgement of a player even involved investigating his genetic background. In assessing youngsters, he would always ask about the height of the mother. He could then determine a youngster's ultimate height.

The strength of the Saints enabled the East Midlands to reach the county championship final for the third time in its history against Cheshire at Birkenhead Park in 1950.

East started strong favourites, but despite the presence of nine Saints and an egg breakfast, supplied by farmer Berridge, they failed to produce their best and went down 5-0. The Saints men were: Alan Hall, Cannell, Hyde, Gray (captain), Berridge, Trevor Smith, Jack Whiting, Hamp and White.

The 1949/50 season saw the debut of Ron Jacobs, who was to make 470 appearances over the next 16 years, while the Wanderers and Crusaders sides were started. The Crusaders had an emphasis on youngsters in the 16 to 19 age group. White, Gray, Knapp and Whiting would visit junior clubs to help with coaching, creating a strong rapport between the Saints and the clubs down the scale.

The Saints were in the early throes of a golden era, and in 1950/51 the East Midlands made up for their lapse by claiming a second county championship. With the aid of home advantage, the East beat a Middlesex side containing four present and several future internationals 10-0. Nine Saints figured in the side but not the unlucky Hyde, who injured a leg in training in the week leading up to the game. Bailey came in, passing up an invitation to sit on the reserve bench for Ireland in the game with Wales at Cardiff. The Saints nine were: Gray, Macnally, Bailey, Jacobs,

Late starter Trevor Smith

Smith, Whiting, Hamp, Hawkes and White.

The 1934 championship-winning skipper Bernard Gadney, who had seen Middlesex beat Yorkshire in the semi final, sent a two-page dossier on Middlesex.

"The thing you have to understand is that Middlesex are so terribly keen. They have made a dead set on winning the championship.

"I loathe people who write giving information, but I thought this might be useful for none of you have seen Middlesex in the last two championship games."

A player unearthed two years earlier was hooker Trevor Smith, real name Trellevyn Harvey Smith, who was already 29 when he joined from Kettering in

1949, after a trial in a junior county match. Smith was one of those players to have his formative rugby years blighted by the war, and had settled for junior rugby when the call came from the Saints. Within two years he was an international – against Wales in Swansea.

While Smith was having a belated tilt at top class rugby, the Saints were looking to invest in the future. Sturtridge spearheaded a campaign to buy the Lotus sports ground on Harlestone Road for £5,000.

The Lotus ground was a prime acquisition. It was a twelve and a half acre site with two full-sized rugby pitches and a practice pitch, six rink bowling green, six tennis courts with a pavilion, groundsman's bungalow and a small cricket pavilion.

The Saints sold it in 1965 for £90,000, which initially went towards buying more land on the outskirts of town. Soon after Northampton was designated a development town and planning permission was revoked. The club was still able to put the money to good use by installing floodlights and building a modern clubhouse, naming it the Sturtridge Pavilion as a tribute to the Aussie, who had died in 1964.

The 1951/52 season ushered in the career at Franklin's Gardens, that of schoolteacher Jeff Butterfield. The Scout later wrote: "to say he is the find of the season would be an understatement."

Early in the season there was a chance for six players to emulate those heroes of the Thirties when a combined Midland Counties side faced the Springboks at Welford Road. Speculation centred on whether Bailey, Cannell, Berridge, Smith, Whiting and White could follow the glorious example of Billy Weston and the rest. They could not, although it was close. They had the satisfaction of preventing a Springbok try, the first time it had happened on the tour, and only going down to a lone penalty.

The club's annual report lamented the retirement of scrum-half Eddie O'Mullane "'a scrum-half we consider to have no superior in the game, possessing all the qualities that go to make a first class player, his position will indeed be hard to fill, for we have no ready-made substitute."

A shy Irishman O'Mullane, an anaesthetist at Northampton General hospital was never seen at training.

"He just didn't take the game seriously," said half-back partner, Ronnie Knapp. "He didn't train and after games would simply return to the hospital and get on with his work. He cut a strange figure in the dressing room. During a team talk, he would sit in the corner with his collar and tie on and a long overcoat, smoking his pipe. He'd be like that until virtually kick-off time. But he was a tremendous player with an enormous pass."

His skill as a doctor also came in useful the day George Adkins dislocated a shoulder during a game. O'Mullane came over to the stricken full-back, put a muddy boot into his back and wrenched the shoulder back into place.

The scrum-half problem lasted only a few months for Richard Eric Gautrey Jeeps joined the club. Dickie Jeeps CBE went on to win 24 caps for England (13 as captain) and become a British Lion, chairman of the Sports Council, an England selector and president of the RFU. He also had three wives, was a county councillor, magistrate and restaurateur.

And if O'Mullane hardly ever said a word, Jeeps

R. O. Pell

Bob Pell - one of the first to be capped after the war but had to wait until a supplier could be found

spent the entire game yapping at his forwards.

Knapp and Gray hung up their boots in 1952. Knapp was 33, having joined the Saints at 27. Like Adkins he had an eventful war, twice being dumped in the Mediterranean. On the second occasion he had to swim for miles before being fished out of the water. A huge duffel coat was given to him by one of his rescuers, which helped keep him warm and alive. He never threw it away.

As a schoolboy, Knapp, born in Cardiff, had played with the legendary Wilf Wooller, who dissuaded a teenage Knapp from playing for the Saints before the war.

"I had some distant relatives in Northampton," explained Knapp, "and Jerry Gordon got to hear of me going up to Cambridge University. He wrote suggesting I play for Northampton but Wilf Wooller told me they were just a team of hard slogging forwards. He told me I should play for Leicester, which I did."

Knapp was one of the first to work on radar during the war. He continued to do so afterwards and the Admiralty sent him to Washington, where every weekend the British would gather on a piece of grass behind the White House to keep their hand in at rugby. By coincidence when he returned home, Knapp got a job with British Timken and this time he did join the Saints.

The war put Knapp's career in the what-might-have-been category. He is probably unique in being the only person to play in an Oxford-Cambridge varsity match and not get a blue and in a Wales-England international and not get a cap. The matches were in 1940 and traditional honours were not bestowed on the players; a quirky sporting fact that had Knapp's name appearing in 'Did You Know' newspaper strips of the period.

He became known as Ronnie 'Four Tries' Knapp after the varsity match. Playing on the wing, he was

51

confronted with a forward after Oxford had to reshuffle through injury. He was able to skate past his makeshift opponent to touch down four times.

Knapp was quite often at the heart of the mischief-making in the Fifties, but the motor bike episode with George Adkins cost him a game with the East Midlands.

"The prank backfired on me because when we got into the Salon there was a rather grandiose ball going on. It turned out to be the Pytchley Hunt Ball, and among the guests was Sir John Pascoe (head of British Timken) and his wife. He called me into his office the next day to give me a rocket and when the next East Midlands game was on I couldn't get time off."

Knapp became great friends with Gray and was one of the guests at the Scotsman's wedding on the morning of a match. "We turned up for the game full of champagne, and we were really fizzing in the first half. But as we approached half-time the champagne began to wear off. We were all feeling pretty grim, when the water bottles came on but they were full of champagne. It was a marvellous touch by Doc Sturtridge."

The 1952/53 season ushered in the start of the Dickie Jeeps era – and yet the Saints only got him by default. As a Bedford Modern player, he should have been earmarked for Goldington Road.

Bedford were accused of missing out on Jeeps, but at the time they had an England trialist scrum-half in Murray Fletcher in the first team.

Pin-up boy Dickie Jeeps and (below) about to take a fierce challenge from Bryn Meredith

Jeeps' first contact with the Saints came via a telephone call from Jerry Gordon, inviting him for a pre-season trial. He didn't exactly jump at the chance because it meant missing a cricket match. Jeeps was an excellent cricketer, who averaged 100 as a schoolboy batsman.

The trial, recalled Jeeps, was a little frustrating. He barely saw any action and remembers thinking: "I've missed a game of cricket for eight minutes of rugby."

In his first season, Jeeps was invited to appear in a Dai Gent XV versus Cornwall, but Jeeps was none too keen.

"If I go," thought Jeeps, "I won't get back into the Saints side. Don White told me to play. He said Dai Gent doesn't pick 'non internationals'."

Jeeps won the first of his England caps in 1956 and was already a veteran of four British Lions tests in South Africa.

In those days the Jeeps family had a fruit farm in Willingham, Cambridgeshire, which preventred him from training.

"I think the only time I trained was before the two matches against Coventry. They were always our big games. Other players couldn't get to training either, like Ron Jacobs, who was farming in Peterborough, and Jeff Butterfield who was at Worksop College," he told me back in 1992.

His father, a former chairman of Cambridgeshire County Council, was only an armchair rugby fan, preferring to watch his son on television with a bottle of whisky. The only time he changed his routine was for Jeeps' final international – against Scotland – in 1962. "I told him I had a shoulder injury and intended packing in after this game, so he came to watch that one."

Jeeps was convinced the match that got him on the Lions tour of South Africa was an epic Saints victory over Cardiff. It had been seen by Haydn Tanner, a Welsh scrum-half in the Thirties. Tanner happened to share a railway carriage with two Lions selectors, so the story goes, and when he was asked who he considered was the best scrum-half around he replied: "The best I've seen is a kid called Jeeps, playing for Northampton."

In South Africa Jeeps partnered Cliff Morgan for all four Tests, two won and two lost.

Jeeps revelled in the big match atmosphere. He gave a flawless exhibition of orthodox passing, allowing the mercurial Morgan all the time he needed to display his full repertoire. The pair won enormous praise from South African critics, and Jeeps was to reign, not always supreme, until the end of the 1962 season. He still had to endure quirks of selection policy, but captained England 13 times and followed Eric Coley as an England selector (1965-71) and was RFU president in 1976/77.

He unashamedly admitted that one of his yardsticks for forming an opinion on a player's suitability for England was: would he get into the Northampton side?

It was a fair question as Jeeps had played alongside some top players at Northampton such as Jeff Butterfield.

In 1953 Butterfield won the first of 28 consecutive caps for England, scoring in a victory against France, a game he almost missed through injury. He pulled a hamstring in a knockabout game at Wellingborough Grammar School during half-term. In dismay he went to see Cobblers physio Jack Jennings.

He was told not to train and prescribed a daily breakfast of two raw eggs mixed with sherry. He got the eggs from his team mates, the Whiting brothers, and religiously followed his cocktail diet before seeing Jennings again the morning before the match.

"Jack told me under no circumstances to do any sprinting – I had been cycling under his orders for two weeks – and to just take my time. I was to wait until I got on the pitch before I did any running.

"I suppose I played under an alcoholic influence and I didn't feel the hamstring at all. I got through the game and I prepared on eggs and sherry ever after.

"I owe a great deal to Jack; we had no-one like him at the Saints."

Butterfield, Jeeps and Frank Sykes toured with the Lions in 1955. Butterfield was a keen observer of the sport and political system.

Under 'INTERNATIONAL APPROACH, he noted five reasons for South Africa's success at the top level during that period:

■ Fanatical. Lead is set by D C (Danie Craven) and their life is winning Tests.

■ Always one (official) and often more at our games. Craven travelled to our first five (matches) – 1000 (miles) in each direction.

■ They selected people to play on our weaknesses – they controlled the game from the touch line.

■ International teams meet on Tues. Had Danie to coach them – professionalism??

One of the greats: Jeff Buitterfield

■ Trained hard and intensively for two hours – 'Moonlight' training.

Then under 'CLUB AND PROVINCIAL' he wrote:

■ Each club has a manager and coach. They train seriously and play to instructions.

■ At 4.00 the whole team turns up for training – regardless of any other commitment.

■ They have wonderful facilities. Stands, showers etc.

■ Clubs would have many teams. Without trying as many as 10 teams.

Butterfield headed one page: 'RACIAL PROBLEM'. Effect on us – NONE.

■ Colour bar is positively evident, more in the Transvaal than in Cape district.

■ They are the workers. The white is the boss – the native has social standing only in his own class.

■ Partition is again positive. All speeches, invitation cards written in dual tongue. What a lark! They hate English control.

Jeeps and Butterfield starred in a dramatic 23-22 first Test win at Ellis Park in front of 100,000 spectators. Butterfield scored a try, which was listed as one of 'FIFTY-TWO FAMOUS TRIES', written by respected rugby writer Clem Thomas.

"Jeff Butterfield received one of the many untakable passes W P C Davies delivered with Olympian elegance in the First Test against South Africa in '55. He appeared to catch the ball behind him somewhere between his liver and his kidneys, and while running at full pace, transferred it under his arm, and finally onto his chest, while at the same time sweeping infield to score the vital equalising try. The pass was not even remotely takable and its translation into a try for the Lions had a remarkable effect on team morale."

He was to follow that up with a left foot drop-goal and another try as the Lions won the third test 9-6 before the Springboks hit back to square the series.

Butterfield, born in the tiny Yorkshire mining village of Heckmondwike, had an uncanny ability to take a pass, was an immaculate passer and an elusive runner. Team-mate Bob Leslie, comparing Butterfield and Cannell, said: "Jeff was superb to play with – he made everything so easy for the person alongside. He was a marvellous passer of the ball, but he was, if you like, conventional. Lewis, on the other hand, was nowhere near so predictable, which made him a dangerous opponent. He was a great individualist."

Sykes, who was encouraged by Butterfield to join the Saints, is reported to have pleaded: "Jeff, for God's sake let me do a bit towards scoring some of the tries occasionally."

His 25th cap, against Wales at Cardiff, on January 17, 1959, was his first as captain. He held the job for all four home internationals. They won one and drew two but the team did not score a single try.

He was replaced as captain in 1960 by Jeeps, who went on to lead England 13 times with a record of W5 D4 L4.

Sport ruled Butterfield's life. He went to Cleckheaton Grammar School, where he was a star athlete and swimmer. Nearing the end of his school life, Butterfield was summoned to see the headmaster about his future career and burst into tears. "I didn't have a clue what I was going to do. All I did was play sport. Then I saw a copy of The Picture Post, showing Loughborough College, where I was told I could get a diploma in athletics.

"Going to Loughborough was a big step for me. A Yorkshire mining village is another world, a very tight knit community."

Butterfield grew up watching Bradford Northern Rugby League club, where he saw Willie Davies, a pre-war international fly-half. "Willie always carried the ball with both hands in front of him and continued to run straight when he passed. I modelled my game on Willie's technique but discovered when I joined Northampton that I did not kick well enough to be considered as a first class outside-half."

At Cleckheaton Rugby Club, a young Butterfield found it hard to even get into the second team as many senior players were returning from the war.

After getting the job at Wellingborough, he was to become part of a dream three-quarter line, although it was not often that the Saints could field all their internationals at the same time.

'How many Butterfields do you see striding a rugby field like a colossus?'

Butterfield was one of the few players to go straight into the Saints first team and for two seasons he took all the training sessions. It was a job he was well trained to do as Cliff Morgan explained when analysing his contribution to the 1955 Lions tour.

"It was not just his skill in creating tries as a centre, but his ability to organise the team training," wrote Morgan. "There was a tremendous amount of individual talent in the party, but in those days a coach was not appointed. Therefore we were fortunate to have Butterfield. He was not only the fittest member of the team but he also had a marvellous tactical brain. This, combined with his background as a physical education teacher, helped him to take training and develop a unified team approach."

Even in 1980 the name Butterfield was still revered in South Africa. Former Springbok Wilf Rosenberg wrote in the South African *Sunday Express*: "Butterfield and Phil Davies. Those Lions centres gave me many problems. Butterfield the man with the magician's bag of tricks…Davies the human battering-ram. Man, they were a handful. How many Butterfields do you see striding a rugby field like a colossus?"

The arrival of Butterfield had a snowball effect on the Saints. Sykes followed him, and then came more college boys in Roger Hosen (Loughborough), Ricci Winn (Oxford) and Phil Taylor (Loughborough).

In 1952/53 White was still the lynchpin and in the Playfair annual he was one of only two Englishmen named in a World XV, along with eight South Africans, three Welshmen and two Irishmen.

It was another magnificent season, six games lost from 41 matches with six drawn. The side ended with 99 tries for the season, 13 going to the fit-again Hyde.

The club was annoyed that the Midland group of the county championship had reverted to Saturday county matches, which meant under-strength Saints sides lost to inferior opposition. A greater measure of the club's ability was the first win at Pontypool for 18 years, draws at Cardiff and Bristol and a one-point defeat by Aberavon on the Easter tour.

The Saints of the White era were a sublime mixture of forward power and creative back play. One game underlining all that was best about the Saints of that period is still vividly etched in all the players' memories. Butterfield reckoned it got him into the England side, and Jeeps on to the British Lions tour. It was in October, 1953, against a Cardiff side captained by Welsh great, Bleddyn Williams. The Saints won 22-9 and had the critics purring with praise.

Roy McKelvie (*Daily Express*) wrote: "**Northampton and Cardiff played one of the finest rugby matches I have seen for years…It is a sign of the times when an English side, even great Northampton, can tan Cardiff, a few years ago almost unbeatable by such a margin…**"

The Times said: "**This was rugby at its best, played at a tremendous pace and in the last minute it was as fast as it had been in the first…it was amazing how the two packs stayed the course.**"

Michael Melford (*Daily Telegraph*): "**Anyone whose faith in rugby football has been at all disturbed by modern trends should have seen yesterday's match at Northampton.**

"**The quality was all one could ask from two of the best club sides in the four countries, the pace was astonishing.**

"**Let it be said at once that Cardiff took a full measure of the honours. Their difficulty was that whatever they did, Northampton did just a shade quicker.**"

The *Chronicle & Echo* proclaimed: '**EPIC GAME AT THE GARDENS**'. "**Even the best-versed writer of schoolboy fiction would find it difficult to describe adequately yesterday's epic clash between the Saints and Cardiff at Franklin's Gardens. I commiserate with absent supporters; they missed a match that will live in my memory as long as I follow rugby football…it was a magnificent struggle for every one of the 80 minutes.**

"**Although defeat stared the side in the face from the first minute when Colin Pickford landed that 45-yard penalty goal Cardiff's great reputation as the premier British club never faded.**

"**Rarely have I seen the likes of a player such as plucky little Cliff Morgan striving might and main with brilliant side-step and uncanny intuition to turn defeat into victory.**

"**Those who question the strength of the Cardiff side may be reminded that five were members of last year's Welsh team, and that several more were Welsh trialists.**

"**They were handsomely beaten by a combination, whose skill, speed and elan fitted them for comparison with the England side itself.**"

White, by then a veteran of 14 internationals and countless representative games, told the *Green 'Un*: "It's the best game I have ever played in. We have played in any number of spectacular matches but never in one with so much brilliant combination from both sides. It was hard but there was no quick tempers.

"I am sure it was a game that all the players will remember for the rest of their days as one of the highlights of their playing careers."

Saints president, Dr Sturtridge said: "This was a beautiful game. I take my hat off to Cardiff."

Former player Tommy Gray beamed: "The finest game I have ever seen."

The side (internationals in CAPITALS) that day was: John Hodgkins; Don Macnally, JEFF BUTTERFIELD, LEWIS CANNELL, JOHN HYDE; Ray Williams, DICKIE JEEPS; MIKE BERRIDGE, TREVOR SMITH, RON JACOBS; Dick Hawkes, Colin Pickford; Hector Woolnough, David Bland, DON WHITE (capt).

The scorers: Tries – Hyde, MacNally, Butterfield (3); Penalty – Pickford; Conversions – Pickford (2).

Four players – Butterfield, White, Hawkes and Jacobs – were in Cardiff later in the season, when the Barbarians took on the touring All Blacks. The New Zealanders won 19-5 but White was the pick of the pack, making his omission from the England side even more inexplicable.

Neither Hawkes nor Jacobs were internationals at that stage, and indeed Hawkes never did get England recognition. There was no doubting he had the ability, but all his contemporaries point to one big weakness – laziness. "He would do one lap of the pitch and that was his training over with for the evening," recalled Knapp.

Hawkes, from Yeovil, had moved to Northampton to work for Travis & Arnold, and although he made the Somerset county side, it was at the Gardens that he won a big reputation as a lineout specialist.

He regularly appeared in England trials but never made the breakthrough. His lack of motivation exasperated plenty of his team mates, particularly skipper White.

Hawkes, who continued his career with Bristol, lost out in his quest for England honours to another Saints lock in 1954, Stanion-born Vic Leadbetter, who made just 54 appearances for the club between 1950 and 1956. A Cambridge Blue, Leadbetter played much of his rugby in Scotland with Edinburgh Wanderers. In 1954 he played against Scotland and France, but did not add to those caps.

Leadbetter was also in the combined Leicester and East Midlands XV that ran the All Blacks to 3-0. He was joined by Hodgkins, Macnally, Hosen (then at Loughborough College), Jacobs, Smith and Hawkes. White was missing through injury, but the Saints skipper still managed to add another notch to his fame without playing for England by being named in Springbok captain Hennie Muller's 'Best XV I Played Against', which listed seven New Zealanders, four Welshmen, two Australians an Irishman and White as the sole Englishman.

In 1954 the Saints built covered accommodation on the east side of the ground at a cost of £4,019. It was named the Gordon Terrace in recognition of the secretary's 25 years in office. The Supporters' Club donated £2,515 towards the cost, and the Mayor, Councillor J V Collier did the opening honours.

A new, exciting name appeared in the team in the 1954/55 season – one James Gilbert George Hetherington, who had played in a friendly at Wellingborough at the back end of the previous season as a guest of fellow Cambridge University student David Bland. At the time, Jim Hetherington was rather more interested in trying for a soccer blue. The game at Wellingborough changed his mind although not exactly for sporting reasons.

"David was asked if he could bring someone along to make up the numbers. I had been planning to watch so I agreed to play. We had a few pints in the Dog & Duck pub, followed by the cheese and pickle rolls, and then

The Saints squad of 1957/58. Back row (left to right): R Dickerson, A L Canham, J Butterfield, P J Taylor, D Coley, C P Daniels, A G Johnson, G J A Head. Middle (standing): I D F Coutts, L C Rowe, R R Winn, F C Matthews, A R Turnell, T O'Connor, F Hobbs, P Stewart, E J Gordon (Hon Sec). Middle (seated): F D Sykes, J G G Hetherington, R E G Jeeps (captain), Mr G S Sturtridge (President), D F White, C R Jacobs. Front: R W Hosen, A P Pearson, R Townsend, J P Hyde

the crumpet arrived. I thought this is the game for me," said Hetherington.

"Don White asked me if I was going for my Blue, and I said I was but not at this game. I had a leaning towards soccer at that stage. I had scored nine goals in one game and two against Mike Pinner, then the England amateur goalkeeper, who went on to play for Queens Park Rangers.

"My father had played for Everton as an amateur, so there was something of a tradition in the family.

"Don told me to forget about soccer and concentrate on rugby. I was rather flattered by that. I had followed rugby and knew of the fame of the people I was sitting with in the pub. I rather liked the idea of playing with them, so I took Don's advice.

"I didn't know whether the club would follow up that conversation but they did with a most marvellous letter from Jerry Gordon.

"I think it was an unwritten rule at the time that nobody went straight into the first team, and at the start of the following season (1954/55) I was carded for the Crusaders at Harlestone Road.

"The following week I had the most amazing thrill to be picked to play against Llanelli at Stradey Park. It was absolutely wonderful but I couldn't believe my eyes when Haydn Tanner wrote in the *News of the World* that he had seen someone destined to go on to play for England. I thought he was up the creek."

Those first impressions were spot on. Hetherington's England debut came three years later.

In October, with Hetherington still away at Cambridge – now seeking and getting a rugby Blue – the Saints started a tradition that died out with league rugby – the Irish weekend. It was the first time the squad had travelled by air, and it took three chartered planes from Birmingham airport to ferry them across.

Two games were played, and both were drawn: Bective Rangers, 6-6 and Cork Constitution, 3-3, a fixture that lasted just the one trip.

The Saints decided to field another XV on the same weekend, an unwise move as Old Millhillians came to Northampton and won 17-3, one of only five defeats and the widest losing margin.

Berridge, in his last season for the club, was rewarded with the captaincy to interrupt White's seven-year reign that dominated the Fifties.

The side lost 16 of 42 matches, more than in the two previous seasons put together, so it is perhaps not surprising to read in the annual report that: "The falling off in the team's standard of play after such a promising start must have been a bitter disappointment to him (Berridge), although on and off the field he always endeavoured to overcome the handicaps in a true captain's manner."

The defeats were all the more surprising as Saints added two more names to their international roll of honour: Yorkshiremen Frank Sykes and Phil Taylor.

No 8 Taylor played against Wales and Ireland in 1955 and was then out in the cold for for seven years – some say because of a doughnut-throwing incident when chairman of selectors, Howard Catcheside, was the accidental victim of the missile. In his recall season he played in all four home internationals.

Sykes was given similar treatment. He played in the other two 1955 internationals and didn't play again until a 1963 tour of Australasia. On the Lions tour of 1955 he was not selected for any of the four tests.

Harry Weston and Claude Palmer died during the season just as Palmer's son Peter had taken over as president of East Midlands.

Saints celebrated their 75th anniversary at the outset of the 1955/56 season with a dinner at the

Salon for 300 people, including W C Ramsey, past president of the Rugby Union, and guests from Ireland and Wales. Gordon was presented with an antique writing desk from Don White to mark his 25 years as honorary secretary

Ramsey told his audience: "It has long been an accepted fact that Northampton is one of the great leaders of the game throughout the country."

No-one in the room was going to dispute that, especially as yet another Northampton player joined the international hall of fame, Ron Jacobs.

It had taken the Peterborough farmer seven years to reach the England front row, but once there he proved difficult to dislodge. Following his debut against Wales, an inauspicious 8-3 defeat at Twickenham, Jacobs had a 13-game unbroken run at prop. The selectors ditched him in 1959 for Bedford's Australian-born, Larry Webb, who never relinquished his Aussie passport and who died in a private plane that went missing over the English channel in 1978. Jacobs had no idea why he was suddenly out of favour but he was back the following season for a nine-match run.

In 1963 he toured New Zealand and Australia with England before a final fling of four caps in 1964, including one game as captain, in the Stade Colombes. It coincided with England's only win of the season, 6-3, with a try from Malcolm Phillips and a penalty from Roger Hosen. The front row was supreme, hooker Bert Godwin taking six strikes against the head.

Jacobs joined Northampton after finishing at Nottingham University, where he took a degree in agriculture. In the holidays he played for Peterborough, where Berridge had been instrumental in helping the club back on its feet after the war.

Jacobs wanted a crack at top class rugby, and was undecided whether to write to Leicester, Bedford or the Saints for a trial. He plumped for Northampton.

In his first season, 1949/50, he managed 16 games and after that he was an established first team man, without ever getting a regular partner. He had a variety that included Berridge and Jack Whiting, who died young, Peter Haddon, Fred Matthews, Roger Turnell and David Powell.

He kept fit by working on his farm, so fit that he packed 470 games into a 17-year career, a mirror image almost of Ray Longland, who was retiring just as Jacobs came on the scene. "Ray didn't think I could do a thing right," mused Jacobs, who retired in 1966, almost on a whim. "It was a very young side, and all my contemporaries had gone. I just got up on the spur of the moment at the annual meeting and announced my retirement. It was only when Barry Newcombe wrote a piece on me that I realised how near I was to 500 games. Had I known I probably would have carried on."

His flat mate at Nottingham University, plant scientist Ian Ford, who won a couple of caps for Wales in 1959 in the second row, did go on to break the 500-barrier for Newport, but they never met on the football field.

Jacobs became president of the Saints, the RFU (1983/84) and England Colts.

Despite the ever growing band of stars in the Fifties, membership of the Saints had actually gone into steady decline for some seasons, and in 1956/57 an appeal was put out for existing members to recruit others to the cause. There was some consolation in that average gate receipts went up from £91 to £102 a match.

By the mid-Fifties there was a flood of student talent flowing into the club, a policy initiated by Butterfield. Loughborough College was a major source of talent.

They were like a club within a club. Graduates Jim Hetherington, Phil Taylor, Frank Sykes and Roger Hosen lived, ate and drank together.

Hetherington described what it was like. "After being thrown out of our digs (21 Billing Road) for misbehaviour (and poisoning the goldfish unwittingly with marmalade), Phil Taylor, Roger Hosen and I teamed up with Frank Sykes to find another place of rest.

"We found a wonderful flat above a lady hairdresser, whose brass plaque – Norah Panting – was on the front door. This was the object of much celebration but we quickly realised that we needed someone to feed the inner man.

"We placed an advertisement in the local paper calling for a housekeeper to attend to the needs of 'Four Hungry Saints'. This produced a flood of replies and the need to interview applicants. We made the great mistake initially of putting some undue emphasis on fanciability rather than culinary prowess. The inevitable result was that we ate badly, or not at all, while one of the four 'went out ' with the lady, who had been selected for her curves.

Ron Jacobs – 17-year career with the Saints

Classy trio: Frank Sykes, Roger Hosen and Jim Hetherington

"It took two months to realise that we needed someone of mature years who was good with the saucepan and not so enticing. We found her – Mrs Barnes – a lady who ruled us and built a solid career as a housekeeper and adviser on life in that memorable little flat above Norah Panting."

Cornishman Hosen was the last of the quartet to arrive. He would go on to make his name as a prodigious kicking full-back, after starting his Gardens career as a centre.

"Recruitment was the club's strength in those days. I would go home to play for Cornwall in the county championship and the Yorkshire contingent would do likewise and there was such a plethora of talent at the club we would quite often find ourselves in the Seconds for a week or two," said Hosen. "You could even find yourself dropped after being at an England trial! Training was not the scientific approach it is today. In fact, it was pretty ordinary – a long way short of Loughborough standard – so the ex-college boys would do extra training at the superb stadium they had at Timken.

"It meant that when it came to matches we were still as fit with 20 minutes to go as we were at the start. We used to whistle up Jim Hetherington from full-back and double the score in those latter stages (this practice was frowned upon a little by the club who described Hetherington's play as 'of a high standard even if adventurous')."

Conveniently for Hosen, Phil Taylor left teaching to join Travis & Arnold, allowing him to get a post at Northampton Grammar School. By an amazing coincidence, Hosen came under Jack Searle, who had taught him at Falmouth Grammar School.

Hosen, who went on to teach cricket and rugby at independent schools in Warwick, Rugby and Cheltenham before a hip replacement in 1986 forced him to give up, learned his kicking technique at Falmouth, where he played both soccer and rugby.

He was constantly practising. "It was like smoking. I was a 40 a day man – 40 kicks from different angles. As a teacher, there was always plenty of rugby balls available."

As he moved up the teaching ladder, Hosen always made sure he was near enough to get back to Northampton, hence the moves to Warwick and Rugby. But his career at Northampton came to a slightly premature end, after taking a post at Cheltenham College.

"We had Saturday morning school, which meant I was leaving at mid-day. I was arriving sweaty and uncomfortable after driving like hell. It was time to move and I joined Bristol. In fact, the change did me good. The fresh challenge stimulated me and I got a full set of caps in 1967."

He had to wait for Hetherington to retire in 1960 before being considered No 1 at the club at full-back.

In 1956/57, Hosen was still a star in the making; Jeeps was the man to catch the headlines nationally as well as locally. He was acclaimed the Player of the Year by the national press as England won a Grand Slam.

The Saints theoretically could play a back division containing Hetherington, Hyde, Butterfield, Cannell, Sykes, Hosen and Jeeps. But they never did. Between them they won 93 England caps.

In January, 1957, another international fell into the club's lap. Joe Gaston, a doctor, arrived in Northampton, but he was not seeking to further his rugby career, which had already earned him eight caps for Ireland. He came first to Creaton Hospital and then Northampton General. From Cloughmills, Ballymena, Gaston stayed in the area for a year, making 18 appearances, before returning to Ireland. A left winger, he was only considered an understudy for Hyde. Gaston happily turned out for the Wanderers, and apparently helped to swell attendances for those games.

Despite this glut of talent, the Saints still suffered their low spots, none worse than the 11-8 defeat by Moseley, the first success at Franklin's Gardens for their Midland rivals since 1906/07.

Inconsistency continued to dog the Saints in 1957/58, and the club was getting a bit fed up with the invitations that were flooding into the big names. Teams minus the stars kept the fans away. The club went as far as protesting to the Rugby Union, and it worked. The RFU brought in legislation restricting the number of invitation matches.

On the other hand, Saints were only too delighted when players were missing through England calls, and in 1958 Hetherington fulfilled the predictions made when his career was in its infancy.

He was still only in his fourth season of top class

England international Phil Taylor

rugby when he was picked to face Australia in what turned out to be a bloodbath. In the eyes of the press, Australia, having been beaten by Wales and Ireland, were determined to make up for those losses by resorting to intimidation against England.

On the eve of covering his 300th international Pat Marshall, the late, respected rugby writer for the *Daily Express*, picked this game from the other 299 he had seen, to kick off a look-back series 15 years after it had taken place on February 1, 1958. This is how Marshall recalled it under the heading:

Gory, glory boys
How battered
England tamed
strong-arm Aussies

"The stark fact that England won 9-6 matters little. What does matter is that for the first time booing was heard at Rugby Headquarters as the tough Aussies crashed into England with stiff arm tackles, knuckles and boots.

"They had a disappointing tour and had already lost to Wales and Ireland. They were not going to bow to the despised Pommies...well, not without a fight.

"The first Englishman to suffer serious damage was fly half Phil Horrocks-Taylor, a new cap. He was led off the field in the 25th minute after a kick had cracked his shin-bone.

"No substitutes in those days. England were down to 14 men, and Jeff Butterfield, who had already been stretched out cold twice by stiff arm tackles, moved into fly-half...

"The Wallabies kept up their physical barrage and exploited England's confusion behind the scrum. By half-time they had gone into a three-point lead...and knocked out Butterfield for the third time and full-back Jim Hetherington for the second.

"Ashcroft went back into the pack after half-time and was replaced in the centre by flanker Peter Robbins. The switch worked. Robbins performed just like an international centre and within 10 minutes helped set up an equalising try for another new cap Malcolm Phillips.

"That really riled the Aussies. They became even more physical.

"Butterfield was laid low for the fourth time. And this time it was serious – a partial dislocation of his right shoulder. He was lifted on to a stretcher and carried almost the whole width of Twickenham. Suddenly the bearers halted. Butterfield, with help from an attendant doctor, had replaced his shoulder. He dismounted wearily from the stretcher – and resumed.

"Australia again went into the lead with only a few minutes left...it seemed England would lose for all their gallantry.

"Skipper Eric Evans thought otherwise. He'd called for one last great effort from his tired, bruised and bloodstained side. Their response is now history.

"The forwards smashed into Australian territory. Half a dozen times it seemed they must score a try.

"Finally, the dazed and severely concussed Hetherington levelled the score on the stroke of full-time with a 40-yard penalty he was to know nothing about for 48 hours.

"England went mad as they strove for the victory they felt they deserved. It came in the dying seconds of injury time.

"The pack won possession way out towards the left. Jeeps to Butterfield to Robbins to Phillips to Jackson on the right. He had 25 yards to go and three men to beat...

"He handed off one man, swerved round the second, side-stepped outside the third and dived for the corner, the winning try and glory.

"Full-back Hetherington raised one hand and collapsed unconscious."

That colourful account was not quite how Hetherington, 35 years on, remembered it. Hetherington said: "I got a packet but these things happen. There was nothing dirty about it; I was just unlucky."

It was a baptism of fire and two years later he was finished with rugby, even though he played a full complement of matches in the Five Nations in 1959.

He said he was retiring because of a head injury but later admitted it was only an excuse.

"The truth is I was getting married, starting a new career and moving to London. It was going to be tedious slogging to get to training on a Tuesday and a Thursday. Without sufficient training my form would have started to go and I couldn't face the thought of playing in the second team."

The Saints produced sublime rugby in 1958/59, a record breaker with 696 points, nearly a third (219) from the deadly accurate Hosen. It was the biggest tally of points in the club's history both from the team and an individual.

For a man who played with style and panache, it was fitting that Hetherington bowed out after a famous win over Bristol, another major force in the land. He had been in the game only six years, but it had been champagne rugby all the way.

Butterfield soldiered on for another three seasons before calling it a day. As a student of the game, it was appropriate that he should have a major input in the first-ever coaching manual produced by the RFU.

For all the excellence of his rugby, Butterfield was equally well known for his geniality, underlined by the

Heading off for Ireland by plane for the first time. Three were needed for the trip

fact that he became proprietor of the Rugby Club of London in Hallam Street, near Oxford Circus.

Butterfield indulged his passion for socialising at the Saints by running a series of barbecues, known as Sundowners. These were aimed at raising funds for the club to help pay for such things as the trips to Ireland. He also came up with the idea in 1961 of a players' bar underneath the old main stand. Past president, Ron Slinn, took great pleasure in building – with 'help' from many of the big names of the era.

Butterfield, John Hyde, Sykes and a young newcomer, Martin Underwood, all past or future internationals, lent carpenter Ron a hand in its construction – with some extraordinary consequences.

"One Sunday morning there was a knock on my front door in Wycliffe Road and there stood Jeff Butterfield," said Slinn. "I could not quite believe my eyes. Here was this great England centre standing at my door, asking for help. He told me the players were keen to have a bar under the main stand. At the time players and spectators had to go the clubhouse at the Harlestone Road ground, which from a social point of view was a complete waste of time.

"We met with architect Peter Haddon and it was not long before 'we' set to work. It took at least 12 months to complete, working one night a week and Sunday mornings."

The lack of DIY expertise caused a few problems.

"Frank Sykes had the job of nailing the joists. Unfortunately he nailed them just a wee bit too close and got stuck between two of them. I had to knock one out to get him down," explained Slinn.

The team was only a week into the project when Slinn discovered the scheme had not been agreed at

all levels. Sturtridge came wandering through, and was aghast.

The quietly spoken Aussie declared: "What the bloody hell is going on here?" When told it was a bar for players and members, he was not impressed. "Players are here to play rugby on that field out there not build bloody bars."

The work carried on regardless and the bar saw several years service before the clubhouse was built – in honour of Sturtridge.

Butterfield was also secretary of the newly-formed players committee, designed to further the social life of the club. It is clear from the annual report of 1961/62 that this development was only grudgingly accepted.

"To administer these (social) activities a subsidiary club has been formed known as the Northampton Saints Club for which a separate membership is required, subscription 1/- (5p) per annum, thus allowing everyone attending the matches at Franklin's Gardens the privilege of joining. This however is not the players' main objective but rather a means towards an end. The players hope that by their devious ways of raising money sufficient funds will eventually accumulate to enable them to embark upon a scheme to build a new club house at the Harlestone Road ground. Their programme is an ambitious one to raise £10,000 to £15,000.

"There has undoubtedly been a great change in the after-match attitude in recent years, but the fact that we are a rugby football club and not a social club must always be borne in mind."

So Butterfield, apart from helping to revolutionise Saints on the pitch was also instrumental in establishing the bonhomie of the period.

60

Chapter Seven
Taylor spearheads new generation

Gardens goodbye to two giants, Dickie Jeeps and Don White

SAINTS

DINNER TO **DICKIE JEEPS**
FRANKLIN'S GARDENS, NORTHAMPTON
TUESDAY, 9th OCTOBER, 1962

DINNER AND PRESENTATION TO **DON WHITE**
FRANKLIN'S GARDENS · NORTHAMPTON
TUESDAY 16TH MAY, 1961

FEW people in rugby doubted the Saints were at the pinnacle of the game, and they started the Sixties by smashing through the 800-point barrier, 837 to be exact. Hosen, who had got his first century two seasons earlier, was responsible for 225 points to beat his own record.

The Saints were pulverising the opposition with a running game in which every player was encouraged to join in. Records tumbled but these were purely incidental to the style in which they were achieved. Thirty four matches were won in 1959/60, the highest total since 1897.

Jeeps succeeded Butterfield as England captain, and refuted suggestions that he was about to retire. The style of Saints play was described as "almost carefree" with a flair for the unexpected. For several seasons now the club had set the benchmark by which future generations would be judged.

With so many players to choose from, selection meetings could go on for ages. The story goes that Sturtridge would let the others argue and then toss a piece of paper on to the table and say "this is the side".

The great warhorse of the Fifties, White called it a day in 1961. His 447th and last game after a career spanning 18 years was also the last of the 1960/61 season, against Old Alleynians, a 51-16 victory. The players chaired him off the field.

Alleynians skipper Chris Howland presented him with a tankard and White told the crowd: "Thank you for your loyal and warm-hearted support. Thank you for all you have done for me."

In the programme, secretary Gordon wrote: "Don's retirement brings to a close an outstanding, colourful and controversial playing career, which has given pleasure and also disappointment to all, for I am sure his triumphs and omissions were felt by everyone.

"A keen student of the game, his ability, allied to that of his colleagues, many of whom were players of comparative stature, enabled the Saints to re-start after the war and reach the standard we now enjoy."

The 1960/61 campaign was one of 'misfortune, miscalculations and mistakes' – not the greatest for the legend to bow out on.

The biggest misfortune befell Hosen, who shattered a knee-cap at Twickenham in October and didn't play again that season. Having scored 450 points in the previous two seasons, the loss was acutely felt. His deputy was former Rugby full-back Ken Taylor, son of ex-Saint Bill Taylor, who turned professional in the Thirties. Taylor took umbrage a year later on being dropped and promptly left for Coventry. It was a move that inspired Michael Tebbitt, who had replaced Barry Newcombe as the *Chronicle & Echo* rugby writer, to liken Taylor's career to a British Rail timetable "Northampton to Coventry, calling in at Long Buckby and Rugby."

Jacobs, who won another five caps, had a magnificent season, using his granite-like power to protect the youngsters around him. His play was inspirational as was that of vice-captain, Phil Taylor, whose finest 80 minutes came when he led a reserve-strewn side to victory over Harlequins.

Perhaps this game convinced the players that Taylor should be the man to succeed Jacobs, and in 1961/62 the campaign was every bit as spectacular as those in the late Fifties.

Taylor revelled in the responsibility and his form was such that after a seven-year gap he was recalled to the England flock for all four internationals as pack leader. He was joined by a player, who shot to fame: Adrian Martin Underwood.

The St Luke's College graduate arrived in Northampton as yet another member of the Northampton Grammar School staff, burst through the trials into the Saints team in the centre and, amazingly, straight into the England side on the wing.

Thereafter it was said that he lost interest in domestic affairs, making just 18 appearances that season and three the next. The Golden Boy who captured the imagination was gone within 12 months.

Underwood played once more for England in 1964 and went on to become a member of the RFU coaching panel.

The final game of the season, again against Old Alleynians, saw Sykes create a club record – seven tries in one match. With five minutes to go he equalled the six scored by Mobbs set in two matches, and in the last seconds clinched the record. Barry Newcombe suggested it would have been more with better service.

In the same game Hosen went through the 1,000 points career barrier, while the Saints, for the first time in their 82-year history, were unbeaten at Franklin's Gardens.

The 1962/63 Saints fell from grace as the side grew old together. It was the winter of the Big Freeze, 10 weeks lost to the snow, and a great side simply melted away through retirement, injury and unavailability. Of 34 matches, only 16 were won and 15 lost.

But the season was not without hope. Another Gardens legend was unearthed from the 13 players who made their debuts – Robert Bainbridge Taylor, burst on to the scene as a raw 20-year-old.

Taylor always gave the impression he was keeping something in reserve, and that exasperated even his most ardent admirers, among them Don White, who was to become his England coach by the end of the decade.

Taylor owned up to his weakness but never found a way of overcoming it. Like all great players, he always seemed to have that little extra time. In 1962 he was just a raw player from Northampton Grammar School, the son of a Cumbrian-born policeman, who was an all-England wrestling champion. His father was a soccer man, and hoped his son would be a good enough to turn professional. He had the chance but turned it down. Said Taylor: "I played for the Cobblers as a youngster and was asked to sign for them, but all my friends played rugby and I didn't fancy it. My dad used to take me to the Cobblers and would have been chuffed if I had given soccer a go.

"I rarely watched the Saints as a boy and didn't have any boyhood heroes. My heroes were Tommy Fowler and Jack English at the Cobblers – Tommy crossing the ball and Jack banging them in at the far post."

Gardens legend Bob Taylor: Not interested in rugby as a schoolboy, dreaming instead of being a winger with the Cobblers

Taylor made 22 appearances in his first season, displacing vice-captain Steve Wilcock as openside flanker. The side was packed with stars but he didn't feel under any pressure.

"Pressure is the biggest bullshit word there is. I didn't feel it at all. It was just lovely to play. Nobody sets out to play badly. Even after you have achieved things in the game, there is no way you can get big-headed because players will always take the mickey if you start to get your head in the air."

Taylor was not the only future international to emerge on the scene in 1962. Farmer Michael James (Jim) Parsons, showed huge promise at lock and

Two international giants: England's Bob Taylor goes after Gareth Edwards of Wales

No 8 Taylor nudged the selectors first and at 20, England chose him for the New Zealand tour trial game at Leicester.

He didn't make it but veteran winger Sykes did, leaving even the player dumbfounded. Eight years after winning caps against France and Scotland, Sykes got a plum trip to the southern hemisphere at the age of 35. "It's incredible," said Sykes, who was originally only a reserve for the trial game.

Selection to New Zealand for Sykes, Jacobs and Hosen made up for the glaring absence of any Northampton men in the Five Nations.

Rebuilding the side was overdue, and it had to be done without Phil Taylor, who moved away from the area and decided to retire. He immediately switched from playing to refereeing. Within two years he was in the London Society of Referees. At the time it was seen as setting an example for other top players to follow. It was a difficult transition. "My biggest difficulty in the first few months was not to get involved. I remember seeing one move start and I thought, 'There's going to be a try here', and I set off for the corner flag" said Taylor.

"Sure enough, the winger came through and I was the only one near him. I was set to thump him into touch and how I let him score I'll never know."

Dick Turnell was handed the onerous task of seeing the Saints through another transitional season, 1963/64, a disastrous nine months which started badly with the death of president, Gordon Short Sturtridge.

The consultant obstetrician and gynaecologist at Northampton General hospital died on his 58th birthday, September 16, 1963. He had been president of the club he had grown to love for 13 years.

Newcombe wrote of him: "Rugby was Mr Sturtridge's life and lifelong hobby. No-one can ever

remember him missing any committee meeting held by the Saints – an achievement in itself. He loved Franklin's Gardens and everything connected with it.

"This man embodied everything that is good about the game – determination, sense of purpose, clear thinking, sportsmanship and comradeship. He was a man's man in everything."

At the end of the season Gordon was elected president at the annual meeting, while continuing as secretary. He just made it to the highest office. A year later he, too, was dead.

New talent continued to filter through to the Gardens, several destined to become internationals. From Leamington Spa came Keith Savage, whose future exploits were to interest gossip columnists as well as sportswriters. He had a startling turn of speed, which the team would come to exploit to great effect in the years ahead.

Strangely, one player not to be mentioned in end-of-season despatches was a young farmer, David Lewes Powell from Daventry Grammar School.

Seeds were being sown for the future. To nurture them along, farmer Jacobs was restored to the captaincy, and Newcombe predicted: "...a fine year lies only a summer away."

His optimistic prediction amid the ashes of a season that had brought 21 defeats in 39 games was based on a finishing burst of six straight victories, including a 39-8 crushing of Bristol.

They continued in 1964/65 where they left off. From the depths of despair, the new-look side produced the best set of results for 67 years; just four matches were lost – to Cardiff, Coventry, Bristol and Leicester.

The youngsters had one big helping hand, the return of Jeeps, brought back for one last hurrah from Cambridge. He brought with him a team-mate, Andrew William Hancock. Like Underwood, he was to

Keith Savage scoring against Bath in 1965 (main picture) and defending against Coventry (1964). Before going on to lead a high-profile life Savage was a sports teacher

step straight into the England team. There would be only three appearances, but he left his mark with a stupendous try against Scotland that snatched an improbable draw from the jaws of defeat. Even the Queen was there to see the longest run for a try in the history of the game in the March gloom of 1965.

As pipe-smoking Hancock said later, he just ran and ran. Bedford's Iain Laughland alone gave chase and launched himself into a despairing tackle as Hancock threw himself over the line in the corner. Hancock became an overnight hero, inundated with telephone calls and telegrams from complete strangers.

Less than four months later, Hancock married Heather Cameron, who, as her name suggests, was

Scottish. They even had their honeymoon in Scotland.

After his great try, Hancock was left pondering whether he should have done more.

"I will always wonder whether I should have tried to go round the posts. Iain Laughland just managed to flick my heels as I crossed the line. I sensed others were covering too. I had to make the decision – an equalising try for sure, or the risk of a defender knocking the ball from my hands as I turned in for the posts. I settled for the certain try."

Jacobs, renowned for his dry wit, commented: "We'll give him the ball on our own line and see what he can do for us."

64

Wonder try: Andy Hancock for England against Scotland

The answer was 28 tries in the season, the icing on the cake for Saints fans, who were treated to a dramatic recovery in fortune.

Hancock has relived the try many times over the years on various rugby programmes. He went on playing for years after leaving the Saints, leading Staffordshire to the county championship over Gloucestershire in 1970 at Burton-on-Trent.

If it had not been for Jeeps, he doubted that he would ever would have tried his luck in senior rugby.

"I'd had a few seasons at Cambridge City and was very happy. I had thought about moving to a bigger club but had never done anything about it. If Dickie had not come back to Cambridge I don't think I would have bothered."

He first made his mark with three tries in 27 minutes at Pontypool, which brought the superb *Green 'Un* headline 'Hancock's Half Hour'.

After early home defeats by Cardiff and Bristol in 1964/65, the Saints went on an 18-match unbeaten streak, 16 wins and two draws. Hancock and Bob Taylor were the most influential players, with Jeeps the inspiration.

David Powell: Meteoric rise

Like the now-retired Butterfield before him, Taylor's training as a PE teacher made him the ideal person to organise training sessions.

The 1965/66 season was disappointing but rewarding for individuals – a British Lions tour to Australia and New Zealand for Savage and prop David Powell, who had made a meteoric rise through the ranks.

Five players, Savage, Powell, scrum-half Trevor Wintle, Hancock and Taylor were all called up by England, but on the domestic front 15 games were lost and it took a last-match hammering of Old Alleynians to enable the club to creep past 500 points.

Powell went from the Wanderers to British Lions in just four months. Dropped during the season by England, he was the only English forward in the party and it was on the tour that he was dubbed 'Piggy'.

When the 1965/66 campaign opened his prospects of making the Saints first team, let alone England and the Lions, were slim until fate took a hand, when Roger Turnell dislocated a shoulder at the end of September.

Powell, who had reached the Saints via Long Buckby and Rugby, seized the opportunity with three tries in October to underline his mobility. Powell used his daily routine as a farmer to help his rugby. On his father's farm at Potcote, Mondays and Wednesdays were regarded as training sessions, running up and down hills wearing heavy boots and carrying a one and a half hundredweight sack of rolled barley on his shoulders, building up his neck and shoulder muscles.

England selector Micky Steele-Bodger was in the crowd at Coundon Road to see a non-stop performance against Coventry, and when the side for Wales was announced Powell, Savage and Taylor were all given their international debut.

Powell and Savage survived the 11-6 defeat, Taylor did not and was snubbed for the rest of the season. Powell was axed after a draw with Ireland, but Savage stayed the distance in what was a disastrous campaign, three defeats and a draw, the worst since 1948. It was hardly surprising that England players did not figure prominently on the Lions tour.

Savage, however, was a certainty. Since his debut for the Saints in October, 1963, he had been dubbed, predictably, the 'Leamington Flier' and it was surprising that he had not been snapped up by Coventry, having had a trial at Coundon Road.

Savage taught soccer at Delapre Secondary Modern School, and his Saints team-mates were in awe of his dribbling skills. He could trap a rugby ball as if it was round and beat three or four players with the ball under close control. Although capped on the wing, Savage was often used in the centre by the club, something he preferred on a cold winter's afternoon because of the greater involvement.

Wintle had barely donned a Saints jersey before being called up for the Calcutta Cup match. At Cambridge University, Wintle had been all the rage but his medical studies limited his rugby chances, and his university understudy, Simon Clarke, got into the England side instead, winning 13 caps.

Wintle, from Lydney Grammar School in Gloucestershire, had a brilliant schoolboy reputation but on an England tour to Australasia in 1963 he had to play second fiddle to Clarke. On completing his

England scrum-half Trevor Wintle makes a break against Old Alleynians, shepherded by Dick Pearcey and Mike Mason (1969)

medical studies, Wintle moved to Northampton General Hospital and the Saints. At the age of 26, after playing in eight England trials, he was named to face Scotland, the third scrum-half in four games. He was immediately cast into the international wilderness until 1969, when he had a full set of games.

Off the field, the Saints had been thrown into turmoil in the early part of the season with the sudden death of Jerry Gordon. He collapsed and died on October 21, 1965. The annual report carried a front page obituary:

"It is impossible to evaluate the enormous contribution that he made towards the high esteem in which the club is now held. He was honorary secretary from 1929 and president as well from 1963, a record that is unlikely to be bettered. His quiet but most charming personality endeared him to all who came in contact with him, and for this reason he was an outstanding ambassador for the club. The Saints was his life's greatest interest, and his dedicated loyalty was quite remarkable."

The Gordon family had also lost one of their two daughters, Rosemary, in a road accident less than a year earlier.

Veteran centre, Bob Leslie, who had just been elected on to the committee as a playing member, took over.

Leslie recalled: "I didn't know what I was letting myself in for. I used to take hugely long minutes, but I was quickly put straight by Peter Palmer and Marcus Jelley. The minutes got much shorter over the years."

Although not in the Gordon class, Leslie stayed in the job for 17 years before handing over to Geoff Allen in 1983. On Gordon's death a new post of team secretary was created, filled initially by George Adkins, to share the workload around.

The side was to be in the doldrums again in

1966/67, although Taylor, Savage and lock Peter Larter shared 10 caps, and all three were chosen to go on England's autumn tour of Canada.

Taylor had the unenviable task of following in the captaincy footsteps of Jacobs and he was to last only one season before Powell embarked on a successful five-season run, blessed initially with success.

The 1966/67 squad lost 25 of its 44 matches and very nearly finished with a points deficit. 427-411; statistically it was the worst in the club's history.

"The leadership probably came a bit too soon. I would have liked another chance but it never came," said Taylor. "There were a number of problems. For a start I got an horrendous ankle injury, which meant I missed a lot of the early games. Also my priority at the time was getting England recognition."

The Saints selectors were accused of persevering with reputations and disregarding current form. Hancock's form had completely deserted him, having lost the turn of foot that had brought him so much success, while hooker Andy Johnson had a depressing list of injuries.

A new breed of player, reflecting the changing times, emerged such as 'Beatle Boy' Barry Oldham. Confident and jaunty while playing for the Wanderers, players became tentative on being upgraded because, it was suggested, the youngsters knew they had no long-term future in the side. A lack of morale set in, coupled with absenteeism at training sessions.

Yet the club was able to call on eight past, present and future internationals, among them Devon-born junior technician in the RAF, Phil Larter. He was an all-round sportsman, with plenty of ability at basketball and in the boxing ring. Ironically for an area boxing champion, Larter was accused of lacking the stomach for a fight. Even after winning 24 caps, Larter never fully shed the Gentle Giant tag.

He never attempted to disguise the fact that he was not naturally aggressive. "Basically rugby is a skilful ball game, which I enjoyed and I liked the physical side. But if I wanted to raise my fist in anger all the time I would have taken up boxing.

"You learned to live with it. Occasionally, of course, you got involved and you were tempted to let one go, but I preferred to get on with the game."

His chance to play for the Saints came when he was stationed at North Luffenham in Rutland.

Larter, who played on and off at the Gardens for 16 years until 1980, was also an excellent left foot kicker, amassing 324 points.

The season 1966/67 season had kicked off in style with the opening of the Peter Haddon designed Gordon Sturtridge Pavilion, marked by a floodlight game between the Saints and an R E G Jeeps XV.

Haddon, by then in the veteran stage and captain of the Wanderers, was rewarded by being chosen to play in this showpiece game, although it was a dubious pleasure as Jacobs, John Pullin and Phil Judd formed an all-international front row in opposition.

Haddon's original design saw the Sturtridge standing on stilts with no ground floor, allowing spectators to continue to stand behind the goal.

The pavilion began to rival the Salon as a Saturday night venue, following the introduction of live music from committee man, Roger Horwood.

The Sturtridge was the perfect boy-meets-girl environment, and the dances between 1967 and 1970 were a great financial success. "They were not popular with the committee because once the music started there was nowhere for them to stand and talk," said Horwood. "It took two years to get approval for the dances, and it was only when I guaranteed them we would make £500 a year profit, that they relented. I think the first dance, after all the expenses were paid, made £14. But the dances soon became popular and we had no trouble meeting our target."

It was all good, clean cut fun but at the first hint of trouble, the dances were brought to an abrupt end.

The pavilion enhanced the Gardens reputation for being one of the finest rugby grounds in the country, but excellent facilities were irrelevant without a team to match.

Taylor lost the captaincy in 1967/68 to Powell, who was to prove himself in the Don White mould for commitment and thorough preparation. Powell's approach was in stark contrast to the easy-does-it style of Taylor. Results were not achieved at the expense of international honours. Quite the reverse in fact. Several of the internationals played only a handful of club games.

Against Wales, the club provided both wingers for England in Derek Prout and Savage, both locks in Parsons and Larter and a young wing forward, Bryan West. Neither Taylor, dropped after defeat by the All Blacks, nor Powell could force their way into the national side, but that was all to the benefit of the Saints cause.

Powell led by example, missing only three matches, and insisting that training sessions be taken seriously. The team entered the season super-fit and it showed as they reeled off nine straight victories, including a 35-9 thrashing of previously unbeaten Blackheath, before losing at Cardiff.

Powell brought a professional approach to the job, analysing the strengths and weaknesses of the opposition. He minimised the role of the three-quarters, even though they had the likes of Savage, Prout, Wintle, Oldham and Glenn Robertson to call on. Powell felt he could not trust a back division that lacked a quality centre and stand-off, the Cinderella spot in the team since the retirement of Tommy Gray.

At least half a dozen players to be tried in the playmaker role, including John Cooley who had moved from Bedford because they would not always play him at stand-off. The Saints followed Bedford's example of playing him in the centre, where his destructive qualities of tackling were so effective. He threatened to quit the Saints as well, but relented to play 221 games in a nine-year spell.

Touch judge George Adkins keeps an eye on things as Roger Horwood leads a charge against Rugby

Northampton-born Bryan West walks off after the England match with Wales (1970) and (right) three years earlier 18-year-old West in action against Penarth

Powell proved to be deeply committed to the captaincy role, and enlisted the aid of former rugby prop Ieuan Jones, who had taken over at Northampton Grammar School from Frank Sykes, by then teaching sport in a school in Boston, Massachusetts.

Jones was part of the Gardens' backroom staff, including a 'professional' medical attendant, John McVey, an appointment seen as another pioneering move by the Saints. For the previous 20 years they had paid an honorarium to Cobblers trainer, Jack Jennings, but McVey, a remedial gymnast, would be a track-suited trainer at Saints games as well as being available to players at Tuesday night training sessions and Sunday morning clinics.

He stayed 10 years at the Gardens before being recommended to Leicester City FC by former Arsenal manager Bertie Mee. He spent 12 years at Filbert Street before going into private practice in the shadow of the Tigers ground.

The find of the season was Bryan Ronald West, who before he had turned 20 was a Northampton, England and British Lions wing forward. Fitness fanatic West came under the influence of both Martin Underwood and Frank Sykes at Northampton Grammar School, and in his early years searched in vain for his best position: centre, full-back, stand-off. Eventually West made the school 1st XV as a flanker, and from then on it was success all the way.

"My best friend, Tony Knight, had reached the England Under 15 side, when I couldn't even get into the Town side. That motivated me a great deal. You tend to be in awe of England players, but here was my best mate getting that far. If he could do it, so could I," said West.

At the age of 16, West got into the England Under 19 XV before starting a PE course at Loughborough, where he got no further than the 2nd XV in an injury-interrupted year. He made his debut for the East

Midlands – against North Midlands – even before his Saints debut, and was soon hailed as the new Bob Taylor.

In January, 1968, Bob Taylor and Budge Rogers made way in the England side for West and another 19-year-old, David Gay, of Bath.

"In the final trial it boiled down to myself or Budge Rogers. At 19 I could not care less about reputations. I was not intimidated at all that Budge was England's most capped player at the time. The arrogance of youth, I suppose," said West. "I just thought I was bigger and better than him. I was playing for the Possibles and we stuffed the Probables. I was fortunate enough to get a few headlines, and that helped to push me into the team."

Like Butterfield before him, West ran into problems before his debut. The day before the game he started to come out in spots, the beginning of German measles.

He sought the advice of skipper Colin McFadyean, and between them they decided he should play. England drew, West came through unscathed, and was on his way to winning eight caps and a Lions tour at the end of his first season.

Although an original pick for the tour to South Africa, West was left at home because of an ankle injury, the decision coming the day before the party flew out to Johannesburg. Scottish flanker and future Saint, Rodger Arneill, then with Edinburgh Academicals, was called up as a late replacement.

"I had been measured up for the blazer and so on but I had to give it to Rodger, who was about my size. I was actually at Heathrow to see them off and straight afterwards took a taxi to see a Harley Street specialist," recalled West.

Within a week the injury had cleared up and West thought he was first reserve if problems should arise. Instead Ireland's Ken Goodall was called into the party only to break two bones in his right hand,

Saints of the Sixties:
Top: Dick Turnell, Mike Mason, Peter Larter and Roger Turnell battle through the Llanelli defence.
Centre: John Cooley makes his presence felt in a game against Coventry in 1964.
Centre right: Keith Allen tries to break clear against Llanelli (1969).
Bottom: Peter Duffy about to offload against Penarth on Boxing Day 1967, a 55-0 win for Saints.
Bottom right: Bob Kottler is snagged by Cardiff's Gareth Edwards.

paving the way for West to make a belated appearance in South Africa.

West did not instantly go on to greater things in 1969. He was overlooked for the whole of the home internationals, but in December of the following season he took part in the first ever England win over the Springboks, 11-8 at Twickenham, along with Taylor and Larter, who scored one of the tries.

England had waited over 60 years for this result, and much credit was given to England's first official coach, Don White. The selectors picked a 30-man squad and White had them training every month from August onwards.

West, still only 22, was made an offer to join Wakefield Trinity Rugby League Club. For a teacher earning less than £1,000 a year, the package of around £7,000 was irresistible. It was made up of a three bedroom chalet-style bungalow worth £3,500, a signing-on fee of £1,000, a retainer of £750-a-year plus wages. They also found him a PE job at Crigglestone County Secondary School.

The house was particularly welcome as it came just as prices started to go through the roof. It meant that West and his new bride Judith started married life without a mortgage round their neck.

Unfortunately for West the actual rugby was not a great success. He saw out only 18 months of his contract. The club put a £2,500 price tag on his head and he moved to York for a further 18 months, commuting from his Wakefield home for training and playing.

Said West: "I had just got married, when I moved to Wakefield with a new job, a new house and a new sport. It was all a bit too much. As a flanker in rugby union I'd been doing the hitting. Now I was the one being hit, one round the legs, the other round the head."

His brief taste of rugby league finished with a dislocated elbow, but he did have one day of glory as Wakefield won the Wills Embassy Rugby League Sevens in front of BBC Grandstand cameras. He collected £25 and a table lighter for his efforts.

At 25 he was finished with both codes of rugby, save for one game at Haberdashers School, Masters v Pupils. He had to write to the RFU for permission to play. They wrote back saying he could, but not to regard it as a precedent for the future.

West was not the only Saint to be approached. Bob Taylor got a call from a man claiming to be a representative of Wakefield. "You don't immediately say no to someone who might be offering you something nice, so I agreed to speak to him," explained Taylor. "He came to a Saints game and offered me £3,000. I told him I wasn't interested in living near Leeds. Now had he offered me a club near the Lake District I might have been willing to listen. But he didn't and that was the end of it. I never heard from an agent ever again."

A new name came to the fore in 1968, full-back Ian Moffatt, who had loads of England trials but never made it into the side.

He was a quality full back, who joined the Saints from Richmond and during his seven-year stint, he became the first Saint to top 300 points, 315, in a season.

The revival of 1967/68 was followed by yet another dramatic slump in fortunes, primarily because the

Ken Taylor: From Rugby Lions to Northampton to beat the breathalyser

1968/69 side just could not win away.

The Lions quartet of Taylor, Larter, Savage and West made only 28 appearances between them, while Moffatt top scored with just 91 points.

Savage's lack of appearances in the black, green and gold finally rubbed the Saints up the wrong way. He was described as the "most controversial player ever to wear a Saints jersey" and towards the end of the 1967/68 season the club refused to pick him for any side.

Secretary Leslie told the press: "He has played only 104 games over five seasons and that is not enough. Our relationship with Keith over the past two seasons has been difficult to say the least. Now we have told him that we shall not select him again and that it would be better for him to find another club."

Savage and the Saints patched up their quarrel in February, 1969, but by then South Africa had become something of a lure, not least for an on-off romance with a model. He spent 15 months teaching out there before returning to England and having spells with Harlequins and the Saints again before retiring.

In 1968/69 the dynamic leadership of Powell was not quite what it had been. He returned to the England fold to play in all four internationals as did Wintle and Larter with Taylor missing only the defeat in Ireland. International duty possibly blunted his commitment to the Saints.

It was also a time of social change, full-back Ken Taylor, who lived in Northampton, returning to the club from Rugby Lions "to beat the breathalyser".

Taylor said at the time: "Before the breathalyser was introduced I was twice stopped by police on my way home to Northampton after playing for Rugby. On both occasions they accepted my explanation that I was travelling home but now they might give me a little bag to blow in, which would be very dodgy."

Chapter Eight
Glenda and Doris

THE new darling of the crowd as the club entered the Seventies was winger Barry Oldham. In 1969/70 the Saints beat every Welsh club they met and Oldham scored 33 tries in as many games.

Bad weather caused the games with Cambridge University, Wasps, Penarth, Pontypool and Gloucester to be cancelled. But for that the club could easily have beaten their all-time points-scoring record of 838. Instead they had to be satisfied with 713.

Apart from Oldham's try-scoring spree, the Saints also found a top quality fly-half at long last, when Ian 'Stumpy' Wright joined from Rosslyn Park. Wright collected 218 points in his introductory season.

Welsh legend Barry John described Wright as "the best fly-half I have played against in Britain for several seasons."

Without the bad weather, Oldham feels he would have posted a target of at least 40 tries.

Oldham's exploit on the wings kept the Saints crowd happy. Cousin of Dick and Roger Turnell, Oldham was in the Towcester Grammar School 1st XV at 13 as a scrum-half, and briefly attempted to fill Jeeps's boots at Northampton. He was quickly converted to winger.

Oldham got his Saints career off on totally the wrong foot. It was the 1964/65 season and he turned up for a Wanderers game in ice-blue, drainpipe denim jeans, floppy sweater and had long hair 'by rugby standards'. "After the game," recalled Oldham, "Don White came in and started to congratulate people. I didn't have a clue who he was, and he said something like 'well done, lad, but if you want to make it at this club you'll have to do something about your clothes and your hair'.

"I was pretty bumptious, even as a 16-year-old, and I just told him that if my ability was good enough, it shouldn't matter what I looked like."

Oldham played 337 games for the Saints and scored 185 tries. "I played all those games for the Saints, yet I felt I played every one of them under pressure. I could never be sure of my place."

Oldham collected the nickname 'Shirley'. "I was given that by Piggy Powell, who followed the school of thought that all backs were tarts. The forwards did all the work and the backs got all the glory, which is why I was Shirley and Glen Robertson, Glenda.

"Then after one mediocre game, Ron Jacobs was reading the riot act, and referred to the wingers as Glenda and Doris. From then on I was always Doris."

If Oldham was pin-up boy, hooker Andy Johnson was the player most admired. He got a kick on the head in the game against Blackheath in the 1966/67 season, which led to a blood clot on the brain and an 18-month absence from the game. Doctors warned of brain damage but he fought back to prolong his career until 1974.

A schoolboy international, Johnson got on the reserve bench in 1969/70, and many observers

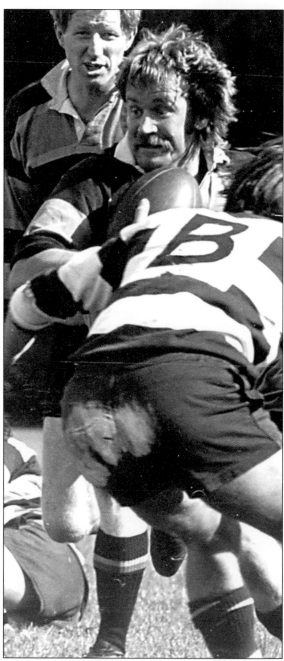

Darling of the crowd: Barry Oldham

thought him better than England incumbent, John Pullin. Johnson was dumbfounded to get the reserve card as it was five years since he had been a trial reserve.

A back injury finally forced Johnson to admit defeat at the age of 36. After a career dogged by injuries to the head, neck, ribs, hand and fingers, he had had enough.

There were seven Saints on view on November 8, 1969, as Midland Counties (East) took on the South Africans at Leicester, the controversial tour disrupted by anti-Apartheid protesters. This was the second game, and went ahead, while a battle raged outside

Outstanding stand-off Ian Wright running out at Franklin's Gardens and (above) lending support to Bob Taylor against Bristol in 1971

between demonstrators and police. Under such volatile conditions, the Springboks lost a number of games, but with virtually a full international side they scraped an 11-9 win over the Midland Counties, although personal glory went to Robertson and Peter Sweet with tries and Larter with a penalty.

This was a prelude to England's historic first win over the Springboks at Twickenham on December 20 with Larter crashing over in the corner for his one and only England try. A future Saint, Chris Wardlow, then with Carlisle, came on as a replacement for full-back Bob Hiller.

The victory was regarded as a triumph for England coach White, but the result flattered to deceive. England finished bottom of the heap with one win – over Ireland – and three defeats.

The international season ended with Taylor taking over the captaincy from Hiller for the French game in Paris, following in the footsteps of Mobbs, Butterfield, Jeeps and Jacobs. He marked the occasion with a try but England flopped to a huge 35-13 defeat.

"There were too many chiefs in the side," said Taylor, "and a few players turned out to be one cap wonders.

"Our biggest problem was that we didn't have 15 players pulling in the same direction. You can have 15 blokes all doing the wrong thing and you can win, but if you have five doing the wrong thing, five doing the right thing and five treading a middle path it is a recipe for disaster. That's what we had in Paris that day."

Nevertheless on October 3, 1970, Taylor was given the captaincy of a joint England and Wales side that played Scotland and Ireland to mark the centenary of the Rugby Football Union. Taylor's side contained J P R Williams, Gareth Edwards, Barry John and David Duckham. The captaincy was a thank-you for his services. Taylor, 28, was not picked for England again.

At the end of the 1970/71 season, Don White was relieved of his England coaching duties, Jeff

Butterfield was dropped from the selection panel, and Jeeps followed him a year later. Mike Tebbitt wrote in the *Green 'Un*: "...this could lead to an anti-Northampton backlash. I may be entirely wrong but personally I shall be a little surprised if either David Powell or Bob Taylor play for England again".

Of five internationals, Taylor, Powell, Larter, Wardlow and Wright, only Larter hung on to his place, and none of them made it on the Lions trip to New Zealand in the summer of 1971.

Wardlow was originally picked for the tour but he had his jaw broken playing for Northern Counties against Coventry, his place going to Scottish international Chris Rea, former presenter of BBC's Rugby Special and a frequent visitor to Franklin's Gardens.

Wright, who had chosen the Saints in preference to Bedford in his quest for England honours, seemed to be so affected by playing behind a dismal England pack that his club performances suffered as well.

In his first international, Wright was on the receiving

Peter Larter outjumps team-mate John Lacey in an England trial

Larter on the charge for the Saints

end of a 30-9 Welsh hammering at Cardiff Arms Park on January 16, 1971. "I stood about eight yards back for the first scrum," he recalled. "I looked down and the next thing I knew the English back-row was level with me."

He played in the next two internationals (a win against Ireland and draw with France) but was never called up again. Each time he partnered John Jackson Page, soon to be his team-mate at Franklin's Gardens.

Wright's decision to join the Saints came as a direct result of being a student at St Luke's College in Exeter with Peter Sweet and Robertson. A resourceful, inventive stand-off and intelligent kicker, Wright stayed nine seasons and amassed 631 points.

The last of the Sixties breed of international wingers, Derek Prout, called it a day to run a sports hall in Southampton. Holder of two England caps, he arguably won them for being at the right club at the right time. Prout even realised he might not get into the Saints side, when he wrote this letter to the club:

"…Northampton have very good wings at the moment and if I find it difficult to break in I might be forced to look elsewhere for a game with a club not so well blessed in reserve strength in the wing positions."

Prout first came to prominence with Redruth and Cornwall, winning the county 100 and 220 yards

championship. He came to Northampton to take up a post with Northampton College of Technology's sports hall. He had been one of a long line of disappointments in the 1970/71 season.

In 1971/72, the Saints came round to the view that they needed a coach – Don White, after all, had done the job for England, a precedent if ever there was one. In so doing they were following the example set by other leading clubs. Their first coach was a White, not Don but Barry, appointed a few months after the club had been attacked for their short-sightedness by the RFU's technical administrator, Don Rutherford.

White, a schoolteacher, made just four appearances in his Saints career between 1962-67. At the start of the season he was appointed to the club's 10-man coaching panel, and achieved greater powers halfway through. Despite his lack of playing success, White's appointment was welcomed. He lasted until the end of the 1973/74 season, complaining that the committee had not given him sufficient backing. He wanted players to be dropped if they did not attend both training sessions, but the committee was reluctant to take such drastic action.

In 1971 Jacko Page and Scotsman Rodger Arneil joined the club. Arneil had nearly joined Northampton in 1969, when he first moved south from Edinburgh.

74

England international Chis Wardlow about to make a tackle against Rugby at Webb Ellis Road

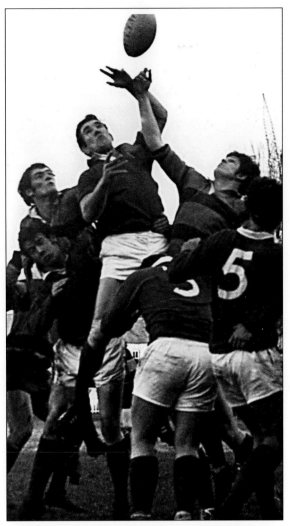

Frank Osborne and Geoff Wright compete for a lineout against Llanelli's Delme Thomas (1970)

But as he had moved to Leicester to work, he opted for the Tigers. When he later set up his own business in Northampton he felt free to switch.

It was not a long stay, 50 games in four years, split in two parts by a work assignment in Frankfurt for seven months.

Page, three years a Blue at Cambridge between 1968 and 1970, played for Bedford during his university days, winning four England caps in 1971. Ambition made him leave Bedford and join Northampton. Instead he was overlooked in his 13 seasons at the Gardens, save for one game against Scotland in 1975, a victorious comeback that critics wrongly assumed would get him a place on the summer tour to Australia.

Page's bald head made him an unmistakable figure on the field and early in his career he chose to wear a toupee. "You are more self conscious of those things when you are young, but the hairpiece didn't last," commented Page. "I worked it out for myself that someone like Piggy Powell was hardly going to let me get away with that. Could you imagine wearing one in somewhere like the Swansea clubhouse at around midnight after a game? It does not bear thinking about."

The introduction of coach Barry White had little affect on results in 1971/72, the first year of the KO Cup. The Saints did not take part in the first year and the competition was shambolic. Clubs were left to sort out a cup date between themselves. In 1974, Gosforth arrived at Northampton on December 28 to sort out their first round match, more than two months after the round had started. It had taken 11 different dates for the first round to be completed.

Then there was a row about kick-off time. Saints wanted 3pm, with lights being switched on if necessary. Gosforth objected and it was left to the RFU KO Cup rules committee to decide that it would be 2pm. The Saints lost 7-4, which meant that the following season three qualifying rounds had to be played before they could even get into the first round.

The committee decided to pull out of the competition on the pretext that the fixture list was becoming overloaded. While five Midland clubs had been seeded into the first round, the Saints, still with a crop of internationals, albeit aging ones, had to sweat it out against teams that would have been considered cannon fodder for the Wanderers not many years earlier. The club's pride took a battering.

The players were unanimous in wanting to take part, and they went on to beat Birmingham, Newbold and Westleigh.

It was an early warning that the Saints were resistant to change. New *Chronicle & Echo* rugby writer, Terry Morris, wrote: "It seemed a marvellous competition when the RFU announced it to a rugby world eager for a little more competition and a few more pounds in the coffers.

"But in the early rounds it is proving to be one almighty yawn and far from the money-spinner it promised initially. There are even stories of some clubs being hundreds of pounds out of pocket even after claiming on the travelling fund."

The RFU was initially against sponsorship, but it soon became the John Player Cup. Team secretary Geoff Allen commented: "There is no incentives for the major clubs to stay in the competition and for clubs to go to the problem of re-arranging fixtures. It costs us money to take part in the KO Cup."

In 1973/74 season a 24-year-old back row man, Mick Roper won a dramatic one-vote victory for the captaincy from Bob Taylor. Peter Sweet beat Wright to the vice-captaincy. Roper was among the last of the Northampton Grammar vintage. Local Grammar schools had produced a steady flow of talent, and occasionally a gem: a White or a Taylor. They also provided teaching jobs for young men with rugby talent. For the Saints the list is endless. When grammar schools died out; the Saints recruitment policy seems to have died with them. The class players coming to Northampton went from a steady stream to a trickle in the Seventies.

Wright, although pipped for the vice captaincy, took over the leadership of the side in 1974/75, and within three months the club lost another of its England connections, when Larter was posted to Germany for three years.

Another second row man was also making headlines – for all the wrong reasons. Geoff Wright was sent off three times in as many years, although the player pleaded wrongful dismissal on each occasion.

"I certainly play hard but I never play dirty," protested Wright, after his third dismissal, a steamy battle against London Scottish. "Things were boiling up all through the game and it suddenly went."

Saints were in a period of rebuilding, particularly in the pack. After five defeats, the Saints faced Bristol in a match shown later that night on BBC2, not a popular move with everyone, particularly those vice-presidents who had to give up their normal seats in the back of the stand for the TV crew. The Saints rose to the occasion with a 7-6 win. It was achieved with a rookie pack, except for Powell in the front row.

Friction was mounting between the players and the old guard on the committee, and in the summer of 1975 a plot was hatched by Oldham and Trevor Crane, egged on by a host of disgruntled, mainly local born players, to oust Don White from office.

"It was a very tame and amateurish effort compared to what came later," said Oldham. "The players had had enough of Don White and we were determined to get him off the committee. We had no grudge against the other committee members; we felt they just followed like sheep.

"Don was standing for re-election and we canvassed behind the scenes to have him removed. Those we could not get to, we handed bits of paper to at the door.

"We had put forward our own representative, John Ebsworth, but Bob Pell in the chair said that Ebsworth was not acceptable as he was not a fully paid up member. We thought we'd blown it but the people at the AGM got the message who we wanted off and voted accordingly. When the result was announced we were jubilant but it was short-lived."

The rebels were outsmarted within minutes of their 'triumph'. White, who had just been elected president of the East Midlands, was co-opted back on to the committee.

By now rugby was being dragged, kicking and screaming, down the road towards a league system, and Coventry match secretary Alf Wyman was the man doing the dragging.

Wyman's plan, anathema to Northampton's committee, was an 18-week league programme between 19 top English and Welsh clubs within a 120-

Famous Five: Peter Sweet, Keith Parker, Ian George, Barry Oldham and Graham Phillips. part of the Midland Counties side that beat the touring Australians, 11-8, in the 1965/76 season

The hugely distinctive John Jackson Page, 'Jacko' to all. He made just one England appearance during his illustrious Saints career spanning over 300 games between 1971 and 1984

Andy Johnson feeds Bob Kottler in a 1971 game against Moseley

mile radius of Bristol. That would leave 16 weeks for traditional fixtures.

It didn't get off the ground, but the Saints, under new coach Andy Johnson, turned failure into success in 1975/76, winning the *Daily Mail* Anglo-Welsh pennant.

The official line may have been anti leagues; the players had a different view. "You pretended they didn't matter, but they did. When we knew we had a chance of winning the Anglo-Welsh pennant, there was no doubt it acted as a real motivation," said Jacko Page.

The Saints lapped up all the publicity in a season, where they could measure their success in semi tangible terms: the *Daily Mail* pennant, the *Sunday Telegraph* English club championship, third in the English-Welsh club title and John Player KO Cup quarter-finalists.

The Saints won 10 of their 13 games in the unofficial Anglo-Welsh table. Decided on a percentage basis, the Saints finished with 76.91 per cent from 10 games compared to Rosslyn Park's 75 per cent from seven games. Results were ground out by uncompromising forwards, backed up by the tactically astute half-back pairing of Page and Wright.

Wyman was at the presentation evening, hosted by the *Daily Mail*, whose sports editor Tom Clarke handed over the pennant. Said Clarke: "We hope that the Anglo-Welsh league develops to the benefit of English rugby. We hope this is the beginning of a successful and sensitive restructuring of the game in England."

The season had an extra gloss for five players, wingers Keith Parker and Oldham, scrum-half Ian George and flankers Sweet and Graham Phillips. They were part of the Midland Counties side that beat the touring Australians, 11-8. Parker twice made something out of nothing to squeeze in for two corner-flag tries.

The following season Dickie Jeeps was president of the RFU, and his first act was to call on English clubs to commit themselves to an open 15-man rugby, flying in the face of the tactics that had been so successful for Johnson and the Saints.

Johnson instantly declared that Jeeps's old club

would faithfully follow that edict – with dire consequences.

Johnson announced: "I want the players to play the game advocated by Dickie Jeeps. This will be a season for the players – and for more adventurous football. If this is what the England selectors want, then the Saints will provide it."

The Saints crashed 25-6 at Bristol in the opening game, forcing Johnson into a hasty rethink. Two days after supporters read of the team's bold intentions, Johnson was furiously back-pedalling: "We have got to decide whether we are going to be an attacking side primarily or whether we are going to shut out the other side. We may have to play a more defensive sort of role."

The 1976/77 season saw the introduction of replacements in domestic games, and it was done in customary shambolic fashion. Clubs could have none, one or two, to be agreed in writing before the game. The law was totally ignored, and there were at least two occasions when heated arguments over substitutes preceded events on the field.

Just how far the club had fallen down the international scale was revealed in December, 1976, when England's chairman of selectors, Sandy Sanders wrote to 100 players, telling them they were in contention for honours. Just three Northampton names appeared on the list: Page, Phillips and Ian George.

Off the field, the club had more success in its search for a second team ground. They found one on their own doorstep, a four-acre former tip on a 60-year lease at the back of Franklin's Gardens with an initial outlay of £9,000.

Seventeen months later, on November 16, 1977, the committee pulled off its biggest coup by buying Franklin's Gardens for a knock-down price of £30,000. Leslie told the press: "We have secured the ground for eternity. It has always been the club's dream to buy the Franklin's Gardens."

The deal was clinched seven years before the lease was due for renewal, and ended any thoughts about moving to another part of town.

Top pictures: Peter Sweet, classy centre and later gritty flanker alongside Greg Wilcox.
Centre: Local boy Graham Phillips in the thick of things against Gloucester and in the wars (above)
Left: Ian George in action for the East Midlands against the Barbarians with Phil Bennett looking on

Chapter Nine
Gary props up sleeping giant

GARY STEPHEN PEARCE, a trainee quantity surveyor from Aylesbury, came for a month's trial in February, 1978, and went on to make 411 appearances for the Saints.

He made his England debut against Scotland on February 3, 1979, he was still strong enough, fit enough and good enough to figure in the 1991 World Cup game against the United States, a total of 36 caps later.

Pearce has a tackle on Fran Cotton to thank for his illustrious career. A Buckinghamshire side had been put together as cannon fodder for England during a training session at Bisham Abbey. Pearce tackled Cotton from a tap penalty and put him out of the first two internationals in 1978. Pearce had never had any aspirations of playing senior rugby, but word spread of the tackle that made Cotton reel, and the Saints got in first with an invitation.

Pearce played in all four home internationals in 1979 but was then overlooked for the Grand Slam campaign of 1980, losing out to Phil Blakeway, missing out on appearing in the front row with Cotton.

Pearce regained his spot on the tour to Argentina in 1981, caps being awarded even though the South Americans were not part of the International Board. He played eight of the next 11 internationals before giving way to Blakeway again but then went on an unbroken run of 17 internationals up to the end of the 1986/87

season.

Throughout this period he was given little credit by the critics. Said Pearce: "It's difficult for some people to see me up there as England's most capped prop. They have never associated my name with the all-time greats even though I must be in that league. Many people are not aware of what I have achieved."

It was a different story for Saints fans. They made him their Player of the Year, when the Saints won Courage League Division Two in 1989/90.

"It's something you don't expect. I'm in a position where I don't score tries, it's not a charismatic role on the field so to win the award was super," said the modest Pearce.

Looking back over a glittering career, Pearce said: "I was invited up to play four games in the Wanderers, which was the system in those days, after which they made a decision to keep you on or send you back to your junior club. I was picked for the Aberavon game on Good Friday and to all intents and purposes have never been dropped since."

His fondest international memory is England's 1983 victory over the All Blacks, the first since 1936, all the more sweet because Pearce had an ear virtually ripped off inside the first 10 minutes. He was stitched up and sent back on only to sustain a broken nose.

Back at work on Monday, Pearce was alarmed as the ear began to swell up, and he finished up needing plastic surgery and wearing a turban for six weeks. It

A legend in the making: Long-haired Gary Pearce (left) with hooker Jon Raphael

A look of resignation or anguish (from the left): Trevor Crane, Gary Pearce, Jon Raphael and Bobbie Smith endure a hammering from old rivals Leicester

left him with his one cauliflower ear.

A practical joker, Pearce was only on the fringes of the infamous aftershave drinking episode at the post-match banquet in Paris in 1982. Colin Smart needed hospital treatment after drinking a cocktail of after-shave and wine. It was a joke that could have turned horribly wrong, but Pearce's quick thinking got Smart to a Paris hospital where he had his stomach pumped. "I was trying – unsuccessfully – to make him vomit when I noticed his breathing was very shallow. He had been having a red wine drinking race with Marcus Rose, after drinking a lot of beer and, of course, the aftershave. He saw Maurice Colclough apparently drink his but what he didn't know was that Maurice had emptied out the contents and substituted red wine."

Apart from Pearce, 1977/78 also marked the arrival of another key forward, former Oxford Blue and Harlequins hooker, Peter Johnson. In a meteoric rise, Johnson was appointed skipper the following season, and made his presence felt immediately with a get-tough message to players to get fit. The ex-parachute regiment captain prepared the players with military precision – literally. In August they were taken to Aldershot for a weekend of Army manoeuvres. If the players needed any convincing that all this exercise was good for them it came two weeks later in the first match, a scorching 26-14 win at Bristol, the first opening day win for three seasons. He left at the end of that season to be replaced as skipper by Peter Sweet.

In September, 1979, past and present players were among an audience of 450 for the centenary dinner,

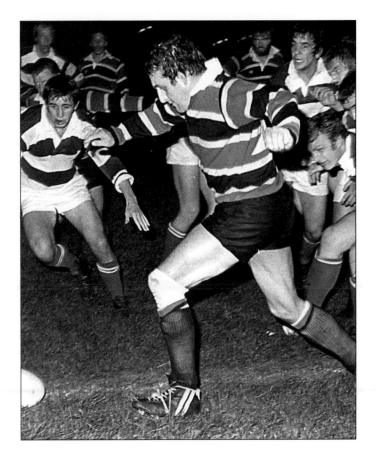

Quick promotion: Former Oxford Blue and Harlequins hooker Peter Johnson was appointed skipper in his second season

Gary props up sleeping giant

Centenary Saints: The 1979/80 squad, back row (left to right): Peter Bignell, Nigel Fox, Jon Surguy, Jon Desborough, Dave Pinches, Charlie Causebrook, Jon Cubitt, Keith Parker; Middle row: Geoff Allen (team secretary), Andy Street, Greg Wilcox, Clive Folwell, Dave Mason, Geoff Wright, Steve Russell, Chris Mackaness, Bob Taylor (coach); Front row: Paul McGuckian, Bobbie Smith, Jon Raphael, Peter Sweet (captain), Don White (president), Jacko Page (vice captain), Gary Pearce, Vince Cannon, Bob Leslie (secretary)

an occasion for much back-slapping. It was left to a Welshman, the incomparable Cliff Morgan, to pay the most articulate compliment. "I pay homage with great humility, warmth, love and affection to the great club of Northampton. May Northampton flourish, may it never become too sophisticated or too aloof. May I wish you well – this club has given so much to so many for so many years."

Don White was president for this memorable year. He told the audience: "To me the Saints is the best club in the world. I never wanted to play for anyone else and my sentiments remain absolutely unchanged."

Dickie Jeeps, by now chairman of the Sports Council and past president of the RFU, said: "This club has had a fantastic number of international players and I really believe we don't need to creep to England selectors. Our club can stand second to none in its contribution to English rugby."

Centenary chairman Hector Woolnough got all the significant *Chronicle & Echo* rugby writers since the war to commit their thoughts on the club to paper.

Michael Tebbitt (1964-73) gave the most graphic account of what life was like for a young reporter. "First let me put the record straight, strictly speaking I am not an ex-Scout. By the time I succeeded Barry Newcombe in 1964 the rugby correspondent was already writing under his own name. Nevertheless the *nom-de-plume* was perpetuated because the old guard such as Ron Jacobs and Dicky Jeeps always signalled their willingness to grant me an audience with the words 'Oi, Scout'.

"In those days the Easter tour – Aberavon on Good Friday, Llanelli on the Saturday and Bristol on the way home on Easter Monday – was the playing highlight of the season. A far more eagerly awaited social event though was the visit to Dublin, home of Bective Rangers, every other year.

"The Saints made their HQ at Jury's Hotel, close to St Stephen's Green and not far from the Post Office, traditional meeting place for Republicans ever since

the abortive Easter Rising of 1916. Irish politics are strictly for the Irish as far as most rugby players are concerned, but one year we became inexplicably caught up in an IRA anniversary.

"With nothing to do on the Sunday afternoon after the match, several players and myself decided to visit Croke Park in Dublin to watch the annual Gaelic football match between Dublin and Tipperary. None of us at that time was fully aware of the nationalistic undertone of the Gaelic sports. 'Northampton Football Club' we proudly announced at the main gate and were promptly ushered to gratis seats in a stadium containing upwards of 50,000 Irishmen.

"What was to follow made our hair curl. Before the game, speaker after speaker stepped up to the microphone to condemn the 'barbarous British for their bloody acts of murder and treachery'. We couldn't believe our ears! After all, they had let us into the ground without paying. Peter Larter started to make a comment and immediately the rest of us chorused: 'For God's sake, shut up! Don't let anyone know we're English'.

"It transpired that the annual Dublin-Tipperary clash marks the anniversary of the original 'Bloody Sunday' of 1920 when the Black and Tans climbed the walls of Croke Park and without warning shot several players on the pretext that they were members of the IRA. It was a wonder we got out of the ground alive!

"Mention of Jury's Hotel reminds me of one of the rare occasions on which team secretary George Adkins inadvertently loosed the purse strings. The master plan was simple really – not surprising this as it was dreamed up by a second row forward known more for his brawn than his brain. He sauntered up to the hotel reception desk and enquired, 'could you tell me the number of Mr Adkins's room, please?' Back came the reply, 'yes soir, it's No 28'. Now for the most difficult part of the plan. Half a dozen of us sat down to a four-course meal, plus wine. When the waiter presented our bill our intrepid lock forward replied,

Successive skippers: Paul McGuckian (left) handed over the reins to Vince Cannon in 1982/83

'oh book it to room No 28's account'. It worked...but poor George nearly threw a fit when presented with his bill on returning from a day's outing to the Wicklow mountains.

"Hancock, Taylor, Savage, Powell, Larter – these were the household names of the Sixties and early Seventies but some of the lesser lights were equally newsworthy at times. I wonder how many Saints supporters remember the name of piano playing Scotsman, Jock Elliott, an ex-Merchant Seaman who joined the Saints after being released from a Spanish jail. He served a six-month sentence for making rude remarks about Franco while drinking in a Spanish bar.

"As a journalist, though, I had even more reason to feel grateful to Keith Savage. His play-boy image brought him constantly into conflict with the Establishment but provided me with hundreds of column inches of good copy. The 'will-he, won't-he' saga of Savage and the South African heiress was as intriguing as the Christina Onassis story.

"Understandably, the players did not always take

Gary props up sleeping giant

Prolific scorer: Keith Parker

kindly to newspaper criticism and some rough justice was administered on occasions, although I avoided some of the greater atrocities inflicted upon Michael Green and Barry Newcombe. I learnt early on never to hand in my room key at a hotel reception desk. My opposite number at Coventry, David Irvine once returned from a night out to find his bed, wardrobe, chair etc. neatly laid out in the car park."

Jeeps brought an international XV to play a showpiece game on a Sunday in December, and the curtain came down on the festivities with a ball at the Saxon. An appeal was also launched to raise the £30,000 cost of purchasing the Gardens, all the subscribers having their names penned into a black and green hard back book embossed with gold lettering and the club's crest. By the end of the season, the figure topped £23,000.

Peter Sweet had the honour of leading the side, but the season turned sour for him, when he was injured halfway through, landing Page with the job from January onwards. The centenary celebrations failed to inspire the team beyond the by now familiar mix of inconsistency, the low point being a 3-0 John Player KO Cup defeat to Nottingham, their first-ever win at Franklin's Gardens.

Just 17 of 38 games in 1981/82 were won as the frustration that ultimately led to the 1988 revolution began to set in. It had got off on the wrong foot when arbitrarily drawn up leagues were announced, putting Saints into Division Three with Blackheath, Broughton Park, Exeter, London Welsh, Roundhay, Sale and Wakefield.

Leslie went on the attack: "We don't need or want leagues. Standards have fallen in rugby but that has nothing to do with whether we want leagues or not. There is nothing wrong with the game.

"The Rugby Union will have us professional in 10 years the way we are going. With so many competitions, sponsorship and players going into games at such a fierce level, with all the preparation that includes, they are bound to say: 'there has to be something in it for me'.

"As far as I am aware the majority of senior clubs are not interested in leagues – they want to make their own fixture lists. We are completely opposed to leagues in rugby union. The RU can introduce what they like but they cannot force anybody to participate if they don't want to. If we were able to play in leagues what would happen to our list. Where would our Welsh fixtures go?

"Our best fixtures would be thrown out of the window. How would that improve the England side.

"It has just been a quirk of history that Northampton Football Club happens to have become a very strong club that entertains strong opposition. By playing strong opposition and over the years playing attractive football, we have attracted crowds which have enabled us to develop our playing standard and build stands and a clubhouse.

"How many senior clubs can there be? Leagues would be the death of the Northampton club as it now stands."

Secretly Gardens officials must have been furious at only being accorded Division Three status.

The other suggested groupings were: **Division One:** Bristol, Gloucester, Gosforth, Leicester, Moseley, Orrell, Rosslyn Park, Wasps, Waterloo. **Division Two:** Bath, Bedford, Coventry, Fylde, Harlequins, Liverpool, London Irish, London Scottish, Richmond.

The 'divisions' reflected the team's performances of that particular period. No-one seemed able to offer the necessary lead. The 1981/82 team secretary and coaching co-ordinator, Geoff Allen, bemoaned the lack of success: "We have got better players than our results do us credit for but I don't know how long we can keep saying that. The players need welding together. If they don't possess the skills of Phil Bennett they need to get very fit. The players were not as fit as when they won the *Daily Mail* Anglo-Welsh pennant a few seasons ago. The club is very conscious that we have to do better."

One ray of sunshine was the form of first season winger Nigel Underwood, whose 10 tries made him the leading scorer. The 21-year-old, a national schoolboy hurdles champion, quit athletics to concentrate on his rugby career.

It was indicative of the lack of success that a close defeat at Cardiff, 26-22, was regarded as the highlight of the season. The low point was a bloodbath at Stradey Park, during which Llanelli's full-back Kevin Thomas collapsed and temporarily stopped breathing. It was a pure accident but the Saints players suffered a terrible mauling, and Allen fumed afterwards: "The Llanelli match left a bad taste. It was an awful exhibition of niggling football.

"For the first 20 minutes of the second half there was no football played at all. I don't know if Llanelli are always like that or just when they play Northampton."

Terry Morris's report in the *Chronicle & Echo* said that "one senior player almost walked off in disgust". Morris claimed the Welshmen indulged in punching, kicking and straight-arm tackling. The unnamed

A touch of glamour at the Gardens in 1979 when 'Dregs & Co' performed at a Saints revue. From left to right: Maggie Crane, Tracey O'Connell, Carol Burwell, Glynis Jenner, Maggie Sweet and Teresa Duggan.

Top: Matthew Ebsworth, who amassed 513 points in his Saints career.
Left: A hairy Phil Pask the player who became (above) the shaven-headed Saints, England and British Lions physio.

player was quoted as saying: "It was nauseating. We all have to go back to work after the match."

Pearce had his nose broken and club chairman Don White offered his own insight into the violence. "It is only the weak who get attacked in this world today. People don't do things when they can't get away with it. If we were a little stronger we would get more respect."

The season was only weeks old when the club took the decision to play a unique double header, two first team games Franklin's Gardens one after the other – with the fans paying twice.

The Saints took this bizarre decision because the Rugby Union would not allow a John Player Cup tie to be played on a Sunday and yet the club also wanted to honour what they thought would be their last fixture with Blackheath after a 79-year run. It was wrongly thought that a re-arrangement of the fixture list would mean the axing of the Blackheath date.

Blackheath were beaten 13-4 and Kettering 31-0 as the resources were balanced between the two games. The fans literally had to file out and come in again, while the Sturtridge Pavilion windows were blacked out to avoid unpaid peeping.

Paul McGuckian handed over the captaincy to lock Vince Cannon for the 1982/83 season, which turned out to be one of the worst in the club's history. Cannon could not be faulted for commitment, but the season left him more angry than depressed as he handed over the hot seat to Northampton GP and permanent England reserve hooker, Jon Raphael.

"If we had had a more successful season I might have carried on. I am a singular player in that my own performance means so much to me. I don't think I have been a bad captain but captains are judged on results as managers are in soccer. To some people captaincy is a hindrance, to me it was an annoyance because I wasn't getting the results I wanted," said the Kettering-born second row, who made his debut in 1974 on an Easter tour and went on to the verge of the England side.

Cannon questioned some players' commitment to the club. "You have to make sacrifices. You have to give up things playing at this standard that ordinary people would take for granted. It is hard work, to stay at the top is even harder."

In 1983/84 false hope emerged under the Raphael leadership as the team suffered just four defeats in the opening 17 games.

Yorkshireman Dick Tilley was now in charge of coaching and for the first half of the season there was a mood of optimism. In the New Year, defeatism crept

in and training attendance dropped off.

Raphael was forced to give up the game in April 1984 because of a neck condition at a time when he was contemplating a second season as captain. The alternative was to risk spending the rest of his life in a wheelchair. Raphael, then 31, was warned that one more tackle or one more scrummage could leave him permanently paralysed.

X-rays had revealed that the doctor's strained neck had suffered a fractured vertebrae and that two had fused together, which had led to severe pain in the shoulders, arms and back. The powerfully-built six-footer said he had the neck of a 60-year-old but the lure of the game had been so great he had resisted the temptation to retire earlier.

He had been in the first class game since he was 17 and went on to play for England Schools and captain his country at Under 23 and B level.

In January, scrum-half Steve Worrall, then a 22-year-old weapons technician with the RAF and veteran of the Falklands War, was flattened by Rosslyn Park prop Paul Curtis. His jaw was shattered and he spent a week recovering in hospital, after an operation to repair the damage.

The incident led to a dispute between the two clubs, which resulted in the return fixture in March being scrapped. Park officials were adamant that it was an accident. Allen wrote to Park asking for them to take disciplinary action against Curtis but none was forthcoming, so the Saints scrapped the fixture.

Worrall, who spent a total of 11 days in hospital, said: "I am pretty pleased that something has actually been done about it. But it is a pity that Northampton had to take action and not Rosslyn Park."

David Woodrow succeeded Raphael as captain for the 1984/85 season, and started with six straight defeats in September. Hooker Bob Gardner and prop Ian Heywood played in all 39 games.

At the end of the season a six-man committee was set up, under the leadership of Ronnie Knapp, "aimed at dragging the Saints out of the dark ages". Knapp was joined by Don White, Bob Taylor, Fred Hobbs, Don Macnally and Peter Haddon in investigating the playing, coaching and selection at the club.

Terry Morris criticised the composition of the committee with a hard-hitting attack. "It is hard not to feel that the running and management of Northampton Football Club has become as exclusive as a trades union closed shop or a masonic lodge with admission strictly controlled. A generation gap has emerged

Vintage performance: Peter Sweet holds aloft the champagne after Saints were named *Sunday Telegraph* Team of the Week for winning 15-7 at Llanelli at Easter (1980)

The way we were: Saints players set out for pre-season training, circa 1980

Graham Poole secures possession in a local derby with Leicester

with a them-and-us attitude."

A year on Morris reported that the findings of the Knapp committee had never been made public.

For the 1985/86 season, Powell, replaced Tilley as coach with Trevor Crane his right hand man. Still success proved elusive. Morris was unrelenting in his campaign for change. He said the Saints had gone backwards; the players lacked direction, organisation and inspiration.

"The imminent introduction of leagues will finish Northampton Football Club if the decline is not halted. The Saints will disappear from the first class circuit," wrote Morris.

At the annual dinner, Crane kept up the momentum: "In two years Northampton will either wind up a powerful side or this great club will be nowhere to be seen."

Chairman of selectors Dick Turnell commented: "It was a miserable season and a lot of us were happy to see the end of it."

Amid all the gloom of the Eighties, Pearce continued to build up his collection of England caps. By the end of the 1985/86 season they numbered 27 and he was asked why he had not joined a more successful club.

"I don't know," said Pearce, "but I don't think I would have achieved any more by going anywhere else. It would, of course, be great to play for a successful club, but Northampton is going to be successful next season, isn't it?"

In the summer of 1986, it was announced that South African ace, Naas Botha, would be joining the club in September.

There was an outcry in the town as the press went into Botha's Mr Nasty reputation. Borough councillors slammed the idea, even sports-loving deputy mayor, Trevor Bailey. "The council are appalled by this signing and we hope that by making our feelings clear we can persuade the club to reconsider," said Bailey. "It detracts from our (anti-apartheid) campaign when one of the town's leading sporting clubs does something like this."

Councillor Bailey and the rest need not have worried, Botha didn't get anywhere near Northampton.

The side did get a boost with the form of local boy Frank Packman, who scorched in for 33 tries from 36 games in 1986/87.

Under skipper Graham Poole, the Saints almost won

promotion from Merit Table B in 1986/87, while a strong youth side, under the guidance of ex-hooker Paul Bryant, was emerging.

In the summer the players went off for a Spanish break to mix rugby with pleasure.

Trouble started when local youths began laying into 35-year-old sales manager Chris Morgan, a centre who had been with the club since 1971. John Cubitt, David Elkington and Nick Grecian had gone to Morgan's aid at which point the local guardia intervened, hurling all four into the cells. Morgan spent three days in jail, the other three just the night.

On their return, Morgan described what happened. "We were set up by local thugs. They pushed us into a fracas and the police swooped. They were heavy handed – every time one of us spoke in English we were hit with a baton about the back. I was put in solitary and the first cell was a hole.

"One of the guards told me the previous prisoner was an AIDS sufferer. The blankets were covered in blood and slime. I kept thinking to myself that I couldn't let myself become unnerved, it would all turn out right in the end."

Morgan ended up in court but was released. Tour manager Geoff Wright said: "It was an excellent tour and we made a lot more friends than enemies."

The following season the self-appointed Senior Clubs sub committee of the RFU came up with a properly structured competition in 1987/88, sponsored by brewery giants Courage. The Saints were placed in Division Two and were not even good enough for that, finishing bottom of the heap. Fortunately, the RFU decreed there would be no relegation in the first season, so the side escaped dropping into Division Three.

Although there was the nucleus of a reasonable side with the likes of Pearce, Packman, Elkington, Ben Ward, Peter Roworth, Paul Alston and Phil Pask, the results in the first season of the Courage League were lamentable: Richmond 3-16; London Scottish 3-50; Bedford 16-17; London Irish 15-13; London Welsh 14-16; Blackheath 12-19; Saracens 6-22; Liverpool St Helens 9-13; Rosslyn Park 0-22; Headingley 3-38

The side that ended the season was: Gray; Packman, Woodrow, Trotman, Ward; Larkin, Elkington; Cox, Roworth, Pearce; Mason, James; Alston, White, Pask.

It was time for a revolution.

Chapter Ten
Revolution

A packed Franklin's Gardens hears the debate that led to the ousting of the committee in 1988

ON July 6, 1988, seven men drove home from Franklin's Gardens at around 10pm – mission accomplished. They had succeeded in overthrowing the committee of Northampton Football Club, mostly fine ex-rugby players who had given blood, sweat and tears for the Saints.

Men like Don White, who had skippered the Saints for seven seasons, played for England and been the first coach of the England side. A successful shoe manufacturer, who hated being beaten in sport, in business, in life.

Men like Bob Leslie, a Scottish trialist, who was told he would never play again but defied doctors to have a career lasting 17 years. He had gone on to be a tireless worker as secretary and then chairman of the Saints. The accolade for such a lifetime of work was going to be the presidency of the Saints, a coveted and prestigious title.

Men like Ronnie Knapp, a pugnacious Welshman, who had been fished out of the Mediterranean twice during the war and who had gone on to become head of British Timken Europe. He resigned as a trustee in the wake of the coup.

But the Gang of Seven as they became known were convinced of one thing as they plotted to take control of the club: there could be no compromise. These men and most of the others had to go.

From that day people who shared in triumphs and consoled each other in adversity, would never speak to

each other again.

Five of the 1988 rebels had played for the club with varying degrees of success.

Roger Horwood was always considered second best to Andy Johnson as a hooker, but he was good enough to make 209 first team appearances in a 17-year span. He had been a hard working committee man, but had quit several years before 1988.

Jon Raphael was another former hooker. His Northampton career ended prematurely in 1984 with 159 games behind him.

Peter Haddon was yet another front row man. The men he was helping to overthrow were personal friends. He was a playing contemporary; not in the same class, perhaps, but with over 100 appearances to his name.

John Shurvinton got only 46 games in seven years in the golden age of Saints backs in the Sixties.

Mike Roper had led the side in the early Seventies and had gone to work for the old committee. But by 1988 he was as disillusioned as the rest.

The other two were solicitor Murray Holmes and Bob Carvell, who rose from bricklayer to make a fortune in building and property development, played for a host of junior clubs, Scouts, Heathens, Daventry.

As a group they would occasionally wander down to Franklin's Gardens, invariably see a disappointing game, and join in the general post mortem in the Sturtridge Pavilion afterwards.

Carvell had the initial idea of producing a

Bob Leslie chairs the crucial annual general meeting of 1988, when the consortium of seven took control of the Saints. Four of the seven are pictured (from the left) John Shurvinton, Roger Horwood, Murray Holmes and Jon Raphael

document setting out a major plan for recovery. He was thinking evolution, not revolution as probably all the rebels were, when they sat down for their first informal chat.

The consortium's proposals were put to the annual meeting in July 1988. It was proposed by Raphael, seconded by Shurvinton and supported by Holmes.

The committee's response was proposed Keith Archer, seconded by Bob Taylor and supported by Jacobs and Frank Sykes.

The vote was overwhelming: 228 for 76 against – a 75 per cent majority in favour. The stark fact gives no hint of the night's emotion and tension. The human pillars of Franklin's Gardens were swept out of office, and the self-styled Gang of Seven were installed with a mandate to make Saints great again.

The Sturtridge Pavilion was bulging with 311 members, after both camps had waged a war of words, particularly in the *Chronicle & Echo*.

From a great and glorious past, the Saints had turned into something of a joke because of its inability to find a winning formula.

"We would go down to the Saints and stand in the bar over a pint bemoaning the fact that the club was now the pits," recalled Horwood. "It was just the honest reaction of rugby fans, who were desperately sorry to see what was happening to a once great club. We found like minds in Jon Raphael and Mike Roper.

"Whether we would ever have done anything about it I don't know but for Bob Carvell. He sat down and compiled a list of all the things that had to be done, then showed it to Colin Richardson (*a local businessman who would have made it a gang of eight but dropped out early through pressure of work*), who polished it up a bit before Bob sent it to the rest of us.

"We met for the first time in February. From the start we were all very positive. I don't think there was one dominant character, but we tended to push Jon

Key players in the revolution: *Chronicle & Echo* **rugby writer Terry Morris (above) and disillusioned player Nick Grecian**

Raphael as the figurehead because he was someone with whom the players could relate and we very much wanted them on our side. We met the players, and they were very apprehensive at first."

Veteran prop Nigel Fox summed up that mood of suspicion. "You'll end up just like the last lot."

Said Horwood: "They didn't believe we wanted to make a team off the field as well as on it. In the Sturtridge at the time the committee room was cut off from the main bar area and inside was all the club memorabilia. None of the ordinary members could see it, and we all vowed the first thing we'd do was to rip down that wall!"

After that initial meeting events moved swiftly. Horwood kept records of their meetings in orderly fashion, sowing the seeds for him eventually becoming club secretary.

Holmes leaked their plans to the newspaper. It had been agreed from the start that the club needed a professional administrator. Two names emerged – former Welsh international and British Lion, Terry Cobner, a schoolmaster at Oundle, and Barrie Corless, a former England international who was working for the Rugby Football Union as their top coaching adviser in the Midlands.

They decided not to approach Cobner but Corless. He basically wrote his own job description, which was sent to RFU secretary Dudley Wood. Confirmation that it met with Twickenham approval, with one or two minor

amendments, came only on the morning of the annual general meeting.

The consortium was dismissed by the old committee. They seriously under-estimated the professionalism and determination of the seven.

"We were determined to leave nothing to chance. We used to practise what we were going to do at the meeting. After all, we had to get it right because we were only going to have one shot at it," said Horwood.

"We asked for a list of members and we were given one; again we could not believe our luck. We contacted as many as we could by telephone. A lot of members were very edgy and many of them asked if the vote would be taken on a show of hands. We said we thought it probably would and some said they would not be able to vote for us if that was the case. We decided to propose that it was a ballot vote and that got through as well."

It had all the trappings of a by-election, and the *Chronicle & Echo* gave both camps equal space on the eve of the AGM. Both sides were offered 500 words to tell members their side of the story. Chairman and president-elect Leslie put forward the 'Establishment manifesto', Raphael fronted the case for the opposition. The two 'candidates' were ringed by a rosette and the story appeared under the headline: 'Showdown at the Gardens'.

Holmes, veteran of countless courtroom scrummages, had the unenviable task of addressing the meeting. All the rebels agreed he gave a masterful display, smoothly putting their case; tearing to shreds the opposition.

A heavy smell of rancour filled the upstairs room of the Sturtridge Pavilion. Friendships ended that night.

There was a tremendous roar from the players at the back of the hall when the vote was announced.

"It was the same sensation I got when I ran out on to the pitch at Franklin's Gardens. The roar of the crowd always produced a shiver down my spine," said Horwood. "I think we all realised this was going to change us very much indeed for the rest of our lives. I remember driving home with a wonderful feeling of achievement."

Annual meetings would normally attract just over 100 members. On the night of July 6 they were hanging from the rafters. Frank Sykes, the former England winger, flew in from the United States to have his say. When Sykes learned the full story he became a supporter of the new regime.

Disenchantment had been rife among the players for years. It was summed up by a young player, Nick Grecian, who had studied at Nene College and stayed in Northampton to play for the Saints for four seasons.

In January, 1988, he wrote a two-page letter to the committee. "It is with regret that I write to advise you of my intention to resign from Northampton Football Club. This decision has been reached after long consideration. Although there is no doubt that I have enjoyed good facilities, some good rugby and many good friends at the club, these factors are outweighed by the frustrations currently experienced in being involved with Northampton FC.

"It is unforgivable that a club with Northampton's heritage and tradition now finds itself in a position whereby the morale and motivation of the players must be at an all time low and the subsequent departure of a number of these players has met with little or no apparent reaction.

"Recognising the time that I have spent at Northampton I feel it would be discourteous to leave without elaborating to some extent on the principle reasons for my departure. Who knows, the points I raise may provoke some reflection and thought and enable the club to act in a manner which may rekindle the kind of enthusiasm required to stay in the top echelons of English club rugby?

"I have long been astonished at the lack of communication in the club, particularly between the senior members (*i.e.* those that run the club) and the players. Seldom, if ever, was advice offered to individual players to adapt their game or individual skills to blend more effectively with the team's style or tactical base.

"Rarely, again if ever, were players informed of the reasons for their being dropped, or promoted for that matter. I believe that the barrier between senior members and players can best be illustrated by the apparent need and obvious enthusiasm for a Committee/Presidents' Bar in the club whereby the same gentlemen and their associates can avoid the nuisance of having to talk to the young men upon whom the future of the club is dependent. This particular aspect of the club's social scene merely nurtures a 'them and us' atmosphere which, in my opinion, is endemic throughout the club.

"I know that all of the current players have respect and admiration for the club's former internationals. This would only be enhanced if the same gentlemen condescended to spend a little time with the players and through chatting in the bar after a game gave us some cause for confidence in the fact that they understood and appreciated the requirements and demands made on individuals and teams in the modern English game. To generate the support or

Thumbs up for a new start: Barrie Corless, the country's first full-time director of rugby, Geoff Allen, who became chief executive and consortium member Bob Carvell, who introduced Keith Barwell to the Saints

Ron Slinn: Threw his support behind the rebels

'hearts and minds' of the people around you is a basic feature of man-management. Most of these people are professional men who will adopt these principles in the course of their business. I have never been able to understand why they were so lacking in the management of the club.

"Team selection at Franklin's Gardens has always been an intriguing process and at times a highly entertaining one, with the players surnames and connections apparently carrying more weight than ability and current form at selection meetings. Again, the situation we have experienced recently, whereby the 1st team skipper and club coach are of little consequence at a selection meeting is frankly ludicrous."

"I can only hope that every effort will be made to address the situation before a club with Northampton's unparalleled reputation finds itself with a fixture list which is perhaps novel but certainly humiliating. We have all seen the rapid changes taking place in English rugby over the past year or so. Are Northampton going to keep pace with all these changes or fall by the wayside?"

Grecian, who left to become part of the London Scottish side that won promotion to Division One in 1992 only to slip back after one season, has only one regret – that the contents of the letter appeared in the press before the committee had had a chance to study it.

The ousted Leslie, who was due to become

president, said: "They were prepared to buy success, and the way things are going I cannot see how the game will remain amateur.

"They have gambled on success; they said they would produce a side to win games and they have done that. But at what cost? I dread to think what will happen if they have two poor seasons."

Outgoing president Ronnie Knapp said: "I think the fun has gone out of the game. It is going professional and nothing looks like being able to stop it.

"In 1988 I didn't want to see rugby go down the same road as tennis and athletics. If a player is good enough and wants to make a living out of the game, then he has the opportunity through rugby league.

"I'd had great fun in my playing days, and if you think something is good you want to hang on to it. When you are a lad and chasing after girls it is great fun but it is amateurish – you don't go to a brothel.

"That's where the game has now gone – to a rugby brothel. As I see it now you cannot a) play for the Saints, b) have a good family relationship, and c) have a career. Something has to give, and I think it is very sad because it was a marvellous game as it was.

"The world is a less better place for the loss of real amateur rugby. The game has become a spectator sport rather than a players sport."

Geoff Allen, who had been secretary for five years, had to withstand fierce verbal attacks in the weeks leading up to the meeting. He had no regrets.

Said Allen: "We couldn't get people to do any of the jobs. When the consortium came to me, they knew my views because I had expressed them for some time. Their ideas made a lot of sense, and I also recognised it needed a complete change of personnel. I was called Judas but my only loyalty was to Northampton Football Club."

In the immediate aftermath of the revolution Allen was made president (and chairman) instead of Leslie, rubbing salt into the old committee's wounds.

Allen insisted that he offered his resignation to the old committee, but that the offer was rejected. For a month leading up to the meeting he was in the crazy position of preparing the defence for the committee, while desperately wanting the rebels to win.

Said Allen: "I played it straight. When I was with the committee I worked to the best of my ability. I had not kept a guilty secret for months and months. I had only been approached with a matter of four or five weeks to go to the AGM."

For 18 months Allen was president and chairman but when he left his job with Northamptonshire County Council to work in London the jobs were split up, with Holmes moving in as chairman. "I don't think the presidency/chairmanship was a patronising gesture towards me. Although the consortium had new ideas, they wanted someone with a knowledge of the workings of the club from the inside," said Allen.

The rebels' trump card, though, was Barrie James Corless, who was capped 10 times by England, between 1976 and 1978, scoring on his debut against Australia. He played for Coventry and Moseley and went to St Peter's College, Saltleigh, Birmingham, before teaching PE for 14 years at Moseley Grammar School and Solihull Sixth Form College.

The RFU appointed him their first divisional technical

administrator in 1980, which meant he did coaching stints around the clubs including Northampton. "The players were very receptive and it was obvious they had some good players here," said Corless. "I found tremendous enthusiasm amongst the players but they lacked any sort of leadership or guidance. There was no real coaching and no tactical awareness. Fifteen blokes just went on to the field with no game plan and no real direction.

"At the time I was looking for a change. John Shurvinton rang me for some advice on what the job should entail, and then he asked me if I knew of anyone who might be interested. I said that I might be.

"I met the Gang of Seven for lunch but didn't build my hopes up because I didn't think they had a cat in hell's chance of taking over – for two reasons: 1) not many people turned up for annual meetings 2) people are loathe to make sweeping changes.

"The rebels, though, had obviously touched a nerve but I didn't know until a few days after the AGM that they had actually won. I was impressed with them from the start. They had common sense business ideas and knew how to put them into practise.

"I knew Jon Raphael and Mick Roper from my playing days and they were all of an age that I could relate to; usually committees are like grandparents.

"I did not see the job as a soccer-style manager. The press give you tags like 'supremo', which make me cringe, but I saw it more as a development officer."

Corless did not start until November 1988 but he was in regular contact with the two club coaches, Terry Burwell and Paul Bryant. He had become the country's first full-time administrator but under the archaic rugby union laws could coach 14 or 16 players but not a XV.

He inherited some above average players: Gary Pearce, Harvey Thorneycroft, David Elkington, Phil Pask, Duncan Frankland and Paul Alston.

The new regime got off to a lucky start. The talented young blood the side had been crying out for landed on their doorstep in the first season – Tim Rodber and Ian Hunter.

The most stagnant aspect of the club in the years leading up to 1988 had been in recruitment. Yet for almost 100 years the Saints had searched for players with a carnivorous appetite. They were recruiting players from Wales before the turn of the century, when the club was not even 20 years old.

"Somehow the committee had lost sight of recruitment. They just seemed to think: 'This is Northampton, players should want to come and play here'," said Allen. "It just doesn't work like that. To get a player of any note to come to a club requires time and effort – more time than a bloke in his spare time can devote."

Corless was brought in to bridge the gap. Initially he had to find a way round the fact that as Northampton had finished bottom of Division Two the previous season, players were not stampeding through the gates of Franklin's Gardens.

"The line that we used then was Northampton are a First Division side in the Second Division, but we were moving up," said Corless. "We had to try to find good students and develop them. We had nothing to offer established players."

Bunny Ingram, Roy Gordon and Paul Witty in full cry. Following the revolution, the fans wanted something to celebrate – they did not have to wait long

Chapter Eleven
A new beginning

TERRY BURWELL was the first major casualty of the new regime, unceremoniously sacked a month from the end of a first season that offered hope for the future but still showed a playing record in the red.

Burwell, the first of several sackings, was accused of having an abrasive style of man management, and not accepting the role of a full-time club administrator.

New president, Geoff Allen said: "He has, on a number of occasions, publicly and openly criticised the role of the club's administrator. That is a dangerous road to tread with a committee that is so committed to the concept."

Burwell wrote: "…great care needs to be taken with regard to his (Barrie Corless) coaching role as we are sailing very close to the wind in that area.

"The breaking of RFU regulations here would lead to relegation from Division Two and the hard work over the last 12 months by all of us would be for nought."

The timing of Burwell's letter coincided with RFU secretary Dudley Wood's speech at the club's annual dinner. "It is marvellous," said Wood, "to see what is happening in the Northampton club. I am very happy with what they are doing. It is all for the good of the game."

The following Saturday the players and fans stood for a minute's silence at Old Deer Park for the Hillsborough victims as Saints played their final league game at London Welsh. It could also have been a mourning for a great rugby club, for the Welsh were already doomed to Division Three. The Saints swept the dirt over the coffin by winning 22-0 for a final league place of third behind worthy champions Saracens and Bedford, the latter promoted with a points difference of minus 46. The Saints, along with Sale, Coventry, Headingley and Blackheath all finished in credit. The Saints annihilated Bedford 42-3.

The first season following the revolution had been encouraging. On January 21, a Friday night, an athletic 6' 6" lock, Tim Rodber, made his debut. Morris

reported: "He displayed more than enough athleticism, ball skill and durability to suggest he is the key to Saints' lock problem in the long term."

In the same week another new player joined from Nottingham, Ian Hunter. An England Under 21 international, Hunter had been recommended by England Colts coach Graham Smith. Corless said that "Hunter gives us more cover in the squad." By the end of the following season his electrifying displays marked him as a future international.

The new regime had the satisfaction of seeing an opening day friendly victory over Harlequins at Twickenham, 22-13, watched by Don White from the committee box.

Pearce had been named captain in the summer in place of Guy Steele-Bodger, and the side he led out that day was: Gray; Packman, Thame, Burns, Woodrow; Steele, Elkington; Rhymes, Frankland, Pearce; Newman, Cannon; Alston, Charles, Tebbutt.

Mark Charles and Rob Tebbutt had been wooed away from Leicester, ironically by Dick Turnell, a short-lived team manager, appointed three months before the takeover.

The key name in that line-up was John Steele, recruited by Burwell from the Army. He was thrown in at the deep end. No-one at the club had ever actually seen him play. The game was a personal triumph for the stand-off, who had never played rugby at the top level before, but who had built up a reputation in the Army sufficient to interest several first division clubs, including Moseley.

In explaining his decision to join Northampton, Steele gave the committee its first thumbs-up. "The whole attitude of the club was positive. The way I was recruited, the way they spoke to me, the way they explained what the club was aiming to achieve, everything was right.

"If someone puts themselves out for you, you want to put yourself out for them. The whole thing is contagious and that is important."

Those words struck just the right chord. Steele

Casualties: Terry Burwell and Paul Bryant with former Cobblers' bosses Graham Carr and Clive Walker – all four got the sack from the two Northampton clubs

Collision course: Tim Rodber battles for the ball with another England back row forward, Ben Clarke

Sheer class: England and Saints full-back Ian Hunter

scored a try, kicked two conversions and two penalties. The Saints were on their way…

Changes now came at a rapid rate. Corless, who moved into the administrator's chair in November, succeeded in axing the Easter tour. They went out with a bang. On Good Friday they won 13-9 at Aberavon and the next day ended Llanelli's eight-match winning run, 24-16. On Easter Monday they beat Bedford 18-7 to complete a double over the Blues.

There was a three-year timetable for promotion – only two were needed. Yet the initial signs in that second season were not good. The Saints had suffered heavy defeats to Leicester, Nottingham and Cambridge University in friendlies and a disastrous league defeat at Headingley.

A 28-12 defeat at Bristol was the catalyst for a change of fortunes.

"Bristol put out a side that contained most of their star players, and while we were never on a par with them, after an hour we had crept to within one score. But that was it," said coach Paul Bryant. "After Frank Packman's super break-out try we never touched the ball again. They scored and took the game away from us, after we had been breathing down their necks at 16-12. I went mad at the boys. I told them they could play second division rugby all their lives or when they got close to the big boys take the game by the scruff of the neck and go for it.

"We were still harbouring the thought that we were playing a first division side and we were supposed to be gallant losers rather than fighting winners. I was disappointed that having got so close to them we seemed to be completely clueless as to what to do.

"Our behaviour off the field that weekend was equally disappointing and the whole side was showing a very bad attitude towards discipline."

The crunch came at Tuesday night's training session. "I told the players that they had to get themselves out of the hole – nobody else could. They could carry on as they were or make the effort and turn the season round. We could go on playing

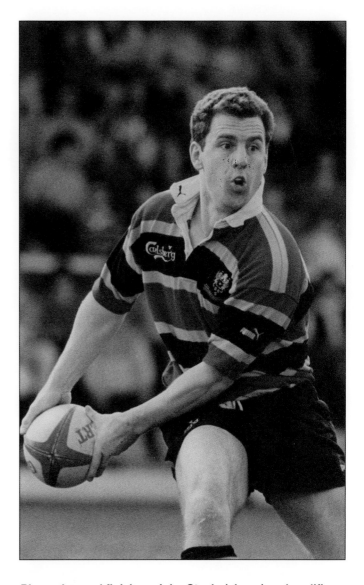

Playmaker and finishes: John Steele (above) and prolific try-scorer Frank Packman

nonsense football and pick up a win here and there or we could make a real go of it.

"Myself, Barrie Corless and the committee had set targets but the players hadn't, and they were the only people who could really achieve anything."

A week later Saints travelled to Sale and gave a committed display to win 16-3. They never lost another league game, dropping just one more point in a 13-13 draw at Liverpool St Helens.

The game that clinched promotion was at Gosforth's compact Percy Park ground. The players were subdued until No 8 Nick Dyte turned in a powerhouse second half display to inspire a 22-15 victory. When the game seemed to be ebbing away, Corless urged the Saints fans to greater noise. They were magnificent. "The fans went wild. In 15 years of watching Saints I had never seen anything like the uncontrollable joy and emotion from the fans, who hugged every Northampton player as he entered the clubhouse," wrote Terry Morris.

It was as if they were exorcising all the ghosts from the Gardens cupboard; these were the fans who had stuck by the club through some of its darkest days. Now they had something to celebrate.

On April 28, the sun shone gloriously, the crowds flooded into the Gardens and neighbours Rugby were beaten 41-25.

Representatives from Courage brewery were on hand to present the trophy, although if the Saints slipped up Liverpool St Helens could still take the title.

In the Pilkington Cup final quarter-final, Saints produced the result of the season, a 23-7 win over former winners and great rivals Leicester. It meant a cup semi-final place against Gloucester at

Franklin's Gardens.

In less than two years the Gardens had been turned into a vibrant arena again. League and cup games attracted a new following. It was one pressure game after another – and the players thrived on it.

Against Gloucester the Saints almost defied the odds. The lead changed hands five times, Gloucester prevailing 17-12 including a memorable try from Hunter. A year later the team would go one better.

But first there was the business of establishing the side in Division One. The sport was now about winning league matches. In just three seasons they had galvanised the domestic scene to the extent that defeats in friendlies at Coventry and Leicester were looked upon as minor irritations rather than a major cause for concern as the team approached their first campaign in Division One.

The first Division One fixture was on September 22, 1990, Saracens at Franklin's Gardens. It was negotiated successfully, 15-6, with the honour of scoring the first try in Division One going to Frank Packman, the local boy who had survived the lean years.

There were just two new faces from the previous

Saints fans rose to the occasion to will the team to victory at Gosforth when the game was slipping away

Inspirational: Nick Dyte

Tim Rodber gives his all in the cup semi-final clash against Gloucester at the Gardens

season. England and Harlequins hooker John Olver replaced Duncan Frankland and Steve Shortland, just out of college, was a contender for the second row. He lasted three league games before losing his place to John Etheridge.

Olver had taken a job at Pitsford's private Northamptonshire Grammar School, and was also about to lose his Quins place to England's No 1 Brian Moore. Frankland went off to Rugby in search of first team football.

A win at Liverpool had the Saints flatteringly sharing top spot but on October 13 the team faced the ultimate yardstick – Bath. They had 10 internationals to Northampton's one, Bath won 16-10. England manager Geoff Cooke, who had masterminded England to the Grand Slam, was there to give the match his personal stamp of approval. "If all English rugby was played to these standards, England would have no problems."

Orrell brought the Saints down from the clouds with a 60-0 hammering, watched by former All Black captain Wayne Shelford. The player who had never lost a match while leading his country was to instill that same mental toughness into his new team mates.

Of the Orrell defeat, Corless said: "Since we started from the bottom of the Second Division it has been one success after another. This is the first real setback, but I don't think it is cause to push the panic button. We have a very young, inexperienced side and we were shown up for that by a very big, experienced side."

A far from convincing win over Bristol was followed by three straight defeats. This time the panic buttons were pushed – if not in the dressing room then certainly in the committee room where they dare not not contemplate the repercussions of relegation. They called a halt to work on the Carlsberg Suite, a plush three-storey addition to the Sturtridge Pavilion.

The club had already built eight hospitality boxes, paid for by sponsors up front to flank one side of the Sturtridge Pavilion. The Carlsberg Suite was going up on the other side, enabling the club to woo even more sponsors.

The committee knew there would be an alarming drop in the number of corporate spectators if the team plunged back into Division Two. It was Shelford to the rescue.

Without Olver, Hunter and Rodber, a Shelford-inspired Saints grabbed a vital point at Wasps in a

101

21-21 draw, having led 18-3.

Corless, now working under the title of director of coaching, said: "We had a chat to the players and clarified their positions and warned them that everything they had achieved was in danger of slipping away.

"I was worried that we might be putting them under extra pressure but they went out against Wasps and showed they wanted to play in the First Division. We won one more point than the rest of the rugby world thought we would, and that has to be a bonus."

Shelford had cajoled his young troops to a superhuman effort. What's more it had been achieved away from the fanatical support of the Gardens.

Two more points were still needed to ensure first division survival and they had three games in which to get them – only one was at home, against Nottingham. They had not lost to the Saints for 11 years.

For sheer emotion, the script was just about perfect. Man-mountain Shelford led by example with two tries, taking ball and several opponents, over with him. In the end the team finished above Saracens, Bristol and the two relegated clubs, Moseley and Liverpool, a healthy eight points clear of trouble.

A week before the Nottingham game, the Saints had, in front of a full Gardens house, reached the Pilkington Cup final with an 18-10 win over Orrell amid almost unbearable tension. Steele was unflappable as he stroked over six penalties to erase the memory of that 60-0 defeat.

Etheridge summed it up: "I honestly believe Orrell thought they had already got to Twickenham and that all they had to do was turn up. They didn't realise we wanted it more."

Over 18,000 tickets were sold by the Saints for the final. From humble beginnings, the Knock Out Cup final had grown into a Twickenham sell-out.

The mixed emotions of a great day were brilliantly summed up by flanker Phil Pask in another Saints souvenir brochure. Worksop-born Pask had drifted down to the Gardens to try his luck, the limit of his ambition to get one game in the first team. Pask survived the carnage of the post-revolution period and the influx of new players to take his place in the Twickenham line-up.

In the brochure he recalled what final day was like, starting from the moment he left his Bozeat home at 8am, giving himself an hour to get to the ground.

"The importance of the occasion really hit me when I arrived at the Gardens to see 22 coaches rarin' to go. Suddenly you felt important, that you were carrying the hopes and aspirations of the whole town of Northampton. It was a great feeling to have such a burden on your shoulders and to understand the magnitude of the whole thing.

"There must have been a thousand people to see us off as we had a police escort to the motorway. There was an electric atmosphere on the coach, particularly when cars honked their horns. It was great see the green, black and gold scarves draping out of car windows.

"You could feel your chest grow an extra three inches by the time we got to the ground. Once there, people flocked to the coach, banging on the windows to wish us well. But our thoughts were firmly fixed on the game; it was 100 per cent concentration. It was a legacy from Wayne Shelford – to block everything else

out of our minds.

"Even my wife Janice would not have been able to distract my thoughts. I know I was thinking of nothing else. It was not a time for cracking jokes. I was mentally rehearsing what was about to happen. There was no need for motivation in the dressing room – we were all totally together.

"The singing of the National Anthem was one of the greatest moments of my life, something I will never forget long after the match details have become blurred. It is something I have always wanted to do but never thought I would ever get the chance; it was quite unbelievable and I could tell the other boys were going through the same experience. You are engulfed by the occasion."

The Saints were just six minutes away from upsetting the favourites, Harlequins. It was the 20th final in the competition's history, and the first to go to extra time. Without Shelford, who had gone back for an abortive attempt to make the 1991 New Zealand World Cup squad, the Saints gave a magnificent defensive display.

Harlequins, studded with internationals, were light years ahead as an attacking force, but a refusal to buckle almost created a shock win. Tries from Richard Langhorn and Andy Harriman plus a David Pears conversion and penalty had cancelled out a breakaway try from Peter Moss and three Steele penalties. The contest was over within seconds of the re-start with a Simon Halliday try and another from Rob Glenister, both converted, to leave a final scoreline of 25-13.

Shortly after the final, Corless took coach Bryant out to lunch, thanked him for all he had done, and fired him. Bryant was, understandably, bitter. He had never got the recognition he felt he was due. All the praise for Saints' success was laid firmly at the door of full-time administrator Corless.

Bryant, on the other hand, had a full-time job as a schoolteacher. If he wanted to take the kudos, which like any normal person he did, he wasn't available at the end of a telephone to cultivate it.

Shelford came back for a second season at Northampton, followed by another New Zealander Glenn Ross, the schoolteacher who had transformed the fortunes of New Zealand provincial side, Waikato.

No-one at Northampton had heard of Ross, very few of Waikato. But if Shelford said he was a good coach, then he was a good coach. And the players soon found out he was a good coach. They liked his ideas.

Shelford's arrival at Northampton was a slice of good luck for the new hard-working committee, wo were full of innovative ideas. None of them, according to Bob Taylor, were particularly new or original but they were backed up by a determination to make them work.

"It was not the ideas that were so good," said Taylor, "it was the energy being put into them. The old committee had had its fun. They had built the Sturtridge and bought the ground. But they had run out of steam."

Taylor also reckoned the acquisition of Shelford had been the best thing to happen to the club for years.

"His legs had gone, of course, but the others players learned so much from him," said Taylor, installed as club president for 1993/94, having been president of the East Midlands in 1992/93.

A New Zealand-born Saints supporter, David Coleman, and committee man Mick Roper, travelled to Llanelli to chat up Shelford, who was in the middle of

In the twilight of his career All Black Wayne Shelford had a
brief but powerful impact at Northampton and also
recommended fellow countryman Glenn Ross (right) to the
club as coach. Shelford's clash with England ace Dean
Richards was memorable

Try scored by   12 P. MOSS

A rolling ball is gathered by Moss: Saints centre Peter Moss claims his piece of club folklore with this Cup final try against Harlequins that very nearly created a major upset

leading the All Blacks through an undefeated tour of Wales and Ireland. Coleman's high-powered recruitment meeting was held over a few beers and went like this:

DC: What are you doing in the New Zealand off-season, mate?

WS: Nothing, why?

DC: You should come over and play for Northampton. It's a great set-up.

WS: Yeah, alright. Set it up.

Shelford not only helped the players believe much more in themselves, he gave the club just the sort of high profile it was looking for, commanding thousands of column inches in the national press.

At the end of what was thought to be his one and only season, there was a memorable tribute to him by Gardens fans. Geoff Allen gave an emotional send-off to Shelford over the public address system, while an adoring crowd sang 'Now Is The Hour', the traditional Maori farewell, after the two-try performance against Nottingham. The returning Shelford was not seen at the ground for a the first month of the 1991/92 season as domestic rugby played second fiddle to the second World Cup, this time being played in Europe. He had a

media role for the competition.

Olver and Pearce were part of the World Cup squad, and joined in the elation at England reaching the final against favourites Australia.

Clubs were pleading poverty as attendances during the World Cup were very ordinary. Only the real diehards watched the non-league games. The Saints success had attracted a whole new audience, but only for league matches.

It was so nearly the season when the club sat at the very top of the rugby pyramid. It was also the start of new international careers.

In 1991/92 Rodber and a new recruit from Bedford, Martin Bayfield, took their place on the club's honours board as England players. They forced their way into an aging pack in what was another Grand Slam campaign.

Bayfield had started to make a name for himself on England's tour of Fiji and Australia, winning two caps. Before the trip he had already announced his intention to quit Bedford and join Northampton. There were rumours that the England hierarchy had pressured him into the move but it was, he said, completely his own

Top division status was secured with a win over Nottingham thanks to a man-mountain performance by Wayne Shelford who then said his farewells to the fans

decision.

"I had thought about moving the previous season, when Bedford were relegated from Division One. I decided to give them one more season, but at the end of that I knew I had to move on to a more successful club.

"I wanted to stay in the Midlands and the choice rested between Northampton and Leicester because I felt at either club my rugby would improve. I chose Northampton because of the presence of Wayne Shelford and Glenn Ross and I have no regrets about my decision. This is a very good Northampton side. What we have to do now is become a great one; there is no doubt we have the ability to do that."

Bayfield played in all the 1992 and 1993 England Five Nations games, and his selection for the Lions tour to New Zealand was inevitable. He was one of the stars of the tour, particularly in the 20-7 win in the second Test.

His former lineout partner Wade Dooley was full of praise. "I take my hat off to Martin Bayfield. He played the sort of game in the middle of the lineout I could only dream of. Even in my hay-day I doubt that I dominated in the way Martin did.

"His supremacy was such that the All Blacks had to resort to mauling the ball out of their own 22, rather than kick for touch and concede the throw. They pulled off the man against him at half-time, and even though it was a blatant tactical substitution and against the laws, it was a compliment of sorts."

There was nothing at the start of the 1991/92 season that suggested the Saints would come within one victory of actually lifting the Courage title.

There was a win at Saracens, a draw at home to London Irish and a defeat at Bath. England ace Jeremy Guscott likened Northampton's performance to a soccer side playing for a goalless draw. That was on December 7. The team did not lose again in the league until April 11 and an agonising defeat it was. On a beautiful sunny day in Nottingham, the chance

was there to lift the title. Bath had opened the door by fielding an ineligible player and being docked a point.

Saints beat northern heavyweights Orrell to trigger off a sequence of wins over Bristol (A), Harlequins (H), Rugby (H), Gloucester (A), Wasps (H) and Leicester (A).

The game at Nottingham came four days after a titanic struggle at Welford Road in which the Saints had scraped a 22-19 success, draining them mentally and physically.

Hunter was out injured and the team was shorn of its main cutting edge at a critical time. But the real problem was that the team as a whole was a spent force. The ultimate prize was within their grasp but they were comprehensively beaten by a side fighting for survival. In the end both teams lost out. Saints finished third behind Bath and Orrell, Nottingham still went down, pipped by Rugby. News of Rugby's win over Harlequins reached Beeston as the crowd were still celebrating their team's shock win. Ross tried to rationalise by saying that Northampton were not the best team in the country, and that Bath were still some way ahead of the rest. Every word true but irrelevant.

The 1991/92 vintage ranked with the best in the club's history. The team topped 1,000 points for the first time (1,137), while John Steele smashed every record in sight: most penalties (80); most conversions (73); most points (425); most kicked points (401). The one blot on the landscape was a first round Cup exit at the hands of all-conquering Bath. The Gardens heaved under the strain of 8,000 fans, who saw the game go into extra time. Bath won a cliffhanger 13-9.

Towering presence: Martin Bayfield in a Saints jersey and (below) playing for the East Midlands against the Barbarians in pursuit of a youthful Lawrence Dallaglio

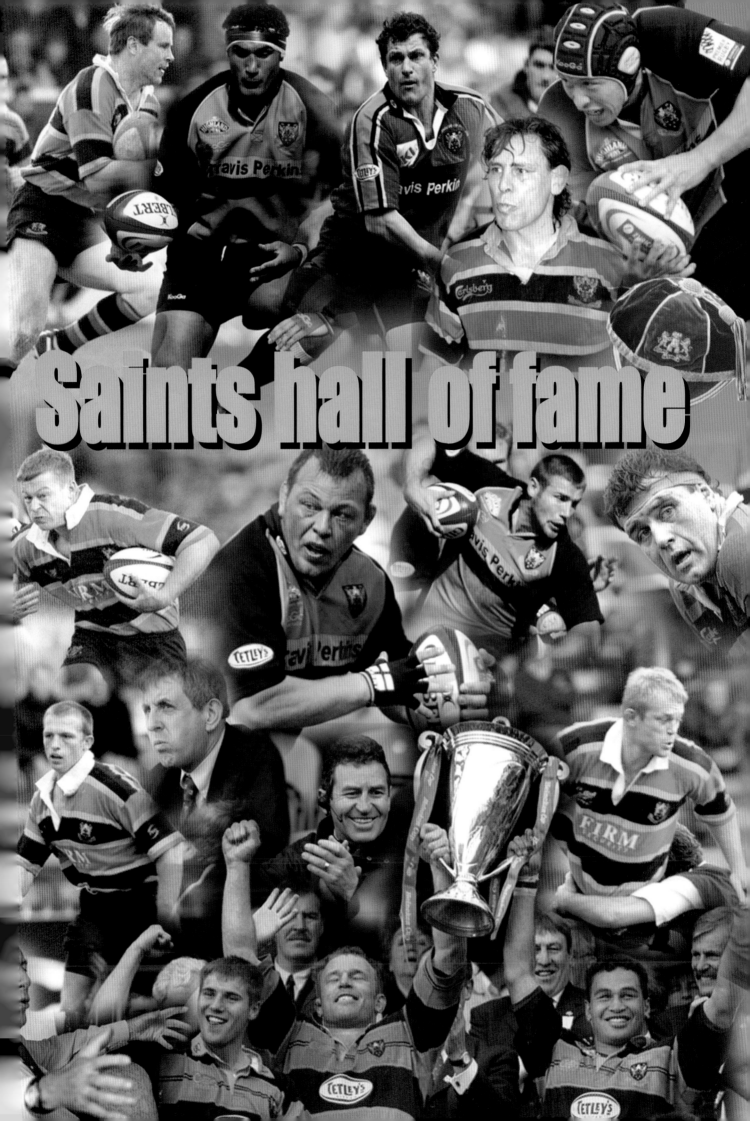

Saints hall of fame

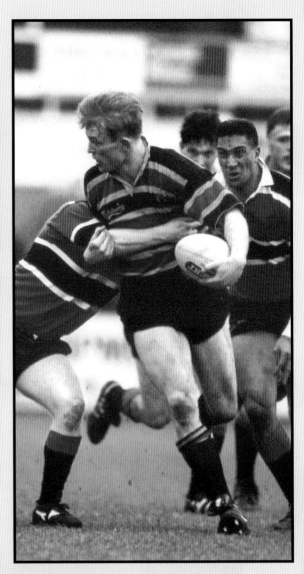

The first three giants of the modern era: Gary Pearce (above), who was in the veteran stage when Tim Rodber (right) and Ian Hunter galvanised the post 1988 Saints

The first taste of glamour for modern-day Saints – the 1991 Pilkington Cup final at Twickenham, which ended in defeat to set something of a trend. Pictures (clockwise from top left) scrum-half Richard Nancekevill dresses up in Harlequin outfit for the sake of the press, England flanker Peter Winterbottom is shadowed by Paul Alston. The fans enjoy their day in the sun, Phil Pask in the thick of the action and John Thame collars former England skipper Will Carling.

Changing times: Saints are one of the first to go down the international recruitment route with the signing of former All Black skipper Wayne Shelford, a big hit with the Gardens fans. Nearer to home Saints signed Martin Bayfield (above) from Bedford. Right: Matt Dawson fulfilled his early potential by going on the Lions tour of South Africa in 1997. This is the run that led to one of the great tries in Lions' history. Below: terrace hero Harvey Thorneycroft

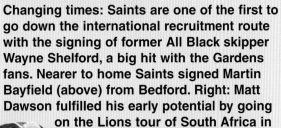

Friends and rivals: Paul Grayson and Gregor Townsend who shared a dressing room with the Saints and British Lions but were deadly opponents with England and Scotland

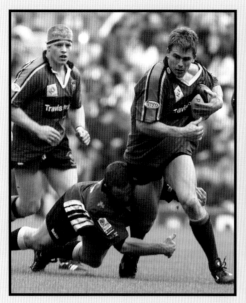

The Twickenham hoodoo that had seen domestic Cup final defeats by Harlequins and Wasps continues against London Irish. Pictures (clockwise from top) Grant Seely, Peter Jorgensen, owner Keith Barwell and wife Maggie look on anxiously, Steve Thompson and Matt Dawson swallowed up by Irish defenders.

John Steele and Matt Dawson celebrate the moment of Heineken Cup triumph and (below) the Saints match-winner Paul Grayson with one of his three successful kicks. Centre pages: Ben Cohen, Tim Rodber and Pat Lam salute the fans after the 9-8 win over Munster

Blossoming talents, Budge Pountney and Grant Seely, in the early part of their playing careers and (below) seasoned campaigner Tom Smith, now on the coaching staff

Here we go again: Saints go down to Gloucester at Twickenham. Andrew Blowers confronted by a sea of Gloucester defenders, words of consolation to Blowers from Keith Barwell, and Wayne Smith and Tim Rodber watch and hope.

South African international Garry Pagel battles with his 1995 World Cup winning captain Francois Pienaar in a Saints-Saracens cup semi-final clash at Franklin's Gardens and (left) a great Saints servant Jon Phillips, who clocked up more than 300 games before switching to neighbouring Bedford

Leading from the front: Steve Thompson (left) and scrum-half Mark Robinson

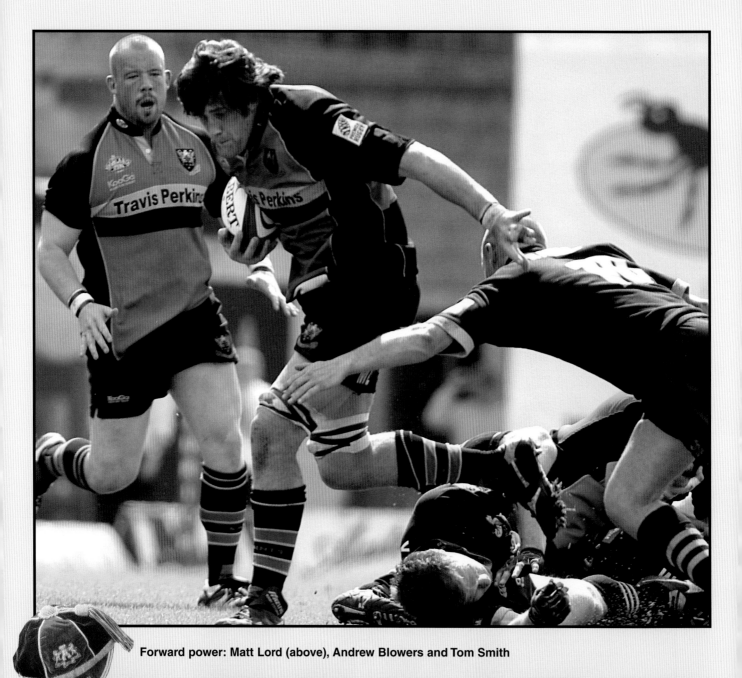

Forward power: Matt Lord (above), Andrew Blowers and Tom Smith

Rugby has become a league of nations: Former South African captain Corne Krige (above), English World Cup star Ben Cohen (above right) and the most exciting player of recent seasons, New Zealander Bruce Reihana

Carlos Spencer – King Carlos. Can he reign supreme at Franklin's Gardens?

The season unearthed an outstanding new talent in Matthew Dawson, the England Under 18 scrum-half. He had started the season hoping to play a couple of games in the Wanderers, but ended up playing 15 in the first team with no less a judge than Bob Taylor claiming he was the most talented footballer in the club.

Youth coach Geoff Wright was delighted at Dawson's promotion: "We are competing with every other big club in the country for the best young talent. It does not hurt our cause at all to be able to hold Matthew up as an example of what can be achieved."

By the season's end, Nick Beal, like Dawson from High Wycombe, had also been snapped up. A year later he would be a sensation as England, against all the odds, lifted the World Sevens crown. In the 10-man squad were Beal, Dawson and Rodber.

For Rodber the Sevens success made up for the frustration of seeing his international career nipped in the bud after two games – against Scotland in Murrayfield and Ireland.

The Army officer injured his neck in an accidental collision at Murrayfield, and lay motionless for a time before being replaced by Dean Richards. Surprisingly given the all-clear to play against the Irish, Rodber helped England trample all over them at Twickenham but then found himself out in the cold for the rest of the season. In 1993 he again had to be content with the replacement's bench.

Rodber was not a product of the schoolboy star system. He was playing, seemingly unnoticed, at No 8 for Oxford Old Boys, until his old maths teacher tipped off former Saint John Ebsworth. Rodber was immensely talented but always insisted that rugby was only secondary to his Army career with the Green Howards.

In January, 1992, the growing reputation of the club was underlined by its increased sponsorship value. A new four-year deal was signed with Carlsberg worth £150,000, four times the value of the one it replaced. The Carlsberg Suite had been opened three months earlier.

The Saints empire was growing fast. The club bought the lake and bowling green behind the far end to develop in the future; a 125-year lease was signed with the borough council for the pitches at the rear of the Gardens; and the council also unanimously approved an interest-free £50,000 loan.

Conservative leader Alwyn Hargraves, who played a major part in the Cobblers moving to the Sixfields Stadium and thus becoming Saints' neighbours, said: "We have been extremely impressed by everything that has been going on down at Franklin's Gardens. As an amateur club they have made tremendous strides."

At the end of the 1992/93 season Corless left for a new job at

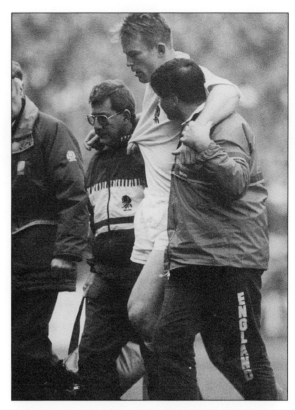

It did not take Tim Rodber long to break into the England side but his debut against Scotland ended painfully. He was to have many titanic battles with Leicester's Dean Richards

Gloucester. The committee said it was over money; Corless implied he was forced out. The *Chronicle & Echo* said Corless had done his job too well, that he had become redundant because the Saints had reached the top – or near enough. They didn't have to beg for players anymore.

Corless's last season as director of coaching was a curious one, many people feeling the game was ruined by the lawmakers. Normally law changes only arouse minor comment, but those introduced in 1992 altered the whole face of rugby. Designed to create attractive rugby, English players were slow to grasp the concept.

There was also the decision to reorganise the composition of the divisions in one fell swoop: four teams to be relegated from Division One, seven from Division Two. Every team in the country, except Bath, faced being sucked into an end-of-season dogfight.

Skipper Olver said he had never known so much tension in the build-up to a season. The result was a series of negative battles as fear prevailed. Entertainment value was well down the list of priorities for players and coaches. In the new commercial world of rugby survival was the name of the game.

Bristol and Saracens were beaten in the opening games, but they were niggly, miserable affairs. The players were terrified of making mistakes. Back-row forwards formed human barriers to ward off waves of individual battering-ram surges. It looked like rugby league.

The team lacked conviction and they were clumsy and leaden-footed in defeat at London Irish.

Just seven days later champions Bath caught a furious backlash. Wounded pride was an important motivational weapon as Saints tenaciously clinched an 11-8 win, thanks to an opportunist Nick Beal try.

Two splendid away wins at Orrell and at Harlequins again put the team in the championship hunt. But the league season fell apart with a 13-12 home defeat by Leicester, the Tigers leading for the only time of the game with Neil Back's injury-time try.

Defeat was only narrowly averted at Rugby, a game watched by the players of the England women's team,

who trod the hallowed Franklin's Gardens turf the next day for an international with Wales.

Gloucester, embroiled in the relegation mire, and Wasps, battling for the title, had too much fire in their bellies as the Saints season slipped away alarmingly, which caused Ross to call a clear-the-air meeting before the final home league game with West Hartlepool. The upshot was 47 first half points for Saints. The thrashing of West Hartlepool was seen as just the tonic needed before the crunch game of the season, a Pilkington Cup semi-final at Leicester. There was a carnival atmosphere at a packed Welford Road and BBC cameras showed all 80 minutes live on Grandstand. By half-time it was all over as Tigers led 23-3. They comfortably kept Saints at arm's length in the second half.

Attitudes had changed so much at Northampton that a season of fourth in the league and a Cup semi-final spot was not nearly good enough.

For all the drama of the league and cup, one man very nearly succeeded in casting a shadow over it all; the moody, charismatic Ian Hunter, who started the campaign as if he was going to conquer the world and ended it injured, disillusioned and depressed.

Eddie Butler in *The Observer* said Hunter had the greatness of silence, the ability to hold a crowd spellbound. But after scoring two magnificent tries for England against Canada at Wembley, another for the Barbarians against the Springboks, and an opportunist one against France, Hunter was dumped after a defeat in Wales.

An injured Hunter was plucked from his misery to be named in the Lions party to tour New Zealand along with Bayfield, but there was a proviso. He had to play in the final Saints game against London Scottish to prove his fitness. He was a shade tentative, but had the final say with a try in the corner. He would be on the plane, but if he hoped to leave his bad luck with injuries back in Northampton, he was wrong. The jinx struck in the first game when he dislocated his shoulder in a freak accident, catching his hand in an opponent's pocket.

New kids on the block: Tim Rodber, Nick Beal and Matt Dawson with their World Sevens gold medals

Chapter Twelve
The McGeechan years

Ian McGeechan, an all-consuming passion for rugby

AFTER the explosive annual meeting of 1988 and the recriminations that followed, club president Bob Taylor did remarkably well to bring both sides together for the launch of *Oh When the Saints*, the history book that charted the club's fortunes from 1880 to 1993.

The bandwagon towards professionalism that the Saints had helped to start and which was so abhorrent to the older generation of players, was now getting into top gear. Bayfield, writing in the club programme, said it was time for top players to be able to cash in on their fame. Rugby was rapidly moving towards a soccer-style structure with the introduction of home and away league games.

Skipper John Olver warned that the physical demands on players could become intolerable.

The 1993/94 season turned out to be the third and last for coach Glenn Ross. He promised a "dynamic new approach" from the side but that proved to be some way wide of the mark.

Positive noises emanated out of Franklin's Gardens, particularly bullish was new stand-off Paul Grayson, signed from Waterloo, who came with a big reputation. The former Accrington Stanley footballer declared: "We have a young side, and who knows, youthful arrogance may take us to the title. How about a league and cup double?"

Stirring stuff not quite backed up by events on the pitch, although the opening game with Leicester was a 19-10 win that partially erased the memory of the previous season's Cup defeat.

The Saints were put firmly in their place at The Recreation Ground, Bath, but then came a sparkling first 40 minutes at Bristol, inspired by the first appearance of the season from Hunter. The Saints fell away alarmingly in the second half, Bristol almost snatching an unlikely win and confidence ebbed from the side.

A shoulder injury sustained in a defeat at

Gloucester threatened to put Tim Rodber out of the England side to face New Zealand at Twickenham. He managed to get off the treatment table to punch huge holes in the All Blacks as England won 15-9.

Injuries started to play a depressing part in a disappointing season. Flanker Rob Tebbutt quit on doctors' orders with a neck injury and a January defeat to Leicester at Welford Road spelled the end of Olver's career with an Achilles tendon problem.

A young Irishman, Allen Clarke, took over as hooker and Rodber as captain, initially until the end of the season. He led out the side at London Irish with a clenched fist demand for maximum effort. He was rewarded with a 16-13 win, a week after an 11-6 Cup defeat Gloucester.

There was a devastating blow in March when dynamic centre John Fletcher, signed from Tynedale after a summer tour with England A, broke his leg in just his 20th game for the club against Harlequins. Fletcher had been compared to England captain Will Carling – now his career had been shattered.

News of Ross's impending departure leaked out and the committee were now on the trail of widely-acclaimed Scottish coach Ian McGeechan. Martin Bayfield was given the job of selling the club while on a Lions tour. McGeechan did not immediately indicate that he was willing to quit a secure job in insurance for full-time rugby involvement but he was eventually won over.

Continuing their desire to move forward, the club announced plans for a million pound stand at the Lake End and an extension to the Gordon Terrace.

The curtain came down on the season with a win over Newcastle Gosforth amid a tidal wave of emotion as Gary Pearce and Phil Pask announced their retirement. John Steele also left for a career in land management but resurfaced at London Scottish as a player and then coach.

All would return to the Gardens in one guise or another: Pearce was prised out of retirement the following season for the final few games as relegation loomed; Pask became club physiotherapist and fitness adviser before landing the same job with England; and Steele would succeed McGeechan as director of rugby.

But as careers closed, so others were about to start. The East Midlands beat Surrey 34-21 to win the

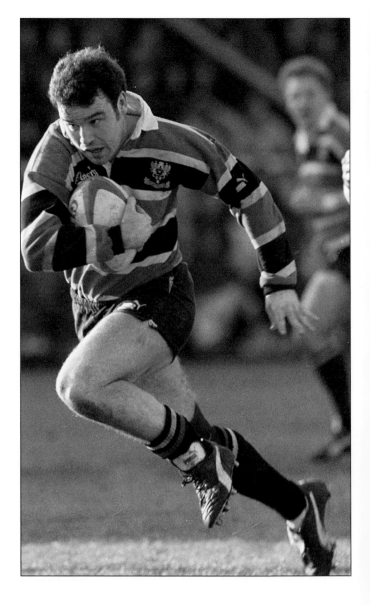

Tragic end: Dashing centre John Fletcher had his Saints career ended in sad circumstances with a broken leg against Harlequins. Club doctor Barry Nuttall (extreme left) looks on as Fletcher's face is etched with pain

Top: Peter Walton, Martin Bayfield and Allen Clarke give Gary Pearce a raucous farewell, although as it turned out his Saints days were not yet over. Right: Gary holds aloft the silver salver presented to him at what he thought was his final appearance at the Gardens. Above: Phil Pask hangs up his boots

Under 21 County Championship with all 15 players and six replacements from Northampton. Among the players in that side were Budge Pountney, Grant Seely, Matt Volland and Craig Moir – all would go on to have substantial careers with Northampton.

The feeling of anxiety that pervaded through the Gardens was reflected in the secretary's comments in the annual report.

Roger Horwood wrote: "We were told 'not to panic' by our coach and players but we remained somewhat unconvinced and with a hollow feeling in the stomach. After all we had achieved in five years, were we about to see it all fizzle out?"

Later he wrote words that would come back to haunt him: "Let us not forget we are still the only side to be promoted from Division Two to One and stay there."

Ouch! The desolation of relegation was etched into every paragraph of Horwood's report a year later.

The cracks that appeared in the squad in 1993/94 became yawning chasms even with McGeechan at the helm.

After an appearance in the final of the Middlesex Sevens, the architect of that success Paul Larkin was invited on to the coaching staff for the 1994/95 season by Ross. Before he could start the Kiwi had gone and with McGeechan not officially starting until October, the squad may have lacked a little in direction.

Whatever spin is put on it, the stark fact is that the first six league games were all defeats, the sequence finally broken with a 9-6 win over Gloucester at the Gardens.

As with the previous season, the campaign started against the two best sides, Leicester and Bath, both heavy but fairly predictable defeats. What happened at Sale (6-41) against Bristol (12-15) and Harlequins (16-23) at the Gardens were a devastating shock to the system as was the 13-10 defeat at Orrell.

For the first four games Grayson was the only scorer: 14 penalties, one try and one conversion. Hunter broke the trend with a try against Harlequins.

Before the Bath game, 100 invited guests saw the plans for the new Lakeside Stand, a project that was put on hold as the club faced the prospect of life in Division Two the following season.

Pountney, who was to become a huge favourite with the Gardens faithful, made his home debut having been given his first league start at Leicester a week earlier. He had impressed on a pre-season trip to Lanzarote and would go on to make the openside flanker spot his own over the coming seasons. For his home debut the programme referred to him as Anthony, which quickly made way for Budge, a family nickname from an early age.

A new 'player' in the domestic rugby scene made its bow at the Gardens on October 8 – Sky television cameras. At this stage the viewing figures nationwide were reputed to be no more than 30,000 but it was a sign of things to come.

A freak try helped Harlequins to victory when Justyn Cassell charged down a Hunter clearance, somehow clung on to the ball and streaked clear. Less than a month later, the flanker was pulling on the black, green and gold for the Saints and did as much as anyone to try and stem the relegation tide.

Harlequins, led by England hooker Brian Moore, would not win a league game again until March 25 – against the Saints in a virtual relegation decider at The Stoop.

Cassell scored on his Saints debut against West Hartlepool, the team everyone expected to fill the one relegation place, and warmed to the Gardens atmosphere. "I was mobbed football-style by the players when I scored, which was something I was not used to and the crowd gave the try a great reception."

As the Saints sat rooted at the bottom, the plot was

Flanker Rob Tebbutt (above) forced to retire through injury. Below: Justyn Cassell, recruited from Harlequins

Promising newcomer: Paul Grayson arrived from Waterloo with a positive attitude

further complicated by England's preparation for the 1995 World Cup in South Africa. It was Rodber's main priority but now he found himself leading a side that was in great danger of the drop.

He popped up on Sky's midweek rugby magazine programme and was pushed on whether he would desert Northampton if the club went down. While insisting the club would not go down, he was also adamant that he was going nowhere.

But he and Martin Bayfield were supposed to be putting their feet up ahead of the World Cup not scrapping for points in a relegation dogfight, while Hunter was again on the sidelines with a dislocated shoulder.

Hunter returned to have another inspired game at Bristol which brought just the third league win of the season on March 4 only for the white flag to be shown at The Stoop as the Saints crashed 10-9 to Harlequins in a match riddled with tension. Moore's victory jig on the whistle underlined just how important the victory was.

Dismayed by how tension had paralysed the players, McGeechan issued a message of defiance: if we go down we go down fighting.

Relegation was so nearly avoided. April brought three league wins and defeat by one point at Gloucester.

Elegance and style: Scottish ace Gregor Townsend

Celtic connection: Irishman Jonathan Bell (left) and Scotsman Michael Dods joined the Saints despite the drop into Division Two

On the final Saturday Saints had to win at West Hartlepool, which they did 21-12, and Harlequins had to lose or draw at Gloucester. They won by a country mile and the Saints were down.

The Saints had won six of their 18 league games, the same as Hartlepool, Harlequins, Gloucester and Orrell. Sale, in fourth place, had just four points more than Saints.

Gary Pearce was persuaded to play in the last four games, replacing the injured Mark Lewis. Pearce had been on a rugby pitch just once since retiring – playing for Aylesbury Old Sociables. At 39, Pearce was still a force to be reckoned with and did not miss a single training session. Alongside him at Hartlepool were a bunch of kids (eight under 22) in place of the absent Rodber, Bayfield, Hunter, Peter Walton, Nick Beal and Frank Packman.

McGeechan, who had coached the British Lions in New Zealand the previous summer, now had the task of restoring his reputation and propelling the Saints straight back to Division One. He told supporters: "I've never been a loser, I don't intend to start now…"

None of the stars left, indeed three more internationals joined: Scottish duo Gregor Townsend and Michael Dods and Irish centre Jonathan Bell.

The season had not kicked off when the biggest decision in the history of the game came in August, 1995 – the International Rugby Board declared the sport open. Paying the players, the development dreaded by all the diehards, was about to change the game forever.

The news was announced two days before club secretary Roger Horwood gave a party at his Billing home and for the men at the gathering there was only one topic of conversation: how were they going to tackle professionalism?

The club was just in the process of setting up offshore accounts for the players in a bid to keep them at the club. Internationals and top club players were to benefit by between £30,000 to £50,000 at the end of their career.

The wage bill at the time was modesty itself. John Shurvinton and Shobha Aranha were in the commercial department, Denise Davies was part-time in accounts, Ian Grimes was bar steward and David Powell groundsman. And that was about it.

In the last year as an amateur club, the Saints made £80,000 profit. At that stage Horwood was convinced the game would stay semi-professional with players continuing to have outside jobs. As that idea became obsolete the committee set up a think-tank of Horwood, Murray Holmes and Ian McGeechan, who decided to form a consortium of businessmen who between them would invest one million pounds.

A meeting was arranged for Thursday lunchtime at Hanrahan's restaurant to draw up a list of possibilities and high on that list was self-made millionaire, newspaper proprietor Keith Barwell.

On the morning of the meeting Horwood was at home when the telephone rang. It was Keith Barwell.

"I remember the conversation clearly," said Horwood. "He said 'I understand you are having a meeting today with Ian McGeechan and Murray Holmes to think over the future of the club and that you are looking for people who might be willing to put money into the club. I don't want to appear big headed but I am £7million richer than I was yesterday because I've just sold a business. I wondered if you might be interested in a million.'

"I went rushing down to Hanrahan's where the other two were waiting and they asked me if I wanted a drink. We got a bottle of wine and raised our glass to

New faces: Budge Pountney (above) and Grant Seely

Breaking through: Youngsters Craig Moir (above) and Matt Volland

Mr Barwell."

Barwell had first been introduced to the club by gang-of-seven member Bob Carvell and had quickly become a major behind-the-scenes player. He was the main reason why the club was able to bring over Wayne Shelford, who was on the payroll of one of his companies, Firm Security, along with the likes of Matthew Dawson, Tim Rodber and Martin Bayfield.

The committee was naturally bowled over by the offer after hearing Barwell's plans first hand and on Sunday, December 10 at the Moat House Hotel the offer was put to the members at an extraordinary general meeting.

A deputation, including trustees Jack Dove, John Linnell and Tony Cooper, went to Barwell's Cheyne Walk office to collect the million pounds.

A board of directors was formed with Barwell as chairman and six others, roughly split into two camps: Barwell's son Leon, Tony Hewitt and Firm Security managing director Mick Owen were the owner's pick with Horwood, Holmes and Jon Raphael representing the members.

"Keith has proved to be tremendous for the club and not afraid to spend his own money," said Horwood.

Meanwhile, on the pitch it was a total mismatch as the Saints, a team of internationals, faced journeymen players.

From the obscurity of Courage League Two, the Saints managed to develop new international players and get more than their share of column inches in the national press. They also shattered every record in the book with an exhilarating brand of rugby that was almost contemptuous of the opposition.

McGeechan had been inspired by the rampant, running style of the beaten finalists in the 1995 World Cup, New Zealand, and looked to follow suit.

After helping Leicester to unveil a new stand at Welford Road, the Saints faced up to life in Division Two at London Irish on September 9. The Exiles were expected to be the main challengers and people listening out for the result on the radio would have had apoplexy when the scoreline started: 'London Irish 32' but then came 'Northampton 65'.

It set the pattern for a season in which vice-captain Martin Hynes, signed the previous season from Orrell, suggested the Saints could top 1,000 league points. They finished not far short on 867 for an average of 48 points in each of the 18 league games. Just 42 of those points came from penalties as the Saints ran the opposition ragged with 125 tries, 20 from centre Matt Allen.

For the second league game of the season against Moseley, Dods replaced virus-victim Hunter at full-back. The Scotsman had captained Gala the season before and on his debut scored a breathtaking try that brought the Saints fans to their feet. "The reception made the hairs on the back of my neck stand on end," said Dods.

The real jewel in the crown was Townsend, who scored on his league debut at Bedford and went on to get 13 tries in eight appearances. Against such modest opposition, Townsend displayed a repertoire of tricks that mesmerised defences and thrilled supporters. His high-risk style of play would later be punished in Division One.

The almost manic determination to run the ball and not kick penalties had many an old player raising his eyebrows in surprise but McGeechan wanted the style of play to be relentless.

Times were changing and Sir John Hall, fresh from reviving Newcastle United's fortunes, signed England stand-off Rob Andrew from Wasps to build a championship-winning side at the city's rugby club. He succeeded from a starting-point of joint bottom in Division Two.

Newcastle improved dramatically from being drubbed 52-9 by Saints in October to only losing 26-5 at the Gardens in April. By then Andrew's team contained as many internationals as McGeechan's, and they won a victory of sorts, forcing Saints to rely on two drop two goals and kick two penalties from Grayson to keep them at arm's length.

Missing all the fun was the immensely talented Nick Beal, who had suffered two horrendous years with injuries. He quietly slipped back into the picture against Oxford University and was a real force by the end of the campaign. In the early weeks as Saints were running riot Beal remarked: "It was miserable being in the stands. I was easy to spot – I was the only one with a long face."

A 54-11 win over second-placed London Scottish meant the Saints had set a new points record for Division Two with just nine games gone.

The Pilkington Cup gave Saints the stage to show a wider public their dynamic new style and in the fourth round they were drawn away at Bath. From the lush pastures of Franklin's Gardens, The Recreation Ground was ankle deep in mud in December. Neither side scored a try but the Saints showed their mettle in going down 12-3.

Half-backs Matt Dawson and Paul Grayson made their England debuts against Western Samoa on December 16 and would go on to play a full part in the Five Nations championship to make 1995/96 a vintage season for the Saints.

The attacking platform the Saints had in Division Two was a shop window for Dawson, Grayson, Townsend, Dods and Bell to establish their international credentials.

But it was a graveyard for the ambitions of Rodber and Bayfield, who were relegated to the support role of the substitutes' bench, victims of the less physical demands of the lower division in the eyes of the England management.

One player did emerge from the pack to claim international recognition and that was Allen Clarke, who made 9 appearances for Ireland starting with Fiji on November 18.

Scotland were the team of the season, beating France, Ireland and Wales before England ground them down at Murrayfield. In that match Saints provided both stand-offs in Grayson and Townsend, leaving McGeechan with mixed feelings. He said he was hoping for blinders from the England half-backs but a win for Scotland. Grayson kicked six penalties; Dods three.

Dods scored three tries in the championship and

Matt Allen

Northern grit: prop Martin Hynes

Irish roar: hooker Allen Clarke, flanked by Matt Stewart, in full throttle. Both players went on to international honours after joining Saints, Clarke with Ireland, Stewart with Scotland

was then a shock omission for the summer tour of Australia and New Zealand accompanied by a "he's not good enough" slight from coach Jim Telfer.

For Dawson it was the start of a bumpy road journey with England and the British Lions – enormous highs, culminating in the 2003 World Cup success – interspersed with the occasional lows.

Australia's World Cup winning No 9 Nick Farr-Jones described Dawson as a scrum-half around whom England could build a side. Dawson fulfilled that prediction, fighting off the persistent challenge of Kyran Bracken, Andy Gomarsall and Austin Healey.

Along the way he has evolved into a sporting celebrity as a pundit on BBC television, a quiz show captain and a national newspaper columnist, fulfilling another prediction, this time from Keith Barwell who, as he watched Dawson going through his pre-match routine, commented: "There's rugby's first future millionaire."

While Dawson was making headlines, two World Cup winning team-mates, Ben Cohen and Steve Thompson (or Steve Walter as he was then known) merited just a line or two in the youth section of the annual report: "Simon Hepher, Ben Cohen, Kelvin Todd, Gavin Waters, Steve Walter and Matt Birke played for the Midland Divisional side…"

After a scintillating season, the Saints management team faced up to two challenges in the summer, preparing for Division One and professionalism. McGeechan, very much steeped in the traditions of the game, did not seem to relish the latter part of the equation.

He made it quite clear that he was not going to spend Barwell's money just for the sake of it. "Money will not win you things. You have got to play for each other. What really matters is how much you want to win for the people around you.

"I have turned down eight internationals because we don't need them. They would not enhance the team and I don't believe in accumulating players for the sake of it. You run the risk of destroying what we have built here.

"The money being paid for some players at the moment is crazy. The level of salaries is just not sustainable."

That was underlined when a potential signing's agent arrived for talks about a possible to Northampton. Coach Paul Larkin had been left in charge of negotiations and took a huge gulp when the all-important question of salary quickly came around. "The player – from another Premiership club and not an international – was asking for silly money. I pointed out to the agent that there was not a single player at Northampton earning that sort of salary."

The Saints devised a sliding scale of pay for the players depending on status. There was equality in the amount of appearance money and win bonus, while the contracts allowed players to be released for 'higher grade' games. Club-v-country issues, never a problem before, lay ahead.

McGeechan suggested that players should remain semi-professional. "I like players to have another interest – it keeps their minds fresh." The snag was that he still wanted them to be available for day-time training.

Bayfield had already signalled his intention to be a full-time professional, the first in the country, and McGeechan expected only a handful to follow suit.

Amid all the euphoria of runaway victories and the glamour of international calls, the fans named Budge Pountney as their Player of the Year.

Vice-captain Hynes said of him: " He is the new

Peter Winterbottom, all perpetual motion and a bloke who never has a bad game."

His ambition was to play for England, which he may well have done, had he not made a startling decision to switch allegiance by exploiting a selection loophole. Without a trace of Scottish blood in his ancestry, Pountney made himself available to play for Scotland by virtue of the fact that his grandmother came from the Channel Islands, allowing him to play for the country of his choice. At the time his path to the England No 7 jersey was blocked by Leicester's Neil Back but his chances of breaking into the side would surely have improved as his reputation grew.

The 1996/97 season was the first real taste of things to come in the professional era. There were four competitions to go for: Courage League Division One, European Conference, Pilkington Cup and an Anglo-Welsh competition. Of the four, the Anglo-Welsh was of least importance as reflected in the sides that were picked and the margins of victory, 107-5 against Caerphilly for example in which centre Matt Allen set a new club record by scoring seven tries.

The most glamorous competition was the European Conference and when the last eight was reached, it consisted of seven French clubs and one English, the Saints.

The team got off to a magnificent start, winning 38-29 in Toulon, their first home defeat for four seasons, and the Saints went on to top a group that contained English, Italian and Irish opposition as well as French.

The quarter-final tie against Narbonne was a huge anti-climax, the Saints losing 23-22, but the French fans brought a touch of colour to the Gardens as did the visiting press pack, who mostly ignored the no-smoking rule in the stand to get stuck into the Gauloises. There was partisanship and bonhomie in equal measure.

The competition required a punishing schedule: games in France, Northampton and Ireland all in the space of eight days during October. There was no denying that European competition was a welcome addition to the fixture list and one with a big future.

The game may now have been open but there was still nothing to stop the nomadic player turning up on the doorstep from foreign parts looking for a game. One such player was Don Mackinnon, a blindside flanker from Australia who arrived at the Gardens via French rugby and was in the starting line-up for the opening league game of the season against West Hartlepool.

He wasn't the only Aussie signing in these infant professional days, when recruitment was still not that sophisticated. Any proper scouting system would never have reached the conclusion that Australian lock John Hearn was worth signing. When he arrived McGeechan's assessment was that the club had to get him fit. Unfortunately, they could not actually add any rugby skill to his undoubted bulk.

A far more impressive signing was that of Western Samoan flanker Shem Tatupu, the first player to be plucked from rugby league by the Saints. He had not fitted into the scheme of things at Wigan and did

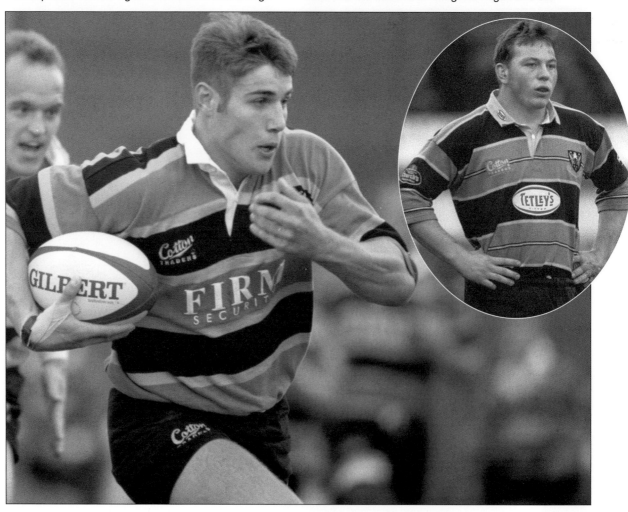

Fresh faces: Ben Cohen and Steve Thompson (inset) early in their Saints careers

not need much persuading to switch back to union. His 20 games that season of wholehearted effort, strong running and aggressive tackling made him Player of the Year.

On September 10, a skinny 18-year-old winger made his first appearance for the Saints and was instantly spotted by the likes of Tim Rodber as a potential future international. Ben Cohen, nephew of 1966 England World Cup soccer hero, George, was on the left wing for the 51-8 win over Treorchy in the Anglo-Welsh competition. He didn't get on the scoresheet but in March he scored in successive games, first against Newport on the 22nd in the Anglo-Welsh and then at Orrell a week later on his Courage League debut.

Cohen's debut coincided with the first away league win of the season at the eighth time of asking. The 50-14 win was the only away league success in contrast to the home form which included victories against Bath (second), Leicester (fourth) and Sale (fifth).

The 22-19 win over Leicester on January 11 was the high point of the season for Kiwi lock Jason Chandler, who outplayed Martin Johnson in the lineout. Chandler was drafted in as Bayfield's season was mainly spent in the treatment room. Bayfield was not seen in a league game until April 26 against Wasps at the Gardens – the day Wasps were crowned the first champions of the professional era under the leadership of Lawrence Dallaglio.

Bayfield was unable to press his international claims but Rodber won his place back and was named the outstanding member of the England pack by manager Jack Rowell.

Two new internationals were created in the season,

Beal winning a lone cap for England against Argentina, and former Blackheath prop Matt Stewart, invited to join the club by Rodber, forced his way into the Scotland side. Rodber had played alongside Stewart for the Army. Soldier Stewart, born in Blackheath but with a grandfather from Dunfermline, made his way to the top of the props' pecking order at Northampton and won five caps in his debut season.

Townsend, who started the season as *Rugby World* magazine Player of the Year, was a marked man at club and international level, alternating between centre and stand-off for both but at 23 he became Scotland's youngest captain for 45 years.

On the down side, Dawson and Grayson were left out of the autumn friendlies. Grayson managed to oust Mike Catt at No 10 to play in three matches in the Five Nations but a knee injury at the wrong time left Dawson as England's fourth choice scrum-half for a time. So there were some raised eyebrows when British Lions coach McGeechan named Dawson, Grayson, Beal, Rodber and Townsend in the party for South Africa. There were accusations of club bias, which were hard to counter. Controversial the choices may have been but McGeechan was totally vindicated in the months ahead.

Dawson, Rodber and Townsend played major parts in an historic 2-1 series win over the Springboks and Beal impressed in the midweek fixtures.

The one sad aspect was the injury to Grayson that saw him return home very early in the tour. Jeremy Guscott and Jason Leonard took him out for a few beers before the journey home, leaving Lions officials to persuade England manager Jack Rowell to release

Overseas quartet: Above (left to right): Aussie John Hearn, Kiwi Jason Chandler and Samoan Shem Tatupu. Below: Don Mackinnon, New Zealand-born and Aussie raised

PRIDE OF LIONS

Ian McGeechan picked five Saints to tour with the British Lions in South Africa. Top: Nick Beal was limited to the mid-week side. Centre: Gregor Townsend's battle with Paul Grayson for the stand-off jersey did not materialise because of Grayson's injury. Bottom left: Matt Dawson, mixing it with the Springboks. Bottom right: Tim Rodber lines up for the first Test alongside Saints prop Tom Smith, then of Watsonians

Mike Catt from the tour of Argentina. It was no easy task and McGeechan later made it clear he was far from impressed with Rowell's attitude.

Dawson, who looked to be Rob Howley's understudy at best, got into the side when the Welshman got injured and scored a never-to-be-forgotten try in the first test on the way to a 25-16 victory. The Lions clinched the series with an 18-15 win before a much-changed side lost 35-16 in the final test.

For the 1997/98 season the players were now fully fledged professionals. Some like Justyn Cassell had good jobs outside of the game and turned down the opportunity. Inevitably players like that fell by the wayside.

For pre-season McGeechan was still coming down from the Lions tour and day one of the professional era saw his deputy Larkin and physio Pask responsible for training schedules.

Larkin had quit his teaching job at William Parker Comprehensive in Daventry and was on a learning curve as much as the players.

McGeechan would later admit he was tetchy towards the players immediately following the tour. Having worked with the cream of British Isles rugby, he had to readjust to operating at club level again.

There were four domestic goals: the Premiership, now sponsored by Allied Dunbar, the European Conference, the Tetley Bitter Cup and the space-filler, the Cheltenham & Gloucester Cup, replacing the Anglo-Welsh.

Success in any of the first three competitions would represent a good season. It was not to be. Slow-starting Saints lost four of their first five league games, the exception a thumping 25-6 win over Leicester.

After the success of the Lions, speculation was rife that McGeechan would take over the England coaching job from Rowell. The Saints made it clear they would expect compensation and this, apparently, cooled England's ardour. Former England coach Dick Best was less than impressed with Twickenham's reticence to pay up. In a national newspaper column he said that if McGeechan was considered the best man for the job they should be willing to pay for him. Still the thought of McGeechan, born in Leeds but "Scottish through and through",

Who would you pick for England, Ron? Clive Woodward sitting next to former Saints president Ron Slinn

being England coach was hard to swallow even for modernists. England settled for a rookie, Clive Woodward, and that turned out to be an inspired choice.

One of his first decisions was to recall Grayson for an autumn international against New Zealand amid howls of derision from the critics. That, too, was inspired as England served notice that good times lay ahead under Woodward. Grayson, told to perform or forget about an England career, responded with a display full of imagination and character as New Zealand looked doomed at 20-3 down.

They fought back to take the lead and Grayson then held his nerve to kick a match-saving penalty.

The wheel of fortune had turned full circle for Grayson, and indeed for Dawson, who from the heights of South Africa, found himself dumped by Woodward in favour of Kyran Bracken to trigger off a rivalry that was still in the balance prior to 2003 World Cup.

Grayson brought that confidence back to the Gardens to trigger a mid-season flourish from the side and in May he was named Saints Player of the Year. Grayson had started the season at full-back, Townsend having gone on record as saying he only wanted to be considered as a stand-off. For the first four league games he partnered Dawson at half-back but then switched to centre (apparently without a murmur) to make way for Grayson.

The Scotsman could not quite win over the Gardens fans and at the end of the season he packed his bags for French club Brive when his contract with Saints ran out. His heart was not in it at Northampton but in the new world of rugby he could not simply walk away from his contractual duties. A transfer would mean a fee.

With the prospect of another relegation battle looming, the Saints targeted the game at London Irish to reverse the losing trend. Appearing in his second game for the Saints was South African prop Garry Pagel, a susbstitute for the rainbow nation for

Coach Paul Larkin

Running battle: Scrum-half Matt Dawson and Saracens No 9 Kyran Bracken were constantly battling for supremacy at international level. In the main Dawson stayed one step ahead

the 1995 World Cup final, and a massive influence for the Saints in the ensuing seasons. His form and that of Chandler meant only rare outings for Tatupu because of the restrictions on playing overseas players.

The 51-10 win at Irish sparked a run of five league wins in six games before inconsistency set in again and only limited success in the other competitions.

On a rain-sodden day in October, the Saints lost 20-15 to Irish side Connaught to go out at the group stage of the European Conference but the Tetley Bitter Cup saw Saints at their best.

In the quarter-finals, an epic clash ended with a win over league champions-elect Newcastle, 16-7, having lost to Rob Andrew's men a month earlier at the Gardens in a titanic league encounter. McGeechan described the cup win as the highlight of the season.

An injury to Rodber before a Gardens semi-final with Saracens was a huge psychological blow. Winger Jon Sleightholme, signed for an undisclosed fee from Bath (later revealed as £50,000), scored a try but Sarries were infinitely superior and fully deserved a 25-10 win before taking the cup in convincing fashion against Wasps.

A poorly structured season meant seven games between April 18 and May 17, five of them defeats, to finish off the campaign, although rugby seemed inconsequential in light of the floods that devastated homes in the St James area in the early part of April.

People died and others had to be rescued by dinghy from houses surrounding the Gardens. The London Irish game was postponed but 10 days later when the game was played on a Wednesday night the Saints pitch was in perfect condition.

Missing for most of the season was Bayfield and in May, 1998, he took the reluctant decision at 32 to quit the game on doctors' orders following a neck injury sustained when diving into a tackle bag.

He stayed with the Saints as coach to the Academy side and started to develop a career on the periphery of the game as an excellent after-dinner speaker, newspaper columnist, pundit and 'actor'. By chance he got a part in the first Harry Potter film as Robbie Coltrane's body double.

At the other end of the scale, Dawson had the honour of captaining an experimental England side to tour to Australia and New Zealand. Three heavy defeats left the tourists, who also included Nick Beal and Phil Pask as assistant physiotherapist and fitness advisor, branded as "pitiful" but Dawson's reputation was relatively unscathed and a promising fly-half had been unearthed in Jonny Wilkinson. Back in Northampton there was speculation during the summer of 1998 that Keith Barwell might be planning a ground-share scheme with the Cobblers at a new, improved Sixfields holding 15,000 spectators. This got a frosty reception in the Letters' Page of the *Chronicle & Echo*.

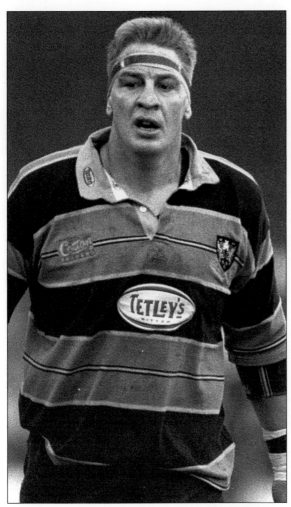

Great acquisition: Springbok prop Garry Pagel

For the start of the 1998/99 the Saints released a massive 18 players and signed just four. Among those to go were Bayfield, Rob MacNaughton, Cassell – retired; Townsend – Brive; Bell, Clarke – Ulster; and Tatupu – loan to Wasps.

The four signings were Western Samoan captain Pat Lam, the Premiership Player of the Year for his part in Newcastle's championship campaign, Federico Mendez, the Argentinian hooker who had laid out Paul Ackford in a Test match and who had vowed never to play for an English club after a torrid time with Bath, French centre David Dantiaq, from Pau, and at 7' 1" the tallest player in the country, Richard Metcalfe, also from Newcastle, an England and Scottish A team lock.

Newcastle boss Rob Andrew was to come in for a barrage of abuse from Geordie fans over the sale of Lam for a reputed £100,000 and his frustration was to spill over on to the pitch when the two clubs met at Kingston Park.

Barwell promised a £500,000 top-up to the players' fund if the side achieved a top-four finish but McGeechan warned that any one of eight clubs, in his opinion, could take the title.

There was fighting talk from the players before the opening game at Vicarage Road against one of those eight, Saracens. Rodber said they were now a "leaner and meaner" squad of players with the capacity to take on board McGeechan's vision of the game, while Dawson spoke of the desire to to get rid of the "under-achiever" tag.

The words were barely out of their mouths when the side had to stomach an unpalatable 34-7 defeat with 27 points conceded in a disastrous opening 27 minutes.

McGeechan was forced to go on the defensive at his first post-match press conference of the season: "Write us off at your peril" was the message.

Barwell used this defeat as the springboard for a stark warning to everyone connected with the playing side in his programme notes for the start of the Franklin's Gardens campaign against Harlequins.

"This season the first team are going to perform well. Success is a journey not a destination – not that we have ever arrived. But I am not going to just let this season meander on.

"I am investing big money, the team are big names, and we have an enormous local support that I am proud of…but it is time to deliver.

"I shall not be afraid to put pressure on players and coaches this year – no matter how big their reputation. There is a voracious appetite for success at Northampton. I shall not hesitate to take action sooner rather than later…"

Whether it was those words, McGeechan's coaching or the influx of quality new players – or a combination of all three – the Saints would deliver as the season unfolded although silverware did prove an elusive commodity once again.

England propping legend Jason Leonard was sent off for raking as Saints eased past Harlequins 25-6 but Leicester proved too strong at Welford Road (35-25). Sin-binned duo Grayson and Andy Northey took no further part in the game, being replaced once their 10-minute punishment was over.

October 3 was a significant date in the career of Tim Rodber as he started the game at Sale in the second row. Rodber, who had been left out of the first England training squad, won enormous praise for his performance in a 37-17 win, especially from Sale coach John Mitchell, who was also Woodward's right hand man with England. "He can add value to our squad in that position. I was very, very impressed," said Mitchell.

But while one architect of the modern-day Saints was getting a new lease of life, another, Ian Hunter, was reluctantly saying goodbye.

Before the Bedford game on October 17, Hunter waved farewell to the Gardens faithful. He had suffered one injury too many, dislocating a shoulder crashing into a tackle bag in the summer.

"I think I realised straight away that was it. Once I had removed the emotion from the situation and talked it through with specialists, I knew it would be difficult to have full confidence in the shoulder again. I

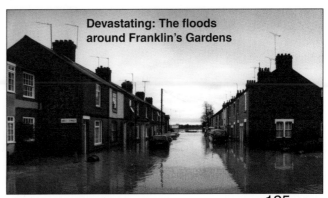

Devastating: The floods around Franklin's Gardens

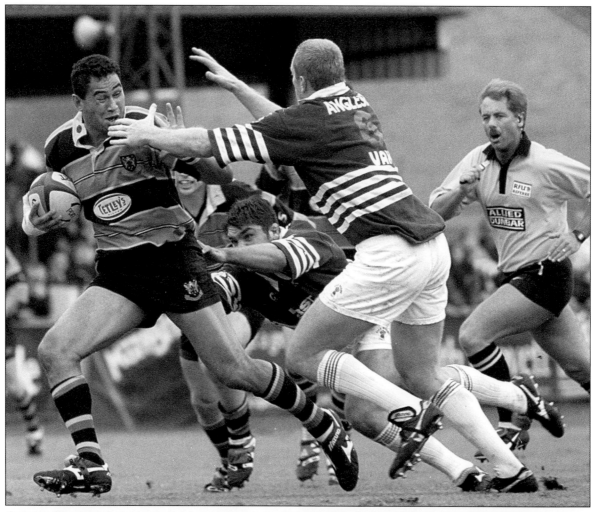

Outstanding trio of signings: Pat Lam (above), Freddie Mendez (below left) and Jon Sleightholme

Frenchman David Dantiaq: Charming off the field, not too impressive on it

had prided myself on the quality of my defence and I did not want to let myself down nor my team mates. I did not want want to replace fearlessness with hesitancy. Rugby is now professional and if I could not do it at 100 per cent then I was no good to the club."

In his *Chronicle & Echo* column, Bayfield wrote: "He has had his fair share of criticism, all of it misplaced because his injuries would have ended a lesser man's career years earlier.

"He had the courage and dedication to come back time and again. Injuries robbed him of a glittering international career."

He retired with just seven caps.

A 33-22 win at London Scottish the previous week was the first on opposition soil in the league since January 1997 and was the second of six straight league successes.

Barwell's programme notes, mostly pungent and provocative, were also prophetic for the October 31 game with Gloucester (a 22-8 win). In welcoming Rob Fisher, president of the New Zealand Rugby Board and vice-chairman of the International Board, Barwell described his vision of a strong England side with its roots in club rugby. Barwell wrote: "Currently coaching Allied Dunbar sides are the likes of Geoff

Cooke, Ian McGeechan, Dick Best, Francois Pienaar, Zinzan Brooke and Rob Andrew to name but a few. With this quality of coaching, a world cup-winning side could emerge for 2003."

A 26-21 win over Wasps marked 100 games for Grant Seely and a week later Pountney pulled on a Scotland jersey for the first time in a non-cap match with the New Zealand Maoris at Murrayfield.

Lam and Metcalfe returned to Kingston Park, where a six-match winning streak ended with a 45-35 defeat. Emotions spilled over when Rob Andrew's high tackle on Lam sparked a brawl between the previous allies.

Much more palatable was the 44-27 win over Richmond that took Saints joint top of the Premiership with Leicester for the first time in their history on November 21 but now the players had to wait almost a month before seeing league action again.

It didn't stop Saints making the news, although it was an agonising time for big-hearted club man Jon Phillips, sent off against Moseley in the resurrected Cheltenham & Gloucester Cup for allegedly elbowing the referee Trevor Fisher.

This was a career-threatening offence if proved but at the hearing on December 16 attended by Phillips and coach Paul Larkin, who farcically had to take with him his own television and video machine, the player was cleared in 10 minutes. Video evidence totally exonerated Phillips and the referee apologised.

On December 5 England faced a South African side at Twickenham going for a world record 18th straight test win. Rodber, Dawson and Beal made major contributions to a 13-7 win that included two penalties from Dawson.

Clive Woodward did not pick a specialist kicker and sent Dawson into the game with this hollow endorsement: "Who else is there?"

Grayson gave him a few tips before the match and Dawson commented: "When one of the great kickers of the modern game gives you advice about landing penalties you do what he says."

In layman's terms he held his nerve but it was not to be a long-term job.

A week later came another historic win – Northampton's first at Bath's Recreation Ground. Bath old boys Jon Sleightholme and Freddie Mendez were in the Saints side, Mendez stirring the pot with a public attack on the club that had sacked him.

Saints won 15-9 with tries from Pountney and Dawson and the Argentinian hooker, who had vowed never to play English club rugby again, declared that "coming to Northampton was the best move of his sporting life."

Statistics showed Saints had made 150 tackles and headlines began to appear like: "We can win the title" – and the players making those headlines were previous championship winners Sleightholme and Lam. The tackle count, said Lam, was evidence of the all-important team spirit, which ultimately counts for more than wage packets.

Unfortunately, the team's aspirations were about to be sabotaged from an unlikely source – London Irish. On January 5, the first home league game for two months, the Irish recovered from an early bombardment to win 32-8 to prevent the Saints

127

Martin Bayfield on the charge against Newcastle. He was the first player in the country to become a full-time professional. Bayfield used his newspaper column to pay tribute to Ian Hunter, who suffered one injury too many. Here he bids farewell to the Gardens fans

leading the table outright.

Four days later Saints won 47-31 at Sale (a week after winning there in the league) and, remarkably, they were handed the chance of quick revenge over Irish by drawing them in the fifth round at Franklin's Gardens on January 30.

A week earlier, Steve Walter (later to change his name to Thompson) made his league debut in a 19-14 win over West Hartlepool. It was his only senior start of the season but a glittering career was about to unfold.

For the Saints a lacklustre period set in with five defeats in seven games in various levels of matches, starting with a 21-6 defeat by the Irish followed by a 21-18 home league defeat by Saracens that handed the title initiative to Leicester, especially when this sequence of results ended with an injury-time 22-15 setback at the Gardens.

Inevitably emotions ran high as the title itself was almost at stake and Tigers had both Pat Howard and a snarling Martin Johnson sin-binned. But the most critical dismissal was that of Mattie Stewart three minutes from time and Tigers took full advantage with a late try.

Off the field, there was also a shock when Mick Owen, who had taken over as chief executive two months earlier, was forced to stand down through illness. Owen, a long-time business associate of Barwell, had arrived with bold statements about turning the Saints into Europe's greatest club. Sadly he died before the Saints went a long way towards fulfilling that dream by winning the Heineken Cup in 2000.

Serious injuries to Grayson (pelvic stress fracture) and Metcalfe (slipped disc) gave Ali Hepher and Jon Phillips a prolonged run in the side, which picked up impressively with five straight league wins, including the first-ever on Wasps soil, 24-15. It came at a price as flanker Don Mackinnon sustained a broken jaw.

Times were now changing fast. The Saints went live on the internet in March and the April 17 game with London Scottish brought the first Ladies Day at the Gardens, complete with beauty therapy and make-up demonstration. What would the pioneers of the past made of that?

Of rather more significance was the unveiling of plans for a revamped Gardens to hold 20,000 seated spectators and the news that four or five other sites close to the M1 were being considered.

Barwell had bought the Ritzy nightclub in 1998 and the neighbouring Express Lifts had shut down in 1996, so the St James site was ripe for redevelopment.

A glorious 40-17 win over Bath to give Saints a double over the side that had dominated English rugby brought down the curtain on the Gardens season. Before the game Mendez was named *Chronicle & Echo* Player of the Year, having gone full circle, from unwanted foreigner to a highly-prized asset. Mendez, who had talked about being homesick weeks earlier, even scored a try and the elaborate celebrations reflected his roller-coaster emotions.

The season petered out with defeats at Richmond and Gloucester but in the immediate aftermath the Saints signalled there would be no complacency.

British Lion centre Allan Bateman was signed on a two-year deal from Richmond and the Gardens pitch was torn up so that drainage could be improved.

McGeechan was named Coach of the Year in the Allied Dunbar Premiership. It turned out to be his last.

Coach of the Year: Ian McGeechan

Great servant: Lock Jon Phillips, who developed from raw teenager to solid professional

Chapter Thirteen
Champions of Europe

ENGLAND players, among them Matt Dawson, rallied round disgraced skipper Lawrence Dallaglio, after lurid headlines appeared in a Sunday newspaper, a scandal that led to the Wasps man standing down as leader.

Dawson was high on the list of candidates to replace Dallaglio but closer to home another bombshell was about to go off – McGeechan was leaving the club.

After five seasons at the Gardens – and only the Division Two championship to show for his efforts – the Leeds-born Scot was going back to international rugby.

The decision took all bar Keith Barwell by surprise. His right-hand man Paul Larkin had no inkling of the June 10 announcement made at a press conference in Edinburgh. McGeechan became Jim Telfer's right hand man leading up to the 1999 World Cup and would then take over the reins completely.

It was, said McGeechan, the only job that would tempt him away from Northampton and Barwell generously allowed him to leave without compensation being paid for the remaining four years of his contract.

Barwell, who declined an offer from McGeechan to stay until after the World Cup, said: "We shall try to get someone better than Geech and that will be a tall order."

Then, significantly, he said he would be talking to his senior players and checking out their views. "I shall be very much guided by the players before making a decision."

The subsequent appointment of former Saints stand-off John Steele a month later suggested a strong influence from senior players like Rodber and Dawson. Before the appointment came the inevitable speculation, much loved by newspapers and supporters. The first name tossed about was utterly predictable, that of Wayne Shelford, who had been such a powerful force for the club in his short stay. The *Chronicle & Echo* postbag threw up another in the recently retired Martin Bayfield, but neither of these names were in the frame as the annual meeting loomed when the new man would be unveiled.

The usual suspects were in there: Geoff Cooke, Dick Best, Rob Andrew along with New Zealanders Alex Wylie and Mike Brewer and former South African coach Ian McIntosh. No mention of Steele, the 34-year-old ex-soldier, who had done a splendid job as director of rugby at London Scottish. So it was a surprised audience when Steele was introduced at the annual meeting from the 20 applicants. Another revelation was that Barwell's love for the club had so far cost him £5 million – "money that I am never going to see again."

It also turned out that McGeechan's opinion had been sought over his successor and that Steele was the preferred option. Explaining the decision, Barwell

All smiles as old international adversaries, Geoff Cooke and Ian McGeechan meet up before a Saints-Bedford clash. Cooke was mentioned as a possible successor to Geech at the Gardens but McGeechan recommended John Steele

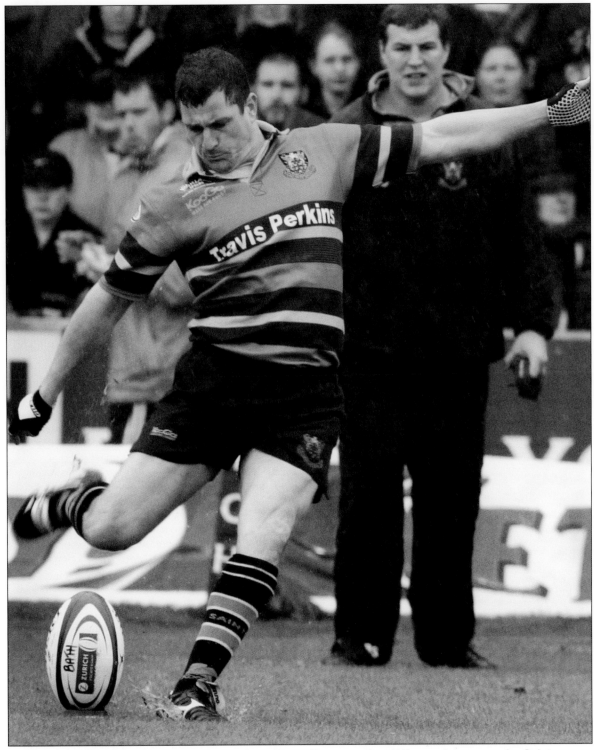

Grase and power: Paul Grayson took over from Roger Hosen as the all-time points scorer for Saints

said: "What the players told me was that they didn't want someone coming in who felt they had to make a name for themselves by changing things. The players feel they are on the fringe of doing great things. It is like a relay race. They want the baton changing over smoothly."

Away from the Gardens there was an appalling tragedy when Jon Desborough, who made 41 appearances between 1977 and 1981, died after a freak injury, when he fell on the blunt end of a javelin during a PE lesson at his Liverpool school. He was speared in the eye as he gave a lesson on safety.

On July 30, Saints finally got their man when Argentinian prop Martin Scelzo signed for the club

after locating the whereabouts of his Italian passport but another overseas player, David Dantiaq, returned to French club Pau, having failed to make much of an impact.

The early part of the 1999/2000 season was dominated by the World Cup featuring Saints men Beal, Dawson, Grayson and Rodber (England), Pountney (Scotland), Lam (Western Samoa), Scelzo (Argentina) and Bateman (Wales). Mendez was ruled out by injury

On August 9 Rodber announced that he was standing down after five years as captain and it surprised nobody that Lam replaced him. Don Mackinnon, the New Zealand-born, Aussie-raised flanker, who had just wandered into the Gardens looking for a game, would lead the side during the World Cup.

The campaign opener against Leicester in September lost much of its quality with 17 players absent on World Cup duty but none of its ferocity. Saints appeared to have stronger resources by walloping Tigers 48-24 but then came defeats at Bath and at home to Saracens and Gloucester in three of the next five games.

Meanwhile, none of the Saints men got further than the quarter-finals of the World Cup, England losing to South Africa, Scotland to New Zealand and Wales to Australia. The others had gone out before then and Lam announced his retirement from international rugby after a 35-20 defeat to Scotland.

So by late October all the players were ready for Saints action except Dawson who came back with a hamstring injury. They were all picked for the Gloucester game on October 30 before which doyen of the press box, Terry Morris, was presented with a Saints shirt to mark 25 years of rugby writing for the *Chronicle & Echo*. There would be no spectacular

Stand-in skipper Don Mackinnon

132

victory to mark the occasion, just the opposite. Long before the end of a 25-9 defeat the Gardens faithful had resorted to chants of "What a load of rubbish" – not quite the homecoming the players had anticipated.

It was time for another icy blast from the throne little more than a year since the "I shall not hesitate to put pressure on" programme notes from Barwell. In the programme for the game against London Irish, Barwell's message was pointed straight at Steele. Perhaps fearing he had got the wrong man, Barwell wrote: "John Steele knows here at Northampton that if he fails he will be replaced. It is as simple as that." For good measure Barwell said that Woodward should be relieved of the England job. Steele reacted to Barwell's comments by saying: "It comes with the territory. You are judged on results. What Keith said is absolutely fair. There is no point in worrying about it."

What followed was quite extraordinary as Saints won 14 out of 15 games, all bar one coming after Barwell's warning. The run had started eight days earlier at Bristol (29-19) on November 5 and came to an unexpected end on February 12 at the Gardens, 23-19, to Bristol. By then the Saints were chasing a fabulous treble of league, Tetley Bitter Cup and Heineken European Cup.

On November 20 an epic adventure began with a 21-12 win over Neath in the first pool match of the European Cup that also marked the debut of scrum-half Ian Vass, a Northampton teenager of whom great things were expected. At that stage he was no higher than fourth choice No 9 behind a trio of Dawson, James Bramhall and Dom Malone.

A week later the Saints played Mackinnon's old club, Grenoble, against the stunning backdrop of the Alps. The side came close that day to scaling the heights, leading 18-10 midway through the second with tries from Cohen and Allan Bateman only to go down 20-18 as the French scored a try four minutes from time.

On December 4 Grayson chalked up 11 points in a 41-17 win at bottom-club Bedford to draw level with Roger Hosen at the top of the scoring charts on 1,466 points. He lasted only 15 minutes of the next game, a 32-8 Heineken Cup win over Edinburgh Reivers but not before he edged into the lead with two penalties.

Six days later Dawson took over the kicking in the return game and landed six conversions to go with three tries for a 27-point haul in a 47-8 win. Indeed Grayson was not missed at all on the kicking front as Dawson claimed six penalties in a Boxing Day 37-5 win over Newcastle Falcons and the same again in an heroic 21-15 win at Wasps three days later. Somehow the Saints successfully defended eight scrums on their line to preserve a victory achieved without Lam, who had returned to New Zealand for personal reasons. The Saints were now top of the table with 20 points from 11 games.

Harvey Thorneycroft, who had a testimonial game at the start of the season, was dragged out of semi retirement to make his 250th appearance on Boxing Day and at the same game Martin Hynes received a watch from the club to mark his enforced retirement at the age of 31 because of an elbow injury.

The new millennium kicked off with a record score, 118-3 against Nuneaton in the Tetley Bitter Cup, featuring 17 tries, four each for Sleightholme and

Mendez. With Mendez as a role model and former Scottish hooker Colin Deans on the coaching staff, Steve Walter was developing rapidly and he got the fillip of being named in a 35-strong England coaching squad along with Ben Cohen.

The winger celebrated with a 60-yard solo try in a 27-16 European Cup win over Grenoble and a 39-25 success at Neath ensured the Saints would have a home tie in the quarter-finals. Bateman returned to the Gnoll for the first time since leaving Neath to go into rugby league and gave his old supporters a try to remember him by.

The Saints were racking up one big score after another: 38-16 (Bedford, league), 44-20 (London Irish, league), 34-32 (Saracens, Tetley Bitter). Irish coach Dick Best said: That is the strongest team we have played this season by a country mile." It was a team minus Rodber, dropped for the first time in his career with Metcalfe and Phillips preferred in the second row.

In the Cup win at Sarries, Saints survived an injury time scare when teenager Matt Leek's drop-goal attempt was deemed to have missed by referee Steve Walsh. It was a very, very close call.

Cohen's selection for England's opening Six Nations game against Ireland proved particularly newsworthy as Uncle George had been one of England's 1966 World Cup football heroes. The old Fulham right back had, said Ben, been a big help in advising about coping with the pressures of top class sport.

Cohen had no problem coping with the Irish, scoring two tries in a comprehensive 50-16 win under the guidance of skipper Matt Dawson, although his football-style celebrations caused a few arched eyebrows at Twickenham.

The warm glow of success was rudely shattered on February 12 when Saints inexplicably went down to Bristol at the Gardens despite taking a 19-16 lead with a minute of normal time remaining with a

Dawson penalty. In injury time Wellingborough-educated winger Spencer Brown scored the try that ended 11 straight victories.

Dawson and Cohen continued to conquer in the Six Nations, France 15-9 in Paris and Wales 46-12 at Twickenham, while Saints broke down the resistance of Second Division London Welsh 35-26 in the Tetley Bitter Cup quarter finals.

A superb 35-11 win at Gloucester showed that lasting damage had not been done by the Bristol setback. It was the first win at Kingsholm for eight years.

Dawson, clearly revelling in leading his country, and Cohen scored two tries apiece in a 59-12 win over Italy that left just McGeechan's Scotland in the way of a Grand Slam.

Amid all this pomp and glory came the shattering news that Andy Blyth, who had left Saints for Sale in the summer, had sustained serious spinal injuries in the first minute of a game at Saracens raising fears that he might be forced to spend the rest of his life in a wheelchair as a tetraplegic.

Saints and Sale met at Franklin's Gardens on March 25, when Saints changed their pre-match routine in a bid to elevate their home form. At Lam's suggestion the team boarded a coach and went to a hotel outside Northampton to replicate in part the ritual of an away game. The outcome was a 26-7 win for Saints, although a magical try from Beal had a more direct bearing on the result than any pre-match bonding.

On April 1 Scotland made fools of England by winning 19-13 against all the odds, thus Craig Moir, Richard Metcalfe, Matt Stewart and Budge Pountney had local bragging rights over Matt Dawson and Ben Cohen even if most of the season had been a disaster for the Scottish squad.

More importantly from a club perspective, the Saints lost Dawson with a rib injury just as the season was

The all-out aggressive style that made Harvey Thorneycroft a legend on the terraces

reaching its climax on three fronts.

Malone stepped into the breach for the Tetley Bitter Cup tie against London Irish at the Madejski Stadium. where both semi-finals took place one after the other. Wasps beat Bristol 44-31 and Saints enjoyed a third win that season over Irish, 24-17.

Steele shrugged off stamina concerns, insisting the squad could cope with a punishing schedule but there were clear signs of fatigue as Saints won a smash-and-grab Heineken Cup quarter-final over Wasps, 25-22, at Franklin's Gardens.

Lowly Harlequins took full advantage of that tiredness three days later with a 29-17 mid-week victory and the title chance vanished completely when Bath claimed a 17-13 win at the Gardens to leave Saints seven points adrift of Leicester Tigers.

Suddenly Saints were in danger of missing out on Heineken Cup qualification as the league season fell apart with a third straight defeat, 26-21 at Leicester.

Although the wheels were coming off in the league, there was still all to play for in the cup competitions and on May 7, again at the Madejski Stadium, the Saints faced Llanelli for a place in the Heineken Cup final. At half-time, Saints were 19-9 down and long odds against making it. The players dragged up reserves of courage to win 31-28 with Grayson, a late replacement, kicking a penalty from 40-metres out.

Absurdly the Saints and Wasps were forced to face each other in a league encounter four days before their Tetley Bitter Cup final and the clubs responded in completely different ways. Wasps fielded virtually a full-strength side, the Saints a second string. Wasps won 54-12.

So the stage was now set for Northampton's first appearance in a Twickenham cup final since 1991 – only nine years earlier but light years away in rugby terms. Gone were the part-timers for whom rugby was a diversion from the classroom or pounding the beat. Now two fully-professional teams would go head-to-head. Tim Rodber was the sole survivor from the side of 1991. Keith Barwell had sat in the stand watching the final with Harlequins. Would his millions at last bring a significant trophy to the Gardens?

He said he could not contemplate "the wretchedness of defeat" and was in bullish mood in a Sky television interview, predicting a 30-point margin of victory.

The interview was picked up by the newspapers and Wasps head coach Nigel Melville pinned up the headlines in the dressing room before the game.

The side picked to start the final was: Beal; Cohen, Allen, Bateman, Moir; Grayson, Dawson; Pagel, Mendez, Stewart; Newman, Metcalfe; Rodber, Pountney, Lam.

Six Grayson penalties and a Pountney try left the Saints one point adrift at 24-23 as the final whistle approached but then a Mark Denney try put the seal on a Wasps victory, 31-23.

Barwell was hauled before a players' jury and Judge Tim Rodber to stand trial for his comments and his 'fine' cost him a very large drinks bill. "I was also forced to drink something very horrible," said the Saints owner.

The league campaign dragged on and four days later Saracens inflicted a fifth straight defeat to seriously leave Heineken Cup qualification in the balance. Heartbreakingly, Beal broke a leg and Dawson dislocated a shoulder. Beal's season was

An horrendous injury to Andy Blyth was a sobering reminder of the perils of playing rugby

over, Dawson's chances of appearing in the Heineken Cup hung by a slender thread.

With both domestic trophies now gone, the Saints were massive underdogs against Munster for the May 28 Heineken Cup final. But a significant step towards achieving a nail-biting success came a week earlier when a 31-13 win at Newcastle in the final league game of the season dramatically guaranteed a place in Europe for the 2000/01 season. A huge weight had been lifted from the players' shoulders, although yet another injury marred the win. Grant Seely, the forgotten man of the season, broke his jaw to ruin his chance of a call-up for the final.

A boost came when Pat Lam's wife Stephanie delivered their fourth child four days before the final. It was impeccable timing from Mrs Lam because her husband had insisted that family matters would come first, leaving his participation in the final in doubt.

The coaches of the other Heineken Cup sides were polled and unanimously chose Munster as the likely winners. The Irishmen came into the game fresh, not having had a game for three weeks, while the Saints had been on a treadmill of matches at the end of a long season. Fitness advisor Phil Pask struck a pessimistic note. "We have penalised ourselves for being too successful and this should never happen again. Rugby is like no other game. It takes a physical toll."

Much was made in the media of the club's supposed failure to deliver when it matters, a somewhat phoney argument since for most of the club's history there had been nothing tangible to actually play for.

Munster, like Saints, had lost just one pool game on

Guilty as charged: Keith Barwell appeared before Judge Tim Rodber at a players' court after the Cup final defeat by Wasps

their way to the final and having overcome French aces Toulouse, they were considered more likely to handle the big occasion.

With no Dawson nor Beal, Grayson moved to full-back and Steele opted for the rookie half-back partnership of Ali Hepher and Dom Malone. The starting line-up was: Grayson; Cohen, Allen,

Bateman, Moir; Hepher, Malone; Pagel, Mendez, Stewart; Newman, Rodber; Mackinnon, Pountney, Lam.

In front of 68,441 spectators at Twickenham the Saints won 9-8, just reward for an outstanding season as opposing skipper Keith Wood generously conceded after the game. "If I was an impartial observer if Northampton had come away from this season without any silverware that would have been a travesty. Northampton have been the best team in England," said Wood.

Saints won with three penalties from Grayson against a Jason Holland drop goal and David Wallace try. Ronan O'Gara had the chance to snatch victory for the Irishmen with a penalty two minutes from time but was off target.

Rodber, disappointing in the Tetley Bitter final but outstanding in this one, was delighted to be a winner with the Saints at last. "To play for England and the British Lions is fantastic but to do something with people you train with every day represents the highlight of my career."

Before the game Andy Blyth visited the dressing room to wish the players good luck and at the end Pat Lam got the boys into a huddle on the pitch for an impromptu prayer.

The cup was displayed to a passionate rugby town two days later in an open-top bus ride with the bells of All Saints' Church greeting the players. For some this was the end of their association with the club.

Mackinnon and Metcalfe joined Edinburgh Reivers, Northey and Chris Johnson departed for newly promoted Rotherham and Mendez signed for Begles Bordeaux.

In June three signings were announced, the most spectacular Olivier Brouzet, joining from Begles along with Luca Martin, winner of 23 Italian caps. Capped 44 times by France, Brouzet, son of an Olympic shot putter, signed a two-year contract as

Rookie European Cup pairing: Half-backs Dom Malone (left) and Ali Hepher

A wet night did not dampen the mood as the players toured Northampton in an open-top bus to celebrate winning the Heineken Cup, held aloft by Ben Cohen and Pat Lam. There was a minor hiccup when the bus was about to leave Franklin's Gardens without the cup. Press officer Tom Sears had left it in his office and was duly despatched to get it amid acute embarrassment…

French connection: Olivier Brouzet

did Joe Shaw from Sale, utility forward Rob Hunter from London Irish, and Steve Brotherstone from Brive, capped four times at hooker by Scotland.

Hepher, meanwhile, was drafted into the England tour of South Africa as understudy to Wilkinson.

Under the new sponsorship banner of Zurich, the 2000/01 season saw some tinkering with the points system. There would be four points for a win, two for a draw; a bonus point for losing by seven points or less and a bonus point for scoring four tries. Generally the reaction was favourable.

Little more than three months after the camaraderie and back-slapping came distinctly un-rugby like brickbats from Steele and Lam, following a 33-19 defeat at Leicester.

Steele called the players "stupid, lazy, indisciplined and thoughtless", while Lam threatened to give up. "I am not here to put my body on the line if players are going to waste my time."

Victory over Harlequins was followed by a 34-23 defeat at Sale, where former Saints coach Glenn Ross had been recruited from Connacht. The squad was being stretched to the limit by an astonishing injury-list to the backs. Dawson, Allen, Hepher, Shaw, Mark Tucker, Beal, Sleightholme were all in the treatment room at the same time.

In the circumstances a 24-13 win over Bath was highly satisfactory but it was followed by a 53-17 thumping by Wasps, bouncing back from conceding 59 points to Newcastle.

With the league campaign stumbling along, the Saints sought inspiration from the defence of their Heineken Cup. It turned out to be an even bigger nightmare.

French champions Biarritz were first up and only two Saints tries in the last minute gave the scoreline a look of respectability at 37-30. That was no cause for alarm but there was a week later when Don

John Leslie – Saints stepped in when Newcastle decided they no longer wanted the Scottish international

Mackinnon brought his Reivers side to the Gardens and won 23-22 with an injury time drop goal from Duncan Hodge, the Saints having led 16-3.

The Saints' problems paled into insignificance with the shattering news that Ben Cohen's dad Peter had been beaten up at Eternity nightclub in Bridge Street, Northampton, that left him critically ill in hospital. A month later, just three days after Ben had scored a hat-trick of tries against Birmingham-Solihull, Peter died at the age of 58. Ben had just been named in the England side to play Australia and the news of his dad's death was broken to him during a training session. He was driven back to Northampton by Matt Dawson and withdrew from the international. Black armbands were worn and a minute's silence observed before the international. The Australian party sent a letter of condolence to the Cohen family.

A week after the Reivers defeat the Heineken Cup defence lay in tatters as Leinster won 14-8 in Dawson's comeback game from the shoulder injury that had kept him out since mid-May. In the return game in Ireland six days later Pountney, who had just been named Scotland captain for the autumn internationals with USA, Australia and Western Samoa, was red-carded after just 12 minutes and Saints slumped to a 40-31 defeat. Four games, four defeats, bottom of the pool. The Saints were in urgent need of a boost. Enter Andrew Blowers.

The 25-year-old Auckland Blues back-row man was hailed as the "new Pat Lam" and the Samoan had played a large part in the 11-times capped All Black joining Saints. When it was circulated that Blowers

was available, Steele and Larkin put him top of the club's wanted list. In years gone by southern hemisphere players would mainly be known by reputation. Now they can be seen on television on a regular basis and Larkin, a keen student of the Super 12 competition, was eager to push for Blowers' signature. Bristol were the main challengers to Saints but a telephone call from Lam persuaded Blowers that his immediate future lay at Franklin's Gardens.

Perhaps fearing that he had signalled his own end at Northampton, Lam went public in saying that he was keen for one more season.

Blowers arrived on Wednesday, November 1. On November 4 he donned the black, green and gold for the first time and played for 58 minutes in the Tetley Bitter Cup tie against Leeds, a 73-35 win, having trained for just 30 minutes before his debut.

In a quirky calendar of fixtures, Saints played the next round a week later against Birmingham-Solihull, which afforded a debut for centre Chris Hyndman, who two months earlier had been working in a chemical plant in Middlesbrough as an apprentice mechanical fitter. A 47-14 win included a hat-trick of tries for Cohen in 16 minutes before the tragic news of his father's death a few days later.

As an England player Cohen then became embroiled in a huge bust-up when the players effectively threatened strike action over a pay row, which, they claimed, had been dragging on for months. Team-mate Dawson, skipper Martin Johnson and Lawrence Dallaglio were the players' negotiators, while coach Clive Woodward could only look on

139

Highly recommended: All Black Andrew Blowers

impotently and fume. Four days before England were due to play Argentina there seemed a distinct possibility that the game would not go ahead. Or if it did, with a bunch of hastily gathered replacements. Barwell came out decisively on the side of the players.

A deal was struck with RFU inside 24 hours and England went on to win 19-0 with Cohen scoring a try followed by a shriek to the heavens that left no-one in any doubt as to who he was thinking of in that moment of joy.

On the same day Saints beat Bristol 24-6 and for the first time summer recruit Joe Shaw made a full 80-minute appearance. Shaw, signed to fill the full-back berth while Beal recovered from his broken leg, had been injured in pre-season training, so a number of options had been tried in the No 15 jersey, primarily Grayson. Shaw was on the wing against Bristol. It was not until December 16 that Shaw made the starting line-up at full-back just as Beal was starting a tentative comeback. Veteran Thorneycroft scored his 100th try for the Saints in 34-15 win over Gloucester, this following a 30-10 win at Saracens to make it four league wins on the trot and third place in the Zurich Premiership.

In between Harlequins had ended cup hopes with an 11-6 win at The Stoop. Two days before Christmas Saints took revenge with a 34-25 away win over the London side and four days after that New Zealand-born Scot John Leslie, made his debut in a 15-12 win at Gloucester following an acrimonious departure from Newcastle. Rob Andrew had given Leslie an

ultimatum: sit on your backside as a sub or join another club.

Six league wins in a row had given Saints a sniff of the title but two defeats to start 2001, against Wasps and Bath, left them with no chance and nothing left to play for but pride.

There were academic exercises against Biarritz and Edinburgh Reivers in the Heineken Cup debacle, the French side being beaten with the help of three Cohen tries.

In the same month, Pat Lam qualified to have his overseas status removed but it made no difference as Steele announced the brave decision that the Samoan was not being retained. Lam, who had just returned to the side from a shoulder operation, said he was shocked by the decision but sought consolation in his faith. "God has a plan for me," he declared at a press conference.

At the same time there was the first hint that Rodber would be retiring by choice at the end of the season but Steele insisted he would not be looking for a major back-row signing.

Back on the field, Grayson and Dawson were reunited at half-back for the first time for 10 months against Sale on February 24. It was an emotional occasion as Andy Blyth – not in a wheelchair but on crutches – led out the sides to a great ovation.

Blyth continued to make a remarkable recovery and his name became synonymous with good causes, He donated the Blyth Spirit Challenge Cup to be competed for between Sale Sharks and Saracens, the opposing teams when his accident occurred at

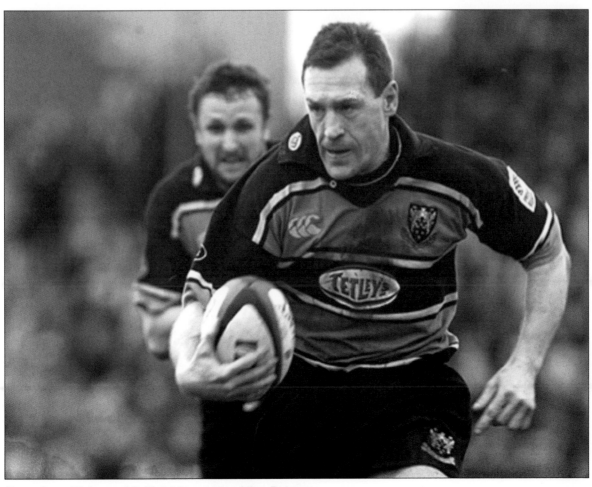

Pure class: Wales and British Lion centre Allan Bateman

Vicarage Road.

For a long time it looked as though he would never walk again but through sheer determination and the dedication and skills of staff at the Royal National Orthopaedic Hospital at Stanmore, Middlesex, he is now able to walk unaided.

The trophy, for annual competition, was Andy's way of acknowledging the support he had received from the players and fans of both clubs.

"I want to extend my warmest thanks to both rugby clubs who have been nothing but brilliant since my accident," he said. "I am particularly grateful to all those who visited me in hospital and gave of their time to attend fund-raising functions throughout the year.

"I also received an overwhelming number of cards and get well wishes from fans and that has been fantastic."

All the money he raises through his Blyth Spirit fund go to the Royal Orthopaedic spinal unit.

Saints marked Andy's presence with a win, 32-26 after conceding two tries in the opening eight minutes.

A bold move by the Saints to stage a match between the champions of the northern and southern hemispheres fell foul of the RFU, which refused to sanction the game against Canterbury, winners of the Super 12 competition. Commercial director Allan Robson, a man from a soccer background, was clearly bemused by the intransigence of the governing body since a date had been found acceptable to both clubs.

An emotional Andly Blyth leads out the teams

A little domestic squabble also flared in the England-Scotland game at Twickenham, when Pountney was sin-binned for kicking Dawson. The England scrum-half said: "It was not an accident that is why he was sin-binned and he apologised after the game."

A week later it was Dawson the sinner, who was fined by the club for 'reckless' play in challenges on Leicester duo Geordan Murphy and Pat Howard, after the England man had received a grilling by Sky TV pundits.

The club's internal inquiry into the incidents concluded there was no malice involved and Dawson accepted the punishment. "I'm hard but fair," said Dawson. Saints lost at home 12-9 to their great rivals in a match that left a lot of people frustrated, none more so than Garry Pagel, who branded referee Robin Goodliffe's display the "worst he had experienced."

It was impossible to keep Dawson out of the news and when he scored a try in a 25-14 win over Saracens he made a very public gesture of kissing the club badge on his jersey. This was his response to Paul Ackford's column in the *Sunday Telegraph* in which he had accused Dawson of being greedy and not caring about his club. "I have been here 10 years and that was outrageous," said Dawson after a game that meant a home play-off fixture against the same opposition.

Before that there was a 46-16 defeat at Bristol to end what Steele called a "disappointing" season. Grayson's playing career seemed to be nearing its end when he signed a new one-year deal that incorporated a kicking coach role. His stand-off place was under threat from Alastair Hepher and James Brooks.

The Saints launched a club magazine, *Black, Green & Gold,* on April 1, a 48-page glossy and Dawson and Cohen were named in the 37-strong Lions party to tour Australia. Cohen was also named Saints Player of the Year.

On April 18 Tim Rodber played his last game at Franklin's Gardens in the play-off against Saracens to a rapturous reception and a host of tributes. Along with Ian Hunter, Rodber had taken the club into a glorious, new chapter following the sterility of the Eighties.

Before the game Keith Barwell ceremoniously took a sledgehammer to the Gordon Terrace to herald in the fabulous redevelopment of Franklin's Gardens. The players then played their part by winning 45-17 to set up a play-off semi-final at Leicester, which ended in a 17-13 defeat. It signalled the end for Rodber, Pagel, Bateman and Lam, who came on for the final 10 minutes after recovering from more surgery on his shoulder. Astonishingly, given the acrimony of his departure, Lam re-signed for Rob Andrew's Newcastle Falcons 10 days later. It was a painful end for Bateman, carried off after an hour, while even before the match plans for the following season had started to fall into place.

Another era was about to unfold but not all were aware of it as players went their separate ways for the summer – Dawson and Cohen to Australia, Steve Thompson to North America on an England development tour, and players like James Bramhall and Matt Volland to pastures new, having been released by the club.

Chapter Fourteen
A Kiwi to the rescue

FOR a side that had lost a wealth of experience in Lam, Rodber, Pagel and Bateman, the Saints only dipped their toe in the transfer market in the summer of 2001. Tom Smith was the man to replace Pagel in the front row and Peter Jorgensen was plucked from Australian rugby league.

London-born Smith, 29, was the holder of 28 Scottish caps when he signed from Brive and he had an early opportunity to find out about the Saints from new team-mates Cohen and Dawson on the Lions tour.

He had made public the fact that he was an epileptic and much of his spare time was devoted to raising money for the charity Enlightenment.

Jorgensen, 28, had been capped twice by the Wallabies in 1992 but had switched codes and was playing for Penrith Panthers when he decided to accept the Saints' offer. A knee operation in 1999 had limited his appearances and he jumped at the chance of coming to England.

As a man who had led England on several occasions, Dawson might reasonably have expected to be the new Saints skipper but he was overlooked in favour of Budge Pountney, who was named on June 6 as the player to shepherd a young squad.

Apart from Cohen. Dawson and Smith on the Lions tour, there was a Northampton representative among the press corps, Terry Morris, from the *Chronicle & Echo*. Not long into the trip he was branding the management duo of Graham Henry and Donal Lenihan as a PR shambles. The comments of a reporter from a provincial newspaper were not going to worry unduly the management but on Saturday June 30, Dawson's column in the *Daily Telegraph* sent shock waves through the tour party. In his *Tour Diary*, Dawson launched an unprecedented verbal assault on individual members of the Lions management team, claiming he "wasn't inspired" by Henry and that Lenihan "treated the squad like children."

Dawson claimed the "mindless" training routines were too long and severe and the squad was being "flogged". He also criticised England coaches Andy Robinson and Phil Larder for being "too distant", adding that their training methods with the Lions differed from their approach with the England set-up.

His comments coincided with a 29-13 Lions victory over the world champions and there were genuine fears that such insubordination would lead to him being kicked off the tour.

Dawson, having apologised for making his feelings public, responded by kicking 15 points in a 30-28 win over ACT Brumbies but the issue did not simply disappear as Englishmen Austin Healey and Dan Luger came out in support of Dawson.

Australia hit back to win the next two Tests, 35-14 and 29-23, Dawson playing in the last as a replacement for the injured Rob Howley.

Back home another experienced player, Matt Allen, quit the Saints to join Cardiff in what he called the "hardest decision of my life." The centre had seen his opportunities decreasing with the signing of Leslie and the promise of Mark Tucker.

Premier Rugby Partnership, an alliance between clubs and players formed in March, announced just before the new campaign that top players would be limited to 32 games, a move welcomed by Pountney, who had been warning of burn-out because of the ever-increasing demands of the modern game.

In the evolving world of professional rugby, England Rugby Ltd was born in August, a move that was set to yield each premiership club £30 million over the next eight years.

So staying in the Premiership was the first priority of every club but the Saints' ambitions were a lot higher than mere survival. They expected to be com-

There were few smiles in the British Lions camp when Matt Dawson launched an assault on the management in his newspaper column

Tom Smith, a British Lions team-mate of Matt Dawson and Ben Cohen before becoming a Saint

peting for honours even with the departure of so many stars.

The intensity of the professional game was borne out after an opening day defeat, 22-9, at Gloucester with phrases like "the heat is on" and "no need to panic" already being used.

A week later, on September 8, the fans got their first look at the £6 million new-look Franklin's Gardens, a great testament first to the 1988 revolu-

tion and then the driving influence of Keith Barwell. The official opening of the Tetley's Bitter Stand, a magnificent edifice that had replaced the ramshackle Gordon Terrace, and the South Stand at the Lake End was still more than a month away but the players christened their new surroundings with a 26-7 win over Bath in front of 10,241 fans, Jorgensen collecting his first try for the club.

Steele summed up the immense pride felt by all

144

Former All Blacks stand-off and coach Wayne Smith had an instant galvanising effect on the Saints

Ben Cohen one of the game's biggest stars at his peak

concerned with the club. "You feel responsible to go out there and do it justice." It would, of course, be just as inspirational to opposition players as to the men in black, green and gold.

Three days later, September 11, 2001, came the devastation of the World Trade Centre in New York. A minute's silence was observed at Leeds where the Saints won 26-6 only to be followed by a 25-20 defeat at Saracens that preceded the season's first foray into Europe against Cardiff. Matt Allen used the opportunity to spice up the clash by claiming that John Leslie had been picked "on name, not ability", forcing him to look for another club.

Cardiff won 25-17 and Allen was a prominent figure, accidentally clashing heads with Beal and setting up a late try that sealed victory. Dawson, who had missed the season so far after knee surgery at the end of the Lions tour, came on as a substitute but then had the discomfort of being savaged in Graham Henry's account of the events in Australia, *Henry's Pride*.

Ian McGeechan and Clive Woodward were among the guests on October 13 for the official opening of the revamped Gardens. Saints took on a Leicester Tigers side going for their fourth successive championship. Tigers scored two tries in as many minutes going into the final quarter on their way to a 21-11 victory in front of an 11,700 crowd.

Rugby in Northampton was now a serious spectator sport with 21st century facilities. All the players had to do was to continually challenge for honours. The immediate reality was somewhat different and it led to a massive shake-up. Having beaten Leeds on October 16, the Saints did not taste success again until December 2, a run of eight defeats and a draw.

After the Leicester defeat, the Saints went on a downward spiral, losing at Sale, at home in the Heineken Cup to Montferrand and being hammered in the return, 50-17.

In the midst of this malaise came Northampton Saints plc's first annual meeting at which Steele came under fire for the team's poor start.

Barwell defended his director of rugby and the players even though the side sat uncomfortably in tenth place in the Premiership and were out of Europe for a second season running. Despite the vote of confidence changes were about to be made.

Barwell called for relegation to be suspended for three seasons to give breathing space to the clubs that were investing millions of pounds on the game's infrastructure.

He outlined his vision for the club. He wanted it to represent a region and not just a town. He saw no reason why the Saints should not attract fans from Peterborough, Cambridge, Ipswich and Norwich.

On November 9 Barwell again used the match day programme to announce to the fans that changes were in the offing but he did not go into detail.

To underline the declining confidence in the team the Saints could only draw 13-13 at home to Harlequins, having to come from 13-3 down with 15 minutes to go to salvage a point.

In the week that followed defensive coach Andy Goodway, who had only joined in August, and former Scottish hooker Colin Deans were sacked and Paul Larkin, who had been with the club since its amateur days, was moved sideways to technical analyst.

Barwell warned that as many as a third of the squad could lose their job.

The immediate effect was a 48-12 disaster at London Irish, a defeat only made marginally respectable by a 12-point burst in the final 10 minutes. Embarrassingly Irish ran in seven tries and the Saints, captained for the first time by Nick Beal, were rock bottom.

There was no respite as Bristol claimed a controversial 23-20 win at the Gardens nine days later with a try four minutes into injury time, awarded only after consultation with a touch judge, which prompted a showdown between the official, John Barnard, and Steele after the game.

Even then Paul Grayson had the chance to sneak a draw but slipped as he took a penalty. The discontent in the camp was perhaps summed up by Grayson's post-match comment: "From playing in the World Cup two years ago to being third choice here is something I find astonishing."

In an earlier time of crisis, the Saints had turned to a New Zealander, Andrew Blowers. Now they did so again with the appointment of former All Blacks player and coach Wayne Smith. From the late 1970s into the mid 1980s Smith was an accomplished New Zealand stand-off, appearing in 17 tests. Originally from Waikato, where he grew up in Putaruru, Smith moved to Canterbury to study and to seek more regular representative chances.

His coaching pedigree was also immaculate. Smith had partly fallen on his sword in losing his All Blacks position to Clive Woodward's former assistant John Mitchell, after a narrow Bledisloe Cup defeat to the Wallabies in 2001. Before that Smith, who had a reputation for being intensely analytical, had guided Canterbury Crusaders to the 1998 and 1999 Super 12 titles.

Steele stayed with the club, switching to a more administrative role, while the mere name of Wayne Smith seemed to galvanise the players. The rot was instantly stopped with a 28-13 win at Newcastle Falcons, Pat Lam having warned the team that there would be no old pals' act. Cohen hit the spot when he said the players were fighting for their jobs.

Smith paid his own fare over to see the players perform and find out as much about the club as he could. Smith said: "I like to be objective and do my own investigations."

The Saints were impressed. "It was not so much that he was being interviewed – he was interviewing us," commented Larkin.

It was a powerful statement of integrity and Smith received a great ovation from 8,000 Saints fans when he was introduced before the game with Wasps on December 8. Saints won 23-10 which brought an honest appraisal from the new man. "We have to be a lot harder, mentally and physically. We have to put pressure on ourselves to do everything excellently. There is a lot of hard work to be done."

Rodber and Hynes were brought into the fold to help coach the forwards but there was almost an unexpected turn of events when Birmingham Solihull led 19-12, and deservedly so, with 22 minutes to go in the Powergen Cup a week later. The Saints rallied to win 32-19 and the first Smith innovation was made

147

Towering presence: Steve Thompson

Front row men Matt Stewart (left) and Chris Johnson – Stewart ran into a series of problems with the disciplinary authorities

- Cohen was tried in the centre.

The first player casualty of the new regime was lock Andy Newman, who was released after receiving a driving ban from Bedford magistrates. At the same time 31-year-old South African lock Johan Ackermann, who served a two-year ban for drug abuse from 1997 to 1999, was brought in to bolster the pack. The former police shooting instructor, capped nine times, was signed from Golden Lions. Inevitably, he was asked about his enforced absence and he explained that a banned steroid had been used to speed up recovery from a knee operation.

The next significant move by Smith before jetting back to New Zealand for Christmas was to talk to the players on a one-to-one basis, leading to a renaissance for Grayson at stand-off. "He asked me how old I was. I told him and he said I have got plenty of rugby to play, which is contrary to what some people have been saying."

Even without Smith in attendance the Saints took revenge on London Irish with a controversial 24-15 win in which two Saints players, Cohen and Stewart, found themselves in trouble. Cohen was accused of foul play, a charge from which he was subsequently cleared by the club. Stewart, on the other hand, was called before an RFU disciplinary committee. He pleaded guilty and was fined £200 for an offence described as at the "bottom of the scale of seriousness". The Scottish prop said he had not expected to receive a ban "as my record speaks for itself of never having been sent off in 250 games."

Amazingly that record changed in the very next game – just two days after the hearing – when Stewart got a red card in the 26-15 Heineken Cup win over Cardiff. He attended a second hearing just two hours after the game and the stain on his record was considered sufficient punishment. The Saints gambled on youngster James Brooks at scrum-half against Cardiff and he gave a Man-of-the-Match performance.

A week earlier, the new year had brought a first defeat for Smith's regime, a Heineken Cup tie against Glasgow Warriors (31-27) at the Partick Thistle FC ground, Dawson being stretchered off with damaged ankle ligaments.

Nevertheless, there was now a mood of optimism and the fixture at Saracens on January 19 was described by Steele as "the season starts here". It turned out to be a dramatic victory, 30-28, sealed by an 80th minute drop goal from Beal.

Shortly after Smith's arrival, Saints and Bedford agreed a deal whereby Northampton would farm out players to their neighbours – players who were on the fringes and those returning from injury.

The first two for whom there appeared no immediate future at the Saints were Ali Hepher and Luca Martin, who made the short journey down the A428 and a lesser grade of rugby. It would become a steady stream thereafter.

A 24-16 win at Harlequins took the Saints from relegation candidates a month earlier to sixth in the table with Ackermann and Brouzet forming an international second row.

The new-found mood of well-being was further underlined with an England debut for Steve Thompson, joining Ben Cohen in the side to face Scotland at Murrayfield, a real feather in the cap for Northampton junior side, Old Scouts. It was ironic that after setting up an academy system to attract youngsters from all parts, the first players to break through to the big time were both Northampton boys.

Thompson, who had been the star of the win over Wasps with Woodward in the stands, gave all the credit to McGeechan for his switch from promising flanker to international hooker. "Geech told me it would be difficult to break into the club's back-row. He told me to get into the Northampton side, become first choice hooker and go on to play for England."

Although McGeechan was plotting England's downfall, he took the time to say that he felt Thompson could become a big name in world rugby. "We moved him from the back-row at 18. He could have been a good club back row player but I felt he could become an outstanding international hooker."

Thompson lined up against club-mates Stewart and Smith and emerged triumphant, playing a big part in a 29-3 win as did Cohen who scored a spectacular solo try. England continued in similar vein against Ireland at Twickenham, winning 45-11. Meanwhile, the Saints hit a blip. They lost 20-10 at home to Sale and then 17-6 at Leicester, described by Smith as the "poorest game of football that I have ever been involved in."

Smith began to show he had no respect for reputations, dropping Brouzet for the Tigers game and then Thompson and Smith for the Powergen Cup semifinal against holders Newcastle. Thompson admitted he was finding it hard to translate his international

149

Great signing – Bruce Reihana soon became one of the most dynamic players in the Premiership

form into his Saints displays. Smith emphasised the point that he was not 'resting' anyone. "I have chosen the team judged on performances."

Far from whingeing about being left out, Thompson reacted in mature fashion. "Wayne has been there and done it and I have great respect for him. He has got my best interests at heart." Thompson said he felt drained when returning from international duty.

The semi-final was supposed to set up a Twickenham final for a host of Falcon internationals,

including Lam, Vaiga Tuigamala, Dodie Weir, Gary Armstrong and George Graham, who were all retiring at the end of the season. Instead the Saints ran riot, winning 38-7, having led 33-0 at half time with an outstanding display of attacking rugby. Seely, fighting for his career, scored two first half tries, with one each for Jorgensen and Moir in front of 11,600 Gardens fans who could hardly believe what they were watching.

Newcastle boss Andrew was stunned. "Nobody has

ever played as well as that in a half against us. Everything they did turned to gold and it was a pretty shell-shocked dressing room at half-time."

Lam was also generous in defeat. "It was a brilliant effort – the Northampton of old. It was very difficult to defend. I was especially pleased for Grase (Paul Grayson) who was pushed aside last year. Wayne Smith has been good for his confidence."

Even Smith was surprised by the display. "I don't know where that came from. If I did, I'd bottle it."

It was the perfect tonic for Keith Barwell, who was watching his first game since being taken ill at the start of the year.

Now London Irish stood between Saints and a first domestic cup triumph. Before March was out the club had sold 20,000 tickets for the final and were pleading for more. They had also followed up with handsome wins over Leeds and relegation-threatened Bath. And in the week before the final, Saints blitzed Gloucester 58-21 with eight tries. The players were in the form of their lives and surely it would be third time lucky in the domestic cup competition.

The Saints were overwhelming favourites even though Irish were above them in the table but there was a bad omen when they lost the toss for a change of strip. They opted for maroon to be the dominant colour with touches of black, green and gold.

The *Chronicle & Echo* again produced splendid coverage with yet another supplement full of optimistic articles from the principals and message of good luck from the supporters. Although trips to Twickenham were becoming fairly frequent there was still only the Heineken Cup to show for the players' efforts.

Paul Grayson had the perfect start to the week when wife Emma produced twin boys, Joel and Ethan, and Smith picked a team of 14 internationals and Grant Seely. It read: Beal; Moir, Jorgensen, Leslie, Cohen; Grayson, Dawson; Smith, Thompson, Stewart; Ackermann, Brouzet; Blowers, Pountney, Seely. The replacements were: Richmond, Morris, Phillips, Rennick, Malone, Tucker and Brooks.

The side oozed class in every aspect of the game. They all had big match experience. They would not be fazed by a Twickenham final. Oh no…

Irish simply blew them away: 38-7. The players were genuinely embarrassed by their collective performance and the headlines underlined the anguish and disappointment:
'SO SORRY'
'NOT EVEN A CONTEST AS EXILES ROMP IT'
'TOO PAINFUL TO WATCH'

The fans at least showed their class in defeat as 1,000 of them made their way to the Rodber Suite of the Tetley's Stand at Franklin's Gardens to drown their sorrows.

Wayne Smith stood on the bar and showed a touch of class as well with these words: **"It is really humbling to be here and see the support today. I want to apologise for that performance. You never have success without adversity. You have to go through these times."**

For Saints supporters they knew exactly what he meant – 1991 (defeat to Harlequins at Twickenham in extra time), 1992 (defeat at Nottingham that cost Saints the league title) 2000 (defeat again at Twickenham to Wasps).

Extraordinarily, Smith received hate mail in the week following the defeat and still the season

Australian World Cup hero Mark Connors – re-routed from joining Bath by signing for Saints

Engine room: Darren Fox and Matt Lord grapple with Trevor Leota of Wasps

dragged on – into June.

Dawson was among those left out for the next game with Saracens when 8,479 swallowed their disappointment and saw Saints win 52-27. Brouzet revealed he was returning to France, which explained the announcement in the immediate aftermath of cup final defeat that Welsh international Steve Williams had been signed from the victorious Irish side.

In the last game of rugby to be played at the Queens Park Rangers FC ground at Loftus Road, Wasps beat Saints 17-6 on May 4 to once again leave Heineken Cup qualification hanging in the balance.

Four days later Smith rallied his troops with this eye-catching comment before a game at Bristol, who were also in the hunt for a play-off place. "Turtles go into their shells when under threat – panthers attack. I want us to be panthers."

And so they were. Despite having Morris and Blowers sin-binned the Saints won 37-27 and followed up with a 24-19 win over Newcastle to end in fifth place to set up a crack at London Irish in the play-offs.

There were some other issues going on at the same time. On May 14 the annual Mobbs Memorial Match between the East Midlands and Barbarians, which had long since ceased to be a meaningful tribute to the great man, was the last game to be played in front of the old Main Stand that had seen its first game on September 24, 1927. Next day work started on its demolition, which prompted requests from supporters to have their old seat as a souvenir. One such request came from Martyn Kiddle, pictured in the press, with seat L12, which was transplanted in his Whitehills home garden. He had watched the Saints for 30 years. Old players gathered in the home dressing room to pose for a picture before the Newcastle game and Terry Morris remembered the old press box with something less than affection.

"It is the end of an era for me and my splintered backside. My seat was perilously close to the old committee. I swear a hole was deliberately drilled in the roof directly over my head."

In a mockery of a match, the Saints beat Irish 38-14 in the play-offs, which brought scathing criticism from Smith. The Exiles did not field a single player from their final line-up and Smith fumed: "The game was a disaster as a spectacle. They have discredited the game."

Saints were, at least, guaranteed a place in Europe for the following season even though they were beaten 32-24 at Bristol to miss out on a final at Twickenham in the play-off final. Nobody was too disappointed about that.

The departure of Brouzet signalled the start of a major reshuffling of the Saints squad. There would be 10 significant outgoing players with only four coming in as Smith streamlined his squad.

Two former Academy players, Andy Rennick and Simon Webster, were next to go – to Scottish district sides - to further their international prospects.

Craig Moir also joined Borders and others to leave the Gardens were Luca Martin, Steve Brotherstone, Tom Kirk, Joe Shaw, Dom Malone and Ali Hepher.

The only new recruits were lock Williams, 31, Spanish winger Oriol Ripol, 26, from Rotherham, No 8 Simon Hepher (younger brother of Ali), returning to the Gardens after two years in France with Colomiers, and, most significantly of all, Bruce Reihana, who was already in England as part of the All Blacks Sevens squad for the Manchester Commonwealth Games.

Capped twice in 2000 by New Zealand, Reihana was given no encouragement that he would be recalled to the squad ahead of the 2003 World Cup and so he decided on a change of scenery. He would not be free to join Saints until November but fans got a taste of things to come when he starred in the 33-15 Commonwealth final win over Fiji.

At 26, Reihana was not looking for easy money in the twilight of a career but still had years of top class rugby in him as Northampton fans would discover. He had scored 44 tries in 71 games with Waikato Chiefs and was a star of the Super 12 tournament.

The New Zealand connection was further strengthened with the appointment of coach Brendon Ratcliffe, who had spearheaded the All Black elite player development programme and had been fitness trainer and technical advisor to the country's Under 21 squad. Ratcliffe had worked with Smith at Hawke's Bay RFU.

Innovator Smith sprang a real surprise in August by naming Pountney and Leslie as co-captains, although exactly how it would work was still to be fully thought out. It was a ploy Smith had used at Canterbury Crusaders when Todd Blackadder and Daryl Gibson shared the role.

Smith said: "I am trying to develop leadership throughout the team. The players understand the rationale behind the idea."

With Springbok lock Ackermann injuring a shoulder in the Powergen Cup final, Saints responded by snapping up Australian World Cup hero, Mark Connors, who had been due to join Bath before the deal fell through. Connors, 31, had won 28 caps for Australia at No 8 but could also play in the second row.

In a pre-season friendly with Stade Francais, Dawson, who introduced fans to the silver boot the previous season, wore the latest must-have accessory, fingerless gloves, much beloved by southern hemisphere players. He was joined by nine other players when the Zurich Premiership kicked off on a Friday night in Sale, which marked Grayson's 200th game, and brought a 24-21 defeat with an injury time Charlie Hodgson drop-goal.

Saints had scored two tries, while Sale had not crossed the line once and uncharacteristically Smith made disparaging remarks about referee Steve Leyshon. "I don't know him from a bar of soap. I bet he has never played the game. He doesn't know the game and at this rate we will all be on the bench and wearing tutus." A last-minute try from new boy Ripol looked to have salvaged a point until Hodgson's dramatic intervention.

Having seen his comments in print, Smith was utterly repentant and said so in his programme notes for the opening home game on September 7 against

Ian Vass: Smart try against Leicester Tigers in an impressive win at Welford Road

Newcastle. "I was not happy with my comments. Making excuses is not part of the culture we are trying to create here."

Connors made his debut in the Newcastle game and Jon Sleightholme, out for two years with a dislocated shoulder during which time he became the club's sponsorship manager, returned to the wing.

Overshadowing the team news was the unveiling of the Church's Stand as the final piece of the £6million jigsaw that had transformed the Gardens from ageing

153

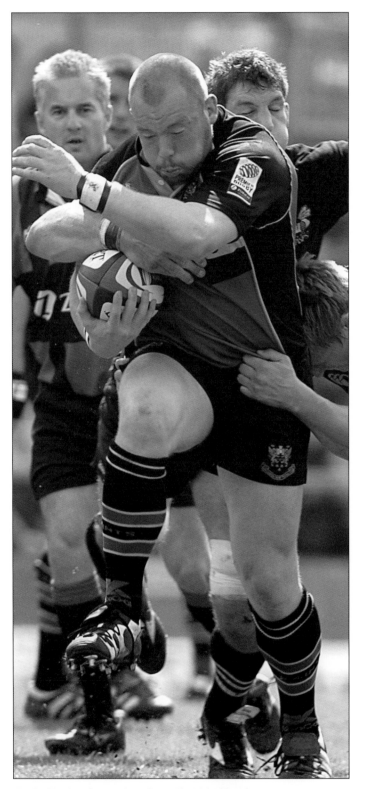

Early England promise: Prop Robbie Morris

October brought two commercial coups for the club – the opening of a retail outlet in Northampton town centre shopping mall, Peacock Place, and a contract with the RFU to stage three A internationals at the Gardens that season.

The month also brought success in league and Heineken Cup action. It brought controversy as well.

At either end of October there were league wins over Wasps and London Irish, sandwiched in between was a 32-9 success over Ulster, in a clash of two former European champions, and an agonising 23-20 defeat at Biarritz. The French won with a penalty seven minutes into injury time after Saints had led 20-13 on the hour.

Leslie did not make the trip because his wife Carmel was expecting their second child, although had she delivered the club was prepared to fly him out on Saturday morning by private jet. The happy event did not happen until the following Wednesday.

Pountney and Stewart were cited by the French but both were cleared by a disciplinary panel as was Biarritz No 8 Thomas Lievremont.

The club's first full trading year as Northampton Saints plc ended with a staggering turnover of £6.7million and a profit of £209,000.

In November the club was stripped bare by the autumn internationals. The Saints lost three players to England, another three to Scotland and one to Wales.

The team lost to leaders Gloucester 18-9 at Kingsholm and then to Leicester when the new stand got its official baptism from David Powell, one of five old players invited to the game: Don White, to represent the Fifties, Ron Jacobs (Sixties), Powell (Seventies), Vince Cannon (Eighties) and Gary Pearce (Nineties). Sadly Jacobs was too ill to attend and died that night at the age of 74.

Powell cut the ribbon and the teams kicked off at noon in front of a full house. The Tigers, also depleted by international calls, had infinitely stronger reserves to win comfortably 16-3. In the second half the fans got their first sight of Reihana. On the same day England beat New Zealand 31-28 featuring a memorable try-saving tackle from Ben Cohen in the dying seconds on Ben Blair.

The streamlining of the club continued with the scaling down of the academy. The Under 18 and development sides were disbanded. Fewer players would be involved and they would train with the first team squad. Too many youngsters were simply making up the numbers without any chance of becoming professional players.

Ackermann's battle to regain full fitness ended in failure and the South African was released after playing just four Premiership games. Matt Lord, 24, was signed from North Harbour with a reputation for being one of the hardest workers in the New Zealand club game and with an English father he was a UK passport holder.

With an expanding injury list and internationals unavailable, flanker Darren Fox, who had overcome two major operations and two years of injuries, came in at Leeds at the age of 22. Saints lost 26-19 after struggling to find 22 fit players.

The deteriorating situation gave fringe players a chance, including centre Chris Hyndman who came in for his first start in two years, while Reihana

relic to 21st Century splendour. It had all been achieved in 33 weeks spanning the summer months of 2001 and 2002. The capacity was now 12,600 and 10,213 saw the Newcastle game in which Sleightholme completed the fairytale with the opening try on 37 minutes on the way to a 31-13 win.

Wins followed over Bristol and Bath before Wayne Shelford's Saracens ended the early season burst at Vicarage Road, former Leicester stand-off Andy Goode collecting 26 points in a 31-19 success.

154

Able deputy: Aussie Shane Drahm proved a fine replacement for World Cup squad man Paul Grayson

played in his third position in as many games to launch his Saints career.

There were no such problems for England as Australia were beaten in sensational style, 32-31, having been 31-19 down, and then South Africa were routed 53-3.

The international players could have returned to a gloomy Gardens but a 35-7 win over Harlequins, described as a "season defining" game, meant there was renewed optimism as winter set in.

That confidence came magnificently to the fore at Welford Road on November 30 when the old enemy suffered a stunning defeat to end one of the greatest records of the modern game. Leicester had gone 57 games and five years unbeaten at Welford Road before Saints, full of cunning and invention, beat them 25-12 with three extraordinary tries.

The first from Pountney followed a mesmeric line-out routine with Thompson, the second was a blistering blindside swoop from Ian Vass, on for the injured Dawson, and the third came from Hyndman, following a dazzling change of direction that caught the Tigers defence on the wrong foot. The Saints had last tasted victory on Tigers soil in April, 1992.

The style of victory convinced many pundits that Saints were on the verge of great things. In fact, it was more significant for exposing chinks in the Tigers' armour that would eventually lead to the sacking of Dean Richards the following season.

Wayne Smith's trait of leaving out high profile players emerged again before the Heineken Cup tie in Cardiff when Tom Smith was punished for missing a players' meeting – somewhat harsh since he had not actually been informed of the meeting.

The Welshmen were beaten 25-11 at the Gardens and the following week Smith was reinstated for the return and was outstanding in a 31-0 one-sided rout. The prop scored two of four tries.

Smith was forced to defend his team selection for a Powergen Cup tie six days later when two-thirds of the side that faced Cardiff were left out for the trip to Division One side Orrell. Smith said he had faith in squad system but that faith was seriously undermined at Orrell, once a force in the land but a club that had been left behind by professionalism.

In an astonishing game the sides finished level at 34-34 thanks to a last-minute try from Jorgensen, only for the northerners to open up a 44-34 lead in extra time. Tries on 95, 98 and 100 minutes rescued Saints from a humiliating defeat and Smith was accused by his opposite number Ross Reynolds of "arrogance".

It was a charge totally refuted by Smith but there was no denying the Saints were fortunate to be in the next round. In the final game of 2002, Gloucester completed a league double by winning 16-13 at the Gardens. The planned assault on domestic honours was again faltering.

Jorgensen, having rescued Saints at Orrell, did it again in the second game of 2003, the return

Heineken Cup tie against Biarritz. Saints squeezed out a 17-14 victory thanks to the Australian's 78th minute try.

This atoned for a home defeat to London Irish the previous week, Smith commenting: "We got back our credibility with the fans after the manner of defeat against the Irish."

Cohen's try-scoring feats with Saints and England inevitably brought media attention but his agent was quick to rubbish reports in *The Sun* and *The Times* that the player might like a crack at American Football when his contract expired in 2005.

Saints entered their final Heineken Cup qualifying game at Ulster, knowing that a narrow defeat would still take them through to the quarter-finals for the first time since winning the competition in 2000. The game ended 16-13 to the Ulstermen, coached by South African Alan Solomons, good enough to top the group ahead of Biarritz. Bookmakers made Saints rank outsiders at 20/1 after the draw pitted them away to Toulouse.

Despite the inconsistency of league results, there was still interest in the Powergen Cup and on February 25 they faced fading giants Bath at The Recreation Ground, where the team's lucky mascot, Peter Jorgensen, struck for a third time. Trailing 29-

Mark Robinson prepares to offload before being clobbered by Wasps skipper Lawrence Dallaglio

Their lives would never be the same again: Steve Thompson, Matt Dawson and Ben Cohen in jubilant mood in the immediate aftermath of World Cup glory and (below) with Phil Pask, one of England's key backroom staff, squad member Paul Grayson being saluted in front of Northampton Guildhall by thousands of fans and Mayor Terry Wire

World Cup winning skipper Martin Johnson sets off in pursuit of powerhouse flanker Darren Fox

23, Jorgensen found the Midas touch in the dying seconds and Grayson's conversion sailed over to give Saints victory by 30-29 it was the only time they had led in the entire match.

Budge Pountney dropped a bombshell the following week when he joined John Leslie in quitting international rugby with a blistering attack on what he called the unprofessionalism of the Scottish RFU.

Pountney, who revealed that he had had a testicle removed after an injury sustained in the London Irish game, said he now had a different perspective.

He walked out of the Monday training session, saying he was no longer prepared to put his body on the line. "I am slogging my guts out and prepared to take risks for Scotland and so are all the players but people around us could not care less."

Pountney accused the Scottish RFU of penny-pinching with no water or food at training sessions and after they had beaten South Africa for the first time in 33 years, a message came through that there was to be no players' tab at the hotel bar.

He said that wives and girlfriends were left on their own "while the blazered brigade have their wives on Scottish RFU accounts."

His old club boss Ian McGeechan, in his last season as Scotland coach, said that Pountney had given "tremendous, unstinting service to the Scotland team." Club and country team-mate Stewart agreed that the players' efforts were not always appreciated.

February started badly with a 16-9 defeat at Wasps, which brought accusations from Smith that the players lacked vibrancy and enthusiasm. They had enough fire in their bellies to beat Saracens, which turned out to be one of Wayne Shelford's last games in charge before he and his coaching staff were sacked.

The A internationals had begun at the Gardens and the performance of prop Robbie Morris, just 22 appearances into his Saints career, prompted an England call from Clive Woodward due to a crop of injuries for the game with Wales in Cardiff. Morris, who won a silver medal in the discus at the Junior Commonwealth Games, won praise from coach Andy Robinson for his contribution to England's 26-9 win.

The Kassam Stadium, Oxford, was used for the Powergen Cup semi-final tie with old rivals London Irish. Games with the Exiles had become feisty affairs but this was as one-sided the previous year's final, this time with Saints triumphant, 38-9. There were tries from Steve Williams, Budge Pountney, Mark Connors, Peter Jorgensen and Darren Fox.

Awaiting them in the final were Gloucester, who would start favourites as they had beaten Saints twice on their way to topping the Premiership table.

Morris won a second cap against Italy and then Grayson's resurrection was complete when he was named in the squad for Scotland for the first time since playing in the 1999 World Cup quarter-finals and six weeks short of his 32nd birthday.

His selection came with monumental praise from Wayne Smith. "He is complete now as a footballer. I have never coached anyone better. He is working hard and now he is being rewarded for it. In Paul Grayson and Matt Dawson we have two of the better brains in world rugby. He (Grayson) is going to make a great coach one day."

He could not quite oust Wilkinson from the team but he sat on the bench while Dawson, Cohen and Thompson all played. Morris did not figure in the 22. England won 40-9.

The month ended with a 42-6 win in Dublin to give England the Grand Slam for the first time since 1995 – the perfect confidence booster for the World Cup in Australia. It was Dawson's 50th cap but to the scrum-half "it was just another game".

At the start of April the *Chronicle & Echo* found yet more words to say about another Twickenham final. Even though it was the fourth final in as many years, the fans did not tire of their trek down the M1. These were two giants of the game, Northampton representing the Midlands and Gloucester from the Westcountry, both with partisan supporters.

Games with the Cherry and Whites stretched back more than a century and the Gloucester boys had generally come out on top. This was to be no different although it was a more competitive performance than the team had given against London Irish. Indeed Saints led at half-time but failed to register a single second half point to lose 40-22.

The team chosen again had 14 internationals, the odd one out being lock Matt Lord. The emergency signing had earned his day in the sun and gave a fully committed performance. "He played like a donkey with the heart of a lion," wrote Terry Morris, which was presumably meant as praise.

The side was: Beal; Reihana, Jorgensen, Leslie, Cohen; Grayson, Dawson; Smith, Thompson, Morris; Lord, Williams; Connors, Pountney, Blowers. The replacements: Richmond, Stewart, Seely, Fox, Howard, Brooks, Hyndman.

Beal, coming towards the twilight of his career, scored a beautiful try and Grayson kicked the rest of the 22 points.

Keith Barwell dipped into his pocket to lay on a free bar for an hour at yet another Gardens wake.

The players had no time to dwell on a numbing day at Twickenham, for there was a Heineken Cup tie in France hard on its heels. Four players were left out and the club's newest international Robbie Morris could not even find a place on the bench. There was to be no great cup shock as weary Saints were dumped out of the competition, 32-16.

With the season now into mid-April there were still five league games to play and with it the annual scramble for Heineken Cup places. Smith's men won four of them, the only blip being a 22-20 defeat at bottom-placed Newcastle, to sneak into third place and the chance to take the championship via the play-offs.

Tom Smith missed the last two games with a broken toe, a freak accident after having a seizure and falling out of bed.

Gloucester topped the table, which in times past would have meant a league and cup double. Instead they could only claim that accolade if they beat either Wasps or Saints in the play-off final. Their eventual opponents were Wasps, conquerors of the Saints 19-10, who then stole the Cherry and Whites' thunder by taking the final.

The rejuvenated Nick Beal took the Player of the Year title, a fitting tribute for a brilliant career often dogged by injury. The news was not so good for Jorgensen, Stewart, Vass, Kelvin Todd and Simon Hepher, who were all released.

Jorgensen was desperately disappointed to go, while Stewart opted to drop down a division to go to Bedford, citing a strange reason. "I had offers from other Premiership clubs but I could not envisage playing against the Saints. I don't think you ever leave this club. You are always a part of it," said Stewart as his seven-year stint at the Gardens drew to a close.

Two players about to get the Gardens experience were Mark 'Sharky' Robinson, whose signing had been announced in February, and former Queensland Reds player Shane Drahm, 25.

Robinson, the 27-year-old former New Zealand scrum-half, and stand-off Drahm, one of many players to leave relegated Bristol, were unveiled on May 24.

With Dawson and Grayson expected to be in Australia for the World Cup, Smith had made sure the club had experienced replacements, admitting the gulf between the England pair and the club's youngsters was just too big.

A third player, French A prop Renaud Peillard, 30, was also supposed to act as a powerful influence during the World Cup but he only started two games – did not complete either of them – and was forced to retire in October with a serious neck injury.

The club got a pre-season boost by winning the Middlesex Sevens with a 31-5 success over Newcastle Falcons in the final. Saints were able to field a powerful squad as the league season kicked off later than normal because of the World Cup. Nick Beal, a World Sevens winner a decade earlier, led a squad of Blowers, Drahm, Fox, Howard, Reihana (winner of two Commonwealth rugby gold medals), Seely, Sleightholme and Tucker.

Apart from the usual pre-season warm-up games, Smith took his troops to Sandhurst Military Academy "to learn the lessons of war". Explained Smith: "We have likened ourselves to a battalion in the middle of a campaign."

There are, of course, casualties in war and the Saints suffered a major loss on August 29 in Cardiff, when co-captain Budge Pountney broke his ankle as he fell awkwardly in a tackle.

At the time it was not considered career-threatening but on February 11, the former Scottish captain admitted defeat in his bid to regain full fitness. It was

a sad conclusion for a dynamic rugby player, who never allowed success to alter his self-effacing personality. His desire to stay in the game was granted when he joined the Gardens backroom staff as assistant to Tim Exeter, who is responsible for the squad's conditioning.

The season kicked off in September on Friday the Thirteenth in a nine-try thriller at Sale, now known as the Sharks, which ended in a high-scoring draw, 37-37, thanks to a Drahm penalty in the tenth minute of injury time, underlining that he possessed a cool temperament.

Jon Sleightholme scored the first two tries of the season as Saints led 20-8 and then trailed 37-27 at Sale's new ground, Edgeley Park, home of Stockport County FC.

The ground came in for scathing criticism from

Nick Beal led a powerful side to success in the Middlesex Sevens

Gardens groundsman David Powell, who called in a "disaster waiting to happen" as the pitch was dangerously close to the spectators, Sleightholme twice being forced to hurdle advertising boards.

Blowers did sustain an injury but it had nothing to do with the proximity of the fans but everything to do with an elbow from Kevin Yates, that brought the prop a meaningless seven-day ban from the RFU. Blowers was taken to hospital with "facial damage" and the already depleted back row lost its most influential player for the immediate future.

Drahm was sought out by the media after his game-saving kick and the Aussie, half aboriginal, hinted that he wanted to be considered for England once he qualified by residence.

The man he had replaced, Paul Grayson, had completed his renaissance from Saints third choice to England international by being named alongside Cohen, Dawson and Thompson in the World Cup squad.

After a steady decline, the former all-conquering Bath invested heavily for the new season and it showed in a 24-6 win at The Recreation Ground, leaving Saints without a win in the opening two games.

That was put right a week later against Wasps, a match that marked the debut of gangly 19-year-old Jon Clarke, still an Academy player who had been snapped up with the collapse of Bristol. His injury time interception try sealed a 27-17 win but there was concern over the number of tries the side was leaking – 10 in three games.

As England prepared for their first World Cup game, Saints took on Rotherham Titans at Millmoor and came away with a 42-13 win. Blowers, back from injury, led the side and Wayne Smith was sufficiently encouraged to outline his plans for the World Cup period. He wanted the side to be in the top five when the players – primarily the English ones – returned.

Once again, London Irish undermined aspirations with a second successive league win at the Gardens (30-24) but it proved to be the only setback in October.

A 33-20 win over Newcastle Falcons at home was the result of a resurgent second half before the club made a little piece of history on October 25. Not since 1973 had the Saints completed back-to-back wins at Welford Road but they emulated that feat in some style. Leicester, tenth in the table and with three straight defeats behind them, were no match for Saints, who won 32-15 in a match that featured two tries from Reihana and an astonishing 60-metre drop-goal from an ebullient Beal. Leicester, who had clearly not brought in sufficient quality to cover for their World Cup absentees, could only respond with five penalties.

Such was the impact of the Robinson/Drahm combination that suggestions were already being made that the Dawson/Grayson combination might find it hard to dislodge them.

The Kiwi-Aussie alliance was under the microscope in the next game, a fiery encounter with Gloucester, which was marred by a mass brawl and the sending-off of Robinson. The scrum-half claimed he had merely gone to Drahm's assistance when the Aussie found himself the target of a clutch of Gloucester players.

At the time Saints led by a comprehensive 27-0 margin and performed heroically in the second half to win 30-17, twice being reduced to 13 players with yellow cards for Blowers and Tucker.

Robinson got his first taste of English justice with a three-week ban, a penalty he described as "harsh". Drahm got a two-week ban, later reduced to a caution, and Gloucester's Andy Hazell was suspended for 21 days.

There was a further ramification when it was revealed Tucker had played for an hour with a broken jaw.

The defensive frailties emerged again with successive defeats to Harlequins and Bath, both of whom posted scores in excess of 40 points. The latter defeat was a bitter pill as it meant an early exit from the Powergen Cup.

A semi-final elimination from the World Cup for the All Blacks led to speculation that Smith might regain his old job as chief coach if John Mitchell was not reappointed. Smith said he was not interested.

World Cup chat was banned in the Saints dressing room on November 22, after England's extra time win over Australia in the final. Smith wanted maximum attention given to the job in hand, which was a win over Leeds. That was achieved without too much fuss, 48-21, and any World Cup disappointment that Australian Drahm might have been feeling was not apparent as he collected 24 points, including a gem of a try.

With exquisite timing Robinson returned to the side for the return game at Gloucester on November 29, when Kingsholm fans had the chance to salute their World Cup trio of Phil Vickery, Trevor Woodman and Andy Gomarsall. The Saints' England quartet had been given time off to unwind but Woodman's introduction in the second half proved decisive as the prop somehow managed to elude three tackles to score a solo try, which changed the course of the game. From being in control Saints lost 29-20 and Smith described the performance as "dumb".

On December 2, Cohen, Dawson, Grayson, Thompson and England physiotherapist, former Saints flanker Phil Pask, who had been mobbed at Heathrow airport on their return, were paraded through Northampton on an open top bus before Mayor Terry Wire gave them a civic reception at the Guildhall.

Three days later it was back to the day job for Cohen, who started the Heineken Cup tie at Llanelli, while Grayson and Thompson were on the bench. Dawson did not figure in the squad. Grayson came off the bench to land two penalties that ensured a bonus point from a 14-9 defeat.

Playing rugby was almost incidental for the England boys as they lapped up a whirlpool of social occasions, the most conspicuous coming on Monday, December 8, when London came to a halt as thousands hailed their heroes from the pavement, office windows and shops. The players reciprocated by recording the event on digital cameras and camcorders, while friends and relatives talked to them on mobile phones in between the hand-waving. BBC and ITV covered the event live, the players met the Queen at Buckingham Palace, and the Prime Minister at No 10. Heady stuff.

A Kiwi to the rescue

All apart from Dawson, suffering with a groin strain, started against Agen as the Heineken Cup campaign continued on December 13 and a hat-trick of tries from Cohen made it the perfect return in a 25-10 win. Agen prop Jean-Jacques Crenca was suspended for a month after getting a red card for a sixth-minute head butt on Thompson.

A silly Twickenham exercise to cash in on England's highly marketable World Cup winning squad on December 20 – a meaningless fixture against the New Zealand Barbarians – was slammed by both Smith and Leicester's Dean Richards. This Mickey Mouse affair robbed Saints of Cohen and Grayson for the league clash with Tigers on the same day.

It made no difference as three Drahm penalties and a Blowers try gave Saints a 14-0 win, after the recently retired Rodber had been invited into the dressing room for a pre-match rallying call to whip up the emotions.

This was a typical Smith gesture, who had a deep sense of the game's traditions and spared no opportunity in trying to instil that attitude into his players. For example, on Fridays after training Smith introduced a jersey presentation at which an old-timer would be invited to say a few words about the club before giving out each player's shirt one by one. The likes of Don White, David Powell, Roger Horwood and even a non-player like Ron Slinn performed the ceremony and were highly honoured to do so.

The returning Dawson failed to see out the first half against Leicester, sustaining a calf injury to continue his low-key return from the World Cup.

The year ended with a 23-19 defeat at Newcastle, featuring four penalties from Wilkinson but also a recurrence of a shoulder injury and he was carted off to hospital for an x-ray.

The warm after-glow given off from the heroics in Australia continued as England were named Team of the Year by the BBC and Wilkinson the Sports Personality of the Year. All the squad received an MBE from the Queen at Buckingham Palace. From then on it was all downhill for England who by the start of the 2004/05 season had fallen spectacularly from grace.

January was a magnificent month for the Saints, starting with a 36-15 win at London Irish and culminating with a truly remarkable win in Agen in thick mud. In between Borders were beaten twice in the European qualifying group, unconvincingly 20-3 at the Gardens and then much more emphatically 39-3 in Scotland six days later before the splendid effort in the Stade Armandie, when Agen were beaten for only the second time in 58 games. Saints emerged 19-6 winners after a masterful tactical triumph achieved by a Reihana try and the boot of Grayson, not only with 14 points but with intelligent kicking for field position.

Because of the Crenca sending-off at Franklin's Gardens in the first game a shadow had been cast on the merit of the Saints win against 14 men for all but six minutes. There was no doubting the quality of the second victory against a shell-shocked Agen.

There could also be no argument about the result on February 1 when a heaving Franklin's Gardens played host to Llanelli Scarlets in a Heineken Cup quarter final in similar muddy conditions.

But where Saints had been so accomplished in France, they were ineffective against the Welsh although it took a freak 58th minute try from full-back Barry Davies to clinch victory. A Grayson chip looked full of attacking promise but Davies skidded in the mud on to the ball, taking him clear of the onrushing Saints players before regaining his footing to sprint clear. The Saints had nothing left to give and it showed six days later when premiership whipping boys Rotherham were only despatched 18-6. At last Dawson managed a full 80 minutes for the club. It coincided with the publication of his autobiography, *Nine Lives*, giving chapter and verse about some of the more controversial moments of his career, including a savage attack on South African World Cup skipper Corne Krige for his part in the violent England-Springboks clash at Twickenham in November 2002.

Of rather more concern to Saints fans was the shattering blow of Budge Pountney's retirement from the game, announced on February 11. The flanker's broken ankle had never sufficiently mended to allow him to return to rugby and the news brought instant tributes from the likes of Rodber and McGeechan, who had first spotted Pountney's potential on a pre-season tour of Lanzarote a decade earlier.

Lock Steve Williams also revealed in the same week that he intended to retire at the end of the season.

On the field Saints won a scrappy game at Saracens 22-19 and the next day, February 16, speculation about Wayne Smith's future ended when John Steele announced that South African Alan Solomons would be joining from Ulster as the new Saints coach.

Out of European and domestic cup competition, Smith had only league success to go for to mark his tenure at the club. Like others before him, Smith's era was destined to be: **so near yet so far**.

The search for the title was helped by an eight-try performance against Sale Sharks with two from Reihana on his way to being named Zurich Premiership's February Player of the Month before the players took what virtually amounted to a March break.

With only one fixture scheduled – on March 27 – Saints and Leicester filled the void with a friendly fixture called the East Midlands Challenge Cup, won by the Tigers 18-5, a throwback to a bygone, pre-professional era.

While Saints took a breather, the month was dominated by cup competitions and the Six Nations.

England's stuttering campaign reached its nadir with a home defeat by Ireland, described by Thompson as "one of the worst days of my life". Suddenly, the man hailed as the greatest hooker of his time was in danger of losing his place.

The list of impending departures continued to grow when the immensely popular Jon Phillips, who had matured from raw tearaway to respected senior lock, finally decided to join Bedford, whose coach Colin Jackson had been trying to get him for two years. Ironically, Phillips' proposed arrival at Goldington Road coincided with Jackson's return to New Zealand. A great club man, Phillips once confided that he did not mind not playing as long as the Saints won. Doubts also started to surface about Matt Dawson's future when speculation mounted that Solomons was interested in bringing Corne Krige to the Gardens. Since Dawson had described Krige as the "thug-in-chief" following the 53-3 England win in 2002, it was difficult to see how the two players could be club mates.

April 1 signalled the beginning of the end for John Leslie's Saints career. His contract was not being renewed and the club's co-captain decided to head back to New Zealand for a final fling with Otago.

Seven days later it was confirmed that one of the club's special sons, Nick Beal, was calling it a day after a roller-coaster career that touched great heights and dark periods of despair. Fifteen England caps were scant reward for a gifted player of scintillating pace, outrageous sidestep and almighty kicking power.

One player to buck the trend was Paul Grayson, who resisted overtures from Newcastle Falcons and other unnamed clubs, saying his heart was firmly at Franklin's Gardens.

Meanwhile, the Wanderers, whose efforts normally warranted just a paragraph at the end of a newspaper story, made their own headlines by reaching the inaugural Zurich A League Championship final, a double-headed affair against Harlequins.

Like the first team, which is good at reaching finals but not winning them, the Wanderers lost the first leg 28-15 and the return at Franklin's Gardens 54-13 for a 72-28 aggregate defeat. Jon Phillips was gracious in defeat: "You always back yourself to go out in a blaze of glory and it would have been nice to win the championship but Quins beat us well in the two games. Hats off to them."

The final matches of the season would determine whether Saints would go into the play-offs and the chance to give Smith a glorious send-off. Their ambitions were undermined by a 31-5 defeat at the newly-named Causeway Stadium, home of London Wasps. In a bid to accommodate all his star players, Smith named Dawson and Cohen as his centre pairings and did so again for the home encounter with leaders

Saints mascot Bernie joins in the farewell to Gardens' great Nick Beal, who retired from rugby to go into the world of finance. Proud son Tom joins him for the final moments of his Saints career

163

Bath 12 days later.

Wet conditions and the high stakes made for a war of attrition, broken just once by a wonderful try from rookie Jon Clarke, in a 16-6 win.

Saints had to win their last two games to fend off the challenge of Gloucester for third spot. On May 1 they won 31-15 at Leeds and scraped home 18-17 against Harlequins as Beal, Phillips, Connors, Leslie and Ripol made their Gardens farewell.

So the Saints were in the play-offs yet again to maintain their consistency for being on the fringes of glory. The only snag was that they faced an away draw at Wasps for the right to meet league leaders Bath in the final at Twickenham.

Despite all the hype surrounding Smith's farewell, the Saints were outclassed 57-20 to bring an air of anti-climax to what had been a brief but quality stay at the Gardens for the New Zealander.

The game was watched by a tearful Matt Dawson, who volunteered for the role of water-carrier. Two days earlier it had been announced that Dawson would be leaving Franklin's Gardens, a story that made front page headlines, probably to join Wasps.

Since the World Cup Dawson had made just four appearances for the club but he was not missed as much as he might have been because of the dynamic performances of the Kiwi who had replaced him, Mark Robinson.

The feisty No 9 and Reihana were two of the five nominations for the Zurich Premiership Player of the Year, eventually named as England lock Simon Shaw.

With his full-time availability to the Saints, Robinson was far better value for money and Grayson, who announced his retirement from international rugby at the same time, summed up how he felt the game was changing.

"Long-term loyalty to one club will become a thing of the past and will be replaced by players coming in from all over the world for two or three years before moving on."

On June 22 it was confirmed that Dawson had signed a one-year deal with the champions, linking up with his British Lions team-mate Rob Howley in an interesting battle for top spot. Dawson would get first bite of the cherry as Howley was due to miss the start of the season because of surgery on an injured wrist. The injury turned out to be terminal for Howley's career, leaving Dawson with an uncontested first-team place. Later he would say that he had been in a "comfort zone" at Northampton and was relishing the fresh challenge.

In July Solomons, South Africa's assistant coach in the Nick Mallett era before reviving Ulster's fortunes, unveiled his coaching team. Australian Frank Ponissi would be skills coach and New Zealander Adrian Kennedy followed Solomons from Ulster as forwards coach.

His initial signings had a distinctly Springbok feel to them: prop Robbie Kempson, winner of 37 South African caps, followed Solomons from Ulster and Selborne Boome came in to form a potential second row pairing with Connacht's Damien Browne, an Irish Under 21 international. Boome arrived with 20 Springbok caps to his name. Former South African A winger Wylie Human joined from Bath with experience of the Cats, Sharks and the Bulls Super 12

squads.

It was then announced that Krige had been released from Currie Cup duties with Western Province in time for the start of the 2004/05 season. He was immediately appointed captain with Steve Thompson as vice-captain.

The end of an illustrious career: Jon Phillips salutes the Saints fans

Chapter Fifteen
Over to you Budge

WAYNE SMITH was always going to be a hard act to follow. For Alan Solomons it proved impossible. And yet the regime started with one of the greatest tries seen in the club's 125-year history, voted the best of the season at the Zurich Premiership awards night. It was hailed by the new coach as the best he had been privileged to witness in a career spanning South Africa, Ireland and England.

It was the most spectacular of false dawns for Solomons, who spent three years at Ulster after his stint as an assistant coach to Nick Mallett with the Springboks. The pair led South Africa to Tri-Nations success in 1998 and to a world record-equalling 17 consecutive test victories.

Solomons also had a successful spell in charge of the Stormers, who achieved a home semi-final in 1999. Western Province also reached the Currie Cup final under his guidance in 1998. That experience counted for nothing at Northampton and he would be on his way out of the Gardens before Christmas with

Anxious times: After a bright start the Alan Solomons regime soon turned sour. After his sacking forwards coach Adrian Kennedy (right) resigned

Charm offensive: Controversial signing Corne Krige won over the fans almost immediately

Alan Solomons makes his exit from Franklin's Gardens leaving Budge Pountney and Paul Grayson to launch a salvage operation, which would go right down to the wire

the Saints facing their biggest crisis of the professional era.

There was no hint of the pall of gloom that would settle over Franklin's Gardens on September 4 when the Saints beat Bath 29-14 on the opening day of the season. Bruce Reihana's brilliant 68th-minute strike guaranteed a bonus point against the previous season's Premiership leaders in front of a 12,000 crowd bathed in sunshine. What made the score all the more remarkable was that it came after seven min-

utes of intense pressure from Bath with Saints leading 22-9. Bath had a five-metre lineout and four close-range scrums. Steve Thompson ripped the ball out of the hands of Andy Beattie as the flanker stretched over the Saints line to launch a try of breathtaking quality. Reihana, who was to be involved three times, flicked on behind his line to newcomer Marc Stcherbina who spotted the space and sprinted clear.

Co-centre Mark Tucker drove forward and found

Marc Stcherbina: The Aussie made an instant impact with a big part in the wonder try against Bath

Reihana, who ignored Ben Cohen outside him and fed Stcherbina inside. The Aussie centre brought John Rudd into the action and although he was held up short, he managed to get his pass to Reihana, who touched down.

Stcherbina, signed from Biarritz, had instantly shown the quality that had him knocking on the door of the Australian side but prior to the 2003 World Cup he had made a calculated decision to join the then French champions, replacing Joe Roff. One of his first games for the French side was against Saints in the Heineken Cup of 2002/03.

The Sydney-born centre was offered new terms for two years by New South Wales Rugby Union but received a far more lucrative two-year offer from Biarritz, where he became the centre partner of former Australian sevens captain Jack Isaac.

Explaining his decision to come to Europe, Stcherbina said at the time: "I was being realistic. I was starting to make my way to the top level with selection for Australia A and having a good Super 12 season. With this in mind I thought maybe I'm a chance of Wallaby selection but I wrote down the names of outside backs for next year. It's getting crowded. You have to back yourself, but at the same time you have to be realistic.

"It would have been a gamble for me to turn my back on this offer from France. I may never get it again."

He was to become a key component in the Saints side yet before long the side found scoring tries an elusive art and dropped to the bottom of the table like a stone.

One critic wrote that the try against was a clear message to the rest of the Premiership that Solomons "is knitting together a formidably tight, inventive unit from a squad that has undergone dramatic changes during the summer."

Solomons said: "The people we chose to come in are quality blokes and the people that are here at the Saints are quality blokes and I just felt there would not be any problem with anyone gelling and that has been the case.

"The people who have come in from outside have been warmly welcomed with a positive environment right from day one. It's a tribute to the players and speaks volumes for them."

A week later Saints inflicted a 45-13 defeat on Harlequins at The Stoop and were the early pacesetters. Solomons spoke of how the emphasis on set-pieces was the key to the flying start that had the pundits predicting big things.

"I believe it is vital to lay a foundation before you play rugby and the foundation has to be laid through your set-pieces," said Solomons.

"There are certain things which I have always said are not negotiable – your set-pieces, your defence and your conditioning, and if you get those right you can then build on your foundation. We try to provide a framework in which the guys play on the day – they have been given freedom within that framework."

The former Ulster coach added: "We've tried to create an environment in which everybody individually and collectively can realise their potential, and part of that is the enjoyment factor. Whatever sphere of life you are in, you do your job better in a positive,

Big blow: Saints had try and stave off relegation without the suspended Mark Robinson

enjoyable environment."

The environment became anything but enjoyable as an 18-12 defeat in September at home to Gloucester triggered a run of nine successive league defeats – eight of them under Solomons – the worst sequence of results since leagues were introduced. In 1987/88 the Saints lost six on the trot in Division Two and repeated that in 1994/95 when the side was relegated from the top division.

On November 22 came the inevitable – Solomons was sacked. It followed a 17-6 home defeat to newly-promoted Worcester Warriors. Keith Barwell made it clear that a victory would not have saved the South

Wasps recruit John Rudd

African. His captain Krige, who had made a favourable impression with the fans amid the despondency, stood down after a defeat that left Saints just one point off the bottom of the table.

In the ensuing weeks the South Africa media did its best to make Saints the villains of the peace with articles from Krige and prop Robbie Kempson criticising the sacking.

An emotional Krige was interviewed in the immediate aftermath of the dismissal, when feelings were running high but not published until some time later by which time he had risen from the ashes of the traumatic period to play a leading role in attempting to keep the team in the Premiership.

Kempson's comments were treated with contempt. In the 11 games he played the prop was rarely seen to good effect. He struggled to get fit and any thoughts that he would be as influential as fellow South African Garry Pagel had been were sorely misplaced.

Barwell and the board entrusted the mammoth task of reviving the season to the rookie coaching pair of Budge Pountney and Paul Grayson.

Pountney had leadership experience with Saints and Scotland, while Grayson had been tipped as top coaching material by no less a judge than Wayne Smith.

Barwell had anticipated great success under Solomons but that mood of optimism quickly turned to despair. Said Barwell: "Alan is a great coach but for whatever reason it has not worked out. The board feels it is now the appropriate time to make a change in the coaching structure.

"Saints now need to look within themselves but the club will be combing the world for another head coach. However, the ideal would be that our new temporary coaching set-up works out."

Following Krige's decision to stand aside, a ballot was held among the players for a new skipper. The South African's name remained in the frame. He very nearly won but was pipped by Steve Thompson to complete the reversion to home-grown values. Krige was named vice-captain.

Pountney's reaction was understandably positive. "This is a great honour for Steve and I know he will lead the team in an exemplary manner. I am also delighted Corne has decided to support Steve, as his experience will be invaluable."

In the wake of Solomons' exit Adrian Kennedy parted company with the club after being recruited as forwards coach during the summer. Kennedy said: "On reflection I felt that was the right course of action given the recent departure of Alan Solomons, my coaching partner for the last eight years."

Amid the league depression, the 2000 Heineken Cup winners had opened this season's European campaign with wins over Glasgow and Llanelli Scarlets. Now, two games into the Pountney-Grayson era, the side faced French aces Toulouse at the Gardens. The new regime had kicked off with a 27-16 league defeat at Newcastle and no-one gave them a prayer against star-studded Toulouse. Against all the odds, and much of the play, the Saints chiselled out a 23-21 win which was somewhat overshadowed by Ben Cohen's contract negotiations.

Cohen was clearly delighted by the change at the top. "I'd love nothing more than to commit myself to the club but I was put in a situation by someone who wanted me out."

Cohen revealed that he had received offers from

Legends of the Gardens: Gary Pearce, Don White and Dickie Jeeps were honoured at the inaugural Hall of Fame dinner. The three other given the honour were Edgar Mobbs, Ron Jacobs and Tim Rodber

Mark Tucker: Season-saving try against Harlequins

three other clubs but John Steele, now with the title of operations director, said: "Ben is valued extremely highly. We are in talks and I will be very disappointed if he plays anywhere else for the rest of his career."

Speaking after the Toulouse win Cohen commented: "This is where I started and this is where I want to finish but it's not down to me. I was unhappy but things have changed and we have found the spark again."

Victory was clinched by a late drop goal from substitute stand-off Shane Drahm and was a triumph for bulldog spirit, which was to resurface a month later at Llanelli.

The Saints lost the return in Toulouse, going down by a respectable 25-12, but could still qualify for the last eight as one of the two best runners-up if they could beat the Welshmen, who strongly fancied their chances at Stradey Park. For most of the game that confidence was more than justified until Thompson scored a sensational late try to give Saints an improbable 22-20 win.

Five days later the new skipper did it again to see off a dogged challenge from Glasgow with an interception try from inside his own half. So from the ashes of a wretched season the Saints had some-

how reached the Heineken Cup quarter-finals. Now came the major priority of saving their Premiership skins. There was also the domestic cup to play for, a trophy that was a far more likely consolation prize than European glory.

Bedford Blues, stacked out with ex-Saints players, were despatched 41-8 in the Powergen Cup and then came vital league wins over London Irish and Leeds Tykes. The 22-21 win over Irish at the Madejski Stadium signalled a welcome change of fortune and stopped the run of league defeats going into double figures.

January, 2005, started with a win over Leeds, against whom the Saints had been drawn at home in the cup on January 22. A semi-final berth seemed to beckon, particularly as the team had ground out five successive workmanlike wins in three different competitions.

Keith Barwell had gone into the cup week with sense of humour still intact by suggesting the Saints were in line for a treble: Winning the Powergen Cup, making a million pounds profit – and being relegated.

Alarmingly the first of those prophecies was shattered as Leeds pulled off a 24-19 win marred by controversy as 'Sharky' Robinson, by now a great

Gardens favourite, was red-carded by referee Chris White on 70 minutes for stamping on the head of former England hooker Mark Regan.

Television evidence was pretty damning but Regan later admitted in a TV interview that he had "milked" the incident, leaving supporters with an immense sense of injustice. Feigning injury has long been part of soccer, where the participants have scant respect for authority, and it was disappointing that a player in rugby had sunk to similar play-acting. The RFU accused Regan of bringing the game into disrepute but it did nothing to help Robinson. He had already been handed a massive 14-week suspension, which left the Saints without a major player in the quest to avoid relegation.

On February 8 Regan was fined £500 after being found guilty of the disrepute charge by a Rugby Football Union disciplinary panel. The hooker was also ordered to pay the £250 costs of the hearing.

He was cleared of a charge that he "intentionally exaggerated the effect of a stamp to his head in an attempt to persuade the referee to send off an opposition player". But he was found guilty of bringing the game into disrepute by stating in a television interview that he intentionally exaggerated the effect of the stamping.

The sense of injustice was compounded when Tykes then beat London Irish to reach the final on April 16 when they faced Bath, who scored an extra time win at Gloucester.

On the same weekend the cup finalists were being decided Saints were triumphing over runaway league leaders Leicester Tigers, admittedly missing a few stars but still with the likes of Martin Johnson and Neil Back running amok. Tigers had inflicted 83 points on Newcastle a week earlier to make a 26-11 Saints win all the more remarkable.

A week later Saints faced a Gloucester side deeply disappointed at losing to their old adversaries in the cup and Saints took full advantage by winning 26-18 at Kingsholm to lift them two places off the foot of the table – temporarily. The next day Harlequins won at Newcastle to enable them to leapfrog over Saints as the battle to avoid the drop started to yield some unlikely results.

The Saints win came without the services of Cohen (now with a new contract), who sustained a fractured cheekbone in a fund-raiser at Twickenham between the northern and southern hemispheres for the victims of the Asian tsunami disaster.

It also came in the week that John Steele announced his shock decision to resign as operations director at the end of the season, although he accepted an offer to stay on the board.

The former stand-off had seven years as a player and was the record points scorer with more than 1,500 points before being overtaken by Paul Grayson. The former Sandhurst-trained Royal Artillery captain, a chartered surveyor, had seen the club float on the stock market to become a plc, and contributed to the club emerging as a profitable business.

Apart from his work with the Saints, the former Perse School pupil had considerable other interests in the game such as being an executive director of Premier Rugby Ltd and a director on the England Rugby board, responsible for managing the elite game in England.

Father-of-two Steele said: "I have been very fortunate to have been a part of the Saints for 13 years. It is a unique club that I have thoroughly enjoyed working for. However, the time has come for me to look for new challenges and although it was a very tough decision, I have decided that I will move on at the end of the season."

Barwell said: "John has been a very loyal servant to the club and a great Saintsman. John will remain as a member of the board where his undoubted experience will be invaluable to us."

The "new challenge" of which Steele spoke came in June with the announcement that he was to become chief executive of UK Sport on 1 July, following three weeks trekking up Mount Everest to raise money for Sport Against Racism and the rugby injuries charity SPIRE.

Sue Campbell, chairman of UK Sport, said: "To be truly world class as an organisation we need world class leadership and this is what John Steele offers. He has a real vision and passion for sport in this country which, allied to his experience at the highest level in rugby, makes him the ideal candidate. We have a tremendously strong team at UK Sport, one that I am very proud to lead, and I know that John will both complement and enhance their ability to bring more sporting success to this country."

UK Sport has three objectives: improving the performance our elite athletes at Olympic and Paralympic level; increasing the UK's impact in the international sporting world and the number of major events held here; and leading the fight for ethical, drug-free sport through both testing and educational campaigns.

Steele was not the only person to leave the Gardens at the end of the season. The magnificent Andrew Blowers announced in November that this would be his last season at Northampton. After the intensity of English club rugby, Blowers had opted for the quieter waters of Japan. He signed a two-year deal with a club sponsored by Toyota.

Said Blowers: "Northampton Saints is home away from home but I feel now is the right time to move on and let some of the younger players come through."

Another expected departure, that of Bruce Reihana, did not materialise. It was announced in September that the flying Kiwi had signed a contract with the New Zealand Rugby Union and was rejoining Waikato.

Said Reihana: "I am a very proud New Zealander, and the opportunity to rejoin some of my old provincial and Super 12 team mates, along with the possibility of playing in an All Blacks jersey again, was too hard to resist."

NZRU deputy chief executive Steve Tew said securing Reihana was a great boost to New Zealand rugby. "To have a player of Bruce's calibre return to New Zealand and bring his experience and talent back to New Zealand rugby is a real win. It also sends a strong message that despite the economic advantages, which are available to our players overseas, there are wider benefits for players who choose to play their rugby here."

Both All Blacks coach Graham Henry and assistant

173

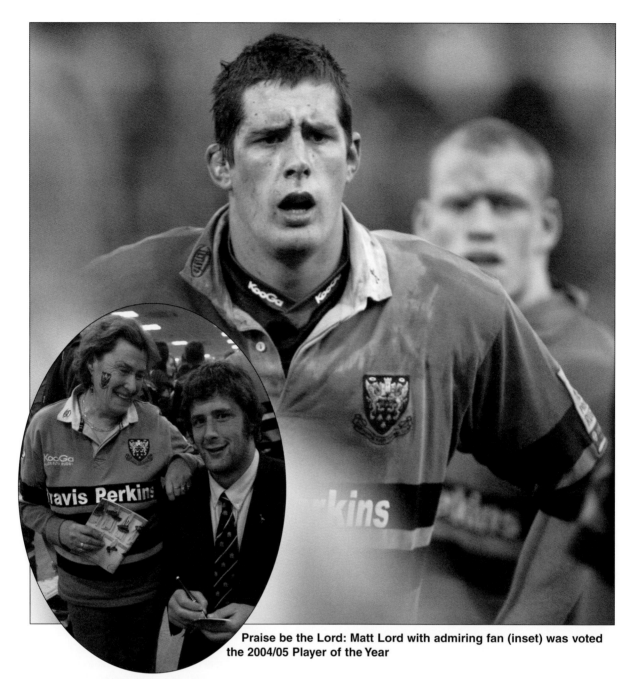

Praise be the Lord: Matt Lord with admiring fan (inset) was voted the 2004/05 Player of the Year

coach Wayne Smith were also enthusiastic at the prospect of Reihana going home.

"Bruce is a class player and his international experience and versatility will be a real asset to our Super 12 and provincial teams. Based on his form in Europe, we will also be interested to see him return to rugby here from an All Blacks selection standpoint," said Smith.

But on February 17, 2005, Saints announced that Reihana had signed a new deal to keep him at Franklin's Gardens for a further three seasons.

Mr Tew said: "He has our full support and we respect his wish now to remain in the United Kingdom. Obviously we were looking forward to having a player of his experience and calibre return to New Zealand but we understand the reasons why he is not able to come back this year."

Reihana said: "It has been a family decision to stay here. The people, the players and the whole set-up here is great and they have helped make my decision

so much easier."

It was great news for the Saints in their bid to stave off the dreaded drop. Reihana, in his short career with the club, had picked up the Zurich Premiership Overseas Player of the Year award, the PRA Players' Player award and was joint highest try scorer in the league, along with Steve Hanley, in 2003/04.

Barwell led the chorus of approval at Reihana's change of heart. "I am absolutely delighted that Bruce is staying. I am sure our fans will be thrilled because as a player, Bruce is irreplaceable, and we all love him dearly."

A week later the new head coach was making headlines and feeling the pain of a £2,000 fine. Pountney was charged with bringing the game into disrepute for comments made about referee Steve Lander in a press conference after the game against Saracens earlier in the month.

Pountney admitted the charge and apologised to an RFU disciplinary committee, which also handed him a six-week suspension from match-day coaching, but dropped the last two weeks. His ban ran until March 24 and prevented him from coaching from the playing enclosure, technical area, and tunnel. He was still able to sit in his usual seat in the Church's Stand and wear his ear and mouth piece.

Pountney had described Lander's performance "a disgrace" following the 21-20 home defeat to Saracens. Tempers flared just before half-time when Saracens coach Steve Diamond pushed Saints team doctor Jon Raphael, after scrum-half Kyran Bracken attempted to leave the pitch to go to the blood bin. Raphael suggested to Lander that the player was not bleeding. Lander ordered Bracken back on to the pitch and Diamond shoved Raphael before officials from both sides stepped in.

"Rugby was a real loser today," said Pountney at the post-match press conference. "Saracens tried to cheat by taking Kyran Bracken off with a blood injury when clearly he didn't have blood and then to have our doctor being shoved and pushed around by Saracens' first-team coach was an absolute disgrace.

"It shouldn't be part of rugby. They were caught cheating and I hope they hold their hands up. I think Steve Lander's performance in the first half was a disgrace and I am not worried about saying it.

"I have warned the Referees' Society that in the last few weeks they have been sending us referees that have not been making decisions. I thought his (Lander's) performance was totally inadequate although his performance in the second half was better."

Diamond denied shoving Raphael and hit back at Pountney by accusing Saints of cheating at the set-piece. "I was getting him (Raphael) out of our technical area – I moved him out of the way," said the Saracens coach. "Northampton's definition of cheating is different to mine. We had four or five scrums on the trot that they collapsed and that is the type of cheating that I would like to talk about."

Pountney had only been confirmed as head coach on the Tuesday prior to the Saracens game. His comments may have been unwise but they were the sentiments shared by the fans, who were perplexed by the amount of first half injury time played, exacerbated by the visitors scoring during that period in a game vital to both sides.

Amid all the tension of trying to stay up, behind the scenes the club was making plans to celebrate its 125-year history and one of the big ideas was to launch a Saints Hall of Fame. Board member Murray Holmes chaired a selection committee comprising of Nick Beal, David Powell, Ron Slinn and myself.

In broad terms I was considered to have most knowledge of the early years based on the research for the book *Oh When the Saints*, published in 1993. Ron has been a supporter since the Second World War, David has been associated with the club since the Sixties and Nick could advise on the modern-day players.

It was decided early on to select an elite group of no more than six and without too much argument we settled on:

● **Edgar Mobbs**, it would be unthinkable to have such a roll of honour without Mobbs appearing in it
● **Don White**, who was such a powerful force in

establishing the great post-War squads
● **Ron Jacobs**, also from the post-War period and the player with the most appearances for the Saints
● **Dickie Jeeps**, one of England's greatest ever players
● **Gary Pearce**, a beacon for the club during the dark period of the late Seventies and Eighties
● **Tim Rodber**, described by Beal as the most influential player at Northampton in the modern era, spanning the last vestiges of the amateur days and into the professional age.

An audience of over 500 was in the Rodber Suite to see White, Jeeps and Pearce receive their awards in person. Mobbs' great-nephew, also known as Edgar, collected his, former president Roger Horwood collected the one for Jacobs and Beal represented Rodber who had taken up a new job in the United States.

The idea is to induct two players each year with no shortage of worthy recipients, both dead and alive. No current players were considered as it was felt their time would come in due course.

The late revival that had started with unexpected victories over Leicester and Gloucester continued against Harlequins on the last weekend in March. On Saturday March 26, the Saints had a Mark Tucker try late into injury time and a Shane Drahm conversion to thank for snatching a vital 22-20 win on the same day that two other struggling teams, Worcester and London Irish, were beaten at home.

A day later there was a collective groan from Northampton, Worcester, Harlequins and the Irish as Leeds Tykes stunned league leaders Leicester Tigers, 23-22, to close the gap at the bottom. A Tykes defeat might just have sealed their fate. With three games to go of a fraught season the smell of relegation still would not go away.

It was, therefore, all the more surprising that it was revealed after the Harlequins success that match-winner Drahm had turned down an offer of a new contract with Saints and had signed for Worcester for the 2005/06 season. Fans were assured that Drahm was totally committed to the cause and yet there was an intriguing last fixture – at Worcester. It might prove to be a relegation-decider, a possibility that grew ever more likely after the round of matches on the weekend of April 9 and 10.

Saints, having gone out of the Heineken Cup in Toulouse 37-9 on April 1, then had three games to clinch survival. It did not start well as the Saints sank to joint bottom spot after losing 30-12 at Bath, while Worcester won at Newcastle, Leeds at Gloucester and Irish at Harlequins. Now just three points separated the bottom five clubs.

The final home fixture came on Friday, April 15, with Pountney portrayed as a Lord Kitchener-type figure on the back page of the *Chronicle & Echo* with a 'WE NEED YOU' headline urging the fans to raise the Franklin's Gardens roof for the 80 minutes against Newcastle Falcons.

The 12,000 fans did not disappoint and the players managed to do their bit…just. Spectators endured the full gamut of emotions, elation when Saints led 20-9 in the first half, to despair when Jonny Wilkinson kicked Falcons into a 22-20 lead, to renewed hope when Drahm edged Saints ahead with

One for the future: Paul Diggin

a penalty, to sheer agony when Wilkinson – on his return from injury – had a late penalty to condemn Saints to defeat and almost certainly relegation.

The only person in the stadium who thought he would miss was Paul Grayson, who knows everything there is to know about kicking at Franklin's Gardens. He assured Pountney that the kick would drift left and so it did. Newcastle also fluffed an attempted drop-goal in front of the posts and so if the fans felt the season's luck had been unkind to the team those final minutes helped to redress the balance.

The relegation issue paled into insignificance for the national media as Wilkinson's performance – coming off the substitute's bench for the final 50 minutes – was seen as far more newsworthy in the week when Sir Clive Woodward had announced his Lions party for New Zealand. He had left out England's World Cup hero with a proviso that if he proved his fitness he would be on the plane.

Steve Thompson was the only Saint to make the squad but that was the furthest thing from his mind as he saluted the fans at the end of a crucial game, when even the Newcastle players sportingly acknowledged the Gardens' supporters for their monumental effort.

Saints fans have always had a reputation for sportsmanship and even in the depths of despair as Wilkinson stepped up to take that vital kick there was a deathly hush in the stadium, infinitely more intimidating than moronic catcalls and booing such as the Saints experienced in Toulouse.

The Heineken Cup quarter-final had been switched to the town's soccer stadium to accomodate the 20,000 fans who wanted to see the game, many from Northampton. The more enlightened Toulouse fans were full of admiration for the commitment to the cause of the Saints supporters. Defeat in France was exacerbated by an injury to Andrew Blowers, concussed at a lineout, which caused him to miss the Newcastle match, before which there was a minute's silence for former full-back Roger Hosen, who collapsed and died while out walking with his wife and daughters in Cornwall. Among those in the crowd was former Saints captain Peter Sweet, who three days later died of cancer.

After the Newcastle win, Barr Construction moved into Franklin's Gardens to begin the next stage of redevelopment, enlarging the South Stand. The redevelopment involved extending the stand over the lake to make room for more seating, seven new boxes, a premium members' club, as well another bar and extra toilet facilities. The extra seating boosted the capacity from 12,100 to 13,600.

In just 10 years of professional rugby union, the Saints were now poised to have a stadium with very nearly double the capacity of its soccer neighbours, the Cobblers. In that time the Saints had more than doubled their fan-base. Doubts that domestic rugby could pull in big attendances were now well and truly dispelled. Each season new fans gave the sport a try, liked what they saw, and stayed.

They were seated in a a modern stadium, with excellent facilities, and watched some of the best players in the world, assuming, of course, that Saints were in the Premiership. For the start of the next 125 years that was so nearly not the case.

Saturday April 30, 2005, was one of vice-like tension with every single Premiership game having a bearing on the championship play-off places or the fight to avoid relegation.

Defeat for Harlequins at Leeds on the previous Tuesday made the London aristocrats favourites for the drop. The bookmakers had Worcester next likely for the drop and then the Saints. It was a fair reflection of the team's chances of staying up.

Saturday's fixtures all kicked off at 3pm on a day when league rugby came of age. Those who would advocate ring-fencing the elite to remove the threat of relegation would simply be making the matches into glorified friendlies.

The fixtures were: Bath (going for third spot and the championship play-offs) versus Leeds (hoping to complete the last part of an amazing escape act as well as proving their Powergen Cup final win over Bath the previous Saturday was no fluke), Gloucester versus Saracens (outside chance of third place), Leicester (second) versus Wasps (first) to see who would finish on top of the table (comprehensively the Tigers), NEC Harlequins (desperate not to tarnish

The man known as King Carlos: Saints fans will be hoping Carlos Spencer reigns supreme

their name with the stench of relegation) versus Sale (hoping to reward a great season with a third place finish), Newcastle versus London Irish (outside chance of going down) and Worcester versus Saints. Worcester allowed Saints just 500 tickets (you could not blame them for that) and my wife, a season ticket holder, tried various scams to try and obtain a ticket, including posing as a teacher from a Worcester school that had returned 50 tickets.

Nothing worked, so she joined thousands of others at Franklin's Gardens, where work had started on the South Stand and the pitch had been dug up, for a specially commissioned Sky TV viewing that cost the club £21,000 to stage.

I 'watched' the game on teletext in a Bedford newspaper office, punching the air with joy or the desk in frustration as the afternoon wore on. Watching it the next morning on Sky Sports confirmed what a nightmare experience it would have been to endure it live. Saints fluctuated from as high as eighth place to bottom spot during the afternoon as scorelines across the country kept changing.

Saints fans were grateful that Harlequins were playing a Sale side with a championship to play for and not out-of-form Gloucester or Newcastle. After all the issues had been decided the most distraught player of the weekend would have been Quins kicker Jeremy Staunton who had a late penalty to keep his side in the Premiership. Like Wilkinson he missed, Sale scraped home, and somehow Saints, despite losing at Worcester, had survived.

In those nervous final weeks they had beaten Harlequins with only seconds to spare and escaped against Newcastle with Wilkinson's missed kick. On television in the days leading up to the Worcester clash Barwell said that he had reconciled himself to the prospect of relegation.

The media had a field day and much of the pre-match publicity centred on whether Worcester-bound Drahm would play. The Aussie made it clear that he was not afraid to play, that there would be no conflict of loyalties, and that he would give his heart and soul to the cause. It was somewhat surprising, therefore, to see him named as a replacement in the team announced to the media.

It was even more of a surprise that long-term casualty Tom Smith and Andrew Blowers, who were also "definitely out", were on the field for the start of the game…along with Drahm. Clearly mind games were at work.

Drahm was as good as his word, kicking his goals and making a try for exciting youngster Paul Diggin, son of a Northampton publican. Near the end any conflict of interest was avoided when he was replaced by Paul Grayson for his final minutes as a Saints player. He kicked his 577th and last penalty in injury time for a total of 2,786 points, made up of 29 tries (145), 419 conversions (838), 577 penalties (1731) and 24 drop goals (72) in a career spanning 259 games between 1996 and 2005.

His last points contribution could not prevent Saints from going down, 21-19, leaving players and supporters to await the outcome at The Stoop, where Harlequins made a dignified exit from the Premiership. One image was particularly impressive, that of Harlequins captain Andre Vos at the end of

the game having the courtesy to sign autographs on the pitch for youngsters, who appeared to be oblivious to the air of despondency engulfing the ground.

None of the 2,000 supporters at Franklin's Gardens moved from their seat until news of the result at The Stoop came through and the relief was overwhelming, particularly for the Saints owner.

"I was at my lowest just after half-time when all the other games were going against us as well," said Barwell. "At the end, I was on the pitch and the players were asking me, but I didn't know until our team manager Lennie Newman came up and told me the Quins result.

"My feeling is one of fantastic relief. Both teams played magnificently, and neither side deserved to be relegated. Staying up is massively important for us, and we have to learn from it. In the second half of the league season, we won six of our last 11 games and picked up three or four bonus points, form that would have put us in the top four."

As one by one the club's South African contingent left, new faces were announced for the 2005/06 season, the most sensational of which was the mercurial No 10 Carlos Spencer.

News that he had visited Franklin's Gardens leaked out before the final game, although the All Black legend had not actually put pen to paper. Barwell was in no doubt that he had got his man with a typically flambouyant interview to the press.

He revealed that the 29-year-old stand-off had committed himself to a future with Saints even if they had disappeared into National League One.

"He hasn't confirmed he is coming, but Carlos's conversation was 'you have committed yourself to me with your offer of a three-year contract – I will commit myself to you, whether you stay up or go down'," said Barwell.

"He asked us to be quiet until the end of the Super 12 tournament. But unfortunately, if you go into the club shop, buy a few Saints shirts and have Carlos and number 10 put on the back, then go down to a bar in town showing off your Maori tattoos, it's obvious what is happening! It's not a done deal yet, but it is 99 per cent."

Ten days later the three-year contract was a 'done deal', potentially the most influential signing of the professional age for Saints. A playmaker was desperately needed when you consider the lack of tries from the backs in all competitions: Cohen (five in 24 games), Human (7-23), Reihana (3-27), Stcherbina (1-29) and Tucker (4-16).

Amazingly the lethal Reihana scored just one Zurich Premiership try in the opening game of the season against Bath. It was rightly named THE try by any player from any club in the season.

The club's Kiwi connection continued to grow with the signing of Sam Harding on a two-year deal from Super 12 champions Canterbury Crusaders to replace Blowers in the back-row.

Harding is the great-nephew of former Wales and British Lions captain Rowe Harding, who toured South Africa with the British Isles in 1924.

Harding, who was born in Perth, Australia, comes from a rugby family with his father and two uncles all playing for Western Australia. Harding won his single All Black cap against Fiji in 2002, aged just 21.

Chapter Sixteen
He tackled the job

The magnificent bronze scuplture that visitors see when they arrive at the main gates in Weedon Road paid for by the Barwell family in recognition of all the help given to complete the stadium redevelopment. There is an inscription on the base under the heading "THEY TACKLED THE JOB"

n the summer of 1996 coach Paul Larkin and physiotherapist Phil Pask sat in the old Trinity pavilion in the absence of Ian McGeechan to work out a training schedule for a full-time professional squad of rugby players.

After careful consideration of the priorities, Larkin said: "Right, that's the first two hours sorted out, what shall we do for the rest of the week?"

The anecdote underlines the learning curve faced by both players and coaches with the advent of full scale professionalism.

Ten years later a player's week has evolved from holding down a job with training on Tuesdays and Thursdays into five days of weight training, skill sessions, practise matches, practising set moves, analysis (of themselves and the opposition), media work and enforced rest.

After the decision of the International Rugby Board in August 1995 to make the game professional, the RFU decreed a moratorium for a season at the end of which no-one was much the wiser as to how the game would adjust.

At Northampton, professionalism is synonymous with the name of Keith Barwell. For a million pounds

he acquired the right to be the major decision-maker in what direction and at what speed the club would go. He was introduced to the Saints by Bob Carvell, one of the gang of seven that led the revolution of 1988.

"I had loosely supported the Saints since school when I used to come to the Mobbs Memorial game," said Barwell. "I knew Bob socially and at the time was living and working in Luton. I told Bob how Luton Town FC built and sold their sponsors' boxes. They cost around £14,000 each and the idea was to get ten punters to put up the money in return for a four-year sponsorship. No revenue would be coming in but the boxes were effectively built for nothing. Bob sold the idea to the new committee and asked me if I'd take the first box which I did."

Barwell's main sporting interest during this period was Northamptonshire County Cricket Club where he ran the membership drive. Despite getting membership into four figures, Barwell was frustrated by a lack of dynamism at the club.

He started to make things happen at the Saints as part of a three-man recruitment committee with Northampton businessmen Tony Hewitt and

Jonathan Howard. Their brief was to find players money-earning opportunities in much the same way that once existed at the cricket club in the days of Sir John Pascoe and British Timken.

One of their first beneficiaries was Ian Hunter, then a student in Leicester. He used to hitch-hike to Northampton for training sessions, so he was provided with a car.

"Players were greatly appreciative of what was being done for them. In Ian's case I still cannot understand why he didn't simply go and join the Tigers, who were on his doorstep," said Barwell.

When the game went professional, Barwell decided to embrace it. He wanted to get involved in the game, but to what extent? Said Barwell: "It was a big decision for me. I live a couple of miles from the Towcestrians ground and if I'd given them £5,000 to £10,000 a year they would probably have erected a statue of me." He decided to go the extra mile or, put another way, the extra £7.5million, about £2.5million of which has simply been written off. In the early years the then chief executive, Geoff Allen, would ring Barwell when there was a cash-flow problem and money would be forthcoming in return for shares

The initial £1million was to get the ball rolling. "The club had backs of the calibre of Matt Dawson, Paul Grayson, Gregor Townsend, Johnny Bell and Nick Beal. I realised we had to get the players on professional contracts or they would be snapped up by other clubs."

He also wasted no time in trying to recruit top calibre players from elsewhere. He tried to lure Martin Johnson from Leicester and had talks with the famous ABC Tigers front row of Darren Garforth, Graham Rowntree and Richard Cockerill. All stayed at Welford Road.

"When I bought the club I had no great plan, no great vision for the future. I probably knew less about rugby than the average fan on the Gordon Terrace. It was important to recognise my weaknesses.

"In the early days we were losing seven-figure sums a year and if you are a reasonable businessman you want to apply reasonable business rules – like making sure income exceeds expenditure.

"Clubs were in a hopeless position because there was nothing forthcoming from the RFU. We were just not getting a fair share of the money that was in the game.

"Traditionally sport in this country has its roots in the upper middle classes or even the aristocracy, be it the Jockey Club, lawn tennis, rugby or cricket. My objective in the early days involved working with other club owners to try and get what we could from the Nigels and Ruperts on the RFU. It was no good trying to do things in isolation. We had to work together."

In the first year of Barwell's reign the club received £425,000 from central funds. It now gets close on £2 million described by the Saints owner as "tolerable".

Barwell inherited Ian McGeechan as coach and soon discovered that hiring and firing did not come easily to the Scotsman. So when McGeechan was away with the Lions in 1997, he sat down with Larkin and drew up a shopping list that included South African prop Garry Pagel, Argentinian hooker Freddie Mendez and Samoan back-row ace Pat Lam.

Keith Barwell: Put the flesh on professional rugby at Franklin's Gardens

Not afraid to show his true colours: Keith Barwell and wife Maggie

"Our squad was based around an English elite of Tim Rodber, Matt Dawson, Paul Grayson and Nick Beal, who felt they were better than the rest. I wanted to upgrade the playing staff and at the same time break up this cosy cartel by introducing quality foreign players," said Barwell.

"I also thought that rugby would follow soccer and introduce a transfer fee system, so I paid Newcastle £100,000 for Pat Lam and £50,000 for Freddie Mendez and the same for Jon Sleightholme. With that squad we should perhaps have done better."

He was also mindful of how McGeechan had operated most effectively with a hard man at his side such as Jim Telfer with the Lions. Barwell set his sights on Sale No 8 John Mitchell and met the Kiwi in cloak-and-dagger circumstances at East Midlands Airport. The deal did not get off the ground as Sale refused to let him go. Considering his subsequent work with England and the All Blacks Mitchell could have been the perfect foil for the Scotsman

181

Modesty to splendour: The old Gordon Terrace that has been replaced by the Tetley's Stand that has more than 3,000 seats and room for 1,500 standing.
Bottom left: The view from the press box and (bottom right) the TV tower, where a bank of closed circuit televisions monitor the ground and where TV pundits are based

The main stand had reached the OAP stage before being replaced by the Church's Stand that can seat more than 3,000 spectators. The new stand is still watched over by the mighty Express Lifts Tower, built between 1980 and 1982. In 2001 Wilcon Homes Midlands Ltd applied for consent to demolish the tower. which was given a Grade II listing in 1997 because it is a unique structure in Britain and is a demonstration of the importance of lift technology to modern tall building construction. It is, of course, also a huge local landmark, famously dubbed the Northampton Lighthouse by DJ Terry Wogan. The tower is now surrounded by a housing estate, which has proved useful to the Saints for providing accomodation for new players, particularly those from overseas.

Front and rear views of the new £3 million tier to the South Stand which required pylons being driven into the lake. The latest redevelopment involves extending the South Stand over the lake into the village area of the ground to make room for additional seating, seven new boxes, a premium members' club, as well another bar. The extra seating will boost Saints' current capacity from 12,100 to 13,600. The players' gymnasium is also being moved there.

As you were: The Sturtridge Pavilion today (above) has stayed pretty much the same as when the bottom picture was taken in 1999

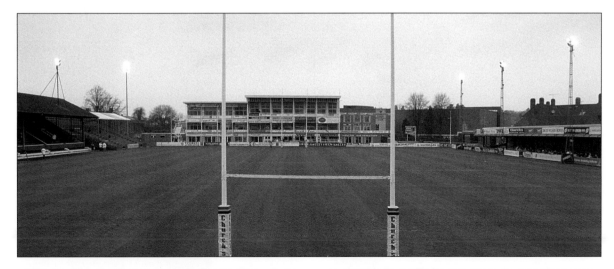

With trophies continuing to elude Saints, Barwell did not stand in the way of McGeechan when he was approached to coach Scotland. He sought the views of McGeechan and the senior players as to a successor and pulled John Steele's name out of a hat that contained a host of international coaches.

As well as being an inspirational leader, Barwell can also be exasperating. He listened as the board members expressed their preferences and then announced that he had already given the job to Steele, at the time director of rugby at London Scottish.

Irrespective of events on the pitch, the lasting lega-cy of Keith Barwell's leadership is the transformation of Franklin's Gardens.

Well into the 1990s, supporters were still expected to use smelly tin sheds as a lavatory. Now those vital calls of nature can be accommodated in style.

Prior to the magnificent revamp of the Gardens at a cost of more than £6 million, the four sides of the ground had evolved from grassy banks to:
■ a main stand, creaking with old age
■ gently sloping terracing on the opposite side
■ the Sturtridge Pavilion, once the club's pride and joy, behind one goal
■ and the Lake End, for the most part still just a

185

The old Franklin's Gardens Hotel, which has stood on the same spot for well over 100 years. Now it plays host to commercial director Allan Robson and his admin staff as well as the club shop that has grown enormously under the management of Jo Norman (above), whose team will take as much as £20,000 on a match day. The shop started life in a tiny room at the entrance to the Sturtridge Pavilion, formerly run by New Zealander David Coleman (right), who persuaded Wayne Shelford to come over. Some want the old hotel building knocked but so far it has resolutely stood its ground.

The portrait of the Rev Samuel Wathen Wigg is surrounded by portraits of all the club's internationals.

Honour Those Who Have Gone Before You: Wayne Smith was fascinated by the club's past and had this board put up at the entrance to the players' tunnel. It is signed by current and immediate past players

grassy knoll until the arrival of temporary seating

It was a hotch-potch stadium which Barwell was keen to develop but where was the money to come from? Having ploughed millions of his own fortune, estimated at £60 million in the *Sunday Times* Rich List, putting him in joint 666th place with, among others, comedian Rowan Atkinson and Sir Mark Thatcher, Barwell and the board decided on a share issue.

From the ordinary Saints fans, the club raised around £1.2million, Tim Rodber and Harvey Thorneycroft's company sold hospitality boxes that brought in a similar figure, Carlsberg-Tetley brewery

put in £1.8million for a stand that replaced the Gordon Terrace, decked out in the brewery's blue and cream colours, Church's shoe company weighed in to replace the West Stand, and the Travis family, who had supported the club for decades, offered the remaining one million pounds still needed to build the South Stand. A discreet plaque says the stand is in memory of Ernest Travis (1874-1937) and his son Ray (1911-1988), both lifelong supporters of the club.

In the space of two summers the redevelopment was achieved. All that remained of the old Gardens was the patchwork Sturtridge Pavilion, that now looks

187

The back wall of the Tetley's Stand records the names of the Saints' founder shareholders, and the other side of the wall is the massive Rodber suite that includes a collection of international shirts donated to the club that adorn the walls near the players' post-match eating area

The plaque that commemorates the opening of the Church's Stand by five legends of the Gardens each representing a different decade: Don White, Ron Jacobs, David Powell, Vince Cannon and Gary Pearce. Sadly Ron Jacobs was too ill to attend

slightly at odds with the rest of the stadium, although there are plans in the pipeline for that as well.

In May 2001, contractors, Barrs of Glasgow, set up camp at the Gardens and had their men at work from 7am. Four months later the Tetley's and South stands were ready for use. The following summer the operation was repeated to create the Church's Stand under which sit the dressing rooms in more or less the same location as their predecessors. The away dressing room is comfortably bigger than at most other grounds and the home facility is positively sumptuous, each changing position being screened from its neighbour. Beyond the dressing room is the treatment centre where the team of physiotherapists and fitness advisers operate leading to a social area exclusively for the players. At the other end of the Church's Stand are the press facilities with an interview room and an area from where photographers can electronically send their pictures from laptop computers.

The press box itself, once a hopelessly inadequate area on one side of the players' tunnel, is now at the back of the stand with at least double the amount of seats. TV and radio are also accommodated in comparative luxury from just a few years previously when cameramen sat alongside committee members and the whole thing was a logistical nightmare.

In the gap between the Church's Stand and the Sturtridge Pavilion is a brick-built structure for use by match day safety officer Ian Edwards with a bank of CCTV screens to monitor crowd behaviour, although having never once seen a policeman in uniform at

the Gardens the cameras must almost be redundant. The 12,000 capacity includes terracing in front of the Tetley Stand, an appeasement to those who just could not face sitting down to watch.

The old Salon dance hall-turned nightclub was acquired for more than a million pounds and demolished to allow the new-look Gardens to be seen from the Weedon Road and the entrance is made all the more grand by an imposing life-size statue of two rugby players, a personal touch from the chairman and his family to thank all the people who contributed to the revamping of the ground under the heading 'They Tackled The Job'.

Barwell's one regret is that there is no room to replace the Sturtridge Pavilion with a stand of equal stature to the other three.

In 2005 Barwell moved into his own suite of offices at the Gardens above the reception area of the Tetley's Stand, where he can oversee his many interests in and out of rugby, including a continuing role in newspapers, an area where he initially made his fortune. And at an age when most people are contemplating retirement, Barwell took on the enormous task of chairman of the West Northamptonshire Urban Development Corporation (UDC), a body set up to drive the growth and regeneration of Northampton, Daventry and Towcester.

A statement from the Office of the Deputy Prime Minister said that Barwell had "proved himself as a dynamic business leader and champion of Northampton's rich sporting and cultural heritage."

Apart from Barwell's work with the Saints, John

Prescott's office pointed to his close involvement with the restoration of one of Northampton's most interesting 20th century buildings, 78 Derngate, formerly the home of the Bassett Lowke family, the interior of which was designed and furnished by Charles Rennie Mackintosh. The restoration spawned a television series shown on satellite TV, presented by antiques expert Eric Knowles.

Jeff Rooker, Minister for Regional Development and Regeneration said: "The UDC provides the opportunity to ensure that Northampton, Daventry and Towcester are enhanced through sustainable, high quality development, and that the history and character of the area is protected. I am confident that Keith is the person to drive forward that process as chair of the UDC."

He has a three-year term of office with a goal of helping the next generation, a worthy project now that he has taken more of a backseat at the rugby club.

Uncomfortable with the role of sugar daddy, he desperately wanted the club to be able to stand on its own two feet. To that end Allan Robson was appointed in January 2000 and has overseen an impressive growth in the business side of the Saints.

With a background in football at Birmingham City and Watford, Robson has spearheaded a campaign that has seen turnover go from £3million when he took over (and a loss of £1.7m) to a turnover of £9.7m (and a profit of £773,000).

In 2000 there were 2,413 season ticketholders. Now there are more than 8,000 and the average gate in 2004/05 was 11,976 with 11 of the 14 home games sold out. Leicester and Gloucester were the only clubs to be watched by more home supporters but the Saints are the most profitable club in the country.

Revenue is derived from three sources:
- ■ Rugby (gates, bars, club shop) brings in £4m
- ■ Premier Rugby supplies just short of £2m
- ■ Sponsorship, hospitailty and conferencing around £4m

As a turbulent 2004/2005 rugby season drew to a close with the Saints still uncertain of their status for the following season, Barwell gave an interview to the BBC in which he outlined his blueprint for the future growth of the game.

Said Barwell: "It's been an interesting time since taking over at the club. Do I enjoy it? Yes. Do I wish I could bail out? Sometimes.

"Running a rugby club is like when you're on a skiing holiday and you find yourself on your bum at the bottom of the crevasse. You think to yourself, 'what the hell am I doing here?'

"Looking at the game as a whole, there's no doubting things need to be sorted out – most notably the club-v-country debate. But the problem is we all have such different agendas.

"We went from a time when rugby was just beer and blokes to a point where England won the World Cup. I understand that England coach Andy Robinson wants access to his players but the clubs obviously have a problem as we share a £30m wage bill between us. That's paid for by our supporters and they want to see their big-name players play. They are customers and they have a right.

"I'm not whingeing here, it's just everyone has to be a bit more realistic, and it's disappointing so far we've not been able to sit around like adults and talk about it.

"People are talking about all these injuries and then blame the Zurich Premiership and the clubs for playing too many games. But Andy Robinson is looking

for too many excuses. Ten years ago there was one pre-Christmas international and four Five Nations matches. Now there are three before Christmas, five in the Six Nations, an extra Barbarians game and then a summer tour. It's not us causing the problem.

"I appreciate we do have to allow England access to their players, but I don't think central contracts is the answer. If that came in, we wouldn't have any England players here. We'd go for more retired internationals and foreign players. And that's not good for the future of the international side.

"As it stands it doesn't make all that much sense to have England players for a director of rugby who is under pressure to win...or get sacked.

"It's difficult to know what the solution is. My fellow chairmen aren't for it but I like the idea of franchising the country – a sort of take on the past proposal of Rob Andrew and Fran Cotton. For example, there's nothing for Devon and Cornwall. What I'd propose is Northampton, for example, to be the team for East Anglia, Leicester representing the Midlands and taking on board Coventry and Nottingham, etc. That way we can finally make rugby a national

First the Jubilee Hall, then the Salon and then various nightclubs and now the Saints staff car park

From fan to commentator: James Knight interviews Paul Grayson at the Madjeski Stadium after the dramatic last-gasp match-winning kick against Llanelli in the Heineken Cup semi-final

which it's not despite what people think.

"I envisage us having 14 franchises, which falls in nicely geographically, and it would certainly be the way to ensure more English players coming through. But this looks unlikely to ever happen. I proposed it to my chairmen and, while there was some support, the majority don't like it. As a result, the game looks likely to fumble on in the dark, which is a shame.

"The other issue I'd like to see changed is the salary cap. It doesn't take a genius to work out that if you are struggling with a squad of 25-30 players, you need a bigger squad. For that, you need more money. I'd prefer the idea of 50-man squads. Therefore players could be changed on a more regular basis and avoid the issue of burn-out."

During the same period Barwell gave an interview to a rugby magazine in which he criticised the end-of-season play-offs that determine the champions. He was promptly fined £10,000 by Premier Rugby, the organisation that runs the top clubs. The fine has been suspended for a year and Barwell has promised to button his lip.

It is a pledge he is certain to break even though it is one he has also made to his new coaching team of Pountney and Grayson. He has also taken the pressure off them by laying down a two to three-year timetable to rebuild the squad.

"I have perhaps been too concerned with making the club self-sufficient. Everybody who has invested in the club wants only one thing in return – success.

"One European Cup win – by one point – is not much to show for 10 years of professionalism and I was utterly traumatised by how close we were to being relegated.

"It is probably going to take two to three years to get back to where we want to be on the pitch. The

perfect Saints side would comprise two or three retired internationals (such as a Back or a Johnson), three or four world class overseas players, a couple of big-hearted players in the Jon Phillips/Matt Lord mould and a crop of homegrown players."

To achieve the latter Saints are reviving their Academy policy with a seven-figure budget for the next three years to comb the country for the best young talent.

The finer details he leaves to others but there is no doubting that he still likes to be at the forefront of the major decisions, like talking terms with agents.

Most players now have an agent, unthinkable 10 years ago when the game went professional, but unlike football they are not in the business of touting their clients around every couple of years.

"In football agents pretty much dictate to players," said Robson. "Everybody in football knows it is wrong but they are powerless to stop it. In rugby there is still a degree of integrity and players are not looking to change clubs all the time looking for the highest bidders.

"The players, not the agents, are the dominant force. I suppose we deal with about three or four agents, who have to be bonded.

"The majority of the players are very good at selling the club, most do community work and many actually enjoy it.

"Off the pitch the players are not superstars and can be relied upon to represent the club in a professional way. It means they stay popular with the supporters even if they go through a loss of form on the pitch."

When Nick Beal joined the Saints he did not have the slightest inkling that a few years later he would have an agent negotiating his contract.

When the game went professional he was making

a twice weekly trip after finishing work in Watford and remembers missing only two sessions – once for bad weather and the other because of a motorway stand-still.

"There was no talk among the players about becoming professionals. We were taken as much by surprise as anyone else," said Beal. "There had been speculation in the press about the southern hemisphere players being so much more powerful and stronger and questioning whether these guys were really amateurs. This became increasingly evident during the 1994/95 season."

Beal and his wife Jo had already moved to Northampton when the momentous decision was made. "When it was decided the squad would become full-time rugby players we were sinply told how much the club intended paying us and we just accepted it. It was not a lot of money."

Beal worked for AXA at the time and to supplement his income the company paid him a retainer. It meant I was no worse off and, of course, I had the option of not going full-time but the chance to improve myself as a player was the real incentive.

"Also the chance to be paid to do the thing you love is everyone's ambition. I did not need any persuading."

Beal was amazed at how quickly his body developed. "I had never done any weight training in my life. Now it was all about weights, recovery, speed. There was specialist skills coaching rather than pure rugby training.

"It meant we were able to catch up with the southern hemisphere pretty quickly and the reason England were able to win the 2003 World Cup."

Beal got himself an agent as more money started to wash around in the game, simply because he had no idea of his worth as a rugby player.

"An agent is able to say to you what your status would be worth to another club – how much they would be prepared to pay you. It is then easier for a third party to negotiate on your behalf and I was never unhappy with what I was offered at Northampton.

"I was never once tempted to leave to play somewhere else and the coaches felt the same way. Geech and Wayne Smith loved their time at the Saints. Wayne was fascinated by the history of the club and constantly instilled into the players how much it means to the town.

Beal paid a huge compliment to Keith Barwell, not just for provinding the financial muscle to power professionalism but also for his passionate commitment to the Saints.

"He is a fan as is Maggie (his wife) and Leon (his son). Win or lose Keith was always in the dressing room afterwards," said Beal.

"As far as I know he has never interfered in team selection – he leaves that to the person appointed to do the job. But if we were having a bad time, he was certainly not averse to spelling out the consequences. He used to refer to it as being in Happy Street or Misery Lane.

"Where the club have been superb is in ring-fencing themselves from the perils of relegation. It would still be a massive blow but by developing the business potential at the Gardens they have made the club self sufficient."

Beal retired on his terms at the end of the 2003/04 season. "I finished when I wanted to finish and not through injury or the club telling me it was time to go.

"I played for 12 seasons and loved every one of them. My body was telling me it was getting harder to recover and I did not want to be hobbling about at 45.

"It was the perfect end. In my last home game we won and I scored with virtually my last touch and my two sons were mascots," said Beal, who had chosen Saints ahead of Wasps when he was making a name for himself at Wycombe as a teenager.

He had no desire to stay in the game and is now a partner with David Williams Financial Services.

He gives the switch to professionalism an unqualified endorsement but what do the fans make of it? One man supremely well able to offer an opinion is James Knight, 47, a supporter since the age of 11.

Now the voice of Radio Northampton at the Gardens, Knight dragged his dad down to a game in 1969 and it was a turning point in his life.

He became utterly besotted with following the Saints and at one stage he and another fan, Neal Roff, were on many occasions during the Seventies and Eighties virtually the sum total of away support.

"In those days the Supporters' Club would occasionally run a coach to an away game. When there was no coach we would go by car together."

It was an exercise in masochism. "Not only did we know the Saints would lose but by 20 to 30 points," said Knight.

When the 1988 revolution came along, Knight was the Supporters' Club secretary which gave him a place on the general committee.

"Some of them were rather patronising towards me and my item was always last on the agenda. There was no doubt in the main they were stuck in the 1950s and if the revolution had not succeeded I dread to think where the club would be today."

Knight was the obvious choice when Radio Northampton jumped on the Saints bandwagon in the aftermath of the 1991 Twickenham appearance against Harlequins in the Pilkington.

From being 50 per cent of the away support, Knight was just one of 20,000 'fans' the club acquired for that game.

Supporters club chairman Ron Slinn asked Knight if he fancied doing some work for the radio station, commentating on Saints matches.

"It was not a lot in those days. A minute or so at half time and at the end and then a considered piece later on," said Knight, who has never looked back.

Still a civil servant, he has travelled to every Saints ties in Europe and now does commentary on the entire 80 minutes with guest summarisers such as Budge Pountney before he became head coach.

He admits he is passionate and biased but he tries not to let that reflect in his commentary.

As for the game, Knight considers it infinitely superior to even 10 years ago and having seen the enormous changes at the Gardens he has no hesitation in saying that professionalism has done nothing but good.

"The entertainment value is – most of the time – superb and the facilities at Northampton are second to none. It is easy to see why so many people have started watching the game. It is a different world to when Neal and I were traipsing around the country."

So what of Roff? in 1993 after the publication of my

first book he gave it a totally unsolicited thumbs-up. "I feel every player should be given a copy to make them realise just what a great club they are coming to," was the gist of his comments.

At the advent of professionalism Roff became disillusioned by how the game was changing and ended his love affair with the Saints.

His is a rare dissenting voice. The staggering attendance figures – more than double that watch the town's football team – and the ever expanding stadium are testament to the growing popularity of rugby in Northampton.

Shortly after he took over, Barwell told then chief executive Geoff Allen that he had no intention of being pointed at in the street as "the man who ruined the Saints". He has been as good as his word.

In the early days Allen would have to hold out the begging bowl when there was a cash-flow crisis, which was a regular occurrence, and money would be forthcoming.

Now the ends more than meet but at the same time the club has remained loyal to its traditions. Even old

wounds have been healed and the likes of Don White and Dickie Jeeps raise a glass to the club's benefactor.

The players wages, although light years away from those of footballers, are starting to reflect the entertainment industry they are in. Many also have outside business interests such as in the case of Ben Cohen (a building company), Steve Thompson (a menswear shop) and Paul Grayson (rugby coaching).

The downside is that future players may become a bit more one dimensional brought on by the tight knit environment of professional sport and the single-minded dedication that is needed to excel.

It is all a far cry from those early pioneers but the desire to make Northampton rugby club great was apparent even then and maybe one day the likes of Albert Orton, player, secretary, treasurer, will be inducted into the Saints Hall of Fame.

There have been lean years but in the main it has been more Happy Street than Misery Lane for Northampton Rugby Football Club.

Here's to more of this: A soaked Keith Barwell drinks from the Heineken Cup in the Saints dressing room. Among the well-wishers were Irish fans and former hell-raisers Peter O'Toole and Richard Harris

193

APPEARANCES & POINTS

1895 to 2005

(records before that destroyed by fire)

Compiled by:

Ian Watson, Bob Taylor and Roy Gordon

Year	Try	Conversion	Drop Goal	Penalty	Mark
1890/91	1	2	3	2	3
1891/92	2	3	4	3	4
1893/94	3	2	4	3	4
1905/06	3	2	4	3	3
1948/49	3	2	3	3	3
1971/72	4	2	3	3	3
1977/78	4	2	3	3	—
1992	5	2	3	3	—

To help evaluate the points scored by players in the following chapter, the above guide illustrates what each type of score was worth, including a 'Goal from a Mark', which has now been abolished

Late greats: Ron Jacobs (left), who was named as one of the inaugural six members of the Saints Hall of Fame, and Jeff Butterfield, who was very close to joining him. Jacobs made a record 470 appearances for the Saints and Butterfield 227. They are seen here at the launch of the first Saints history book in 1993. Both have since died.

Name	Years	Appearances	Tries	Pens	Cons	DG	Pts
ABELL E T	**1895-1900**	**5**	**0**	**0**	**0**	**0**	**0**
ABBEY J	1995-1996	1	0	0	0	0	0
ABBOTT G W	1906-1907	8	0	0	0	0	0
ACKERMANN J	2001-2002	7	0	0	0	0	0
ADAMS A	1909-1910	1	0	0	0	0	0
ADAMS D	1977-1979	4	0	0	0	0	0
ADAMS E	1901-1902	6	1	0	0	0	3
ADAMS JR	1928-1931	17	4	0	0	0	12
ADAMS M	1937-1938	1	0	0	0	0	0
ADAMS P L	1928-1931	5	2	0	0	0	6
ADAMS R A	1946-1947	2	0	0	0	0	0
ADAMS R H	1952-1953	1	0	0	0	0	0
ADKINS G	1945-1951	149	0	5	12	2	46
AITKEN R	1968-1969	2	1	0	0	0	3
ALLAN C	1998-2000	19	3	0	0	0	15
ALLBRIGHT T	1929-1930	2	0	0	0	0	0
ALLEN C	1989-1998	110	0	0	0	0	0
ALLEN G F	1964-1970	24	21	0	0	0	63
ALLEN G R	1962-1972	136	27	1	1	8	110
ALLEN K L	1966-1975	88	28	4	3	4	123
ALLEN M	1994-2002	182	71	0	0	0	355
ALLISON M G	1950-1963	29	3	0	0	0	9
ALLISON W	1931-1936	55	7	0	1	7	51
ALSTON P	1984-1992	195	57	0	0	0	228
AMOS M	1965-1966	1	1	0	0	0	3
AMPS M J	1952-1956	14	2	0	0	0	6
ANDERSON C E	1919-1920	1	0	0	0	0	0
ANDERSON F	1901-1903	9	0	0	0	0	0
ANDERSON J S	1937-1939	2	0	0	0	0	0
ANDERSON K	1955-1956	1	0	0	0	0	0
ANDREWS	1942-1943	1	1	0	0	0	3
ANDREWS A C	1904-1905	1	0	0	0	0	0
ANDREWS E	1946-1947	1	0	0	0	0	0
ANDREWS H	1902-1903	2	0	0	0	0	0
ANDREWS R	1937-1938	1	0	0	0	0	0
ANDREWS R	1895-1896	1	0	0	0	0	0
ANDREWS T	1971-1974	28	10	0	0	5	55
ANSELL H	1938-1939	2	0	0	0	0	0
ARCHER C S	1922-1925	32	11	0	0	0	33
ARCHER R	1942-1943	1	0	0	0	0	0
ARNEIL R J	1971-1975	51	7	0	0	0	28
ATKINSON C B	1919-1920	1	0	0	0	0	0
ATKINSON C B	1906-1907	1	0	0	0	0	0
ATKINSON E G W	1922-1923	14	10	0	0	0	30
ATKINSON R	1939-1940	1	1	0	0	0	3
ATTERBURY F	1895-1896	3	0	0	0	0	0
ATTERBURY H	1895-1904	123	13	0	0	0	39
ATTERBURY J L	1900-1906	63	4	0	0	0	12
ATTLEY R	1958-1959	1	0	0	0	1	3
ATTWOOD G	1919-1920	1	0	0	0	0	0
ATTWOOD JACK	1941-1942	1	1	0	0	0	3
ATTWOOD JIM	1940-1943	20	6	0	0	0	18
ATTWOOD JOHN	1940-1941	9	2	0	0	0	6
AUCKLAND E	1903-1904	4	1	0	0	0	3
AUCKLAND J	1904-1905	2	0	0	0	0	0
AUSTIN W B	1912-1914	32	2	0	0	0	6
BADGER G W	**1962-1965**	**3**	**0**	**0**	**0**	**0**	**0**
BAGNALL D	1967-1969	18	6	0	0	0	18
BAILEY D	1995-1996	1	0	0	0	0	0
BAILEY G H	1930-1933	40	19	0	0	0	57
BAILEY J E	1937-1939	31	7	0	0	0	21
BAILEY N	1947-1954	156	74	0	0	0	222
BAILEY R C	1920-1922	2	0	0	0	0	0
BAILLON L B	1930-1940	17	1	0	3	0	9
BAILLON L C	1902-1903	1	0	0	0	0	0
BAILLON M	1934-1936	4	0	0	0	0	0
BAILLON R O	1930-1942	161	0	17	43	3	149
BAINES M P	1898-1899	1	0	0	0	0	0
BAINES P	1985-1988	4	0	0	0	0	0
BAIRD I	1975-1977	2	0	0	0	0	0
BAKER A	1955-1956	8	0	0	0	0	0
BAKER L	1992-1993	3	0	0	0	0	0
BALDWIN G	1990-1995	105	11	0	0	0	48
BALDWIN G W	1921-1927	42	0	0	0	0	0
BALDWIN K	1967-1969	11	4	0	0	0	12
BANGHAM K	1968-1969	26	1	0	0	0	3
BARAK M	1928-1932	14	3	0	0	0	9
BARBER F	1946-1947	9	1	0	0	0	3
BARBER S	1946-1947	1	0	0	0	0	0
BARKER	1945-1946	1	0	0	0	0	0
BARKER A E	1928-1931	13	1	0	0	0	3
BARKER F	1909-1910	1	0	0	0	0	0
BARKER J W	1928-1929	1	0	0	0	0	0
BARKER N	1965-1966	1	0	0	0	0	0
BARKER T	1948-1952	59	2	0	0	0	6
BARKER T	1984-1988	16	0	0	0	0	0
BARNES H	1910-1911	16	3	0	0	0	9
BARNES L E	1912-1914	14	10	0	0	1	34
BARNES S	1996-1998	23	2	0	0	0	10
BARNETT R D	1952-1953	1	0	0	0	0	0
BARNFIELD T	1898-1905	49	4	0	0	0	12
BARON P	1967-1969	32	4	0	0	0	12
BARRATT H C	1913-1914	5	2	0	0	0	6
BARRELL J M G	1957-1958	1	0	0	0	0	0
BARRETT M D	1954-1956	2	1	0	0	0	3
BARROW M P	1923-1924	4	1	0	0	0	3
BARROW R J L	1980-1983	57	3	0	1	1	17
BARTON C J J T	1910-1913	15	1	0	0	0	3
BARTON C L A	1913-1914	1	0	0	0	0	0
BARTON J	1953-1958	46	3	0	0	0	9
BASS J G	1924-1928	14	0	0	1	0	2
BATEMAN A	1999-2001	49	5	0	0	0	25

Name	Years	Appearances	Tries	Pens	Cons	DG	Pts
BATES G	1901-1902	8	0	0	0	0	0
BATES N	1979-1981	4	1	0	0	0	4
BAXTER B W J	1954-1957	37	1	0	0	0	3
BAXTER D	1950-1955	2	0	0	0	0	0
BAXTER R C	1897-1898	1	1	0	0	0	3
BAYES D	1990-1991	4	0	0	0	0	0
BAYFIELD M	1991-1998	98	9	0	0	0	43
BEAL N	1992-2004	268	74	21	21	3	482
BEALES A	1992-1997	31	7	0	0	0	35
BEARD K J	1950-1952	12	0	0	0	0	0
BEASLEY J N	1903-1921	122	57	0	1	0	173
BEASLEY R N	1904-1914	11	3	0	0	0	9
BEATTIE A G N	1945-1946	1	0	0	0	0	0
BEATTIE R	2004-2005	9	0	0	0	0	0
BEATTY L	1945-1946	1	0	0	0	0	0
BEAVERS A	1963-1964	4	0	0	0	0	0
BEDDALL H B	1902-1903	2	0	0	0	0	0
BEDDOW T	1995-1999	33	1	0	0	0	5
BEEBY C H	1932-1933	1	0	0	0	0	0
BEGBIE E	1908-1909	1	0	0	0	0	0
BEIM D	1967-1968	1	0	0	0	0	0
BELL A P	1934-1949	141	31	0	0	0	93
BELL F	1947-1948	2	0	0	0	0	0
BELL J	1995-1998	41	18	0	0	0	90
BELL J B	1940-1941	7	3	0	0	0	9
BELLAMY C	1968-1969	1	0	0	0	0	0
BENJAMIN C	1994-1995	2	0	0	0	0	0
BENNETT I	1981-1985	40	0	0	0	0	0
BENNETT L	1904-1905	2	0	0	0	0	0
BENNIE D	1953-1954	1	0	0	0	0	0
BENNIE J D W	1960-1961	1	0	0	0	0	0
BENSTEAD G T	1980-1983	16	0	0	0	0	0
BENTLEY J	1928-1930	4	1	0	0	0	3
BENTLEY S	1928-1929	2	0	0	0	0	0
BERRIDGE L	1966-1968	10	1	6	7	0	35
BERRIDGE M J	1945-1955	251	8	0	0	0	24
BERRILL C	1897-1898	3	0	0	0	0	0
BERRILL H E	1899-1901	21	5	0	0	0	15
BERRILL J	1972-1973	2	0	0	0	0	0
BERWICK E	1948-1949	1	0	0	0	0	0
BERWICK E	1940-1941	20	2	0	0	0	6
BERWICK M	1940-1941	1	0	0	0	0	0
EVAN W J	1962-1965	37	4	0	0	0	12
BIDDLES C	1907-1908	1	0	0	0	0	0
BIGNELL P	1972-1981	177	76	0	0	0	304
BINYON J C	1919-1926	122	22	3	1	0	77
BIRCH A	1945-1946	4	0	0	0	0	0
BIRCH E	1945-1951	77	9	0	0	0	27
BIRCH F N	1926-1929	63	15	0	0	3	57
BIRCH J	1906-1913	99	14	0	0	0	42
BIRCH W	1948-1949	1	0	0	0	0	0
BISHOP E W	1895-1896	1	0	0	0	0	0
BLAIKIE R	1979-1988	9	0	0	0	0	0
BLAKEMEN W H	1921-1922	1	0	0	0	0	0
BLAKISTON A F	1919-1926	87	39	0	0	0	117
BLAND D	1951-1958	50	5	0	0	0	15
BLASON A	1939-1940	6	3	0	0	0	9
BLASON R	1945-1946	5	1	0	0	0	3
BLEWITT O	1985-1988	40	12	0	0	0	48
BLINCOW W	1907-1908	1	0	0	0	0	0
BLOOMFIELD J M	1940-1946	2	0	0	0	0	0
BLOWERS A	2000-2005	126	11	0	0	0	55
BLOWERS H	1998-1999	1	0	0	0	0	0
BLUNT G	1905-1907	21	1	0	0	0	3
BLYTH A	1997-1999	25	3	0	3	0	21
BODDINGTON F W	1938-1939	1	0	0	0	0	0
BOOME S	2004-2005	14	0	0	0	0	0
BORDIEU M P	1941-1942	1	0	0	0	0	0
BORRIE H	1931-1932	2	1	0	0	0	3
BOTT J	1911-1913	3	0	0	0	0	0
BOUNDY L M	1934-1937	28	14	0	0	3	54
BOURNE J	1910-1911	1	0	0	0	0	0
BOWLES V	1954-1955	16	2	0	0	0	6
BRADBURY P	1945-1947	29	1	0	0	0	3
BRADLEY J T	1933-1942	90	17	12	39	1	169
BRADSHAW G	1902-1903	1	0	0	0	0	0
BRADSHAW K	1938-1949	38	9	0	0	0	27
BRADSHAW W	1910-1914	53	22	0	0	1	70
BRAMHALL J	1996-2001	44	3	0	0	0	15
BRANSDON J	1924-1925	1	0	0	0	0	0
BREAM W J	1941-1922	16	1	1	16	0	38
BRENNAN J	1954-1956	2	1	0	0	0	3
BRENTON A	2001-2002	2	0	0	0	0	0
BRETT J A	1938-1939	2	0	0	0	0	0
BREWSTER P	1945-1947	30	2	0	0	0	6
BRIDGEMAN D	1984-1985	3	0	0	0	0	0
BROOKES A E	1934-1939	118	21	11	30	4	172
BROOKES F R	1905-1906	1	0	0	0	0	0
BROOKES L	1976-1977	3	0	0	0	0	0
BROOKES L A L	1905-1906	2	1	0	0	0	3
BROOKFIELD E	1945-1946	1	0	0	0	0	0
BROOKMAN F	1951-1954	34	1	1	1	3	17
BROOKS J	2000-2004	58	8	0	0	1	43
BROOKSLEY J	1909-1910	9	1	0	0	0	3
BROOMFIELD E	1945-1954	52	2	0	0	0	6
BROTHERSTONE S	2000-2002	30	0	0	0	0	0
BROUGHTON-BLACK C	1941-1942	1	0	0	0	0	0
BROUZET O	2000-2002	49	0	0	0	0	0
BROWN C H	1897-1898	1	0	0	0	0	0
BROWN H J C	1954-1958	24	8	3	4	0	41
BROWN J	1954-1958	16	1	7	6	0	36
BROWN J F	1926-1927	1	0	0	0	0	0
BROWN K A R	1966-1968	27	3	0	0	5	24
BROWN L	1923-1927	16	5	0	0	0	15

Name	Years	Appearances	Tries	Pens	Cons	DG	Pts	Name	Years	Appearances	Tries	Pens	Cons	DG	Pts
BROWN LOUIS	1926-1927	1	0	0	0	0	0	COCKING H P	1904-1906	3	0	0	7	0	14
BROWN R	1983-1984	1	0	0	0	0	0	CODLING A	2004-2005	2	0	0	0	0	0
BROWN R T	1964-1965	1	0	1	1	0	5	COHEN B	1996-2005	196	81	0	0	0	405
BROWN W	1900-1911	84	4	0	9	0	30	COLBOURNE A	1904-1905	2	0	0	0	0	0
BROWNE D	2004-2005	30	0	0	0	0	0	COLDWELL T	1941-1942	1	0	0	0	0	0
BRUCE C P	1958-1959	3	0	0	0	0	0	COLES F	1920-1921	1	0	0	0	1	4
BRYAN T A	1977-1979	25	4	10	5	2	62	COLES F C	1901-1911	219	60	15	144	12	561
BRYAN T H	1958-1960	6	3	0	0	0	9	COLES M A	1938-1939	19	1	0	0	0	3
BRYANT P	1980-1984	16	1	0	0	0	4	COLES W E	1938-1939	3	0	0	0	0	0
BRYSON A F	1904-1905	2	0	0	0	0	0	COLEY D	1955-1962	166	34	4	17	1	151
BUCKLAND P	1988-1990	2	0	0	0	0	0	COLEY E	1920-1934	292	83	0	0	0	249
BUDGEN C	2001-2005	75	4	0	0	0	20	COLLIER T	1911-1922	45	3	0	0	0	9
BULL A G	1909-1926	220	37	0	0	1	115	COLLINS A	1900-1902	3	0	0	0	0	0
BULLOCK P	1969-1972	34	3	0	0	0	18	COLLINS B	1900-1901	2	0	0	0	0	0
BURDER H G	1908-1910	10	1	0	0	0	3	COLLINS G	1907-1908	1	0	0	0	0	0
BURDETT T	1908-1909	3	1	0	0	0	3	COLLINS J	1907-1908	2	0	0	0	0	0
BURDITT J	1979-1981	2	0	0	0	0	0	COLLINS L	1907-1908	1	0	0	0	0	0
BURGESS B	1990-1995	11	1	4	7	1	33	COLLINS T	1910-1914	121	7	0	0	0	21
BURKE A	1920-1923	12	1	0	0	0	3	COLLINSON H F	1932-1933	6	0	0	0	0	0
BURKE G	1900-1908	200	11	0	0	0	33	COLLINSON W A	1929-1930	1	0	0	0	0	0
BURKE H	1906-1912	117	9	0	0	0	27	COLLIS R	1948-1949	1	0	0	0	0	0
BURKE HERBERT	1911-1914	18	0	0	0	0	0	CONNORS M	2002-2004	51	4	0	0	0	20
BURKE M	1997-1998	2	0	0	0	0	0	COOK E C	1908-1923	263	219	0	1	0	659
BURKE W	1921-1922	2	0	0	0	0	0	COOK H	1945-1946	2	0	0	0	0	0
BURNS C	1987-1992	64	12	0	0	0	48	COOK J G	1932-1933	11	4	0	0	0	12
BURR F N	1908-1909	4	5	0	0	1	19	COOK R	1999-2000	1	0	0	0	0	0
BURROWS P	1945-1946	1	0	0	0	0	0	COOKE D A	1979-1981	18	0	0	0	0	0
BURTON	1907-1908	5	2	0	0	0	6	COOLEY J R	1963-1972	221	52	0	0	24	231
BURTON F J	1932-1936	2	0	0	0	0	0	CORBETT M	1948-1949	1	0	0	0	0	0
BURWELL F G	1942-1943	2	0	0	0	0	0	CORNISH A	1998-1999	3	1	0	0	0	5
BURWELL T	1983-1985	9	0	0	0	0	0	COSBY J	1951-1952	3	0	0	0	0	0
BUSHELL G A	1975-1977	3	0	0	0	0	0	COTTON B	1968-1969	1	1	0	0	0	3
BUSWELL C R	1959-1960	1	0	0	0	0	0	COTTON G	1912-1913	5	0	0	0	0	0
BUSWELL R G	1942-1943	1	0	0	0	0	0	COULSON J B	1934-1941	35	4	0	0	0	12
BUTCHER A	1939-1940	4	0	0	0	0	0	COUTTS I D F	1952-1959	110	13	0	0	1	42
BUTCHER A J	1945-1946	1	0	0	0	0	0	COWAN C D	1941-1942	1	0	1	0	0	3
BUTCHER W	1930-1934	25	1	0	0	0	3	COX A P	1895-1896	4	0	0	0	0	0
BUTTERFIELD J	1951-1963	227	67	0	0	2	207	COX F M	1895-1897	2	0	0	0	0	0
BYRDE E W	1906-1907	1	0	0	0	0	0	COX R I	1977-1989	126	1	0	0	0	4
BYRNE B	1966-1967	5	0	0	0	0	0	COX W M	1895-1896	1	0	0	0	0	0
								CRANE H H	1929-1930	1	0	0	0	0	0
CADE G	1911-1912	1	0	0	0	0	0	CRANE T H	1971-1981	69	14	0	0	0	56
CAMPBELL R B	1903-1904	1	0	0	0	0	0	CRASK H W	1923-1933	23	5	0	0	0	15
CAMPION R P	1961-1962	1	0	0	0	0	0	CREASY R H	1942-1943	1	1	0	0	0	3
CANHAM A L	1956-1962	83	2	0	0	0	6	CRICK P C	1934-1937	18	2	0	0	0	6
CANHAM J	1980-1984	13	1	0	0	0	4	CRISP E J	1919-1921	31	1	1	34	0	74
CANNELL L B	1945-1960	138	97	2	7	2	317	CROFTS R J	1935-1936	2	1	0	0	0	3
CANNON V G M	1973-1989	438	74	0	1	0	298	CROSON A	1982-1983	3	0	0	0	0	0
CAPLAN D W N	1981-1984	51	2	2	4	1	25	CROSS C	1959-1960	3	0	0	0	0	0
CARTER A	1901-1903	4	2	0	0	0	6	CROSS S	1919-1920	2	0	0	0	0	0
CARTER P	1974-1980	59	6	40	31	2	212	CROSS W	1898-1899	1	0	0	0	0	0
CARMELL A E	1958-1959	1	0	0	0	0	0	CROUCH T	1899-1903	23	5	0	0	0	15
CARR W	1988-1991	32	7	0	0	0	28	CROWTHER S N	1902-1903	2	0	0	0	0	0
CARTER S	1992-1993	1	0	0	0	0	0	CUBITT J G	1973-1988	232	43	16	14	2	254
CASSELL J	1994-1998	44	9	0	0	0	45	CULLINAN J	1926-1927	1	0	0	0	0	0
CASSY M J W	1940-1942	5	3	0	0	0	9	CUMMINGS A	1926-1927	1	0	0	0	0	0
CASTLEDENE W	1906-1907	2	0	0	0	0	0	CUMMINS A G B	1899-1903	47	13	0	0	0	39
CATLETT A	1991-1992	2	0	0	0	0	0	CUMMINS N	1926-1927	2	0	0	0	0	0
CATLEY S	1897-1898	29	2	0	0	0	6	CURGENVEN G	1896-1897	4	0	0	0	0	0
CATLIN G	1977-1978	1	0	0	0	0	0	CURRIE J R	1906-1907	4	0	0	0	0	0
CAUSEBROOK D J	1979-1986	24	1	0	0	0	4	CURTIS D	1948-1950	9	3	0	0	0	9
CAVE C F	1895-1900	65	57	7	70	0 (1)	332	CURTIS T A	1920-1925	69	10	0	0	0	30
CAVE G H	1908-1910	17	1	0	0	0	3								
CAVE P	1927-1928	5	0	0	0	0	0	DAKIN R W	1901-1904	2	3	0	1	0	11
CAVE P H	1895-1899	8	0	0	0	0	0	DANGERFIELD T V	1959-1960	2	0	0	0	0	0
CAVE R H V	1919-1920	1	0	0	0	0	0	DANIELL A E	1900-1901	1	0	0	0	0	0
CHALMERS A	1897-1912	436	32	0	1	0	98	DANIELS A D	1928-1937	88	18	2	11	2	90
CHAMBERLAIN S	1958-1959	1	0	0	0	0	0	DANIELS C P	1952-1967	320	27	0	0	0	81
CHANDLER A	1925-1930	19	0	0	0	0	0	DANIELS P	1899-1901	2	0	0	0	0	0
CHANDLER J	1996-1999	51	4	0	0	0	20	DANTIACQ D	1998-1999	22	3	0	0	0	15
CHAPLIN J E	1948-1949	4	0	0	0	0	0	DARLOW J	1903-1904	12	0	0	0	0	0
CHAPLIN S	1921-1922	13	1	0	0	0	3	DAVIDSON J	1989-1990	4	0	0	0	0	0
CHAPMAN W	1926-1928	3	0	0	0	0	0	DAVIES	1970-1971	9	1	0	0	0	3
CHARLES M	1988-1989	35	10	0	0	0	40	DAVIES A	1913-1914	1	0	0	0	0	0
CHATER W J B	1938-1939	1	0	0	0	0	0	DAVIES A W	1940-1941	1	0	0	0	0	0
CHESTER M L	1936-1937	11	4	0	0	0	12	DAVIES C B	1909-1910	4	0	0	0	0	0
CHISHOLM R	1927-1928	1	0	0	0	0	0	DAVIES D	1926-1927	1	0	0	0	0	0
CHORLTON A R	1933-1937	37	24	0	0	0	72	DAVIES G	1934-1935	1	0	0	0	0	0
CHOWN R	1937-1938	1	0	0	0	0	0	DAVIES I T	1921-1923	23	4	0	0	1	16
CHRISTIE G	1936-1937	1	0	0	0	0	0	DAVIES K	1954-1957	15	0	0	0	0	0
CHRISTIE J	1935-1936	1	0	0	0	0	0	DAVIES R L	1929-1930	4	0	0	0	0	0
CHURCHOUSE K	1913-1914	3	0	0	0	0	0	DAVIS C H	1895-1902	81	2	0	1	0	8
CIVIL C	1899-1901	14	5	0	0	0	15	DAVIS D	1931-1932	1	0	0	0	0	0
CLARK B	1985-1991	45	7	0	0	0	28	DAVIS H W	1936-1937	2	0	0	0	0	0
CLARKE A	1989-1998	100	3	0	0	0	15	DAVIS M P	1929-1930	12	0	0	0	0	0
CLARKE D J N S	1972-1978	100	25	0	0	0	100	DAVIS P W	1920-1922	15	2	0	0	0	6
CLARKE F	1925-1927	4	0	0	0	0	0	DAVIS S J	1946-1947	5	1	0	0	1	7
CLARKE G	1932-1933	5	0	0	0	0	0	DAWES A	1932-1933	17	0	0	1	0	2
CLARKE J	1957-1958	9	0	0	0	0	0	DAWSON M	1991-2004	246	66	79	64	1	693
CLARKE JOHN	2003-2005	19	5	0	0	0	25	DAY K	1938-1941	5	0	0	0	0	0
CLARKE J O C	1940-1941	6	0	0	0	0	0	DAYKENE	1900-1902	1	0	0	0	0	0
CLARKE P	1932-1934	5	1	0	0	0	3	DE GROOT K	1987-1988	3	0	0	0	0	0
CLAYSON A	1945-1946	1	1	0	0	0	3	DEANS A	1986-1987	4	2	0	0	1	11
CLAYSON G	1895-1896	6	0	0	0	0	0	DEANS P D A	1960-1961	11	2	0	0	0	6
CLAYTON R C	1933-1935	16	0	0	0	0	0	DEEKS J B	1960-1971	3	0	0	0	0	0
CLEAVER T G H	1929-1932	24	6	0	0	0	18	DEELEY W	1990-1991	1	0	0	0	0	0
CLEAVER W	1900-1901	1	0	0	0	0	0	DEIGHTON M	1963-1964	1	1	0	0	0	3
CLEWLOW F C	1912-1913	6	0	0	0	0	0	DELAP M V	1924-1925	16	3	0	0	0	9
CLIFTON H C	1920-1922	32	0	0	0	0	0	DENNIS C M	1950-1951	1	0	0	0	0	0
CLIFTON R	1928-1929	4	1	0	0	0	3	DENTON A	1899-1900	5	0	0	0	0	0
CLIVE C M	1900-1901	2	0	0	0	0	0	DENTON D	1921-1928	156	13	0	1	0	41
CLOTHIER W	1995-1996	1	0	0	0	0	0	DESBOROUGH G R	1946-1956	42	2	4	2	0	22
CLUES G	1941-1942	2	1	0	0	0	3	DESBOROUGH J E	1977-1981	41	8	0	0	0	32
COATES D B	1962-1963	1	0	0	0	0	0	DEWEY P	1986-1988	18	4	0	0	0	16

Name	Years	Appearances	Tries	Pens	Cons	DG	Pts
DICKENS A	1907-1908	1	0	0	0	0	0
DICKENS A E	1919-1920	2	0	0	1	0	2
DICKENS B	1921-1923	2	0	0	0	0	0
DICKENS C	1901-1902	1	0	0	0	0	0
DICKENS E	1901-1902	1	0	0	0	0	0
DICKENS F	1901-1902	1	0	0	0	0	0
DICKENS J	1901-1902	3	0	0	0	0	0
DICKERSON R	1054-1064	79	19	0	0	0	57
DICKS E	1934-1939	8	1	0	0	0	3
DICKS J	1931-1937	124	17	0	1	0	53
DIGGIN P	2003-2004	1	0	0	0	0	0
DILLION P P L	1930-1931	2	0	0	0	0	0
DIX S	1927-1930	6	0	0	0	0	0
DIXIE-SMITH J W	1901-1903	49	24	0	0	0	72
DIXON W J	1898-1909	75	5	0	0	1	19
DOBBS H	1901-1902	2	0	0	0	0	0
DOBBS R	1900-1901	1	0	0	0	0	0
DOBSON R	1938-1939	1	0	0	0	0	0
DODD H	1925-1926	1	0	0	0	0	0
DODGSON W R B	1924-1926	21	6	0	0	1	22
DODS M	1995-1997	18	9	6	31	0	125
DOLDING, R	1994-1995	1	0	0	0	0	0
DONALD B	1993-1995	14	1	0	0	0	0
DOUGLAS C C	1913-1914	1	0	0	0	0	0
DOUGLAS M	1992-1993	3	2	0	0	0	10
DOUGLAS W S	1935-1936	1	0	0	0	0	0
DOWDALL C E	1895-1896	2	1	0	0	0	3
DOWLING K	1930-1931	2	0	0	0	0	0
DOWNES E J R	1942-1943	4	0	0	0	0	0
DOWSETT J	1936-1942	3	0	0	0	0	0
DRAGE C	1899-1900	1	0	0	0	0	0
DRAGE E	1899-1904	97	0	0	0	0	0
DRAGE W	1899-1900	1	0	0	0	0	0
DRAHM S	2003-2005	55	6	109	64	4	497
DRAKES T E	1930-1933	13	1	0	0	0	3
DREW	1940-1941	1	0	0	0	0	0
DUDBRIDGE W L	1913-1914	3	0	0	0	0	0
DUFFY P F	1966-1975	200	5	0	0	0	19
DUNCAN L	1905-1906	2	0	0	0	0	0
DUNCOMBE D	1953-1954	1	0	0	0	0	0
DUNCOMBE M	1951-1952	1	0	0	0	0	0
DUNKLEY A T	1937-1947	8	1	0	0	0	3
DUNKLEY E	1900-1901	1	0	0	0	0	0
DUNN W M	1946-1947	6	1	0	0	0	3
DURR J	1926-1927	2	1	0	0	0	3
DUTTON D T	1942-1943	3	0	0	0	0	0
DYER H	1923-1930	22	4	1	4	0	23
DYTE N	1985-1991	68	11	11	9	0	95
EAGLE G	1994-1995	4	1	3	7	0	28
EALES R	1983-1988	64	8	0	0	0	32
EARL A	1910-1926	137	11	0	11	2	63
EARL C D	1940-1941	1	0	0	0	0	0
EARL K T	1959-1960	1	0	0	0	0	0
EARLE R	1941-1942	1	0	0	0	0	0
EBSWORTH J L	1961-1968	52	17	2	0	0	57
EBSWORTH J R	1981-1982	4	0	0	0	0	0
EBSWORTH M J	1979-1992	100	17	95	65	10	513
EDE F	1906-1907	1	0	0	0	0	0
EDWARDS A E	1907-1908	5	1	0	0	0	3
EDWARDS D B	1951-1952	6	0	0	0	0	0
EDWARDS I M	1930-1931	1	0	0	0	0	0
EDWARDS N	1993-1995	17	0	0	0	0	0
EDWARDS W H	1895-1903	180	14	0	0	0	42
ELKINGTON D	1985-1996	209	20	0	0	0	81
ELKS D	1948-1949	1	0	0	0	0	0
ELLIOTT J	1966-1967	18	1	0	0	0	3
EMES R H A	1932-1934	52	9	0	0	1	31
EMMS D A	1950-1957	62	8	0	0	0	24
EMMS S	2004-2005	3	0	0	0	0	0
ENGLAND W E	1938-1939	1	0	0	0	0	0
ENGLISH J	1989-1990	7	3	0	0	0	12
ENTWISTLE J	1929-1930	2	0	0	0	0	0
ETHERIDGE J	1990-1996	82	2	0	0	4	9
ETTE A	1945-1946	2	0	0	0	0	0
EVANS C W	1920-1921	1	0	0	0	0	0
EVANS D J	1912-1913	1	0	0	0	0	0
EVANS H K	1912-1913	1	0	0	0	0	0
EVANS J H	1900-1901	1	0	0	0	0	0
EVANS L	2000-2001	1	0	0	0	0	0
EVANS M	1983-1984	1	1	0	0	1	6
EVANS-EVANS E	1933-1939	65	6	0	0	0	18
FACER M J	1926-1927	33	5	0	0	1	19
FACER R G	1919-1925	33	0	1	0	0	3
FALLOWFIELD W	1937-1946	60	13	1	2	0	46
FARAM A	1940-1943	38	0	0	0	0	0
FARMER S	1919-1920	1	0	0	0	0	0
FARR C J	1922-1924	28	1	0	0	0	3
FARROW J	1950-1951	8	0	0	0	0	0
FAULKNER A	1905-1907	4	0	0	0	0	0
FAULKNER D	1974-1975	3	0	0	0	0	0
FAULKNER F	1905-1907	6	1	0	0	0	3
FAULKNER J	1905-1906	1	0	0	0	0	0
FAULKNER J F	1896-1897	1	0	0	0	0	0
FAULKNER M	1969-1974	7	0	0	0	0	0
FEETHAM P	1994-1995	9	1	0	0	0	5
FEHNERT S H	1979-1980	5	2	0	0	0	8
FELLOWS-SMITH J P	1955-1958	26	0	0	0	0	0
FENN J	1986-1989	5	0	0	0	0	0
FENSOME L A	1925-1926	1	0	0	0	0	0
FERNEYHOUGH S	1905-1907	7	0	0	0	0	0
FERRAR H T	1900-1901	1	0	0	0	0	0
FERRAR J E	1900-1902	9	0	0	0	0	0
FIDGETT E	1924-1929	75	9	0	0	0	27
FIDGETT F	1921-1922	1	0	0	0	0	0
0FIELD A	1897-1899	2	1	0	4	0	11
FIELD R	1983-1988	37	1	0	0	0	4
FIELDEN M	1992-1994	19	6	0	0	0	30
FISHER O	1908-1909	2	0	0	0	0	0
FITZHUGH G J	1963-1964	10	1	0	0	0	3
FITZPATRICK L E	1911-1913	14	1	0	0	0	3
FITZPATRICK R	1910-1911	1	0	0	0	0	0
FLAVELL J P	1957-1959	2	0	0	0	0	0
FLETCHER J	1992-1994	20	3	0	0	0	15
FLOYD W	1929-1930	1	0	0	0	0	0
FOALE S	1990-2000	128	25	0	0	0	118
FOLLITT H B	1903-1906	41	4	0	0	0	12
FOLWELL A J S	1966-1971	35	5	0	0	0	15
FOLWELL C W	1979-1986	124	7	0	0	0	28
FORD C W	1941-1942	1	1	0	0	0	3
FOREMAN W G	1900-1903	3	1	0	0	0	3
FORGE A C B	1930-1933	41	14	0	0	0	42
FORWARD W H	1896-1897	1	0	0	0	0	0
FOSTER A	1983-1984	7	0	0	0	0	0
FOSTER M	1993-1995	13	2	0	0	0	0
FOSTER M C	1952-1953	1	0	0	0	0	0
FOUNTAINE M	1996-1997	8	3	0	0	0	15
FOX D	2002-2005	66	9	0	0	0	45
FOX N M J	1973-1990	274	7	1	0	0	31
FOX W	1989-1991	4	0	0	0	0	0
FRANKLAND D A	1978-1991	137	16	0	0	0	64
FRANKLIN C	1905-1906	1	0	0	0	0	0
FRANKLIN D	1952-1957	13	3	0	0	0	9
FRANKLIN H	1897-1898	1	0	0	0	0	0
FRASER G	1898-1900	3	0	0	0	0	0
FREEMAN A	1930-1931	11	0	0	0	0	0
FREEMAN D	1954-1958	4	2	0	0	0	6
FREER A	1912-1914	22	4	0	1	0	14
FREER G	1909-1910	1	0	0	0	0	0
FRIEND J R	1920-1921	4	0	0	0	0	0
FRITH A H	1900-1901	1	1	0	0	0	3
FROGGATT J J	1934-1935	6	1	1	2	0	10
FRY T	1982-1983	12	0	0	0	0	0
FULTON B	2004-2005	3	0	0	0	0	0
FUSSELL P W	1906-1911	77	7	0	0	0	21
GADSDEN G H	1921-1922	2	0	0	0	0	0
GADSDEN J G	1920-1921	10	1	0	0	0	3
GALLAGHER A	1994-1997	19	3	0	0	0	15
GAMES J	1895-1896	1	0	0	0	1	4
GANE G H	1964-1965	3	0	0	0	0	0
GARDNER R	1984-1986	41	0	0	0	0	0
GARLICK J	1930-1931	1	0	0	0	0	0
GARNER J	1951-1954	12	6	0	0	0	18
GARNETT S	1919-1925	20	3	0	0	0	9
GARRATT F	1927-1938	225	29	0	0	0	87
GARRETT G W	1896-1897	1	0	0	0	0	0
GARRETT L H	1932-1934	17	4	0	0	0	12
GARRETT R W	1939-1942	6	0	0	0	0	0
GARRETT W C	1896-1897	1	0	0	0	0	0
GASCOIGNE W	1938-1939	17	5	0	0	0	15
GASTON J T	1956-1958	18	9	0	0	0	27
GAUTRY R	1923-1925	9	2	0	0	0	6
GAWTHROPP A	1903-1904	5	0	0	0	0	0
GEDDES A	1931-1932	2	0	0	0	0	0
GEE W	1983-1984	1	0	0	0	0	0
GEORGE I K	1972-1987	131	32	13	7	4	193
GEORGE R W	1976-1981	41	1	0	0	0	4
GERRARD C H	1934-1938	19	3	0	0	0	9
GIBBS W J	1921-1922	4	0	0	0	0	0
GIBSON A	1897-1898	1	0	0	0	0	0
GIBSON I M	1958-1961	72	34	0	0	0	102
GILBERT G	1909-1910	1	0	0	0	0	0
GILBERT H	1909-1920	19	2	0	0	0	6
GILBERT J W	1952-1953	3	0	0	0	0	0
GILBEY H R	1935-1939	8	2	0	0	0	6
GILLAM J	1911-1914	35	19	0	0	0	57
GILLIAND L J	1962-1963	3	0	0	0	0	0
GLENN R	1987-1993	73	12	1	2	1	58
GODDARD J	1942-1943	10	4	0	0	0	12
GODWIN J	1941-1942	1	0	0	0	0	0
GOLDIE B	1951-1952	15	2	0	0	0	6
GOLDING J	2003-2004	4	0	0	0	0	0
GOLDSWAIN R	1977-1980	15	2	0	0	1	11
GOOD H S	1939-1943	44	28	0	1	0	66
GOOD W E	1941-1942	5	0	0	0	0	0
GOODMAN A	1904-1905	2	0	0	0	0	0
GOODMAN E	1912-1913	1	0	0	0	0	0
GOODMAN T	1928-1935	25	0	0	0	0	0
GOOSEY J T	1928-1938	56	2	0	0	0	6
GOOSEY W H	1913-1921	39	10	0	0	0	30
GORBOLD R	1908-1912	25	0	0	0	0	0
GORDON E J	1921-1929	54	28	0	0	0	84
GOSLING C	1908-1909	1	0	0	0	0	0
GOSSE P M	1940-1941	4	0	0	0	0	0
GOTCH R F	1940-1941	3	0	0	0	0	0
GOTCH S	1974-1975	3	0	0	0	0	0
GRACE W G	1900-1903	18	2	0	0	0	6
GRANDIDGE H B	1905-1906	1	0	0	0	0	0
GRANT D M	1910-1912	5	2	0	0	0	6
GRAY G C	1898-1899	1	0	0	0	0	0
GRAY J A	1939-1942	6	1	0	0	0	3
GRAY M	1987-1990	15	2	1	0	0	11
GRAY R	1938-1941	13	1	0	0	0	3
GRAY T	1946-1951	127	24	26	130	20	470
GRAYSON P	1996-2005	259	29	577	419	24	2786
GREAVES P	1997-1998	1	1	0	0	0	5

Name	Years	Appearances	Tries	Pens	Cons	DG	Pts
GRECIAN N J	1983-1988	67	17	1	1	1	59
GREEN A	1911-1913	13	0	1	0	0	3
GREEN M	1970-1971	1	0	0	0	0	0
GREEN M	1933-1934	1	0	0	0	0	0
GREEN S	1977-1978	2	0	0	0	0	0
GREEN W	1928-1931	44	5	0	0	0	15
GREEN W E	1942-1943	2	0	0	0	0	0
GREENACRE E	1926-1927	8	4	0	0	0	12
GREENALL P	1979-1982	27	5	0	0	0	20
GREENHALGH M	1983-1987	65	21	80	50	0	424
GREENWOOD J	1913-1914	10	0	0	0	0	0
GREGORY S E	1913-1914	7	2	0	0	0	6
GRIFFIN H,	1912-1928	307	34	0	0	0	102
GRIFFITHS-JONES C	1922-1923	13	1	0	0	0	3
GRIFFITHS A N	1981-1986	48	6	26	16	4	146
GRIFFITHS J	1991-1993	29	12	0	0	0	52
GRIFFITHS M J	1933-1934	1	0	0	0	0	0
GRIMSDELL A S	1903-1904	1	0	0	0	0	0
GROOME J	1993-1994	1	0	0	0	0	0
GROSE W	1921-1922	1	0	0	0	0	0
GUEST W	1924-1925	1	0	0	0	0	0
GUILLAUME R F	1940-1943	11	2	0	0	0	6
GURNEY J C	1913-1914	1	0	0	0	0	0
GURNEY R	1953-1954	2	0	0	0	0	0
GURNEY R T	1911-1914	9	0	0	0	0	0
GURNEY W	1950-1953	42	15	0	0	0	45
HABERGHAM W	**1985-1986**	**1**	**1**	**0**	**0**	**0**	**4**
HADDON H W	1898-1899	2	0	0	0	0	0
HADDON P F	1951-1969	111	5	0	0	0	15
HAFFENDEN C L	1919-1921	8	3	0	0	0	9
HAIRST A	1942-1943	1	0	0	0	0	0
HALES P	1991-1996	2	0	0	0	0	0
HALL A	1942-1943	1	0	0	0	0	0
HALL A,	1911-1912	1	0	0	0	0	0
HALL A M	1949-1952	31	6	0	0	0	18
HALL A R	1956-1957	1	0	0	0	0	0
HALL C	1988-1992	88	18	0	0	0	72
HALL H G	1948-1953	34	1	0	0	0	3
HALL W	1912-1913	2	2	0	0	0	6
HAMP W R	1939-1955	212	15	1	0	0	48
HANCOCK A W	1964-1968	73	44	0	2	2	142
HANCOCK W	1910-1913	58	0	1	1	0	5
HANDFORD D T	1919-1920	8	2	0	0	0	6
HANNEN B	1895-1902	92	23	2	19	3	125
HARBAGE I	1988-1992	4	0	0	0	0	0
HARDACRE J R	1942-1943	4	0	0	0	0	0
HARDEN T C M	1976-1978	9	3	0	0	0	12
HARDING A F	1904-1905	1	0	0	0	0	0
HARDING H	1905-1907	21	4	2	4	0	26
HARDY R	1974-1977	4	0	0	0	0	0
HARPER J	1968-1969	3	0	0	0	0	0
HARRIS A	1895-1896	1	0	0	0	0	0
HARRIS F E	1933-1936	43	6	0	0	0	18
HARRIS R D J	1974-1975	5	0	0	0	0	0
HARRIS T	1923-1937	426	110	21	63	0	519
HARRIS W	1902-1906	8	0	0	0	0	0
HARRISON C L R	1929-1934	4	0	0	0	0	0
HARRISON D	1964-1965	1	0	0	0	0	0
HARRISON J A	1936-1937	7	0	0	0	0	0
HARRISON R	1907-1913	99	22	0	10	1	90
HARRISON S R	1908-1910	14	0	0	0	0	0
HART P	1940-1942	12	8	0	0	1	28
HARTELL E H	1913-1914	1	0	0	0	0	0
HARTWELL A	1990-1992	4	0	0	0	0	0
HARWOOD J	1973-1974	35	3	0	0	0	12
HASELMERE E E	1925-1931	162	96	0	6	25	400
HASSELMIER L	1913-1914	1	0	0	0	0	0
HATTON J C	1905-1906	1	0	0	0	0	0
HAWGOOD J	1957-1967	16	1	2	5	1	22
HAWKES R C	1947-1956	171	12	0	0	0	36
HAWKINS C W	1962-1963	5	1	2	0	0	9
HAWTIN L J	1964-1968	59	9	0	0	0	27
HAYES R G S	1900-1901	2	0	0	0	0	0
HAYWARD D	1950-1951	1	0	0	0	0	0
HAYWARD G H	1907-1909	10	0	0	0	0	0
HAYWOOD R	1919-1921	20	2	0	0	0	6
HAZEL B J B	1945-1947	51	9	0	1	1	33
HEAD G J A	1957-1959	25	2	0	0	1	9
HEADLANDS A J	1910-1913	8	0	0	0	0	0
HEARD A D	1908-1909	1	1	0	0	0	3
HEARN J	1996-1997	7	0	0	0	0	0
HEAVER S	1986-1988	31	1	0	0	0	4
HEFFERMAN C K	1947-1948	2	0	0	0	0	0
HEGGS J	1899-1900	1	0	0	0	0	0
HEITMAN K	1994-1996	5	0	7	7	1	38
HELDER G	1903-1904	1	0	0	0	0	0
HELLIER R S	1922-1923	2	1	0	0	0	3
HENDERSON N E	1941-1942	1	0	0	0	0	0
HENNELL J D	1940-1941	4	0	0	0	0	0
HEPHER A	1994-2002	120	27	125	134	7	799
HEPHER S	1997-2004	28	3	0	0	0	15
HETHERINGTON J G G	1954-1960	117	13	31	42	1	219
HEWITT F	1904-1906	2	0	0	0	0	0
HEYGATE J R	1930-1937	22	0	0	0	0	0
HEYWOOD I	1976-1986	143	2	0	0	0	8
HIAM J	1912-1913	1	0	0	0	0	0
HICKIE A G S	1905-1907	3	0	0	0	0	0
HICKLING G	1901-1903	3	0	0	0	0	0
HICKSON G	1899-1903	6	0	0	0	0	0
HICKSON G S	1899-1900	1	0	0	0	0	0
HILL E	1927-1928	4	1	0	0	0	3
HILL J B	1942-1943	13	8	0	0	0	24
HILL R	1963-1965	41	2	0	0	0	6
HILLBOROUGH A	1930-1931	1	0	0	0	0	0

Name	Years	Appearances	Tries	Pens	Cons	DG	Pts
HILLYER R S	1927-1928	2	0	0	0	0	0
HINTON R	1985-1987	22	3	0	0	0	12
HIPWELL F C	1909-1910	1	1	0	0	0	3
HIPWELL M J	1920-1921	1	0	0	0	0	0
HIVES A	1911-1912	2	0	0	0	0	0
HIVES R	1909-1913	79	11	7	45	1	148
HIVES S	1912-1913	1	0	0	0	0	0
HOBBS A J	1900-1906	112	18	0	0	0	54
HOBBS F	1950-1960	62	4	16	26	1	115
HOBBS G	1900-1901	1	0	0	0	0	0
HOBBS H	1900-1902	4	0	0	0	0	0
HOBBS J W	1951-1956	8	0	0	0	0	0
HODGE P J	1907-1908	28	2	0	3	1	16
HODGES A	1935-1936	1	0	0	0	0	0
HODGKINS J	1949-1955	79	1	0	1	1	8
HOGAN R	1954-1956	13	1	0	0	0	3
HOLLINGS W H	1900-1901	1	0	0	0	0	0
HOLLOWELL R	1919-1920	1	0	0	0	0	0
HOLMES M M	1930-1931	21	5	0	1	2	25
HOLMES S	1999-2000	23	6	0	0	0	30
HOMAN M	1961-1962	3	1	0	0	0	3
HOOKER D C	1950-1955	104	19	0	0	3	66
HOPKINS	1910-1911	1	0	0	0	0	0
HOPKINS C	1981-1983	6	1	0	0	0	4
HOPPER R	1987-1988	1	0	0	0	0	0
HORN H	1895-1897	2	0	0	0	0	0
HORNE W	1909-1913	18	0	0	0	0	0
HORNSEY C	1902-1904	9	1	0	0	0	3
HORTON	1904-1905	1	0	0	0	0	0
HORWOOD R	1958-1975	209	9	0	0	0	27
HOSEN R W	1955-1967	250	71	200	295	20	1463
HOSKIN W W	1910-1912	28	6	0	1	0	20
HOSTE A G	1900-1906	38	1	0	0	0	3
HOULIHAN M	1919-1920	1	0	0	0	0	0
HOWARD J	1998-2005	53	4	0	0	0	20
HOWARD J E	1934-1940	77	3	0	0	0	9
HOWES G T	1970-1977	14	2	0	0	0	8
HOWETT R L	1919-1920	2	0	0	0	0	0
HOWKINS J	1956-1957	1	0	0	0	0	0
HOWSON J	1904-1906	2	0	0	0	0	0
HUDSON J W	1919-1920	1	2	0	0	0	6
HUDSON N B	1912-1913	1	0	0	0	0	0
HUDSON R F	1942-1943	1	1	0	0	0	3
HUGHES A	1988-1991	15	0	0	0	0	0
HUGHES A M	1945-1946	2	0	0	0	0	0
HUGHES R	1989-1990	1	0	0	0	0	0
HUGHES W H	1920-1921	2	0	0	0	0	0
HUMAN W	2004-2005	23	7	0	0	0	35
HUMPHREY S H G	1912-1921	15	5	0	6	0	27
HUNTER A	1941-1942	1	1	0	0	0	3
HUNTER I G	1988-1998	155	44	12	17	1	268
HUNTER J	1907-1908	2	0	0	0	0	0
HUNTER R	2000-2004	77	6	0	0	0	30
HUNTER T H	1912-1913	6	0	0	0	0	0
HURRELL R G	1935-1940	95	6	13	15	0	87
HURRY W	1933-1934	1	0	0	0	0	0
HURST H	1920-1922	7	0	0	0	0	0
HUSKISSON J	1940-1941	2	0	0	0	0	0
HUTCHINSON P	1987-1988	3	0	0	0	0	0
HYDE D B T	1980-1981	21	1	0	0	0	4
HYDE E F D	1934-1935	2	0	0	0	0	0
HYDE Jim	1955-1956	7	2	0	0	0	6
HYDE John P	1947-1963	308	163	0	0	0	489
HYND H	1919-1920	10	1	0	2	0	7
HYNDMAN C	2000-2005	40	4	0	0	0	20
HYNES M	1994-1999	95	0	0	0	0	0
ILES J W	**1941-1942**	**1**	**0**	**0**	**0**	**0**	**0**
ILOTT L	1993-						
INGRAM P	1988-1991	16	2	0	0	0	8
IRELAND E	1905-1906	7	0	0	0	0	0
IZZARD W	1912-1913	8	0	0	0	0	0
JACK C W N	**1913-1914**	**10**	**0**	**0**	**0**	**0**	**0**
JACK H W	1913-1914	1	0	0	0	0	0
JACKETT E J	1907-1909	2	0	0	0	0	0
JACKSON A	1907-1909	1	0	0	0	0	0
JACKSON A	1921-1922	5	0	0	0	0	0
JACKSON R	1996-2000	19	4	0	3	0	26
JACKSON T C H	1941-1942	1	0	0	0	0	0
JACKSON W A	1935-1937	48	7	0	0	0	21
JACKSON W M	1927-1937	164	7	0	0	0	21
JACOBS C R	1949-1966	470	19	0	0	0	57
JACQUES R	1951-1952	1	0	0	0	0	0
JAGGARD P	1971-1973	11	3	9	10	0	59
JAMES C	1948-1949	1	0	0	0	0	0
JAMES D	1987-1989	31	3	0	0	0	12
JAMES L	1940-1941	1	0	0	0	0	0
JAMES M	1954-1961	22	9	0	0	0	27
JAMES P	1958-1959	1	0	0	0	0	0
JAMES S	1990-1991	10	10	0	0	0	40
JAMES S T	1930-1931	2	0	0	0	0	0
JAMES W	1935-1936	1	0	0	0	0	0
JEEPS R E G	1952-1965	273	48	0	5	2	160
JEFFCOATE J	1934-1950	183	15	0	0	0	45
JEFFCOATE R	1945-1946	1	0	0	0	0	0
JELLEY J	1926-1927	3	0	0	0	0	0
JELLEY M	1927-1938	156	17	0	0	0	51
JENKINS C R	1929-1931	5	2	0	0	0	6
JENKINS D	1964-1968	45	10	0	0	1	33
JENKINS J	1984-1985	1	1	0	0	0	4
JENKINS L V	1940-1943	13	2	0	0	0	6
JENKINS O F	1900-1906	2	0	00	0	0	0
JENSEN K G	1980-1983	61	4	0	0	0	16

Name	Years	Appearances	Tries	Pens	Cons	DG	Pts
JEPPE D J	1922-1923	8	8	0	0	0	24
JESSOP A W	1971-1973	4	0	0	0	0	0
JEYES J	1919-1924	53	3	0	1	0	11
JOHN E	1926-1927	1	0	0	0	0	0
JOHN H W	1926-1927	1	0	0	0	0	0
JOHNS T T	1940-1941	4	3	0	0	0	9
JOHNSON A	1901-1902	17	1	0	0	0	3
JOHNSON A G	1956-1975	303	7	0	0	0	23
JOHNSON A M	1981-1988	74	7	62	56	5	341
JOHNSON B	1956-1957	1	0	0	0	0	0
JOHNSON C	1995-2000	72	10	0	0	0	50
JOHNSON L H	1902-1907	134	10	0	1	0	32
JOHNSON P	1945-1946	5	3	0	0	0	9
JOHNSON P A	1959-1960	1	0	0	0	0	0
JOHNSON P M	1977-1979	56	4	0	0	0	16
JOHNSON T	1931-1932	3	1	0	0	0	3
JOLLIFFE R L K	1963-1966	21	9	0	0	0	27
JONES A	1902-1904	2	0	0	0	0	0
JONES B	2003-2004	1	0	0	0	0	0
JONES C	1980-1981	1	0	0	0	0	0
JONES D	1992-1993	3	0	0	0	0	0
JONES G	1947-1951	26	3	0	0	0	9
JONES G J	1924-1925	1	0	0	0	0	0
JONES G W	1896-1900	111	18	0	5	0	64
JONES H	1971-1972	21	7	3	3	1	46
JONES H	1920-1926	19	9	0	0	0	27
JONES J I T	1921-1923	6	1	0	0	0	3
JONES M	1998-1999	1	0	0	0	0	0
JONES P	1952-1956	18	0	0	0	0	0
JONES R	1922-1931	231	74	0	0	12	270
JONES R C	1919-1923	91	33	0	0	0	99
JONES R T	1947-1949	19	6	0	0	0	18
JONES Reg	1922-1923	3	0	0	0	0	0
JONES W	1907-1908	3	0	0	0	0	0
JORGENSEN P	2001-2003	49	19	1	0	0	97
JOSEPH I	1982-1986	11	0	0	0	0	0
JUDKIN W A	1896-1899	25	0	0	0	0	0
JUDS S	1993-1995	16	5	0	0	0	25
JULLIENNE E	1932-1933	10	2	0	0	0	6
KALUGHER W G	**1928-1930**	**17**	**12**	**0**	**5**	**0**	**46**
KANE	1925-1926	1	0	0	0	0	0
KEATING R	1979-1980	4	0	0	0	0	0
KENT A	1977-1979	21	4	0	0	0	0
KILBAIN M	1987-1988	1	0	0	0	0	0
KILBEY G A	1919-1921	56	47	0	0	0	141
KILBORN T	1922-1924	2	0	0	0	0	0
KILGANNON J	1945-1946	4	1	0	0	0	3
KIMPTON R	1928-1929	1	0	0	0	0	0
KING C D	1955-1963	5	3	0	0	0	9
KING D	1931-1939	206	72	0	0	0	216
KINGSTON A	1904-1905	1	0	0	0	0	0
KINGSTON F C	1895-1896	2	0	0	0	0	0
KINGSTON H E	1895-1905	264	117	15	97	38 (2)	710
KINGSTON W H	1895-1905	262	207	0	134	7	920
KIRK T	1999-2002	6	0	0	0	0	0
KIRTON L	1956-1957	2	0	0	0	0	0
KITCHENER S	1942-1946	22	0	0	0	0	0
KITCHENER S D	1920-1922	39	4	0	0	0	12
KITCHIN A E	1913-1914	2	0	0	0	0	0
KIPLING J H	1898-1899	2	0	0	0	0	0
KNAPP I	1968-1969	1	0	0	0	0	0
KNAPP E R	1946-1952	147	65	2	9	11	252
KNIGHT C	1907-1908	2	4	0	0	0	12
KNIGHT K A	1975-1976	2	0	0	0	0	0
KNIGHT S	1908-1909	11	2	0	0	0	6
KNOTT J E	1930-1934	50	0	0	0	1	4
KNOWLES C	1994-1995	2	0	0	0	0	0
KNOX I	1989-1990	1	0	0	0	0	0
KOTTLER R	1965-1971	94	7	0	0	0	21
KRIGE K	2004-2005	26	3	0	0	0	15
LACEY J	**1970-1974**	**131**	**7**	**0**	**0**	**0**	**28**
LAM P	1998-2001	78	24	0	0	0	120
LAMB J	1990-1991	4	0	0	0	0	0
LAMBDEN J	1983-1985	41	4	0	0	0	16
LAMBLEY E	1972-1975	2	1	0	0	0	4
LANDON C R	1966-1975	94	7	0	0	0	23
LANE S	1940-1941	1	0	0	0	0	0
LANGHAM N	1987-1988	3	0	0	0	0	0
LANGLEY P J	1949-1951	8	2	0	0	0	6
LANGLEY W	1939-1940	1	0	0	0	0	0
LARKIN P D	1982-1990	170	10	57	51	6	306
LARTER P J	1964-1980	132	4	67	55	0	324
LATHOM H E	1906-1907	1	1	0	0	0	3
LAURIE I	1971-1972	3	1	0	0	0	4
LAW D	1953-1955	9	0	0	0	1	3
LAW M I	1945-1946	1	0	0	0	0	0
LAW N	1994-1997	14	5	0	0	0	25
LAWS K	1955-1957	8	0	0	0	0	0
LAWSON J	1919-1920	1	1	0	0	0	3
LAXON F	1904-1905	2	0	0	0	0	0
LAYMAN F W	1922-1924	39	39	0	0	0	117
LAYZELL S C	1907-1926	37	1	0	1	0	5
LEACH F	1902-1903	1	0	0	0	0	0
LEADBETTER V H	1950-1956	54	7	0	0	0	21
LEAT I	1989-1991	4	3	0	0	0	12
LEDDER V J	1936-1937	1	1	0	0	0	3
LEE Lieut	1929-1930	1	0	0	0	0	0
LEE C	1908-1911	51	3	0	0	0	9
LEE J	1904-1905	1	0	0	0	0	0
LEE P	1995-1996	1	0	0	0	0	0
LEECH E	1902-1903	1	0	0	0	0	0
LEES H A	1931-1932	1	0	0	0	0	0
LEESON J	1911-1912	1	0	0	0	0	0

Name	Years	Appearances	Tries	Pens	Cons	DG	Pts
LEIGH C	1897-1911	336	48	4	45	2	254
LEIGH R H	1913-1914	2	0	0	0	0	0
LENTON A	1963-1964	1	0	0	0	0	0
LESLIE R	1949-1967	265	72	3	2	7	250
LESLIE J	2000-2004	89	14	0	0	0	70
LETT S J R	1979-1982	19	9	0	0	0	36
LEWIS A	1949-1950	1	0	0	0	0	0
LEWIS D	1954-1955	1	0	0	0	0	0
LEWIS G H	1941-1942	2	0	0	0	0	0
LEWIS J	1921-1922	1	0	0	0	0	0
LEWIS J E	1937-1938	1	0	0	0	0	0
LEWIS M	1992-1997	51	5	0	0	0	25
LINDOW E C	1905-1913	18	5	0	1	0	17
LINDOW E D	1913-1922	31	8	1	5	1	41
LINDSAY J S	1948-1949	5	0	0	0	0	0
LINDSAY W O B	1929-1931	11	3	0	0	0	9
LINDSEY-SMITH	1896-1897	1	0	0	0	0	0
LINES A	1940-1941	4	0	0	0	0	0
LINES R	1943-1944	12	1	0	0	0	3
LINNELL P	1953-1956	7	1	0	0	0	3
LIVINGSTONE S	1913-1914	21	0	0	0	0	0
LLEWELLYN B	1945-1946	1	1	0	0	0	3
LLOYD H	1913-1914	1	0	0	0	0	0
LLOYD I	1913-1914	8	0	0	0	0	0
LLOYD T P	1908-1909	2	2	0	0	0	6
LLOYD-EVANS	1908-1909	2	0	0	0	0	0
LLOYD-GARDINER	1905-1907	20	3	0	0	0	9
LOAKE L	1927-1928	1	0	0	0	0	0
LOMAS J E	1945-1953	222	46	0	0	0	138
LONG M G	1907-1908	1	0	0	0	0	0
LONG R	1982-1984	13	2	0	0	0	8
LONGLAND A	1934-1946	34	1	0	0	0	3
LONGLAND J	1902-1904	11	0	0	0	0	0
LONGLAND L	1945-1947	34	2	0	0	0	6
LONGLAND M	1941-1942	13	1	0	0	0	3
LONGLAND R J	1927-1948	356	17	14	26	0	145
LORD J E D	1932-1933	2	2	2	0	0	12
LORD M	2002-2005	69	1	0	0	0	5
LOVE C	1898-1901	10	0	0	0	0	0
LOVELL J	1946-1949	7	0	0	0	0	0
LOVEROCK R	1926-1930	99	59	0	0	1	181
LOYNES W D	1940-1941	1	0	0	0	0	0
LUCAS J A	1899-1900	1	0	0	0	0	0
LUCK A E	1919-1928	253	38	10	42	0	228
LUCK J C	1895-1896	6	0	0	0	0	0
LUTTER I A	1973-1986	125	1	0	0	0	4
LUYT Dr	1909-1910	7	0	0	0	0	0
LYNN M	1986-1988	24	4	0	0	0	16
LA VILLE T T	1908-1909	1	0	0	0	0	0
McCANLIS M A	**1924-1926**	**14**	**7**	**0**	**0**	**0**	**21**
McCONKEY P	1963-1964	1	0	0	0	0	0
MACDONALD A	1942-1943	1	0	0	0	0	0
McEWEN P	1941-1942	1	0	0	0	0	0
MacEWEN R	1954-1956	12	0	0	0	0	0
MacGREGOR R	1909-1910	2	0	0	0	0	0
McGUCKIAN P T	1977-1985	165	82	0	0	0	328
MACIEJEWSKI J	1979-1982	43	3	0	0	0	12
MacINTYRE A	1935-1936	1	3	0	0	0	9
MacKANESS C W	1975-1982	127	5	6	7	8	76
MacKENZIE A	1937-1938	1	0	0	0	0	0
MacKENZIE J M	1923-1924	7	2	0	0	0	6
MacKINNON D	1996-2000	78	5	0	0	0	25
MacKINTOSH L H	1925-1926	11	2	0	0	2	14
MacLEAN J B	1929-1930	2	1	0	0	0	3
McLOUGHLIN W M	1938-1939	1	0	0	0	0	0
MacMANUS H C	1906-1907	16	2	0	0	0	6
MacMILLAN L	1905-1906	4	0	0	0	0	0
McNAB A	1994-1995	7	0	0	0	0	0
MacNALLY D	1976-1977	1	0	0	0	0	0
MacNALLY Don	1949-1958	166	63	0	0	0	189
McNAMEE B	2003-2004	1	0	0	0	0	0
MacNAUGHTON D A	1900-1901	1	0	0	0	0	0
MacNAUGHTON R	1991-1998	114	22	0	0	0	103
McVICAR C A	1906-1907	3	0	0	0	0	0
MAGUIRE J	1967-1968	9	0	0	0	0	0
MAHONEY J B	1938-1939	5	4	0	0	0	12
MAJOR A C	1974-1975	1	0	0	0	0	0
MAJOR T	1973-1974	1	0	0	0	0	0
MALCOMSON G L M	1936-1937	1	1	0	0	0	3
MALKIN C F	1905-1906	1	1	0	0	0	3
MALKIN H C	1905-1906	1	0	0	0	0	0
MALKIN J L	1905-1906	1	0	0	0	0	0
MALONE C	1926-1927	2	0	0	0	0	0
MALONE D	1996-2002	82	13	0	0	0	65
MALONE P	1927-1928	3	1	0	0	0	3
MANN M	1909-1912	10	3	0	0	0	9
MANNING K	1957-1958	2	0	0	0	0	0
MANNING N H	1968-1975	76	2	0	0	0	6
MANTLE L	1941-1942	1	0	0	0	0	0
MANTON A V	1903-1912	47	9	0	0	1	31
MANTON G	1904-1905	1	0	0	0	0	0
MARAIS C	1982-1983	1	1	0	0	0	4
MARKHAM T M	1920-1922	23	10	0	0	0	30
MARKLAND J D	1929-1931	9	1	0	0	0	3
MARLEY H	1905-1906	1	0	0	0	0	0
MARQUES C	1921-1922	3	0	0	0	0	0
MARRIOTT T J	1948-1958	36	0	0	0	0	0
MARRIOTT W	1901-1902	1	0	0	0	0	0
MARSDEN T	1998-1999	1	0	0	0	0	0
MARSDEN-JONES D	1925-1926	10	0	0	0	0	0
MARSH W E	1942-1943	1	0	0	0	0	0

Name	Years	Appearances	Tries	Pens	Cons	DG	Pts
MARSHALL B	1969-1974	10	0	0	0	0	0
MARSHALL G	1962-1975	54	3	0	0	0	9
MARTIN A	1979-1981	3	0	0	0	0	0
MARTIN L	2000-2002	32	6	0	0	0	30
MARTIN R	1985-1986	2	0	0	0	0	0
MARTIN R A	1948-1949	3	0	0	0	0	0
MARTYN C H	1913-1914	1	0	0	0	0	0
MARTYN R F	1913-1914	7	0	0	0	0	0
MASH J L	1906-1910	39	2	0	0	0	6
MASON D H	1974-1990	190	4	0	0	0	14
MASON E	1901-1902	3	0	0	0	0	0
MASON J	1921-1922	3	0	0	0	0	0
MASON J	1901-1907	142	13	0	0	2	47
MASON M	1968-1969	30	1	0	0	0	3
MASSEY E J	1923-1924	2	0	0	0	0	0
MASSEY W H	1901-1902	5	0	0	0	0	0
MASTERS D	1995-1996	1	0	0	0	0	0
MATHESON	1940-1941	1	0	0	0	0	0
MATHIAS J	1990-1991	1	0	0	0	0	0
MATTACOLA P	1978-1981	12	0	0	0	0	0
MATTHEWS A D G	1927-1936	94	15	1	2	0	52
MATTHEWS F C	1950-1951	85	0	0	0	0	0
MATTHEWS M	1941-1942	1	1	0	0	0	3
MAUNDEN B	1994-1996	1	0	0	0	0	0
MAWBY F C	1913-1920	5	0	0	0	0	0
MAWBY W J C	1941-1943	2	1	0	0	0	3
MAWLEY F C	1912-1913	3	0	0	0	0	0
MAYES L	1940-1941	4	6	0	0	0	18
MAYES L	1925-1933	136	44	0	0	0	132
MEAD F F	1895-1896	9	0	0	0	0	0
MEHAFFEY J	1908-1909	1	0	0	0	0	0
MELLISH A	1948-1949	1	0	0	0	0	0
MELLOR F	1920-1921	4	0	0	1	0	2
MENDEZ F	1998-2000	46	13	0	0	0	65
MERLIN D	1992-1998	67	21	0	0	0	105
MERRIMAN R	1933-1938	6	0	0	0	0	0
MERRY J B	1920-1928	208	17	0	1	0	53
METCALFE R	1998-2000	46	4	0	0	0	20
MICHAEL W L	1921-1922	1	0	0	0	0	0
MILES J H	1900-1907	71	74	3	16	0	263
MILES M	1981-1982	2	0	0	0	0	0
MILES MATT	2002-2004	16	0	0	0	0	0
MILES P	1992-1994	7	0	0	0	0	0
MILES S	1989-1991	8	1	0	0	0	4
MILLER F W	1929-1930	6	0	0	0	0	0
MILLER H	1931-1932	1	0	0	0	0	0
MILLER M E	1981-1982	8	0	0	0	0	0
MILLER M W	1900-1901	1	0	0	0	0	0
MILLER W	1931-1932	4	0	0	0	0	0
MILLETT W L	1941-1942	4	0	0	2	0	4
MILLHOUSE C	1992-1996	28	8	0	0	0	40
MILLIN T G	1927-1928	8	2	0	0	0	6
MILLS A	1910-1912	3	0	0	0	0	0
MILLS J	1900-1901	3	0	0	0	0	0
MILLWARD J	1923-1935	236	43	0	0	1	133
MILLWARD J	1911-1912	1	0	0	0	0	0
MILMAN D K N	1933-1934	1	1	0	0	0	3
MILNE H T N	1900-1902	5	0	0	0	0	0
MILROY A	1934-1935	1	0	0	0	0	0
MILTON J C	1902-1903	1	0	0	0	0	0
MILTON M	1911-1912	1	0	0	0	0	0
MILTON N W	1906-1907	1	0	0	0	0	0
MILWARD F	1919-1921	22	1	0	0	0	3
MINAHAN E	1909-1910	1	0	0	0	0	0
MITCHELL F H	1906-1907	1	0	0	0	0	0
MOBBS E R	1905-1913	234	179	0	2	1	545
MOFFATT A	1987-1988	1	0	0	0	0	0
MOFFATT I	1967-1974	216	34	209	183	2	1113
MOFFATT J	1991-1993	5	1	0	0	0	4
MOIR C	1994-2002	166	37	0	0	0	185
MONCRIEFF F B	1906-1907	1	0	0	0	0	0
MONK A	1895-1897	7	0	0	0	0	0
MORETON J O	1938-1942	7	0	0	0	0	0
MORGAN C D	1971-1978	74	12	0	0	0	48
MORGAN E	1901-1902	2	0	0	0	0	0
MORGAN F J	1907-1909	2	1	0	0	0	3
MORGAN G	1965-1966	2	0	0	0	0	0
MORGAN J	1902-1908	10	0	0	0	0	0
MORGAN K	1993-1997	49	15	0	0	0	75
MORGAN W R	1936-1937	3	0	0	0	0	0
MORING W T	1895-1896	2	0	0	0	0	0
MORLEY H M	1950-1951	2	0	0	0	1	3
MORRIS R E	1969-1975	84	51	0	0	0	196
MORRIS ROBBIE	2001-2005	83	0	0	0	0	0
MORRISON C	1906-1907	2	0	0	0	0	0
MORRISON H S	1898-1899	6	1	0	0	0	3
MORRISON L G	1906-1907	2	0	0	0	0	0
MORRISON N P	1905-1906	3	0	0	0	0	0
MORRISON R R	1952-1959	15	2	0	0	0	6
MORTIMER E	1903-1904	1	0	0	0	0	0
MORTON W R	1920-1923	4	1	0	0	0	3
MOSS E T	1900-1901	2	0	0	0	0	0
MOSS P J	1987-1991	68	20	25	25	1	208
MOSS T C	1896-1898	9	0	0	0	0	0
MOULTON W	1966-1967	1	0	0	0	0	0
MOVEN W	1988-1989	10	0	0	0	0	0
MUDDIMAN F	1907-1920	87	12	10	70	0	206
MUDDIMAN G,	1941-1943	6	4	0	0	0	12
MULLINGS A F	1901-1902	3	1	0	0	0	3
MUNKS W C O	1947-1948	1	0	0	0	0	0
MUNTON J	1911-1913	6	2	0	0	1	10
MUNTZ C	1955-1956	8	0	0	0	0	0
MURBY R A	1958-1961	20	0	0	0	0	0
MURPHY B M	1950-1951	1	0	0	0	0	0
MURRAY W	1955-1957	12	1	0	0	0	3
MYNARD A	1986-1987	11	4	9	8	2	65
MYNARD I	1896-1900	11	1	0	0	0	3
MYNARD J	1900-1901	1	0	0	0	0	0
NAILER H F	**1920-1922**	**33**	**3**	**0**	**0**	**0**	**9**
NANCEKIVELL R	1990-1992	19	5	0	0	0	20
NASH R	1934-1937	45	17	0	0	0	51
NAYLOR C H	1900-1903	41	0	0	0	0	0
NEAL F	1895-1896	56	7	0	0	0	21
NEALE C W	1931-1932	3	0	0	0	0	0
NEEDHAM E	1955-1959	3	0	0	0	0	0
NEESHAM B W	1960-1961	17	1	0	0	0	3
NEGUS E J	1905-1906	1	0	0	0	0	0
NEIL J L	1957-1961	5	0	0	0	0	0
NELSON G	1925-1926	12	5	0	0	0	15
NEVILL G C	1949-1951	5	1	0	0	0	3
NEVILLE R G	1896-1898	32	1	0	0	0	3
NEWITT A J	1906-1908	4	0	1	0	0	3
NEWMAN A	1997-2002	64	2	0	0	0	10
NEWMAN D	1982-1991	125	12	0	0	0	48
NEWTON C W	1896-1898	32	1	0	0	0	3
NICHOLAS A J	1940-1943	3	1	0	0	0	3
NICHOLLS C	1900-1901	2	0	0	0	0	0
NICHOLS M	1957-1958	1	0	0	0	0	0
NICHOLSON I J	1938-1939	2	0	0	0	0	0
NICHOLSON L H	1924-1925	3	1	0	0	0	3
NORFOLK H	1934-1939	70	2	0	0	0	6
NORMAN D R	1948-1951	5	0	0	0	0	0
NORRIS	1969-1970	1	0	0	0	0	0
NORRIS R	1940-1941	1	0	0	0	0	0
NORRIS W G	1940-1942	14	3	0	12	0	33
NORTHEY A	1997-2000	65	2	0	0	0	10
NORWELL R E	1930-1931	1	0	0	0	0	0
NURSER F	1904-1905	18	0	0	0	0	0
O'CONNOR R W	**1936-1938**	**14**	**0**	**0**	**0**	**0**	**0**
O'CONNOR T	1956-1958	29	7	0	0	0	21
O'DONOGHUE E	2004-2005	4	0	0	0	0	0
O'FLYNN F A	1899-1901	19	1	0	0	0	3
OGILVIE J C	1913-1914	1	0	0	0	0	0
OLDHAM B J V	1964-1978	337	185	0	0	0	635
OLVER C J	1990-1994	70	6	0	0	0	28
O'MEARA E	1945-1946	4	0	0	0	0	0
O'MULLANE E J	1947-1952	76	7	3	3	0	36
ORBELL P A L	1946-1948	6	2	0	0	0	6
ORCHARD R S	1925-1927	9	0	0	0	0	0
ORD M	1991-1993	22	6	0	0	0	26
ORMSBY E	1903-1904	4	0	0	0	0	0
O'ROURKE A	1911-1912	1	0	0	0	0	0
ORTON A E	1895-1896	11	2	0	0	0	6
ORTON R	1900-1903	10	4	0	0	0	12
OSBORNE D	1976-1977	2	0	0	0	0	0
OSBORNE F A	1968-1977	123	6	0	0	0	22
OSBOURNE A J	1911-1912	1	0	0	0	0	0
OWENS C	1938-1939	1	0	0	0	0	0
PACKER H E	**1902-1903**	**1**	**0**	**0**	**0**	**0**	**0**
PACKER S R	1921-1922	2	1	0	0	0	3
PACKMAN F E	1983-1996	323	178	2	7	1	771
PAGE B	1963-1969	125	8	61	114	7	456
PAGE G P	1974-1975	2	0	0	0	0	0
PAGE J J	1971-1984	312	15	0	0	31	153
PAGE W	1900-1902	7	0	0	0	0	0
PAGEL G	1997-2001	111	15	0	0	0	75
PALMER E C M	1932-1939	87	35	0	0	0	105
PALMER H A	1903-1907	38	14	0	0	0	42
PALMER H C	1903-1908	87	27	0	0	0	71
PALMER P	1930-1931	1	0	0	0	0	0
PALMER R A	1930-1935	38	13	0	0	0	39
PANTING F C	1907-1909	27	16	0	0	0	48
PARKER G	1937-1939	11	0	0	0	0	0
PARKER G	1899-1900	1	1	0	0	0	3
PARKER K	1972-1983	231	89	0	0	0	356
PARKER R	1902-1905	6	0	0	0	0	0
PARKER W	1899-1900	1	0	0	0	0	0
PARKES	1926-1927	1	0	0	0	0	0
PARKINSON D	1963-1964	4	0	0	0	0	0
PARKINSON R F	1962-1963	5	3	0	0	0	9
PARRY J F	1945-1946	1	0	0	0	0	0
PARSONS C	1941-1943	27	7	0	1	0	23
PARSONS M J	1962-1968	94	6	0	0	0	18
PARTLOW H	1940-1941	1	0	0	0	0	0
PASK P	1986-1994	150	34	0	1	0	144
PATRICK E	1938-1939	1	0	0	0	0	0
PATRICK W	1897-1902	98	45	0	3	1	145
PAY B M	1961-1963	39	5	0	0	2	21
PAYNE G	1950-1952	13	1	0	0	0	3
PAYNE J V	1923-1925	9	1	0	0	0	3
PEACHEY E R	1919-1920	1	0	0	0	0	0
PEARCE C	1932-1933	1	0	0	0	0	0
PEARCE G S	1977-1996	411	31	0	0	0	125
PEARCEY R	1966-1972	63	6	0	0	0	18
PEARSON A S	1957-1961	121	9	0	0	0	0
PEECH F B	1895-1896	1	1	0	0	0	3
PEEL R F W	1933-1934	1	0	0	0	0	0
PEGLEY A	1907-1908	5	1	0	0	0	3
PELL E	1946-1948	13	5	0	0	0	15
PELL J M	1942-1952	139	20	3	2	0	91
PELL R O	1942-1952	183	58	0	0	1	177
PEILLARD R	2003-2004	2	0	0	0	0	0
PEMBER J D	1919-1965	19	5	0	0	0	15
PEMBERTON R	1912-1913	1	0	0	0	0	0
PENNINGTON G A P	1926-1928	38	1	0	0	0	3
PERCIVAL G	1901-1902	3	0	0	0	0	0

Name	Years	Appearances	Tries	Pens	Cons	DG	Pts
PERCIVAL M J	1962-1967	18	0	0	0	0	0
PERCIVAL W J	1925-1935	140	17	0	0	0	51
PERKINS C	1902-1903	1	0	0	0	0	0
PERKINS R	1929-1930	1	0	0	0	0	0
PETTITT H	1911-1920	53	5	0	0	0	15
PETTS S E F	1937-1943	92	4	2	18	0	54
PEYTON-JONES J N	1941-1942	2	2	0	0	0	6
PHILLIPS C	1994-1995	1	0	0	0	0	0
PHILLIPS E	1905-1906	4	2	0	0	0	6
PHILLIPS G N	1971-1978	177	28	0	0	0	112
PHILLIPS J P	1990-2004	322	27	0	0	0	134
PHILLIPS J W	1906-1907	1	0	0	0	0	0
PHILP P	1978-1979	2	0	0	0	0	0
PICKFORD C	1949-1960	196	4	37	70	0	263
PICTON J	1907-1908	1	0	0	0	0	0
PINCHAM M	1994-1995	1	0	0	0	0	0
PINCHES D A	1975-1983	117	11	0	0	0	44
PIPER G J	1920-1922	28	3	0	0	0	9
PITMAN R D	1913-1914	1	0	0	0	0	0
PITT R	1897-1898	3	0	0	0	0	0
PITTS E A	1898-1899	16	0	0	0	0	0
PLANT I	1988-1991	25	0	0	0	0	0
PLATTS A M	1919-1920	1	0	0	0	0	0
PLUMTREE G W	1940-1941	4	2	0	3	0	12
POCKLINGTON V	1988-1991	68	3	0	0	0	12
POLLARD A H	1919-1920	1	0	0	0	0	0
POLLARD C J	1930-1934	33	7	0	0	0	21
POLLARD D J	1939-1940	8	0	0	0	0	0
POOLE G J	1974-1987	246	22	0	0	0	88
POOLE J	1935-1936	3	0	0	0	0	0
POPE R	1971-1972	5	2	0	0	0	8
POPPE G	1922-1923	1	0	0	0	0	0
PORTER J	1942-1943	4	0	0	0	0	0
POTTER F W	1895-1896	3	3	0	3	0	15
POULSON M	1983-1984	9	1	10	3	4	52
POUNTNEY A C	1994-2004	215	45	0	0	0	225
POWELL D L	1963-1978	370	24	0	0	0	81
POWELL R B	1963-1964	4	0	0	0	0	0
POWELL R C	1936-1942	76	2	0	0	0	6
POWELL W C	1934-1936	30	8	0	0	2	32
PRESTIDGE A	1985-1986	1	0	0	0	0	0
PRESTON T H	1901-1909	156	17	0	0	0	51
PRICE J	1994-1995	7	0	0	0	0	0
PRICE M	1941-1942	1	0	0	0	0	0
PRIGMORE C G	1936-1938	29	17	0	0	0	51
PRINCE S	1990-1991	1	0	0	0	0	0
PRITCHARD W F	1938-1939	1	1	0	0	0	0
PROUT D	1967-1971	61	32	0	0	0	96
PULFORD R	1951-1952	1	0	0	0	0	0
PYNE R	1968-1969	2	0	0	0	0	0
PYWELL R H	1936-1938	7	1	0	0	0	3
QUENNELL C	**1935-1936**	**3**	**0**	**0**	**0**	**0**	**0**
QUINN A	1988-1989	1	0	0	0	0	0
RANDALL G	**1902-1903**	**1**	**0**	**0**	**0**	**0**	**0**
RAPHAEL J A G D	1971-1984	159	5	0	0	0	20
RATHBONE J	1975-1976	3	0	0	0	0	0
RAWBONE G	1920-1921	1	0	0	0	0	0
RAY G C	1908-1909	1	0	0	0	0	0
RAYBOULD P	1974-1981	112	8	69	100	0	739
READ C	1921-1922	1	0	0	0	0	0
READ F	1920-1921	4	0	0	0	0	0
READ F	1909-1910	20	0	0	0	0	0
READ G W A	1902-1903	4	0	0	0	0	0
READ J G	1921-1922	3	0	0	0	0	0
REASON A D	1981-1988	52	3	0	0	0	12
REED S	1990-1993	3	1	0	0	0	4
REES A L	1942-1947	6	1	0	0	0	3
REES J	1948-1949	1	0	0	0	0	0
REES J F	1942-1943	1	0	0	0	0	0
REES M J	1965-1966	6	1	0	0	0	3
REES R	1992-1994	8	3	0	0	0	15
REIHANA B	2002-2005	75	21	10	14	0	163
REMMINGER J J	1941-1942	1	1	0	0	0	3
RENNICK A	1999-2002	23	1	0	0	0	5
RENSHAW J	1912-1913	2	0	0	0	0	0
REVITT H	1903-1904	1	0	0	0	0	0
REYNOLDS G	1912-1914	5	1	0	0	0	3
RHYMES R	1987-1992	22	0	0	0	0	0
RICHARDS F	1942-1943	1	0	0	0	0	0
RICHARDS F R	1913-1914	19	1	0	0	0	3
RICHARDS G	1919-1920	6	0	0	0	0	0
RICHARDS H W	1926-1927	3	0	0	0	0	0
RICHARDSON J	1994-1995	4	0	0	0	0	0
RICHMOND D	2000-2005	87	5	0	0	0	25
RIDGEWAY R G	1908-1910	17	6	0	4	1	30
RIDGWAY A	1927-1929	4	1	0	0	0	3
RIDGWAY W E	1927-1928	1	0	0	0	0	0
RILEY J	1945-1946	1	1	0	0	0	3
RIPOL O	2002-2004	37	8	0	0	0	40
RIVETT A	1905-1906	1	0	0	0	0	0
ROBB S	1919-1920	1	0	0	0	0	0
ROBERTS A T	1898-1899	1	0	0	0	0	0
ROBERTS E D	1923-1924	15	1	0	0	0	3
ROBERTS H C	1931-1932	1	0	0	0	0	0
ROBERTS J	1929-1930	1	0	0	0	0	0
ROBERTS P T	1964-1965	12	0	0	0	0	0
ROBERTSON G	1949-1950	1	0	0	0	0	0
ROBERTSON G T	1962-1971	109	90	0	1	2	278
ROBERTSON M A	1948-1950	15	0	0	0	1	3
ROBESON J L	1939-1940	1	0	0	0	0	0
ROBINSON A	1912-1914	4	0	0	0	0	0
ROBINSON A	1895-1899	111	0	0	0	0	0
ROBINSON A C	1895-1897	12	0	0	0	0	0

Name	Years	Appearances	Tries	Pens	Cons	DG	Pts
ROBINSON C E	1906-1908	3	0	0	0	0	0
ROBINSON E	1907-1908	1	0	0	0	0	0
ROBINSON H	1912-1921	33	13	0	0	0	39
ROBINSON H A	1906-1907	10	3	0	0	3	21
ROBINSON H H	1900-1902	3	0	0	0	0	0
ROBINSON K	1927-1928	1	1	0	0	0	3
ROBINSON M	2003-2005	43	6	0	0	0	30
ROBINSON P	1940-1943	6	1	0	0	1	7
ROBINSON P	1992-1993	1	0	0	0	0	0
ROBINSON R A	1947-1949	26	6	0	0	0	18
ROBINSON W	1905-1906	1	0	0	0	0	0
ROBJOHNS D	1987-1988	2	0	0	0	0	0
RODBER T A K	1988-2001	235	41	0	0	0	197
ROGERS A	1895-1896	1	0	0	0	0	0
ROGERS F	1927-1928	1	0	0	0	0	0
ROGERS M	1938-1939	2	0	0	0	0	0
RONCORONI A S	1929-1930	1	0	0	0	0	0
ROPER M J	1966-1977	154	32	0	0	0	118
ROSSITER J R	1929-1930	1	0	0	0	0	0
ROTHWELL T	1903-1904	4	1	0	0	0	3
ROWBOTHAM R N	1906-1907	3	0	0	0	0	0
ROWE L C	1955-1961	36	14	0	0	0	48
ROWE R	1955-1960	11	7	0	0	0	21
ROWORTH P	1986-1996	127	6	0	0	0	27
ROY A H	1912-1913	1	0	0	0	0	0
ROY F	1912-1920	4	0	0	0	0	0
RUDD J	2004-2005	25	4	0	0	0	20
RUDGE W H	1924-1925	1	0	0	0	0	0
RUSH J F	1932-1933	4	0	0	0	0	0
RUSH R E	1936-1937	1	0	0	0	0	0
RUSHTON P	1954-1955	5	0	0	0	0	0
RUSSELL A B	1942-1943	5	0	0	0	0	0
RUSSELL B F	1942-1943	1	0	0	0	0	0
RUSSELL S J	1975-1983	130	18	0	0	0	72
RUTHERFORD C	1926-1927	1	1	0	0	0	3
RUTHERFORD K A	1933-1946	39	11	0	0	0	33
RYAN M T	1962-1965	10	0	0	3	0	6
RYDER L	1946-1949	8	0	0	0	0	0
SALSBURY T	**1985-1988**	**22**	**0**	**0**	**0**	**0**	**0**
SAMBROOK H A	1920-1930	89	13	0	0	3	51
SAMBROOK L C	1920-1921	1	0	0	0	0	0
SAMPSON R G	1932-1934	19	1	0	0	0	3
SAMUEL G	1937-1938	2	0	0	0	0	0
SANTALL E R	1921-1922	1	0	0	0	0	0
SAUNDERS E G	1902-1903	1	0	0	0	0	0
SAUNDERS E W	1902-1903	1	0	0	0	0	0
SAVAGE K F	1963-1972	113	41	0	0	0	123
SAVING T	1975-1976	13	1	0	0	0	4
SAXBY J	1955-1956	2	0	0	0	0	0
SCAIFE C S	1900-1901	1	0	0	0	0	0
SCHULZE D G	1909-1910	1	0	0	0	0	0
SCOTNEY R T	1948-1951	3	1	0	0	0	3
SCOTT J G	1940-1941	8	16	0	0	0	48
SCOTT T	1902-1903	5	0	0	0	1	4
SCELZO M	1999-2001	28	1	0	0	0	5
SEABORNE B	1986-1987	2	0	0	0	0	0
SEABY W	1897-1899	2	0	0	0	0	0
SEAGER J C	1921-1922	1	0	0	0	0	0
SEELY J	1994-2005	249	63	0	1	0	317
SENIOR H H	1942-1943	1	0	0	0	0	0
SERGEANT J	1909-1912	2	0	0	0	0	0
SEVERS B	1900-1901	3	0	0	0	0	0
SEVERS R J	1899-1900	2	0	0	1	0	2
SEXTON C M	1974-1977	57	1	0	0	0	4
SHACKLETON H	1895-1896	1	0	0	0	0	0
SHANNON S	1994-1995	2	0	0	0	0	0
SHARMAN A	1941-1942	1	0	0	0	0	0
SHARMAN D L	1941-1942	14	1	0	0	0	3
SHARMAN J	1945-1946	1	0	0	0	0	0
SHARMAN J R	1937-1938	1	0	0	0	0	0
SHARPE Jerry	1981-1984	20	0	2	0	0	6
SHARPE John	1982-1986	22	2	1	0	0	11
SHAW D G	1942-1943	1	2	0	2	0	10
SHAW D S	1949-1950	1	0	0	0	0	0
SHAW D V	1933-1934	8	2	0	0	0	6
SHAW J	2000-2002	21	4	0	0	0	20
SHAW T A	1919-1921	17	0	0	0	0	0
SHELFORD W	1990-1994	66	18	0	0	0	78
SHELLEY E H	1928-1929	3	0	0	0	0	0
SHEPPARD S	1896-1897	1	0	0	0	0	0
SHEPPARD W V	1933-1934	1	0	0	0	0	0
SHORTLAND S	1990-1991	11	2	0	0	0	?
SHRIMPTON C	1951-1952	3	0	0	0	0	0
SHURVINTON E J	1960-1967	46	9	10	21	1	102
SIMCOE H	1921-1922	1	0	0	0	0	0
SIMCOE J	1896-1904	2	0	0	0	0	0
SIME W A	1929-1936	3	1	0	0	0	3
SIMMONDS F	1897-1908	166	107	16	108	20	581
SIMMONS G	1933-1934	1	0	0	0	0	0
SIMPSON W H	1901-1902	1	0	0	0	0	0
SIPA I	2004-2005	1	0	0	0	0	0
SKEMPTON A	1908-1909	7	0	0	0	0	0
SKEMPTON A W	1903-1905	21	0	0	0	0	0
SKEMPTON L	1907-1910	62	1	0	0	0	3
SKIPP M S	1941-1943	16	6	0	0	0	18
SLEIGHT A B	1902-1904	3	3	0	0	0	9
SLEIGHT K S	1912-1913	1	1	0	0	0	3
SLEIGHTHOLME J	1997-2003	84	22	0	0	0	110
SLINN G	1937-1939	2	0	0	0	0	0
SLOW C	1930-1933	61	14	0	0	12	90
SMART K	1963-1965	7	1	0	0	0	3
SMART S	1940-1941	9	3	0	0	0	9
SMITH A	1983-1984	2	0	0	0	0	0
SMITH A	1911-1912	1	0	0	0	0	0

Name	Years	Appearances	Tries	Pens	Cons	DG	Pts
SMITH A	1895-1900	167	74	0	1	0	224
SMITH A J	1905-1906	1	0	0	0	0	0
SMITH B P	1937-1938	3	1	0	0	0	3
SMITH D	1951-1956	2	0	0	0	0	0
SMITH D E	1942-1948	13	0	0	0	0	0
SMITH H	1934-1935	1	0	0	0	0	0
SMITH H A H	1911-1912	1	0	0	0	0	0
SMITH H R	1903-1908	7	1	0	0	0	3
SMITH J	1937-1939	14	3	0	0	0	9
SMITH J	1913-1914	17	3	0	0	0	9
SMITH J W	1948-1951	49	9	0	0	2	33
SMITH K A	1942-1943	4	1	0	0	0	3
SMITH K T	1963-1964	8	0	0	0	0	0
SMITH N	1995-1996	5	1	0	0	0	5
SMITH P J	1982-1983	1	0	0	0	0	0
SMITH R G	1956-1962	80	8	0	0	0	24
SMITH R H	1954-1957	34	8	0	0	0	0
SMITH R J E	1975-1980	91	0	0	0	0	0
SMITH S	1942-1943	1	1	0	0	0	3
SMITH S R	1957-1958	1	0	0	0	0	0
SMITH T H	1949-1956	150	5	0	0	0	15
SMITH TOM	2001-2005	83	5	0	0	0	25
SMITH W H	1900-1901	14	3	0	0	1	13
SNELL R E	1947-1952	5	5	0	0	0	15
SNODIN P G	1954-1957	2	0	0	0	0	0
SODEN M	2000-2005	88	6	0	0	0	30
SOLOMON R	1938-1941	6	0	0	0	0	0
SOUTHERN N	1977-1980	8	0	0	0	0	0
SOUTHWELL C A	1953-1970	245	14	3	5	0	61
SPANKIE M D	1908-1909	1	0	0	0	0	0
SPANTON R	1913-1914	19	2	0	0	0	6
SPARKES G	1957-1959	9	0	0	0	0	0
SPENCER A	1925-1927	9	5	0	0	0	15
SPENCER C	1979-1980	1	0	0	0	0	0
SPENCER R H	1936-1937	1	0	0	0	0	0
SPILLMAN J L	1942-1943	5	1	0	0	0	3
SPOKES T	1937-1938	1	0	0	0	0	0
STAFFORD C	1905-1907	28	1	0	0	0	3
STAFFORD R C	1910-1911	2	1	0	0	0	3
STANFORD P	1945-1946	1	0	0	0	0	0
STANLEY C	1895-1896	2	0	0	0	0	0
STANLEY F	1895-1897	37	0	0	0	0	0
STANLEY R G	1926-1928	5	1	0	2	1	11
STANLEY W	1895-1898	31	1	0	0	0	3
STAPLETON D	1995-1996	2	0	0	0	0	0
STAPLETON T J	1948-1949	2	0	0	0	0	0
STCHERBINA M	2004-2005	29	1	0	0	0	5
STEEL G H	1895-1896	16	1	0	0	0	3
STEELE C F	1942-1943	1	0	0	0	0	0
STEELE J	1988-1994	149	33	248	221	20	1385
STEELE-BODGER H G	1986-1988	58	0	0	0	0	0
STEFFERT M	1992-1994	28	4	0	0	0	20
STEPHENS J P	1937-1941	25	5	0	0	0	15
STEPHENSON T E V	1956-1958	12	1	0	0	0	3
STERLING A M	1922-1923	1	0	0	0	0	0
STEVENS D T	1959-1960	4	0	0	0	0	0
STEVENS S	1941-1942	1	0	0	0	0	0
STEWART M	1996-2003	169	4	0	0	0	20
STEWART P J	1955-1961	79	25	0	0	0	75
STEWART R D	1927-1928	2	0	0	0	0	0
STEWART W A	1910-1911	3	0	0	0	0	0
STEYN C L	1923-1926	12	5	0	0	0	15
STILL D C	1942-1948	8	1	0	0	0	3
STILL R	1983-1984	3	0	0	0	0	0
STIMPSON G	1932-1947	123	26	2	7	1	102
STIMSON C C	1911-1912	1	0	0	0	0	0
STOLLZ B	1994-1995	1	0	0	0	0	0
STOCK S M	1936-1937	5	1	0	0	0	3
STONEBANK T A	1946-1947	1	0	0	0	0	0
STONEMAN J B	1946-1947	1	0	0	0	0	0
STONEMAN J P	1935-1936	1	0	0	0	0	0
STOPS J F	1896-1899	37	3	0	0	0	9
STORRAR A E	1908-1909	6	0	0	0	0	0
STOUT D	1985-1988	8	1	0	0	0	4
STOYLES A	1989-1990	10	1	0	0	0	4
STRANG P D	1949-1950	9	0	0	0	0	0
STRANGER M O	1897-1898	1	0	0	0	0	0
STREET A J	1978-1988	155	28	0	0	0	112
STRETTON A E	1921-1922	6	0	0	0	0	0
STRIKE P	1990-1991	1	0	0	0	0	0
STRONG D M	1936-1938	2	1	0	0	0	3
STROUGLER W G	1940-1941	1	0	0	0	0	0
STUBBS G	1895-1897	12	0	0	0	0	0
STURGESS A C	1973-1978	9	0	0	0	0	0
STURGESS B	2001-2005	37	2	0	0	0	10
STURGESS G	1966-1967	4	1	0	0	0	3
STURGESS W J	1921-1922	2	0	0	0	0	0
STURTRIDGE G S	1933-1943	118	30	0	9	1	112
SUMMERS M P	1981-1985	60	32	0	9	1	128
SURGUY J E	1977-1984	72	13	47	36	26	333
SUTTON A W	1903-1909	28	0	0	0	0	0
SWAN L	1936-1939	15	0	0	0	0	0
SWANNELL B I	1896-1904	116	16	0	6	0	60
SWANNELL R P	1896-1901	131	8	0	7	0	38
SWEET P R	1966-1982	333	58	0	0	0	215
SWINGLER F	1926-1929	2	0	0	0	0	0
SYKES F D	1954-1965	235	152	0	0	0	456
TANNER P	1989-1992	5	0	0	0	0	0
TARRY J K	1966-1975	56	1	0	0	0	3
TATUPU S	1996-1998	33	8	0	0	0	40
TAUMOEPEAU T	2003-2004	9	0	0	0	0	0
TAUNTON D E	1928-1929	1	0	0	0	0	0
TAYLOR A	1987-1991	2	0	0	0	0	0
TAYLOR A W	1920-1921	1	0	0	0	0	0
TAYLOR B	1990-1998	85	4	0	2	0	23
TAYLOR G	1989-1995	4	0	0	0	0	0
TAYLOR G	1981-1982	18	4	0	1	0	18
TAYLOR J	1965-1966	7	0	0	0	0	0
TAYLOR J A S	1939-1940	5	0	2	7	0	20
TAYLOR K J	1960-1971	71	4	20	47	0	166
TAYLOR L W	1900-1901	10	2	0	0	0	6
TAYLOR P J	1954-1963	224	38	0	4	0	122
TAYLOR R B	1962-1979	313	75	12	3	0	280
TAYLOR W	1927-1931	42	0	4	6	0	24
TAYLOR W J	1935-1938	49	1	1	4	0	14
TEARLE A R	1920-1925	19	4	0	0	0	12
TEASDALE S	1986-1987	2	2	1	7	0	25
TEBBITT C P	1911-1924	147	17	3	60	0	180
TEBBITT G	1932-1934	2	0	0	0	0	0
TEBBITT R	1937-1938	1	1	0	0	0	3
TEBBITT R R	1946-1947	7	2	0	0	0	6
TEBBUTT R	1988-1994	81	8	0	0	0	32
THAME J	1987-1992	111	23	0	0	0	92
THEVERARD T D	1934-1935	1	1	0	0	0	3
THOMAS A	1945-1946	2	0	0	0	0	0
THOMAS A	1984-1986	12	0	9	6	0	39
THOMAS A C	1963-1967	44	4	0	0	0	12
THOMAS A L	1929-1930	1	0	0	0	0	0
THOMAS D	1921-1922	1	0	0	0	0	0
THOMAS D	1984-1986	15	3	0	0	0	12
THOMAS D J	1926-1927	1	0	0	0	0	0
THOMAS H	1957-1958	1	0	0	0	0	0
THOMAS H	1900-1901	1	0	0	0	0	0
THOMAS J W H	1945-1946	6	0	0	0	0	0
THOMAS S	1905-1906	1	0	0	0	0	0
THOMAS T	1964-1965	1	2	0	0	0	6
THOMPSON G	1939-1941	2	0	0	0	0	0
THOMPSON I C	1967-1974	43	2	0	0	0	6
THOMPSON J	1933-1934	10	0	0	0	0	0
THOMPSON P	1907-1908	1	0	0	0	0	0
THOMPSON S	1997-2005	160	19	0	0	0	95
THOMPSON W	1902-1903	1	0	0	0	0	0
THORNE A	1927-1928	1	0	0	0	0	0
THORNEYCROFT G	1897-1900	15	1	0	0	0	3
THORNEYCROFT H	1987-2001	261	100	0	3	0	462
THORNTON B	1900-1901	7	0	0	0	0	0
THRUPP I	1967-1969	5	0	0	0	0	0
THURLOW R	1989-1990	1	0	0	0	0	0
TIMBRELL M	1970-1971	1	1	0	0	0	3
TODD K	1998-2003	31	1	0	0	0	5
TOMLINSON H R	1902-1903	18	1	0	0	0	3
TOMPKINS F H R	1935-1936	1	0	0	0	0	0
TONKIN J	1919-1920	1	0	0	0	0	0
TOSELAND R	1956-1958	5	0	0	0	0	0
TOWNSEND G	1995-1998	64	30	18	5	3	223
TOWNSEND R G	1956-1966	82	29	1	7	0	104
TOWNSEND W	1901-1902	1	0	0	0	0	0
TRASLER F	1895-1896	4	1	0	0	0	3
TRAYLEN G J	1949-1951	3	0	0	0	0	0
TREEN J H	1929-1934	121	40	33	97	1	417
TROTMAN P	1985-1988	11	0	2	1	1	11
TRUSLER W	1895-1896	2	0	0	0	0	0
TRUSSLER F	1895-1896	2	0	0	0	0	0
TRUSSLER W	1920-1921	3	1	0	0	0	3
TUBB S	1988-1994	55	6	47	55	5	294
TUCKER M	1998-2005	105	15	6	6	0	75
TUCKLEY J W	1961-1966	80	30	0	0	0	90
TUNNEY B	1957-1964	83	13	0	0	0	39
TURNBULL F	1923-1924	10	1	0	0	0	3
TURNELL A R	1955-1969	345	38	0	0	0	114
TURNELL R	1982-1983	12	0	0	0	0	0
TURNELL R C	1956-1970	208	20	0	0	0	60
TURNELL W	1945-1947	13	2	0	0	0	06
TURNER A J	1904-1905	2	0	0	0	0	0
TWELFTREE H L	1922-1927	72	3	0	0	0	9
TYRRELL H	1929-1930	2	0	0	0	0	0
TYRRELL W H	1919-1925	28	1	0	0	0	3
TYSALL K L	1975-1977	4	1	9	2	0	35
UDY W H	1919-1922	65	21	0	0	1	67
UNDERWOOD A M	1961-1963	21	14	0	0	1	45
UNDERWOOD C T	1919-1922	7	2	0	0	0	6
UNDERWOOD N P C	1980-1987	147	72	0	0	0	288
UNDERWOOD R	1951-1955	3	0	0	0	0	0
UNDERWOOD T	1959-1960	1	0	0	0	0	0
UNDERWOOD W	1898-1899	1	0	0	0	0	0
UREN E R	1923-1924	13	2	1	1	0	11
VAN WYK J	2004-2005	4	0	0	0	0	0
VANN A G S	1905-1906	6	1	0	0	0	3
VANN D W A	1934-1947	74	18	0	1	0	56
VANN R A H	1939-1940	3	0	0	0	0	0
VASEY P	1941-1942	1	2	0	0	0	6
VASS I	1999-2003	26	5	0	0	0	25
VAUGHAN R	1922-1931	255	2	65	231	1	667
VERWEY J H	1922-1924	8	3	0	0	0	9
VESSEY R	1988-1990	7	0	0	0	0	0
VILK A	2003-2004	6	0	0	0	0	0
VINCENT G G	1898-1899	1	0	0	0	0	0
VINCENT R J	1971-1975	19	0	0	0	0	0
VOGEL H E I	1903-1905	17	0	0	0	0	0
VOLLAND M	1996-2001	123	2	0	0	0	10
WADE F	1912-1913	4	1	0	0	0	0
WAGGETT C	1992-1993	1	1	1	1	0	10
WAITE B	1966-1972	63	16	0	0	0	48
WAKELEY W H R	1926-1927	1	0	0	0	0	0
WAKELIN C	1899-1900	2	0	0	0	0	0

Name	Years	Appearances	Tries	Pens	Cons	DG	Pts
WAKELIN W E	1912-1913	11	1	0	0	0	
3ALDEN S	1937-1938	1	0	0	0	0	0
WALDRON S	1986-1987	14	0	0	0	0	0
WALKER E F	1902-1904	2	0	0	0	0	0
WALKER G A	1932-1933	1	1	0	0	0	3
WALKER G V	1938-1939	1	0	0	0	0	0
WALKER J	1994-1995	4	1	0	0	0	5
WALKER R G G	1929-1930	3	0	0	0	1	4
WALKER W A	1938-1939	1	0	0	0	0	0
WALKER W J	1968-1969	1	0	0	0	0	0
WALSH G	1996-1997	5	0	0	0	0	0
WALTERS G	1995-1996	1	0	0	0	0	0
WALTERS S	1987-1988	3	1	0	0	0	4
WALTON P	1992-1995	51	10	0	0	0	50
WARD B	1986-1996	161	45	0	0	0	193
WARD E M	1930-1931	8	3	0	0	0	0
WARD J	1992-1994	13	1	0	0	0	5
WARD J W	1909-1911	11	7	0	0	1	25
WARD N	1992-1993	1	0	0	0	0	0
WARD R V S	1940-1943	47	2	0	0	0	6
WARDLOW C	1969-1972	37	12	1	0	1	44
WARNER J A	1936-1937	2	0	0	0	0	0
WARR O	1913-1914	1	0	0	0	0	0
WARREN J W	1904-1909	98	9	0	0	0	27
WARRINGTON J M	1904-1909	4	0	0	0	0	0
WARWICK A R	1941-1943	21	1	0	0	0	3
WARWICK K	1939-1940	1	0	0	0	0	0
WARWOOD A	1992-1993	2	0	0	0	0	0
WATKINS A	1940-1941	1	0	0	0	0	0
WATKINS S	1968-1971	7	0	0	0	0	0
WATKINS V	1928-1937	167	18	3	2	0	67
WATSON A	1912-1913	1	0	0	0	0	0
WATSON J	1954-1955	3	1	0	0	0	3
WATSON J R	1912-1914	5	0	0	0	0	0
WATSON S	1974-1978	80	2	0	0	0	8
WATT P N	1945-1947	27	2	0	0	0	6
WEBB R	1922-1931	201	20	0	0	0	60
WEBBER L	1995-1996	2	0	0	0	0	0
WEBSTER G	1992-1996	34	1	0	0	0	5
WEBSTER S	1993-1995	10	3	0	0	0	15
WEBSTER SIMON	2000-2002	14	3	0	0	0	15
WELCH W	1906-1914	169	6	1	44	0	109
WELLS E	1938-1940	3	0	0	0	0	0
WESLEY A J	1919-1920	1	0	0	0	0	0
WEST A	1979-1980	1	0	0	0	0	0
WEST B R	1968-1973	56	8	0	0	0	26
WEST H	1896-1908	76	19	0	1	0	59
WEST J M W	1897-1903	91	14	0	0	0	42
WEST R	1901-1905	59	0	0	0	0	0
WEST W	1898-1908	54	14	1	1	2	55
WESTON A	1895-1896	2	0	0	0	0	0
WESTON H T F	1895-1902	153	4	0	0	0	12
WESTON W H	1922-1938	390	48	8	55	0	281
WHEELER C W	1908-1909	1	0	0	0	0	0
WHEELER W T	1903-1904	1	0	0	0	0	0
WHIGHAM A	1986-1988	8	1	0	0	0	4
WHITE A	1920-1921	1	0	0	0	0	0
WHITE B	1962-1967	4	0	0	0	0	0
WHITE D F	1943-1961	448	116	71	183	1	930
WHITE E W	1899-1913	227	30	0	1	0	92
WHITE F	1907-1908	1	0	0	0	0	0
WHITE I C	1980-1988	170	26	0	0	0	104
WHITE J	1977-1978	1	0	0	0	0	0
WHITE P	1954-1955	20	1	0	0	0	3
WHITE R	1985-1990	4	0	0	0	0	0
WHITE R B	1941-1943	5	0	0	0	0	0
WHITEHEAD M	1966-1967	1	0	0	0	0	0
WHITING F C	1946-1956	58	2	0	0	0	6
WHITING G	1950-1954	43	9	0	0	0	27
WHITING J H	1945-1954	254	13	0	0	0	39
WHITTAKER J D	1895-1896	3	0	0	0	0	0
WICKSON G	1921-1922	2	0	0	0	0	0
WIFFING J	1955-1956	1	0	0	0	0	0
WIGGINS A F M	1940-1941	2	2	0	0	0	6
WILCOCK S H	1959-1963	85	28	3	3	0	99
WILCOX A	1995-1996	1	0	0	0	0	0
WILCOX G	1979-1982	40	1	0	0	0	4
WILCOX N	1948-1949	1	0	0	0	0	0
WILDING F J	1926-1928	2	0	0	0	0	0
WILKINS F	1895-1898	44	0	0	0	0	0
WILKINS H E	1912-1913	1	0	0	0	0	0
WILKINS R C	1958-1967	147	5	1	0	0	18
WILKINSON E H	1900-1909	15	1	0	2	0	7
WILLETT D	1946-1947	1	0	0	0	0	0
WILLETT G	1940-1941	1	1	0	0	0	3
WILLETT H	1903-1912	26	7	0	0	0	21
WILLIAMS A	1973-1975	3	0	0	0	0	0
WILLIAMS D	1924-1927	74	53	0	0	0	159
WILLIAMS G	1921-1922	3	0	0	0	0	0
WILLIAMS R	1952-1958	73	14	0	3	0	48
WILLIAMS R	1896-1897	3	0	0	0	0	0
WILLIAMS R G	1936-1937	3	0	0	0	0	0
WILLIAMS S	1895-1897	65	34	0	1	5	124
WILLIAMS S	1984-1988	32	4	0	0	0	16
WILLIAMS STEVE	2002-2004	26	3	0	0	0	15
WILLIAMS T P	1921-1922	1	0	0	0	0	0
WILLIAMS W J	1941-1943	5	0	0	0	0	0
WILLIAMSON G	1908-1922	118	14	0	0	1	46
WILLIS G	1940-1941	1	0	0	0	0	0
WILLIS H	1909-1910	1	0	0	0	0	0
WILLOWS R G	1933-1935	7	4	0	0	0	12
WILMER J	1998-1999	1	0	0	0	0	0
WILSON C	1993-1994	1	0	0	0	0	0

Name	Years	Appearances	Tries	Pens	Cons	DG	Pts
WILSON F A	1951-1955	2	0	0	0	1	3
WILSON G	1970-1974	30	0	0	0	0	0
WILSON G R A	1980-1982	25	4	0	0	0	16
WILSON H E	1926-1929	11	7	0	0	0	21
WILSON K	1990-1991	4	0	0	0	0	0
WINDSOR-LEWIS G	1956-1957	1	0	0	0	0	0
WINN R R	1954-1961	135	26	0	0	0	78
WINTER E R	1936-1938	11	0	0	0	0	0
WINTLE T C	1965-1969	83	2	0	0	0	6
WOOD A	1934-1939	73	3	0	0	0	9
WOOD C C	1906-1907	1	0	0	0	0	0
WOOD D	1935-1937	5	0	0	0	0	0
WOOD G	1983-1987	36	5	0	0	0	20
WOOD G H	1913-1914	1	0	0	0	0	0
WOOD J	1955-1956	1	0	0	0	0	0
WOOD N	1991-1993	7	3	0	0	0	14
WOOD W	1907-1908	16	2	2	0	0	12
WOODING E	1913-1914	1	0	0	0	0	0
WOODING R	1913-1914	3	0	0	0	0	0
WOODROW D R	1981-1990	213	34	1	7	0	153
WOOLFENDEN P S	1963-1969	57	4	0	0	0	12
WOOLNOUGH A	1945-1946	1	1	0	0	0	3
WOOLNOUGH G A	1921-1922	3	0	0	0	0	0
WOOLNOUGH H T	1948-1955	168	17	0	0	0	51
WOOLNOUGH H	1949-1950	1	0	0	0	0	0
WORRALL S A S	1982-1985	49	8	61	32	2	285
WORTHINGTON A	1902-1903	1	0	0	0	0	0
WRENCH D	1969-1970	9	0	0	0	0	0
WRIGHT A	1896-1903	12	3	0	0	0	9
WRIGHT F	1910-1920	2	0	0	0	0	0
WRIGHT G	1908-1912	60	5	0	3	0	21
WRIGHT G C	1967-1983	246	6	0	0	0	23
WRIGHT H	1900-1901	3	0	0	0	0	0
WRIGHT I D	1969-1978	251	29	73	109	29	631
WRIGHT J	1995-1997	29	9	0	0	0	45
WRIGHT O	1911-1912	2	0	0	0	0	0
WRIGHT W	1898-1906	7	1	0	0	0	3
WRIGHT W J	1945-1946	14	7	0	0	0	21
WYKES A	1940-1942	2	0	0	0	0	0
WYNNE E H	1897-1898	15	7	0	0	0	21
YARDE S C	1940-1942	2	1	0	0	0	3
YELD G G	1903-1904	9	0	1	2	0	7
YEOMAN I	1901-1902	1	0	0	0	0	0
YORK J	1938-1940	10	0	0	0	0	0
YORK N A	1928-1936	126	21	5	14	2	114
YUILL S K	1979-1980	3	0	0	0	0	0
ZIERVOGEL C	1938-1940	9	0	0	0	0	0

D. F. White

Don White: The only player to figure in the top 10 for appearances, tries and points scored – see facing page

Most appearances

Qualification: 300 appearances

Ron Jacobs	470	David Powell	370	Jon Phillips	322
Don White	448	Ray Longland	356	Clive Daniels	320
Vince Cannon	438	Andy Turnell	345	Bob Taylor	313
Alf Chalmers	436	Barry Oldham	337	Jacko Page	312
Tom Harris	426	Cock Leigh	336	John Hyde	308
Gary Pearce	411	Peter Sweet	333	Harry Griffin	307
Billy Weston	390	Frank Packman	323	Andy Johnson	303

Most tries (appearances in brackets)

Qualification: 80 tries

Teddy Cook	219 (263)	Frank Simmonds	107 (166)
Billy Kingston	207 (262)	Harvey Thorneycroft	100 (261)
Barry Oldham	185 (337)	Lewis Cannell	97 (138)
Edgar Mobbs	179 (234)	Teddy Haselmere	96 (162)
Frank Packman	178 (323)	Glen Robertson	90 (109)
John Hyde	163 (308)	Keith Parker	89 (231)
Frank Sykes	152 (235)	Eric Coley	83 (292)
Teddy Kingston	117 (264)	Paul McGuckian	82 (165)
Don White	116 (448)	Ben Cohen	81 (196)
Tom Harris	110 (426)		

Most points

Qualification: 500 points

Paul Grayson	2786	Matthew Dawson	693
Roger Hosen	1463	Bob Vaughan	667
John Steele	1385	Teddy Cook	659
Ian Moffatt	1113	Barry Oldham	635
Don White	930	Ian Wright	631
Billy Kingston	920	Frank Simmonds	581
Ali Hepher	799	Frank Coles	561
Frank Packman	771	Edgar Mobbs	545
Phil Raybould	739	Tom Harris	519
Teddy Kingston	710	Matthew Ebsworth	513

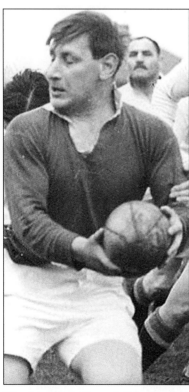

The top three (from left to right): Ron Jacons, heading the appearances chart, Teddy Cook, a fantastic 219 tries, and Paul Grayson, 2,786 points. Will these records ever be surpassed?

RESULTS

1895 to 2005

Records from 1880 to 1894 destroyed by fire.
Results up to and including 1992/93 season include friendlies.
From 1993/94 to 2004/2005 league and cup matches only

ABERAVON

Season	Home	Away
1903-04	3-0	
1921-22	7-0	
1951-52	6-10	
1952-53		8-9
1953-54		0-3
1954-55	9-0	
1955-56		3-0
1956-57	12-19	
1957-58		6-8
1958-59	3-3	
1959-60		10-5
1960-61	6-6	
1961-62		0-0
1962-63	6-15	
1963-64	3-14	
1964-65		11-8
1965-66	15-11	
1966-67	3-9	3-5
1967-68	6-11	6-3
1968-69	12-3	6-19
1969-70	39-8	
1970-71	17-18	18-12
1971-72	24-13	3-8
1972-73	30-15	7-8
1973-74	36-14	9-37
1974-75	15-9	0-6
1975-76	13-3	20-34
1976-77	24-13	15-10
1977-78	17-13	17-32
1978-79	16-8	7-6
1979-80	8-0	12-35
1980-81	16-24	13-20
1981-82	14-27	16-32
1982-83	10-33	14-16
1983-84	29-15	13-21
1984-85	17-8	13-11
1985-86	9-3	0-15
1986-87	15-26	18-12
1987-88	19-9	0-51
1988-89	20-13	13-9
1989-90	13-25	
1990-91	24-27	
1991-92	32-16	
1992-93		12-20

ABERCARN and CWMCARN

Season	Home	Away
1895-96	3-12	
1896-97	10-0	
1897-98	16-0	
1901-02	6-3	
1925-26	37-3	

AGEN

Season	Home	Away
2003-04	25-10	19-6

ARMY

Season	Home	Away
1919-20	39-3	6-13
1920-21	11-5	
1939-40	8-5	
1940-41	50-3	
1940-41	40-3	
1940-41	24-13	
1940-41	27-8	
1940-41	24-3	
1941-42	3-3	
1941-42	18-21	
1941-42	19-8	
1941-42	8-17	
1941-42	45-0	
1942-43	3-19	

ASPATRIA

Season	Home	Away
1897-98	8-4	

AYLESBURY

Season	Home	Away
1940-41	49-0	

BALLYMENA

Season	Home	Away
1963-64		9-14
1965-66	14-0	

BATH

Season	Home	Away
1929-30	4-8	8-10
1930-31	9-3	5-6
1931-32	5-18	6-14
1932-33		5-10
1932-33		12-8
1933-34	22-0	5-9
1934-35	24-8	8-3
1935-36	6-3	0-11
1936-37		0-15
1937-38	11-0	0-11
1938-39	15-3	0-6
1945-46	12-6	5-16
1946-47		13-16
1947-48	14-5	
1954-55		0-3
1955-56	24-0	
1956-57		3-0
1958-59	14-3	
1959-60		10-5
1960-61	32-5	
1963-64		3-9
1964-65	37-0	
1965-66		12-11
1966-67	11-6	
1967-68		3-8
1969-70		30-11
1971-72		6-15
1972-73	23-14	
1973-74		10-3
1974-75	15-3	22-7
1975-76		
1976-77	14-12	
1977-78		3-16
1978-79	10-10	
1980-81	12-6	0-27
1981-82		
1982-83	16-19	6-16
1983-84		
1984-85	9-20	
1986-87	10-12	3-58
1988-89		
1990-91	10-16	6-15
1991-92	9-13	
1992-93	11-8	9-37
1993-94	9-30	6-26
1994-95	16-32	6-26
1995-96		3-12
1996-97	9-6	14-52
1997-98	16-15	3-26
1998-99	40-17	15-9
1999-2000	13-17	13-33
2000-01	24-13	13-36
2001-02	26-7	29-11
2002-03	24-3	27-10
		30-29
2003-04	16-6	6-24
		13-42
2004-05	29-14	12-30

BATLEY

Season	Home	Away
1924-25	17-5	
1925-26	48-0	
1926-27	17-0	

BECTIVE RANGERS

Season	Home	Away
1898-99	11-5	
1902-03	16-3	
1907-08	20-0	
1932-33	11-11	
1933-34	6-0	
1934-35	0-6	
1954-55		6-6
1955-56	5-11	
1956-57		0-6
1957-58	12-8	
1962-63	6-9	
1963-64		14-12
1964-65	12-3	
1965-66		9-9
1967-68	25-9	
1968-69		37-3
1969-70	57-3	
1970-71		13-3
1971-72	21-6	
1973-74	22-12	
1974-75		10-8
1975-76	18-9	
1976-77		26-12
1977-78	27-12	
1978-79		3-0
1980-81		3-6
1981-82	6-11	
1982-83		12-10
1983-84	13-0	
1984-85		14-12
1985-86	24-9	
1986-87		3-19
1987-88	15-6	28-19
1988-89		15-20
1989-90	36-9	
1990-91		14-0
1991-92	40-8	
1992-93		37-15

BEDFORD

Season	Home	Away
1895-96	16-3	0-5
1897-98	9-6	7-0
1898-99	19-0	12-3
1899-00	29-0	14-5
1900-01	7-5	14-3
1901-02	32-0	14-0
1902-03	27-3	8-0
1903-04	31-9	5-6
1904-05	3-8	17-3
1905-06	10-0	16-3
1906-07	28-5	3-9
1907-08	6-16	15-0
1908-09	21-8	10-3
1909-10	14-3	14-8
1910-11	38-3	14-0
1911-12	28-6	20-0
1911-12	19-11	
1912-13	19-8	5-0
1912-13		3-3
1913-14	27-5	5-20
1913-14	0-9	
1919-20	40-5	21-13
1919-20	53-3	
1920-21	25-5	23-3
1921-22	30-3	5-6
1922-23	27-6	3-0
1923-24	17-0	6-6
1924-25	7-0	12-0
1924-25		0-3
1925-26	6-6	9-0
1926-27	22-3	28-0
1927-28	5-6	0-0
1928-29	16-3	16-0
1928-29		20-5
1929-30	13-11	5-0
1930-31	16-19	0-6
1931-32	15-3	6-0
1932-33	28-9	6-3
1933-34	11-0	11-13
1934-35	9-9	0-15
1935-36	0-9	11-14
1936-37	6-12	3-4
1937-38	3-3	6-0
1938-39	3-9	3-10
1939-40	11-8	
1940-41	13-10	0-5
1945-46	11-11	8-10
1946-47		11-11
1947-48	11-3	25-3
1948-49	3-11	0-6
1949-50	17-3	8-3
1950-51	6-6	0-6
1951-52	8-0	0-11
1952-53	6-8	8-3
1953-54	16-3	11-0
1954-55	3-0	3-6
1955-56	8-0	8-3
1956-57	35-10	6-0
1957-58	14-3	9-6
1958-59	20-0	0-0
1959-60	26-6	8-13
1960-61	21-6	14-5
1961-62	31-3	16-3
1962-63	11-16	3-3
1963-64	14-19	6-21
1964-65	15-6	27-9
1965-66	0-8	8-10
1966-67	21-6	6-0
1966-67		0-9
1967-68	6-3	5-5
1968-69	14-11	13-8
1969-70	11-16	6-23
1969-70	12-8	

Season	Home	Away
1970-71	27-3	8-11
1971-72	10-6	9-12
1972-73	21-7	14-7
1973-74	22-7	6-16
1974-75	9-29	16-40
1975-76	9-6	18-15
1975-76	12-30	
1976-77	25-9	6-23
1977-78	12-9	3-9
1978-79	10-0	42-0
1979-80	19-3	17-7
1980-81	7-15	3-6
1981-82	17-13	7-12
1982-83	22-13	16-19
1983-84	13-10	15-9
1984-85	22-7	28-12
1985-86	16-22	20-24
1986-87	15-9	12-21
1987-88	23-6	16-17
1988-89	42-3	18-7
1989-90	37-7	22-20
1990-91	50-7	22-44
1991-92	30-6	23-15
1992-93	33-16	
1995-96	48-0	49-17
1997-98	31-26	
1998-99	34-29	42-31
1999-2000	38-16	41-17
2004-05	41-8	

BEDFORD WANDERERS

Season	Home	Away
1895-96	5-7	
1896-97	22-0	11-0
1897-98	18-0	6-0

BIARRITZ

Season	Home	Away
2000-01	32-24	30-37
2002-03	17-14	20-23

BIRKENHEAD PARK

Season	Home	Away
1905-06	12-5	8-5
1906-07	10-5	3-8
1907-08	12-5	13-6
1908-09	31-6	8-5
1909-10	20-0	11-3
1910-11	28-3	24-4
1911-12	32-5	
1912-13	45-6	27-4
1913-14	18-8	0-9
1951-52	24-3	
1952-53		16-3
1953-54	16-6	
1954-55		3-8
1955-56	37-8	
1956-57		0-6
1957-58	0-0	
1958-59		27-3
1984-85	50-11	

BIRMINGHAM

Season	Home	Away
1922-23	11-8	
1923-24	28-4	
1924-25	12-7	
1925-26	6-0	
1945-46	23-3	
1946-47	30-0	
1947-48	16-3	
1948-49	23-3	
1949-50	14-3	
1950-51	17-3	
1951-52	14-5	
1953-54	33-3	
1971-72	31-3	
1972-73	39-6	
1973-74		27-9
1974-75	20-6	
1978-79	21-15	
1979-80		14-13
1980-81	22-6	
1981-82		14-6
1982-83	48-3	
1983-84		18-6
1984-85	34-13	
1985-86		16-19
1986-87	34-0	
1987-88		36-7
2000-01	47-14	

Season	Home	Away
2001-02	32-19	

BIRMINGHAM OLD BOYS

Season	Home	Away
1920-21	33-11	

BIRMINGHAM UNIVERSITY

Season	Home	Away
1942-43	12-31	

BLACKHEATH

Season	Home	Away
1902-03	0-8	
1903-04		6-24
1904-05	3-3	
1905-06		0-8
1906-07	5-10	
1907-08		0-20
1908-09	22-3	
1909-10		21-14
1910-11	11-5	
1911-12		9-16
1912-13	32-5	
1913-14		0-27
1919-20	6-10	
1920-21		0-9
1923-24	12-6	
1924-25		8-10
1925-26	8-0	
1926-27		4-10
1935-36	8-0	
1953-54	21-0	
1954-55		3-17
1955-56	23-0	
1956-57		6-5
1957-58	21-14	
1958-59		29-0
1959-60	51-14	
1960-61		16-6
1961-62	17-8	
1962-63		13-3
1963-64	12-0	
1964-65		11-11
1965-66	11-9	
1966-67		0-16
1967-68	35-9	
1968-69		11-19
1969-70	27-9	
1970-71		19-3
1971-72	40-9	
1972-73		16-15
1973-74	30-0	
1974-75		10-18
1975-76	4-17	
1976-77		9-13
1977-78	19-10	
1978-79		15-16
1979-80	7-15	
1980-81		9-24
1981-82	13-4	
1982-83	10-20	
1983-84		6-33
1985-86		13-10
1987-88		12-19
1988-89	15-7	
1989-90		10-9
1990-91	43-12	
1995-96	69-14	24-10

BORDEAUX BEGLES

Season	Home	Away
1997-98	25=13	16-23

BORDERS

Season	Home	Away
2003-04	20-3	39-3

BRIDGEND

Season	Home	Away
1928-29	9-3	
1930-31		0-25
1931-32	7-14	
1932-33		11-6
1933-34		5-9
1934-35		0-11
1935-36		6-15
1936-37		4-6
1990-91		9-17
1991-92	53-16	

BRIDGWATER ALBION

Season	Home	Away
1900-01	3-4	0-8
1901-02	19-8	
1903-04	0-9	
1907-08	0-3	
1909-10	29-3	
1910-11	27-3	
1911-12	33-3	
1912-13	36-6	
1922-23	12-6	6-14
1924-25		11-3
1927-28		19-8
1928-29	11-0	18-10
1929-30	20-0	13-3
1930-31		13-0
1931-32		8-6
1932-33		12-5
1933-34		19-3
1934-35		22-5
1938-39	10-23	

BRISTOL

Season	Home	Away
1900-01	17-8	
1920-21	6-0	3-25
1921-22	0-14	0-44
1938-39		0-9
1946-47	0-0	3-18
1947-48	13-0	0-10
1948-49	3-3	0-19
1949-50	11-13	3-11
1950-51	13-0	0-5
1951-52	0-10	3-0
1952-53	14-5	9-9
1953-54	8-5	3-9
1954-55	0-9	3-24
1955-56	6-3	3-13
1956-57		15-14
1957-58	3-11	9-32
1958-59		21-10
1959-60	22-11	13-25
1960-61	3-0	16-3
1961-62	14-14	5-6
1962-63		3-12
1963-64	39-8	3-26
1964-65	11-18	14-13
1965-66		16-18
1966-67	11-17	
1967-68	19-14	12-26
1968-69	16-11	11-33
1969-70	14-3	11-30
1970-71	25-3	11-26
1971-72	12-17	12-22
1972-73	18-6	10-7
1973-74	16-19	4-16
1974-75	7-6	13-7
1975-76	21-14	19-4
1976-77	9-10	6-25
1977-78	9-15	
1978-79	0-3	26-14
1979-80	15-15	
1980-81		12-31
1981-82	16-18	
1982-83		4-30
1983-84	16-18	
1984-85		13-53
1985-86		10-31
1986-87	12-31	
1988-89	16-20	
1989-90		12-28
1990-91	12-9	
1991-92		15-9
1992-93	16-6	
1993-94	22-19	31-22
1994-95	15-18	24-13
1996-97	29-21	11-20
1997-98	35-12	15-22
1999-2000	19-23	29-19
2000-01	24-6	16-46
2001-02	20-23	37-27
		24-32
2002-03	43-13	36-28

BROUGHTON

Season	Home	Away
1896-97	13-0	
1897-98	40-0	

BUCKINGHAMSHIRE

Season	Home	Away
1896-97	3-0	

W. BURKE'S XV

Season	Home	Away
1940-41	67-5	

BURTON-ON-TRENT

Season	Home	Away
1896-97	0-5	
1897-98	3-3	
1898-99	25-0	
1922-23	39-8	6-0

CAMBRIDGE UNIVERSITY

Season	Home	Away
1899-00		0-15
1900-01	8-10	
1901-02		6-6
1902-03		0-30
1903-04	4-6	
1922-23		10-13
1942-43		3-19
1945-46		6-3
1946-47	8-6	
1947-48	11-17	
1948-49	0-14	
1949-50		3-19
1950-51	15-8	
1951-52		10-11
1952-53	8-3	
1953-54		8-0
1954-55	3-8	
1955-56		3-27
1956-57	12-0	
1957-58		11-11
1958-59	9-3	
1959-60		12-8
1960-61	3-8	
1961-62		0-14
1962-63	16-26	
1963-64		0-3
1964-65	9-0	
1965-66		8-0
1966-67	0-8	
1967-68		5-3
1968-69	9-6	
1970-71	12-17	
1971-72		13-26
1972-73	35-7	
1974-75	13-13	
1975-76		20-39
1976-77	15-6	
1977-78	12-3	18-15
1978-79		42-6
1979-80	13-9	
1981-82		13-19
1982-83	20-37	
1983-84		24-17
1984-85	29-26	
1985-86		24-16
1986-87	33-0	
1987-88	35-4	3-12
1988-89	21-28	
1989-90		4-28
1990-91	19-14	
1991-92		27-11
1992-93	46-15	

CAMBRIDGE UNIVERSITY 60 CLUB

Season	Home	Away
1933-34	9-10	
1934-35	18-15	
1935-36	8-16	

CAERPHILLY

Season	Home	Away
1996-97	107-5	

L. B. CANNELL'S XV

Season	Home	Away
1951-52	8-6	

CARDIFF

Season	Home	Away
1925-26	10-14	8-0
1926-27		18-6
1927-28	17-6	
1928-29	29-0	11-8
1930-31	9-20	
1934-35	11-3	
1935-36	13-6	
1936-37	3-20	
1937-38	6-16	
1948-49	12-27	15-8
1949-50	6-3	6-11
1950-51	0-6	3-8
1951-52	0-20	3-6
1952-53	11-6	6-6
1953-54	22-9	9-14
1954-55	6-8	3-6
1955-56	6-3	11-14
1956-57		3-0
1957-58	3-8	3-13
1958-59	14-11	
1959-60		8-9
1960-61	6-6	
1961-62		9-9
1962-63	0-0	
1963-64		6-17
1964-65	6-8	
1965-66		3-17
1966-67	3-6	
1967-68		0-6
1968-69	6-6	
1969-70		7-0
1970-71	14-3	
1971-72		20-24
1972-73	15-4	
1973-74	0-7	
1974-75	9-6	
1975-76		15-19
1976-77	16-20	
1977-78		6-50
1978-79	3-10	
1979-80		4-45
1980-81	7-13	
1981-82		22-26
1982-83	9-40	
1983-84		7-13
1984-85	10-44	
1986-87		4-35
1987-88	7-14	
2001-02	26-15	17-25
2002-03	25-11	31-0

CARLISLE

Season	Home	Away
1899-00	17-3	

CASTLEFORD

Season	Home	Away
1897-98	19-5	
1899-00	37-8	
1901-02	3-8	
1903-04	8-0	
1904-05	26-0	19-8

CATFORD BRIDGE

Season	Home	Away
1903-04	12-0	

CHELTENHAM

Season	Home	Away
1900-01	24-0	6-11
1905-06	6-3	
1907-08	10-13	7-0
1908-09	19-6	
1909-10	18-3	3-11
1910-11	6-0	14-3
1911-12	9-3	0-6
1912-13	6-3	0-3
1913-14	11-10	0-20
1919-20	11-3	6-5
1950-51		3-6
1952-53	11-0	
1954-55		6-0
1955-56	14-5	3-15
1956-57	44-6	17-3
1957-58	30-8	5-12
1958-59	24-3	22-3
1959-60	34-0	35-0
1960-61	34-0	24-0
1961-62	26-3	
1962-63	19-3	
1963-64	8-11	
1964-65		21-3
1965-66	40-3	
1966-67		0-0
1967-68	30-9	
1968-69		13-9
1969-70	20-13	
1971-72	0-15	
1972-73		20-0
1973-74		7-6
1974-75	24-3	
1977-78	15-4	
1978-79		22-0
1979-80	14-7	
1980-81		0-12
1982-83		19-12
1983-84	31-12	
1984-85	30-6	
1985-86		28-9
1986-87		58-10
1987-88	24-4	
1988-89		44-12
1989-90	78-0	

CHICAGO LIONS (USA)

Season	Home	Away
1973-74	76-10	

CINDERFORD

Season	Home	Away
1900-01	31-5	
1901-02	21-3	
1902-03	26-0	
1908-09	6-11	
1922-23	13-15	
1923-24	15-0	
1924-25	29-4	

CIVIL SERVICE

Season	Home	Away
1904-05	15-3	

CLAPHAM PARK

Season	Home	Away
1895-96	14-0	

COMBINED SERVICES

Season	Home	Away
1940-41	11-3	

CONNACHT

Season	Home	Away
1996-97		31-11
1997-98	15-20	13-43

CO-OPTIMISTS

Season	Home	Away
1979-80	18-24	

CORBY

Season	Home	Away
1940-41	35-5	
1941-42	6-5	
1942-43	6-0	

CORK CONSTITUTION

Season	Home	Away
1954-55		3-3

COUNTY DUBLIN

Season	Home	Away
1912-13		5-25
1913-14	0-0	

COVENTRY

Season	Home	Away
1896-97	3-0	
1897-98		7-0
1898-99	18-5	6-3
1899-00	24-0	21-8
1900-01	29-5	11-3
1901-02		18-0
1902-03	19-6	3-8
1902-03	24-0	
1903-04	5-8	11-3
1903-04	11-9	
1904-05	24-5	36-3
1905-06	13-0	3-4
1906-07	6-5	
1907-08	14-0	10-19
1908-09	11-5	6-6
1909-10	0-6	3-8
1909-10	21-5	
1910-11	25-0	10-6
1910-11		8-3
1911-12	16-0	0-7
1912-13	8-5	3-30

(continued)

Season	Home	Away
1913-14	3-0	
1919-20	8-6	8-15
1919-20	9-5	
1920-21	12-0	6-4
1920-21	6-11	3-24
1921-22	19-0	5-36
1922-23	3-0	11-3
1923-24	8-0	8-3
1924-25	10-6	3-14
1925-26	9-11	0-12
1926-27	6-0	0-5
1927-28	6-3	0-0
1928-29	15-6	7-8
1928-29	8-3	
1929-30	6-8	0-14
1930-31	19-5	8-22
1931-32	13-3	3-5
1931-32		8-24
1932-33	14-5	
1933-34		9-3
1933-34	6-6	3-11
1934-35	16-3	3-3
1935-36	3-15	0-6
1936-37	3-7	
1936-37	6-0	6-7
1937-38	9-8	8-19
1937-38		3-17
1938-39	7-7	0-22
1939-40		15-6
1941-42	9-3	
1942-43	0-17	3-40
1945-46	5-15	0-6
1946-47	11-6	
1947-48		8-5
1948-49	6-6	6-11
1949-50	5-12	0-0
1950-51	11-3	3-3
1951-52	12-3	3-8
1952-53	11-0	12-6
1953-54	9-0	8-16
1954-55		3-6
1955-56	11-3	3-11
1956-57	9-3	0-0
1957-58	0-6	3-8
1958-59	12-5	8-3
1959-60	14-8	13-11
1960-61	6-6	10-15
1960-61	24-3	
1961-62	0-0	0-13
1962-63	9-0	0-9
1963-64	3-0	11-19
1964-65	17-0	11-14
1965-66	12-11	8-14
1966-67	3-11	6-19
1967-68	0-14	0-9
1968-69	9-13	9-22
1969-70	24-13	6-0
1970-71	11-18	3-9
1971-72	12-9	7-22
1972-73	19-18	9-24
1973-74	6-11	12-6
1974-75	21-15	11-39
1975-76	12-8	19-11
1976-77	6-16	18-33
1977-78	12-6	
1978-79		12-26
1979-80	37-12	18-40
1980-81	19-9	10-43
1981-82	8-14	6-7
1982-83		17-32
1983-84	23-3	15-23
1984-85		7-36
1985-86	8-13	4-29
1986-87		4-4
1987-88	44-6	12-29
1988-89		10-22
1989-90	24-18	4-34
1990-91		13-15
1991-92	19-11	34-7
		31-7
1992-93	21-26	7-10
1993-94	6-22	29-10
1996-97	26-17	

R. COVE-SMITH'S XV

Season	Home	Away
1927-28	12-8	

CROSS KEYS

Season	Home	Away
1923-24	19-0	10-17

Season	Home	Away
1959-60	41-3	
1983-84	14-7	
1986-87		27-6

CROYDON

Season	Home	Away
1898-99		5-6
1899-00	23-0	
1900-01		10-11

CRUMLIN

Season	Home	Away
1919-20	6-9	
1920-21	11-3	
1921-22	5-5	
1923-24	21-3	

CUBS (BUENOS AIRES)

Season	Home	Away
1977-78	31-4	

G. CURGENVEN'S XV

Season	Home	Away
1896-97	12-0	

DAVENTRY

Season	Home	Away
1895-96	55-0	

DEVON ALBION

Season	Home	Away
1912-13	3-3	
1913-14		3-21

DEVONPORT ALBION

Season	Home	Away
1898-99	3-4	
1899-00		0-17
1900-01	5-6	
1901-02		0-14
1902-03	4-11	
1903-04		3-17
1906-07		6-39
1907-08	0-14	
1909-10		0-16
1910-11	11-3	
1911-12		3-36

DOLPHIN

Season	Home	Away
1963-64		5-0
1964-65	34-9	

DUNVANT

Season	Home	Away
1996-97	48-32	

EAST MIDLANDS

Season	Home	Away
1919-20	11-10	

EBBW VALE

Season	Home	Away
1924-25	0-4	
1973-74	13-7	
1975-76	24-12	
1977-78	19-6	
1978-79		15-21
1979-80	10-12	
1980-81		3-10
1981-82	20-6	
1982-83		7-26
1983-84	24-15	
1985-86	16-10	
1986-87		13-22
1987-88	14-12	

EDGEWARE

Season	Home	Away
1925-26	41-0	
1926-27	54-0	
1927-28	14-3	3-23
1928-29	11-3	

EDINBURGH

Season	Home	Away
1999-2000	32-8	47-8
2000-01	22-23	15-18

EDINBURGH ROYAL H.S.

Season	Home	Away

Season	Home	Away
1905-06	19-0	

EXETER

Season	Home	Away
1904-05	3-3	
1905-06	15-6	6-23
1906-07	16-13	
1982-83		28-15
1983-84	44-15	
1984-85		23-3
1985-86	28-13	

FYLDE

Season	Home	Away
1979-80	16-12	
1985-86	40-11	
1986-87	22-20	
1988-89		12-13
1991-92	46-9	

GALA

Season	Home	Away
1972-73		10-18
1973-74	45-6	
1978-79		16-0
1991-92		34-9
1992-93	41-12	

N. F. GAMBLE'S XV

Season	Home	Away
1940-41	24-0	

GLASGOW

Season	Home	Away
1961-62	18-6	
1962-63		8-9

GLASGOW RUGBY

Season	Home	Away
2001-02	30-9	27-31
2004-05	33-23	13-9

GLASGOW UNIVERSITY

Season	Home	Away
1910-11	22-6	
1911-12	17-3	
1912-13	29-6	

GLOUCESTER

Season	Home	Away
1898-99		8-18
1900-01	10-16	0-17
1901-02	0-9	0-27
1902-03	8-3	0-6
1903-04	0-16	10-11
1904-05	10-4	3-29
1905-06	3-9	6-20
1906-07	9-11	0-15
1907-08	19-9	9-11
1908-09	3-11	0-3
1909-10	12-4	8-10
1910-11	3-4	3-8
1911-12	3-3	3-14
1912-13	8-6	3-6
1913-14	9-3	0-16
1919-20	15-8	
1920-21	11-5	8-14
1921-22	8-24	3-26
1923-24	0-3	3-28
1926-27		3-6
1927-28	4-0	3-9
1928-29		3-11
1929-30	10-5	6-12
1930-31	3-8	11-8
1931-32	3-0	8-10
1932-33	8-18	3-17
1933-34	17-3	0-5
1934-35	13-0	6-5
1935-36	3-0	
1938-39		3-7
1945-46		7-13
1947-48	7-5	
1948-49		0-0
1949-50	6-0	
1950-51		0-21
1951-52	5-3	
1952-53		6-6
1953-54		3-5
1954-55	11-6	
1955-56	19-8	
1956-57		6-12

Season	Home	Away
1957-58	5-9	
1958-59		33-3
1959-60	28-9	
1960-61		11-14
1961-62	17-10	
1962-63		6-3
1963-64	3-6	
1965-66	8-8	
1966-67	16-6	9-16
1967-68	18-8	3-19
1968-69		11-16
1970-71		6-25
1971-72	16-6	
1972-73		3-7
1973-74	17-15	
1974-75		10-51
1975-76	3-20	
1976-77		6-31
1978-79		4-37
1979-80	3-12	
1980-81		7-22
1981-82	7-14	
1982-83		10-12
1983-84	17-14	
1984-85		10-28
1986-87		6-17
1987-88	12-13	
1988-89		12-29
1989-90	12-17	
1990-91	6-7	
1991-92		17-10
1992-93	16-21	
1993-94	19-3	14-19
		6-11
1994-95	9-6	13-14
1996-97	25-27	6-19
1997-98	22-24	15-20
	30-11	
1998-99	22-8	31-43
1999-2000	9-25	35-11
2000-01	34-15	15-12
2001-02	58-21	9-22
2002-03	13-16	9-18
	22-40 (played at Twickenham)	
2003-04	30-17	20-28
2004-05	12-18	26-18

GOSFORTH
(Newcastle Gosforth from 1990-91)

Season	Home	Away
1957-58	33-6	
1960-61		6-9
1974-75	4-7	
1985-86		6-6
(won on away team rule)		
1988-89	13-12	
1989-90		22-15

GRENOBLE

Season	Home	Away
1999-2000	27-16	18-20

GUY'S HOSPITAL

Season	Home	Away
1901-02	20-3	
1903-04	8-11	
1904-05	12-6	
1905-06	11-3	
1907-08	3-8	
1908-09	19-10	
1909-10	6-0	
1910-11	16-0	
1911-12	12-8	
1912-13	21-0	
1913-14	6-16	
1919-20	11-0	
1920-21	3-3	
1921-22	0-9	
1925-26	15-3	
1927-28	11-5	
1928-29		10-0
1929-30	13-0	
1930-31	11-3	10-6
1931-32	22-3	17-5
1932-33		8-13
1933-34	27-13	
1934-35	39-6	
1941-42	0-9	
1953-54	11-6	
1955-56	12-0	

HALIFAX

Season	Home	Away
1962-63	6-6	
1964-65		17-0

HAMPSTEAD

Season	Home	Away
1895-96	25-0	

HANDSWORTH

Season	Home	Away
1895-96	18-0	
1896-97	3-0	8-4
1896-97	29-0	
1897-98	16-0	36-4
1898-99	29-0	
1899-00	24-0	
1900-01	42-0	
1901-02	27-0	
1902-03	20-0	
1903-04	9-3	

HARLEQUINS

Season	Home	Away
1896-97	6-6	
1897-98		18-3
1898-99	13-0	
1899-00	35-0	
1900-01	16-8	
1901-02	21-0	
1902-03	23-5	
1905-06		18-3
1906-07	16-16	
1908-09	29-0	
1909-10		11-27
1910-11	11-18	
1911-12		0-32
1912-13	5-19	
1913-14		0-21
1919-20	22-13	
1920-21	11-19	
1921-22		0-3
1922-23	3-16	
1923-24		6-21
1924-25	26-3	
1925-26		10-25
1926-27	3-6	
1927-28	11-0	
1928-29	9-3	
1929-30	0-3	
1930-31	21-0	
1931-32		0-6
1932-33	7-13	
1933-34		6-21
1934-35	12-6	
1935-36		8-12
1937-38		8-14
1938-39	17-13	
1945-46	5-8	
1947-48	6-0	
1949-50		5-9
1950-51		3-14
1951-52	9-0	
1952-53	0-0	0-11
1954-55	24-0	
1956-57	9-3	
1958-59	27-0	
1959-60	9-14	24-14
1960-61	11-6	24-5
1961-62	20-6	
1962-63	3-0	3-8
1963-64	9-6	
1964-65	19-0	
1965-66	3-33	
1966-67	11-19	6-12
1968-69	9-12	8-17
1969-70	24-13	6-6
1970-71	12-8	30-6
1971-72	12-13	20-6
1972-73	29-14	28-15
1973-74	28-13	21-18
1974-75	12-18	18-16
1975-76	6-4	16-6
1976-77	39-6	16-35
1977-78	19-7	9-9
1978-79	42-3	24-21
1979-80	7-12	
1980-81		10-19
1981-82	27-18	
1982-83		9-27
1983-84	28-12	

Season	Home	Away
1984-85		13-39
1985-86	21-24	
1986-87		0-13
1987-88	15-4	
1988-89		22-13
1989-90	23-7	
1990-91		6-21
1990-91	13-25	
(after extra time, played at Twickenham)		
1991-92	25-14	15-32
1992-93	21-16	12-7
1993-94	15-14	7-15
1994-95	16-23	9-10
1996-97	15-20	16-36
1997-98	23-26	30-5
1998-99	25-6	24-17
1999-2000	29-27	17-29
2000-01	27-20	34-25
		6-11
2001-02	13-13	24-16
2002-03	35-7	31-19
2003-04	18-17	21-43
2004-05	22-20	45-13

HARROGATE

Season	Home	Away
1990-91	50-12	18-4
1991-92		51-0
1992-93	36-14	

HEADINGLEY

Season	Home	Away
1910-11	37-0	
1911-12	32-9	8-5
1934-35	10-5	
1935-36		0-19
1936-37	5-11	
1937-38		6-5
1947-48	34-5	
1948-49		19-8
1949-50	11-3	
1950-51		5-6
1951-52	9-9	
1952-53		21-0
1953-54	18-5	
1954-55	34-9	
1955-56		5-6
1956-57		6-3
1957-58	5-8	
1958-59		26-11
1959-60	14-8	
1960-61		8-25
1961-62	34-5	
1962-63		6-9
1963-64	21-5	
1964-65		21-15
1965-66	30-5	
1966-67	13-11	
1967-68		8-12
1968-69	17-16	
1969-70		14-6
1970-71	21-6	
1971-72		44-0
1972-73	21-13	
1973-74		14-12
1974-75	24-7	
1975-76		10-13
1976-77	16-4	
1977-78		9-13
1978-79	22-16	
1979-80		3-9
1980-81	35-0	
1981-82		18-6
1982-83	30-7	
1983-84		3-23
1984-85	9-21	
1985-86		14-28
1986-87	12-8	
1987-88		3-38
1988-89	19-7	
1989-90		3-15
1991-92		65-0

HERIOT'S FORMER PUPILS

Season	Home	Away
1950-51	9-11	
1951-52		0-0
1965-66		10-11
1966-67	3-10	

HINCKLEY

Season	Home	Away
1982-83	31-4	

HOUSEHOLD BRIGADE

Season	Home	Away
1922-23	30-3	

JEDFOREST

Season	Home	Away
1908-09	6-13	
1913-14	9-14	

R. E. G. JEEPS XV

Season	Home	Away
1966-67	0-27	
1979-80	17-8	

JESUS COLLEGE OXFORD

Season	Home	Away
1895-96	8-5	
1896-97	6-3	
1897-98	38-0	

JESUS COLLEGE WANDERERS

Season	Home	Away
1896-97	31-0	

KENSINGTON NOMADS

Season	Home	Away
1896-97	6-0	

KETTERING

Season	Home	Away
1975-76	38-0 (Midland Preliminary Cup final)	
1981-82	31-0	

KINGS COLLEGE HOSPITAL

Season	Home	Away
1924-25	12-15	
1925-26	12-3	
1926-27	17-0	

LANSDOWNE

Season	Home	Away
1898-99	10-0	
1899-00	14-8	

LEEDS

Season	Home	Away
2000-01	73-35	
2001-02	34-14	26-6
2002-03	28-6	19-26
2003-04	48-24	31-15
2004-05	18-9	21-26
	19-24	

LEICESTER

Season	Home	Away
1894-95	0-11	7-21
1895-96	11-8	0-3
1895-96	5-4	
1896-97	15-11	3-11
1897-98	16-8	0-10
1897-98	8-3	
1898-99		3-6
1898-99	0-4	5-24
1899-00	3-3	0-4
1900-01	0-4	0-0
1901-02	6-11	0-14
1902-03	6-12	0-13
1903-04	5-14	3-14
1904-05	0-0	0-8
1905-06	8-0	10-3
1906-07	3-3	0-11
1907-08	11-3	3-13
1908-09	11-3	0-16
1909-10	3-8	11-3
1910-11	3-14	0-0
1911-12	3-8	3-16
1912-13	5-12	5-18
1913-14	3-27	3-21
1919-20	6-6	0-18
1919-20	6-25	
1920-21	12-0	0-30
1921-22	7-11	4-29
1922-23	3-21	11-14
1923-24	19-16	3-13
1924-25	3-6	3-8
1925-26	18-0	5-11
1926-27	18-9	5-5
1927-28	6-3	3-3
1928-29	11-8	10-8
1929-30	3-18	3-10
1930-31	3-6	10-10
1931-32	18-0	10-13
1932-33	6-9	21-3
1933-34	14-8	3-10
1934-35	11-3	8-13
1935-36	6-0	0-14
1936-37	12-3	3-22
1936-37		11-4
1937-38	16-6	3-10
1937-38	12-3	
1938-39	3-5	3-8
1938-39		14-14
1945-46	5-0	0-6
1946-47		7-5
1947-48	11-0	7-14
1948-49	9-9	8-6
1949-50	14-3	9-3
1950-51	5-14	8-26
1951-52	13-11	5-3
1952-53	11-0	10-9
1953-54	19-5	8-12
1954-55	6-8	9-5
1955-56	19-10	16-9
1956-57	6-13	9-9
1957-58	3-3	11-8
1958-59	22-13	10-3
1959-60	17-14	6-6
1960-61	8-3	9-0
1961-62	29-13	0-5
1962-63		9-12
1963-64	0-11	3-27
1964-65	18-8	3-14
1965-66	3-9	11-16
1966-67	3-8	9-17
1967-68	12-3	6-9
1968-69		17-17
1969-70	29-8	9-14
1970-71	9-8	6-6
1971-72	12-4	24-15
1972-73	22-12	22-12
1973-74	26-7	9-15
1973-74	22-6	
1974-75	20-6	13-13
1975-76	28-12	12-24
1976-77	3-23	13-40
1977-78	26-10	11-20
1978-79	16-9	6-23
1978-79		3-29
1979-80	4-42	
1980-81		21-25
1981-82	22-6	
1981-82	10-23	
1982-83	18-9	10-15
1983-84	0-25	
1984-85		4-24
1985-86	6-14	15-25
1986-87		15-24
1987-88	0-47	9-35
1988-89	19-30	8-42
1989-90	23-7	12-34
1990-91	18-28	3-26
1991-92	21-17	22-19
1992-93	12-13	3-28
		6-28
1993-94	19-10	9-36
1994-95	18-20	15-28
1996-97	22-19	9-23
1997-98	25-6	15-15
1998-99	15-22	25-35
1999-2000	46-24	21-26
2000-01	9-12	19-33
		13-17
2001-02	11-21	6-17
2002-03	3-16	25-12
2003-04	14-0	32-15
2004-05	26-11	13-32

LEICESTERSHIRE HARLEQUINS

Season	Home	Away
1941-42	16-3	

LEINSTER

Season	Home	Away
2000-01	8-14	31-40

LENNOX

Season	Home	Away

Season	Home	Away
1895-96	0-0	
1897-98	8-5	
1898-99	5-5	
1899-00	18-3	
1900-01	17-3	
1901-02	12-0	42-3
1902-03	5-0	18-9
1903-04	5-3	
1904-05	18-6	
1905-06	37-8	
1909-10	62-3	

LITTLEBOROUGH

Season	Home	Away
1898-99	26-0	

LICHFIELD

Season	Home	Away
1985-86	20-13	
1986-87	18-24	

LIVERPOOL
(Liverpool St. Helens from 1988-89)

Season	Home	Away
1971-72	22-21	
1975-76	19-12	
1977-78		4-16
1984-85	101-10	
1985-86		7-16
1987-88	9-13	
18989-90		13-13
1990-91		23-13

LLANELLI

Season	Home	Away
1902-03	5-16	
1904-05	5-0	5-13
1905-06	19-3	3-17
1906-07	0-18	3-12
1907-8	5-0	0-14
1908-09	0-4	0-3
1909-10	0-4	0-3
1910-11	14-3	5-6
1912-13	0-8	0-9
1913-14	6-4	0-12
1920-21		0-12
1921-22	0-7	0-15
1925-26	3-5	0-22
1926-27	10-8	5-9
1935-36	9-10	6-6
1936-37	0-3	0-23
1937-38	8-12	0-21
1938-39	8-11	3-8
1945-46		6-30
1946-47	3-0	3-7
1947-48	8-5	5-9
1948-49	3-0	10-12
1949-50	6-8	13-3
1950-51	9-14	0-3
1951-52	3-6	8-24
1954-55		8-14
1955-56	8-8	
1956-57		0-6
1957-58	27-3	
1958-59		16-6
1959-60	9-8	
1960-61		0-6
1961-62	14-3	
1963-64		8-16
1964-65	11-6	3-9
1965-66	3-9	3-5
1966-67	11-3	5-13
1967-68		0-19
1968-69	12-3	8-23
1969-70	17-6	8-6
1970-71	17-19	9-27
1971-72	21-8	7-36
1972-73		14-46
1973-74		0-44
1974-75	10-24	10-53
1975-76	13-10	16-36
1976-77		15-55
1977-78	0-28	10-21
1978-79	11-3	18-60
1979-80	4-21	15-7
1980-81	12-4	0-31
1981-82	17-17	15-33
1982-83	3-33	0-50
1983-84	8-3	13-61
1984-85	10-7	9-54
1985-86	17-46	19-46

Season	Home	Away
1986-87	18-14	12-27
1987-88	15-24	13-27
1988-89	0-8	24-16
1989-90	13-17	22-37
1990-91	18-30	19-41
1991-92	59-6	11-30
1999-2000	31-28 (played at Reading)	
2003-04	9-18	9-14
2004-05	25-3	22-20

LLWYNPIA TONYPANDY

Season	Home	Away
1895-96	6-9	
1898-99	5-0	
1899-00	0-0	
1900-01	5-0	
1901-02	25-0	

LONDON DEVONIANS

Season	Home	Away
1903-04	32-3	

(played at the County Ground; Franklin's Gardens flooded)

LONDON HOSPITAL

Season	Home	Away
1909-10	11-5	
1910-11	23-9	
1911-12	25-8	
1913-14	23-6	
1919-20	74-0 (club record)	
1926-27	0-12	
1927-28	12-11	
1928-29	8-0	
1929-30	3-12	
1930-31	7-3	
1931-32	32-0	
1932-33	17-3	
1933-34	21-5	

LONDON IRISH

Season	Home	Away
1904-05	25-0	
1912-13	3-3	
1921-22	18-0	
1936-37	22-3	
1951-52		3-9
1952-53	12-6	
1953-54	17-3	
1955-56		15-10
1956-57	6-0	
1957-58		3-11
1958-59	26-14	
1959-60	8-10	10-5
1960-61	20-3	
1960-61	11-10	
1961-62		30-11
1964-65		27-0
1966-67		22-3
1967-68	19-3	
1968-69		9-15
1969-70	14-8	
1970-71		9-17
1971-72	17-8	
1972-73		24-4
1973-74	18-6	
1975-76	18-15	
1976-77		12-11
1977-78	12-6	
1978-79		7-25
1979-80	9-3	
1980-81		3-18
1982-83		21-13
1983-84	30-19	
1984-85		17-24
1985-86	6-15	
1986-87		17-6
1987-88	15-13	
1988-89		10-18
1989-90	33-21	
1990-91		58-6
1991-92	12-12	
1992-93		3-12
1993-94	23-12	16-13
1995-96	65-32	52-24
1996-97	31-21	21-34
1997-98	33-18	51-10
1998-99	8-32	26-10
	6-21	
1999-2000	24-19	44-20
	24-17 (played at Reading)	

Season	Home	Away
2000-01	27-10	10-13
2001-02	24-15	12-48
	7-38 (played at Twickenham)	
2002-03	10-22	14-12
	38-9 (played at Oxford)	
2003-04	24-30	36-15
2004-05	20-21	22-21

LONDON NEW ZEALANDERS

Season	Home	Away
1925-26	40-0	

LONDON SCOTTISH

Season	Home	Away
1903-04	6-5	0-8
1904-05		6-3
1905-06	23-8	
1922-23	27-6	15-10
1924-25		23-11
1925-26	22-0	
1926-27		5-3
1954-55	24-3	
1955-56		6-14
1956-57	14-3	
1957-58		12-6
1958-59	11-3	
1960-61	17-0	
1961-62		8-6
1962-63	5-8	
1963-64		3-12
1964-65	15-8	
1965-66		17-6
1966-67	18-5	
1967-68		11-8
1968-69	23-11	
1969-70		6-20
1970-71	17-5	
1971-72		10-21
1972-73	11-9	
1973-74		16-10
1974-75	13-12	
1975-76		10-10
1975-76		28-16
1976-77	22-12	
1977-78		12-44
1978-79	27-9	
1979-80		19-6
1980-81	6-21	
1981-82		13-37
1982-83	10-12	
1983-84		15-6
1983-84		6-34
1984-85	26-9	
1985-86	6-11	11-19
1986-87	30-0	
1987-88		3-50
1988-89		3-3
1992-93		34-21
1995-96	54-11	59-17
1998-99	44-13	33-22

LONDON WELSH

Season	Home	Away
1895-96	8-5	8-3
1896-97	16-0	
1897-98	38-0	
1900-01	3-3	
1901-02	5-3	
1902-03	12-8	
1904-05	33-3	15-3
1905-06	0-0	
1906-07	6-9	9-23
1907-08	12-5	3-10
1908-0	5-8	
1909-10	0-5	
1910-11	13-0	11-0
1912-13	33-5	
1913-14	15-9	13-8
1919-20	22-7	5-9
1920-21	6-0	
1921-22	10-9	
1922-23	23-3	6-0
1923-24	3-0	0-3
1926-27	43-0	9-17
1927-28		4-0
1928-29	17-3	
1929-30		3-3
1930-31	19-10	
1931-32	18-10	
1932-33	14-9	10-6
1933-34	19-8	20-11

Season	Home	Away
1934-35	15-8	7-5
1935-36	27-3	13-0
1936-37	11-13	
1937-38	3-9	10-8
1938-39	11-3	
1946-47		3-11
1947-48	3-7	
1948-49		5-6
1949-50	8-3	
1950-51		12-3
1951-52	22-3	
1952-53		0-0
1953-54	11-0	
1954-55		0-6
1955-56	16-3	
1956-57		21-0
1957-58	3-0	
1958-59		11-20
1959-60	16-9	
1960-61		6-8
1963-64	8-14	
1964-65		18-13
1965-66	6-5	
1966-67		8-22
1967-68	11-6	
1968-69		8-23
1969-70	28-14	
1971-72	13-6	
1972-73		12-21
1973-74	18-17	
1974-75		18-35
1975-76	22-13	
1976-77		18-3
		11-17
1977-78	3-8	
1979-80	7-4	
1980-81		9-34
1981-82	12-6	
1982-83		7-20
1983-84	7-7	
1986-87		8-19
1987-88	14-16	
1988-89		22-0
1991-92	34-0	
1992-93		37-3
1999-2000		35-26

LONG BUCKBY & OLNEY

Season	Home	Away
1919-20	41-4	

LOUISVILLE (USA)

Season	Home	Away
1987-88	70-6	

LYONS

Season	Home	Away
1926-27	0-3	

MANCHESTER

Season	Home	Away
1898-99	23-3	
1899-00	47-8	
1900-01	23-3	
1922-23	15-0	12-0
1923-24		8-13
1978-79	27-0	

MANCHESTER OLD BOYS

Season	Home	Away
1895-96	54-0	

MANLEY (AUSTRALIA)

Season	Home	Away
1990-91	19-19	

MARKET HARBOROUGH

Season	Home	Away
1940-41	17-5	

METROPOLITAN POLICE

Season	Home	Away
1937-38	6-0	
1938-39	18-0	
1940-41	3-17	
1946-47	11-0	
1947-48	25-0	
1948-49	33-0	
1949-50	14-6	
1950-51	9-3	
1951-52	20-11	

Season	Home	Away
1952-53		0-3
1953-54	11-8	
1954-55	16-0	
1956-57	13-5	
1957-58	11-9	
1959-60	17-11	
1970-71	53-15	
1971-72	16-0	
1972-73	16-3	
1974-75	13-15	
1975-76	34-12	
1976-77	19-18	
1977-78	11-6	
1978-79	14-12	
1979-80	10-12	
1980-81	18-4	
1981-82	16-14	
1982-83	6-7	
1983-84	13-9	
1984-85	19-7	
1985-86	12-3	
1986-87	20-10	
1987-88	12-6	
1988-89	23-6	
1989-90	22-22	16-4
1990-91	26-10	
1991-92	17-18	
1992-93	35-10	
1993-94	81-0	
1994-95	17-13	

MID WEST (USA)

Season	Home	Away
1983-84	20-4	

MIDDLESEX HOSPITAL

Season	Home	Away
1951-52	31-5	

MONTAUBAN

Season	Home	Away
1967-68	9-3	

MONTFERRAND VULCANS

Season	Home	Away
2001-02	18-21	17-50

MORLEY

Season	Home	Away
1981-82	12-7	
1984-85		13-9
1986-87	36-10	
1987-88	44-3	
1991-92	17-6	

MOSELEY

Season	Home	Away
1896-97	3-3	0-14
1897-98	0-5	0-0
1898-99	21-3	0-0
1899-00	3-0	9-6
1900-01	13-6	21-6
1901-02	5-7	11-3
1902-03	14-0	15-3
1903-04	5-7	5-11
1904-05	19-4	8-14
1905-06	11-0	15-5
1906-07	8-21	8-8
1907-08	5-3	3-5
1908-09	18-0	10-3
1909-10	6-3	6-14
1910-11	31-0	14-8
1911-12	12-11	7-7
1912-13	22-5	
1913-14	16-11	3-14
1919-20	27-0	6-0
1920-21	28-6	16-6
1921-22	14-3	
1922-23	3-0	9-9
1923-24	19-0	19-11
1924-25	12-5	8-5
1925-26	14-0	3-6
1926-27	45-15	11-6
1927-28	20-3	11-3
1928-29	22-8	9-3
1929-30	14-6	9-5
1930-31	12-0	13-9
1931-32	19-0	5-22
1932-33	27-5	
1933-34	9-5	6-11
1934-35	21-5	3-15
1935-36	3-3	10-14
1936-37	13-3	0-3
1937-38	8-3	
1938-39		8-0
1945-46	24-0	3-11
1946-47	3-0	3-3
1947-48	28-0	3-3
1948-49	30-8	18-3
1949-50	9-0	8-6
1950-51	25-3	17-3
1951-52	8-3	3-3
1952-53	23-11	6-0
1953-54	17-3	20-8
1954-55	6-6	6-14
1955-56	21-13	5-3
1956-57	8-11	13-12
1957-58	30-3	20-11
1958-59	11-6	25-10
1959-60	27-8	3-6
1960-61	0-6	19-8
1961-62	17-3	15-3
1962-63	17-6	3-8
1963-64	18-6	3-3
1964-65	17-5	31-9
1965-66	3-11	3-19
1966-67	11-14	9-17
1967-68	14-15	21-17
1968-69	22-8	0-24
1969-70	24-14	3-8
1970-71	11-11	0-23
1971-72	6-25	12-25
1971-72		14-25
1972-73	9-12	18-21
1972-73	6-9	
1973-74	20-16	12-19
1974-75	11-21	9-51
1975-76	6-4	23-8
1976-77	12-15	
1977-78		6-34
1979-80	6-15	0-6
1980-81	4-10	3-27
1981-82	19-13	
1982-83	9-13	6-9
1983-84		11-12
1984-85	16-23	
1985-86		13-38
1986-87	7-19	
1987-88		19-32
1988-89	12-3	11-13
1989-90	36-6	21-27
1990-91	10-6	16-10
1991-92	35-12	21-13
1992-93	8-6	13-10
1992-93	37-15	
1994-95		16-6
1995-96	50-7	46-16

MOUNTAIN ASH

Season	Home	Away
1897-98	19-0	

MUNSTER

Season	Home	Away
1999-2000	9-8 (played at Twickenham)	

MYTHOLMROYD

Season	Home	Away
1900-01	23-0	

NARBONNE

Season	Home	Away
1996-97	22-23	

NATIONAL F. C.

Season	Home	Away
1910-11	33-12	

NEATH

Season	Home	Away
1913-14	6-10	3-18
1920-21	8-21	6-21
1922-23	6-6	
1923-24	0-0	0-15
1924-25	6-3	
1925-26		8-41
1926-27	11-11	3-25
1935-36	8-8	
1936-37		3-32
1953-54	0-6	
1954-55		3-0
1957-58		0-27

Season	Home	Away
1958-59	17-6	
1959-60	19-6	
1961-62		0-14
1999-2000	21-12	39-23

NEW BRIGHTON

Season	Home	Away
1973-74	39-10	
1974-75		18-19

NEW ZEALAND

Season	Home	Away
1905-06	0-32	

NEW ZEALAND SERVICES

Seasom	Home	Away
1945-46	6-11	

NEWBOLD-ON-AVON

Season	Home	Away
1974-75	43-3	

NEWBRIDGE

Season	Home	Away
1945-46		0-17

NEWCASTLE
(previously GOSFORTH)

Season	Home	Away
1991-92		12-32
1992-93	33-3	
1993-94	43-23	28-8
1995-96	26-5	52-9
1997-98	17-21	12-37
	17-7	
1998-99	57-16	35-45
1999-2000	37-5	32-23
2000-01	26-18	21-27
2001-02	24-19	28-13
	38-7	
2002-03	31-13	20-22
2003-04	33-20	19-23
		11-12
2004-05	23-22	16-27

NEWPORT

Season	Home	Away
1904-05		3-12
1910-11		0-19
1911-12	0-20	
1912-13		0-33
1913-14	0-13	
1920-21	6-13	3-23
1921-22	5-18	5-20
1922-23		0-19
1923-24	6-3	
1924-25		3-13
1925-26	13-3	
1926-27		9-9
1967-68	14-23	
1986-87		18-34
1996-97		67-19

NICE

Season	Home	Away
	66-7	26-10

NORTH BUCKS

Season	Home	Away
1895-96	18-0	

NORTHAMPTON & DISTRICT ALLIANCE

Season	Home	Away
1940-41	36-0	

NORTHANTS RUGBY UNION

Season	Home	Away
1896-97	20-8#	
1897-98	27-0#	
1898-99	38-0#	
1899-00	34-4#	
1903-04	23-0#	
1904-05	20-5#	
1905-06	5-0#	
1907-08	5-6#	
1908-09	17-0	
1909-10	50-5	
1910-11	65-6	
1911-12	49-8	
1912-13	59-0	
1913-14	68-6	

Season	Home	Away
1919-20	37-6	
# (18 players in Union side)		

NORTHERN

Season	Home	Away
1983-84	13-12	
1989-90	25-4	

NORWICH

Season	Home	Away
1984-85		30-6

NOTTINGHAM

Season	Home	Away
1923-24	9-3	
1924-25	27-0	
1925-26	6-0	
1926-27	18-6	
1927-28	39-3	5-5
1928-29	10-3	
1929-30	11-0	
1945-46	13-0	
1946-47	20-4	
1947-48	18-3	3-0
1948-49	11-9	10-6
1949-50		12-3
1950-51	26-3	3-3
1951-52	27-0	
1952-53	9-6	18-16
1953-54	3-3	9-6
1954-55	24-6	
1955-56		17-9
1956-57	35-3	
1957-58		11-3
1958-59	34-11	
1959-60		9-8
1960-61	12-3	
1961-62	29-3	
1962-63		33-3
1963-64	41-3	
1964-65		43-5
1965-66	21-3	
1966-67		14-3
1967-68	36-3	
1968-69		42-3
1969-70	12-8	
1970-71		16-13
1971-72	27-22	
1972-73		22-10
1973-74	9-3	
1974-75		6-20
1975-76	10-6	
1976-77		15-3
1977-78	25-12	
1978-79	10-7	
1979-80	0-3	11-6
1980-81	18-18	
1981-82		6-7
1982-83	9-15	
1983-84		10-9
1984-85	3-19	3-15
1985-86		0-33
1986-87	9-12	
1987-88		0-22
1988-89	19-22	12-25
1989-90	6-32	16-25
1990-91	22-15	7-27
1991-92	38-3	9-18
1992-93		46-17
1995-96	35-5	43-7
1940-41	3-6	
1942-43	3-16	0-32
1945-46	20-0	0-0
1946-47	30-12	16-0
1947-48	19-0	8-3
1948-49	30-3	32-9
1949-50	11-3	6-17
1950-51	3-13	3-9
1951-52		5-6
1979-80		16-7
1980-81	16-3	
1982-83		27-0
1983-84		10-23
1984-85	19-6	
1985-86		33-6
1986-87	29-6	
1987-88		3-6
1989-90	24-0	
1990-91	62-0	
1991-92		21-25
1999-2000	118-3	

NUNEATON

Season	Home	Away
1895-96	13-0	5-7
1896-97	9-0	
1900-01	16-0	
1901-02	34-3	
1902-03	35-0	
1903-04		13-0
1904-05	41-0	3-0
1913-14	11-8	
1919-20	20-3	50-3
1920-21	6-4	6-6
1921-22	8-6	8-3
1931-32	13-10	
1932-33	18-0	9-0
1933-34	17-14	0-22
1934-35		10-6
1936-37		11-3
1937-38	23-11	
1938-39		6-8

NORTHAMPTONSHIRE

Season	Home	Away
1939-40	31-6	

PETRARCA PADOVA

Season	Home	Away
1996-97	29-9	

OLD ALLEYNIANS

Season	Home	Away
1905-06	17-5	
1923-24	19-3	
1924-25	43-8	
1925-26	38-5	
1926-27	11-8	
1927-28	28-11	
1928-29	17-4	
1929-30	12-3	
1930-31	31-8	
1932-33	11-3	
1933-34	30-18	
1934-35	35-16	
1935-36	29-3	
1936-37	16-10	
1937-38	19-3	
1938-39	18-11	
1945-46	29-3	
1946-47	36-6	
1947-48	21-8	
1948-49	31-0	
1949-50	25-3	
1950-51	16-6	
1951-52	25-3	
1952-53	20-0	
1954-55	39-3	
1955-56	25-6	
1956-57	27-3	
1957-58		23-3
1958-59	29-5	
1959-60	16-22	
1960-61	52-6	
1961-62	34-0	
1962-63	14-3	
1963-64	35-3	
1964-65	24-15	
1966-67	27-9	
1967-68	17-11	
1968-69	18-3	
1969-70	43-8	
1970-71	34-3	
1972-73	27-8	
1974-75	18-0	
1975-76	13-7	

OLD BELVEDERE

Season	Home	Away
1956-57		3-8

OLD BLUES

Season	Home	Away
1923-24	9-9	
1924-25	11-15	
1925-26	50-8	
1926-27	20-8	
1927-28	26-3	
1929-30	17-9	

OLD CRANLEIGHIANS

Season	Home	Away

Season	Home	Away
1928-29	9-5	
1946-47	38-0	

OLD EDWARDIANS

Season	Home	Away
1897-98	13-3	
1898-99	13-0	
1899-00	36-3	
1901-02	14-0	
1902-0	30-0	
1906-07	13-4	
1908-09	22-3	
1909-10	18-0	
1910-11	25-10	
1911-12	22-3	
1912-13	17-11	
1913-14	6-18	
1920-21	31-19	
1921-22	10-5	
1922-23	12-0	
1923-24	26-5	
1924-25		6-10
1925-26	22-5	
1927-28	16-0	
1928-29		43-5

OLD LEYSIANS

Season	Home	Away
1898-99	13-0	

OLD MERCHANT TAYLORS

Season	Home	Away
1899-00	8-0	
1902-03	3-3	
1905-06	22-3	
1906-07	22-6	
1907-08	18-0	
1909-10	5-3	
1911-12	7-11	
1912-13	9-4	
1919-20	43-0	
1920-21	4-11	
1912-22	23-0	
1922-23	12-3	
1923-24	8-3	
1924-25	9-6	
1925-26	24-5	
1926-27	37-8	
1927-28	12-10	
1928-29	13-5	
1929-30	33-11	
1930-31	11-20	
1931-32	11-3	
1932-33	13-3	
1933-34	12-11	
1934-35	6-6	
1935-36	12-8	
1936-37	16-0	
1937-38	6-6	
1938-39	8-6	
1945-46	32-0	
1946-47	24-0	
1947-48	18-3	
1949-50	8-9	
1950-51	15-3	
1951-52		11-5
1952-53	22-3	
1953-54	11-3	
1954-55	16-3	
1955-56	23-0	
1956-57	25-8	
1957-58	20-3	
1958-59	18-0	
1959-60	46-12	
1960-61	22-3	
1961-62	26-11	
1962-63	18-9	
1963-64	17-0	
1965-66	36-9	
1966-67	31-6	
1969-70	53-5	
1971-72	54-6	

OLD MILLHILLIANS

Season	Home	Away
1928-29	27-13	
1929-30	26-0	
1930-31	8-10	
1931-32	9-3	
1932-33	7-3	
1933-34	11-11	

Season	Home	Away
1934-35	5-5	
1935-36	22-8	
1936-37	12-0	
1937-38	3-8	
1938-39	16-8	
1946-47	29-0	
1947-48	49-0	
1948-49	24-0	
1949-50	23-3	
1950-51	43-0	
1951-52	44-0	
1952-53	9-11	
1953-54		11-11
1954-55	3-17	
1955-56	26-6	
1956-57	19-3	
1957-58		17-6
1958-59		3-8
1959-60	16-22	
1960-61	52-6	
1961-62	34-0	
1962-63	14-3	
1963-64	35-3	
1964-65	24-15	
1966-67	27-9	
1967-68	17-11	
1968-69	18-3	
1969-70	43-8	
1970-71	34-3	
1972-73	27-8	
1974-75	18-0	
1975-76	13-7	

OLD NORTHAMPTONIANS

Season	Home	Away
1939-40	16-11	

OLD OUNDELLIANS

Season	Home	Away
1902-03	28-0	

OLD PAULINES

Season	Home	Away
1931-32	12-4	
1932-33	22-10	
1933-34	31-6	
1934-35	16-6	
1937-38	34-13	

OLD UPPINGHAMIANS

Season	Home	Away
1897-98	8-3	

OLNEY

Season	Home	Away
1895-96	6-0	10-0
1895-96	5-0	
1896-97	8-4	20-0
1897-98	19-3	8-0
1898-99	8-3	3-3
1899-00	17-0	18-0
1900-01	16-3	38-0
1901-02	15-0	21-3
1902-03	13-5	
1902-03	14-0	
1903-04	19-6	
1904-05	15-9	
1905-06	6-6	
1907-8	25-0	

ORRELL

Season	Home	Away
1973-74		9-19
1990-91	18-10	0-60
1991-92	12-4	
1992-93		10-9
1993-94	9-13	6-27
1994-95	15-3	10-13
1996-97	41-7	50-14
	61-7	
2002-03		55-44

OTLEY

Season	Home	Away
1898-99	24-9	

OUNDLE SCHOOL

Season	Home	Away
1895-96		6-0
1896-97		27-3

Season	Home	Away
1897-98		
1898-99		
1899-00		
1900-01		
1901-02		
1902-03		
1940-41		
1941-42		
1942-43		

OXFORD GREYHOUNDS

Season	Home	Away
1926-27	5-3	

OXFORD UNIVERSITY

Season	Home	Away
1902-03		3-11
1903-04	0-19	
1904-05		8-15
1905-06	6-3	
1906-07		12-5
1907-08	11-5	
1948-49	9-13	8-22
1949-50	12-0	
1950-51		5-3
1956-57	14-8	
1958-59		5-16
1959-60	40-3	
1960-61		3-33
1961-62	22-8	
1963-64	6-10	
1964-65		9-6
1965-66	19-8	14-5
1966-67		5-8
1976-68	10-9	
1968-69		3-6
1969-70	36-23	
1970-71		31-6
1971-72	21-11	
1972-73		25-6
1973-74	36-10	
1974-75		3-13
1975-76	17-3	
1976-77		47-7
1977-78	33-7	
1978-79		30-15
1979-80	14-9	
1980-81		16-10
1981-82	16-22	
1982-83		20-10
1983-84	27-16	
1984-85		34-14
1985-86	27-11	
1986-87		12-18
1987-88	22-19	
1988-89		18-26
1989-90	26-7	
1990-91		25-14

OXFORDSHIRE

Season	Home	Away
1952-53	16-0	

PENARTH

Season	Home	Away
1904-05	11-8	0-14
1905-06	3-3	5-8
1926-27	16-6	
1928-29	8-5	
1929-30	3-6	
1930-31	11-8	
1931-32	15-3	
1932-33	12-6	
1933-34	6-0	
1934-35	24-11	
1935-36	8-0	
1937-38	35-3	
1949-50	12-5	
1950-51	12-3	
1951-52	3-0	
1952-53	13-0	
1953-54	8-5	
1954-55	3-3	
1955-56	6-6	
1957-58	24-3	
1958-59	3-13	
1959-60	36-6	
1960-61	5-0	
1963-64	16-16	
1964-65	17-3	
1966-67	33-3	

Season	Home	Away
	17-5	
	53-0	
	34-14	
	8-9	
	18-0	
	14-0	
	13-11	
	20-13	
	13-19	

PENRYN

Season	Home	Away
1958-59		13-0
1963-64		9-3

PENYGRAIG

Season	Home	Away
1895-96	8-3	
1896-97	5-0	
1902-03	10-0	

PERCY PARK

Season	Home	Away
1899-00	11-0	
1900-01	16-5	
1961-62	14-0	

PLYMOUTH ALBION

Season	Home	Away
1901-02		11-19
1902-03	3-8	
1903-04		3-22
1906-07	6-5	0-16
1907-08	3-11	0-6
1911-12	5-13	
1928-29	3-0	0-26
1929-30	3-3	3-8
1930-31	16-6	
1931-32	4-3	8-16
1933-34		3-0
1934-35	4-3	
1980-81	56-0	
1981-82		7-15
1987-88		7-14
1989-90	6-4	

PONTYPOOL

Season	Home	Away
1921-22	3-17	0-22
1930-31	11-17	11-11
1931-32	5-9	3-24
1932-33	11-8	0-8
1933-34	6-0	18-5
1934-35	15-0	9-6
1935-36	13-8	6-10
1936-37	4-10	5-8
1937-38	6-8	0-14
1938-39	3-0	0-25
1945-46	19-3	3-30
1946-47	5-14	0-0
1947-48	0-9	9-14
1948-49	0-3	3-9
1949-50	5-3	5-12
1950-51	3-3	3-6
1951-52	6-0	0-11
1952-53	3-6	9-3
1953-54		10-12
1954-55	17-3	
1955-56		8-12
1957-58	22-3	
1959-60		14-3
1961-62	28-6	
1962-63		3-8
1963-64	9-11	
1964-65		6-3
1965-66	26-14	
1966-67		6-8
1967-68	16-3	
1970-71		3-12
1971-72	21-17	
1972-73		7-17
1973-74	101-10	
1974-75		3-16

PORTADOWN

Season	Home	Away
1991-92		28-10

PORTSMOUTH

Season	Home	Away
1896-97	3-0	
1897-98		28-0
1898-99	7-6	
1900-01	14-8	

PRESTON GRASSHOPPERS

Season	Home	Away
1996-97		40-11

PENARTH (continued)

Season	Home	Away
1967-68	55-0	

PUBLIC SCHOOLS

Season	Home	Away
1913-14	19-5	

QUEEN'S WOOLWICH

Season	Home	Away
1895-96	31-0	

QUEENSLAND (AUSTRALIA)

Season	Home	Away
1990-91	3-15	

R. A. F. BOMBER COMMAND

Season	Home	Away
1945-46	22-15	

RACING CLUB of FRANCE

Season	Home	Away
1903-04	10-0	
1924-25	0-3	
1926-27	26-0	

READING

Season	Home	Away
1939-40	26-3	

RICHMOND

Season	Home	Away
1898-99		3-0
1899-00		7-13
1900-01	9-3	
1901-02		0-17
1902-03	19-3	
1903-04		5-28
1904-05	31-0	
1905-06		0-16
1906-07	21-5	
1908-09	8-3	
1911-12		6-0
1913-14	0-0	
1929-30		3-0
1930-31	17-23	
1931-32		10-9
1932-33	6-12	
1933-34		0-16
1934-35	11-3	
1935-36		7-0
1936-37	6-23	
1937-38		16-16
1938-39	11-3	
1946-47	19-3	
1947-48		17-0
1948-49	29-8	
1949-50		14-5
1950-51	24-6	
1951-52		0-3
1952-53	6-6	
1953-54		8-6
1954-55	17-8	
1955-56	15-12 (first floodlit match)	
1955-56		5-3
1956-57	19-10	
1957-58		3-13
1958-59	14-0	
1958-59	19-3	
1959-60		9-5
1960-61	12-5	
1961-62	0-3	12-3
1962-63	9-3	
1963-64		11-13
1964-65	17-8	9-8
1966-67	0-11	
1967-68		13-8
1968-69	21-15	
1969-70		3-6
1970-71	29-3	
1971-72		12-15
1972-73	21-21	
1973-74		26-10
1974-75	3-10	
1975-76		6-13
1976-77	10-15	
1977-78		6-9
1978-79	29-18	
1979-80		11-22
1980-81	27-7	
1981-82		25-12
1982-83	9-20	
1983-84		20-13
1984-85	0-9	
1985-86	19-7	
1986-87		49-9
1987-88	3-16	
1988-89		12-15
		0-6
1989-90	12-6	
1991-92	21-16	
1992-93	14-30	
1994-95	27-6	
1997-98	39-47	24-21
1998-99	44-27	31-19

RICHMOND & BLACKHEATH

Season	Home	Away
1945-46		17-5

ROCKCLIFFE

Season	Home	Away
1899-00	8-21	
1901-02	0-9	
1902-03	3-3	

ROSSLYN PARK

Season	Home	Away
1898-99	31-5	
1899-00	19-13	
1900-01	0-11	
1901-02	20-10	
1923-24	13-0	
1924-25	11-14	
1925-26	22-0	
1926-27	47-0	
1927-28	11-0	
1928-29	12-16	
1929-30	13-6	
1930-31	23-0	
1931-32	30-6	
1932-33	22-0	
1933-34	10-21	
1934-35	6-16	
1935-36	9-6	
1936-37	6-5	
1937-38	21-5	
1938-39	17-11	
1945-46	20-5	8-13
1947-48	15-3	
1948-49	6-8	
1949-50	0-8	
1951-52	26-6	
1952-53	9-3	
1953-54	6-0	
1954-55	12-8	
1955-56	22-5	
1956-57	14-6	
1957-58	6-3	
1958-59	32-14	
1959-60	9-8	
1960-61		14-19
1961-62	22-14	
1962-63	16-0	13-3
1963-64	6-13	
1964-65		34-5
1965-66	14-8	
1966-67		14-6
1967-68	25-3	
1968-69		20-24
1969-70	30-3	
1970-71		9-17
1971-72	12-3	
1972-73		9-14
1976-77		7-18
1980-81		7-23
1981-82	6-20	
1982-83		14-25
1983-84		20-6
1984-85		0-11
1986-87		16-23
1987-88	0-22	
1988-89		15-29
1989-90		17-19
1990-91		0-48
1991-92	20-12	

ROTHERHAM

Season	Home	Away
2000-01	42-0	32-19
2003-04	18-8	42-13

ROUNDHAY

Season	Home	Away
1971-72		20-12
1972-73	20-9	

ROYAL AIR FORCE

Season	Home	Away
1973-74		9-15
1976-77	19-9	
1919-20	21-3	
1919-20	20-0	
1920-21	11-4	
1921-22	0-12	
1924-25	8-10	
1927-28	11-3	
1929-30	21-11	
1930-31	14-5	
1931-32	20-6	
1932-33	21-14	
1933-34	14-5	
1934-35	16-11	
1936-37	3-8	
1937-38	8-6	
1938-39	11-0	
1940-41	20-6	
1941-42	22-9	
1942-43	33-6	
1942-43	36-0	
1942-43	24-3	
1942-43	9-6	
1965-66	8-8	
1986-87	31-6	
1989-90	8-16	
1990-91	25-9	
1991-92	16-43	
1992-93	33-30	

ROYAL NAVY

Season	Home	Away
1978-79	27-4	

ROYAL VETERINARY COLLEGE

Season	Home	Away
1895-96	25-0	

RUGBY

Season	Home	Away
1895-96	13-0	0-0
1896-97	25-0	12-0
1897-98	30-0	11-0
1898-99	14-0	49-0
1901-02	7-5	8-3
1902-03	6-3	5-5
1905-06	43-0	23-8
1906-07	38-0	9-5
1907-08	15-0	16-3
1908-09	21-9	15-0
1909-10	60-4	
1910-11	24-6	21-10
1911-12	9-3	5-10
1912-13	36-0	8-10
1913-14		10-16
1919-20	24-5	8-10
1920-21	19-5	13-6
1921-22	16-3	10-5
1922-23	32-0	0-0
1923-24	11-5	11-5
1924-25	19-0	3-16
1925-26	21-3	17-3
1926-27	23-0	8-5
1927-28	15-0	14-7
1928-29	16-5	22-0
1929-30	12-6	3-8
1930-31	6-8	0-17
1931-32	18-3	6-6
1932-33	3-0	12-10
1933-34	8-5	6-0
1934-35	6-3	11-6
1935-36	12-3	19-5
1936-37	25-0	11-6
1937-38	5-5	11-5
1938-39	11-8	0-9
1940-41	3-5	6-18
1940-41	6-8	6-5
1941-42	9-14	0-5
1941-42	0-0	6-13
1942-43	8-9	0-32
1942-43		3-21
1945-46	9-0	6-3
1946-47	16-3	8-6
1947-48	35-0	18-0
1948-49	26-6	8-6
1949-50	6-3	5-9
1949-50	6-6	
1950-51	18-8	6-0

Season	Home	Away
1951-52	20-3	18-11
1952-53	24-3	11-0
1953-54	28-0	17-0
1954-55	36-3	12-9
1955-56	11-5	3-10
1956-57		5-3
1957-58	14-3	
1958-59		6-8
1959-60	9-0	
1960-61	8-3	23-11
1961-62		19-0
1962-63	12-8	
1963-64		6-0
1964-65	32-11	
1965-66		9-11
1966-67		0-5
1967-68	28-8	
1968-69		0-6
1969-70	18-9	
1970-71		8-3
1971-72	27-3	
1972-73		19-13
1973-74	22-13	
1974-75		6-3
1975-76	36-6	
1976-77		18-4
1977-78	19-3	
1978-79		11-6
1979-80	26-3	
1980-81		21-16
1981-82	49-3	
1982-83		16-9
1983-84	53-12	
1984-85		16-9
1985-86	32-12	
1986-87		15-15
1987-88	10-9	
1988-89		13-19
1989-90	41-25	
1990-91		3-28
1991-92	29-0	
1992-93	76-0	13-7

SALE

Season	Home	Away
1897-98	18-0	
1898-99	27-0	
1899-00	34-0	
1924-25	16-3	
1925-26		11-9
1926-27	0-14	
1927-28	17-3	
1938-39	3-5	
1945-46	14-6	0-6
1946-47	10-16	0-26
1947-48	6-12	15-8
1948-49	9-8	12-8
1949-50	21-0	14-8
1950-51	8-0	
1951-52	11-0	6-9
1952-53	24-9	23-3
1953-54	8-3	
1954-55		15-3
1955-56	21-0	
1956-57		11-5
1957-58		29-0
1958-59	28-8	
1959-60		23-8
1960-61	30-3	
1961-62		24-9
1962-63	26-3	
1963-64		0-15
1964-65	27-0	
1965-66		24-6
1966-67	16-0	
1967-68		14-0
1968-69	6-3	
1970-71	9-8	
1971-72		13-11
1972-73	33-6	
1973-74		0-19
1975-76		9-22
1976-77	15-0	
1977-78		8-19
1979-80		4-10
1980-81	13-20	
1981-82		0-17
1982-83	13-6	
1983-84		16-27
1984-85	9-9	
1985-86		7-21

Season	Home	Away
1986-87	36-9	
1987-88		3-23
1988-89	15-12	
1989-90	16-3	
1991-92	21-0	
1994-95	9-22	6-41
1996-97	30-12	15-31
	9-22	
1997-98	33-14	19-30
1998-99	37-17	39-24
		47-31
1999-2000	26-7	13-9
2000-01	32-26	23-34
2001-02	10-20	14-34
2002-03	27-17	21-24
2003-04	51-12	37-37
2004-05	6-23	24-37

SAN ISIDRO (ARGENTINA)

Season	Home	Away
1979-80	9-13	

SARACENS

Season	Home	Away
1895-96	39-0	
1966-67	6-3	
1970-71	17-8	
1971-72		24-15
1972-73	16-23	
1973-74		15-4
1974-75	3-7	
1975-76	29-15	
1976-77		12-9
1977-78	8-7	
1978-79		9-10
1979-80	22-6	6-14
1980-81	13-9	15-6
1981-82		8-4
1982-83	27-0	19-19
1983-84	13-4	10-7
1984-85	14-4	18-9
1985-86	12-18	
1986-87	20-6	15-17
1987-88	48-12	6-22
1988-89	4-32	
	56-4	
1990-91	15-6	
	16-10	
1991-92		14-9
1992-93	21-17	
1996-97	17-10	23-24
1997-98	13-19	20-43
	10-25	
1998-99	18-21	7-34
1999-2000	8-32	24-29
		34-32
2000-01	26-14	30-10
2001-02	52-27	20-25
		30-28
2002-03	34-25	19-31
2003-04	24-3	22-18
2004-05	20-21	12-23

SAINT BARTHOLOMEW'S HOSPITAL

Season	Home	Away
1895-96	13-7	
1896-97	19-0	
1897-98	43-3	
1898-99	29-0	
1899-00	27-3	
1900-01	24-5	
1901-02	14-3	
1902-03	14-0	
1905-06	17-6	
1908-09	26-0	
1925-26	14-9	
1926-27	13-6	
1927-28		22-3
1929-30		10-10
1930-31	17-6	
1931-32		6-13
1932-33	18-3	
1934-35	23-0	
1940-41	5-5	
1941-42	5-12	

SAINT GEORGE'S HOSPITAL

Season	Home	Away
1895-96	24-3	

SAINT LUKE'S COLLEGE

Season	Home	Away
1972-73	30-22	

SAINT MARY'S HOSPITAL

Season	Home	Away
1895-96	8-0	
1896-97	3-0	
1897-98	20-0	
1926-27	28-0	
1927-28	29-0	
1934-35	11-0	
1937-38	6-0	
1941-42	5-8	
1953-54	20-14	
1954-55	8-6	
1956-57	11-8	

SKIPTON

Season	Home	Away
1900-01	29-0	

SOUTH WALES POLICE

Season	Home	Away
1988-89	29-17	

STIRLING COUNTY

Season	Home	Away
1991-92	27-6	

STRATFORD-ON-AVON

Season	Home	Away
1906-07	28-3	
1907-08	15-5	8-4
1908-09	35-3	3-14
1909-10	28-0	

STREATHAM

Season	Home	Away
1895-96	21-8	
1896-97	18-10	
1896-97	8-5	
1897-98	39-0	

STREATHAM & CROYDON

Season	Home	Away
1972-73	26-9	

STROUD

Season	Home	Away
1910-11	11-10	

SUSSEX

Season	Home	Away
1948-49		21-6
1950-51	38-0	

SWANSEA

Season	Home	Away
1897-98	0-3	
1898-99	0-19	3-34
1899-00	0-9	3-35
1900-01	0-8	
1906-07	3-10	3-16
1907-08	6-13	0-8
1908-09	5-8	7-14
1909-10		3-19
1910-11	18-3	0-9
1912-13	0-30	9-25
1913-14		5-16
1919-20	3-3	
1920-21	0-9	
1921-22	5-17	
1923-24	6-6	
1974-75		0-47

TABARD

Season	Home	Away
1992-93		50-13

J. E. THORNELOE'S XV

Season	Home	Away
1939-40	5-21	5-13
1939-40	8-6	14-22

TIVERTON

Season	Home	Away
1899-00	14-10	

TORQUAY ATHLETIC

Season	Home	Away
1905-06		3-20
1922-23		8-5
1924-25		8-0
1927-28	21-0	6-10
1928-29	7-11	11-12
1977-78		19-9

TOULON

Season	Home	Away
1996-97	38-29	

TOULOUSE

Season	Home	Away
2002-03		16-32
2004-05	23-21	12-25
		9-37

TREHERBERT

Season	Home	Away
1902-03	0-6	
1903-04	4-3	

TREORCHY

Season	Home	Away
1996-97	51-8	

U. C. S. OLD BOYS

Season	Home	Away
1903-04	10-0	
1922-23	15-10	
1923-24	29-14	
1924-25	21-13	
1925-26	25-3	
1926-27	23-5	
1927-28	21-0	16-10
1928-29	26-13	
1929-30	17-0	
1930-31	17-8	
1931-32	40-3	
1932-33	31-3	
1935-36	61-3	

U. S. DEVONPORT

Season	Home	Away
1921-22	5-0	
1922-23	9-8	13-9
1924-25	3-3	5-10
1927-28	6-0	14-8
1929-30	6-11	23-6

U. S. PORTSMOUTH

Season	Home	Away
1906-07	15-9	0-9
1907-08	10-13	6-9
1908-09	17-6	5-0
1909-10	16-3	5-9
1910-11	11-0	3-8
1911-12	20-12	11-24
1912-13	3-14	3-16
1922-23	15-11	9-0
1923-24	9-8	
1924-25		5-10
1929-30	14-8	
1930-31		8-5
1931-32	20-0	
1932-33		15-0
1933-34	16-3	
1934-35	15-13	
1935-36	12-7	
1938-39	11-14	
1946-47	14-6	
1947-48		34-9
1948-49		11-13
1949-50	19-8	
1950-51		3-0
1951-52	25-9	
1952-53		20-9
1953-54	24-3	
1954-55		8-8
1955-56	6-19	
1956-57		8-13
1957-58	43-3	
1958-59		24-0
1959-60	36-6	
1960-61		11-16

ULSTER

Season	Home	Away
2002-03	32-9	13-16

UPPER CLIFTON

Season	Home	Away
1899-00	29-0	

VALE OF LUNE

Season	Home	Away
1987-88		7-12
1988-89	48-0	

WAKEFIELD

Season	Home	Away
1920-21	17-16	
1921-22	6-13	
1922-23	9-3	3-3
1923-24	31-3	8-0
1924-25	52-3	22-8
1925-26	15-0	3-0
1975-76		6-12
1977-78	20-8	
1989-90	22-10	
1991-92		20-15
1995-96	23-0	34-21

WALSALL

Season	Home	Away
1977-78		16-8
1981-82		32-9

WASPS

Season	Home	Away
1895-96	8-0	
1896-97	18-0	
1897-98	14-0	
1940-41	0-0	0-8
1941-42	8-21	0-3
1942-43	11-22	3-19
1946-47	11-0	
1947-48		12-3
1948-49	11-5	
1949-50		9-5
1950-51	0-0	
1951-52		0-3
1952-53	3-0	
1953-54		8-3
1954-55	16-0	
1955-56		0-9
1956-57	8-8	
1957-58		6-11
1958-59	14-16	
1959-60		13-8
1960-61	8-14	
1961-62		0-0
1962-63	8-0	
1963-64		13-6
1964-65	11-3	
1965-66		3-8
1966-67	6-8	
1967-68		9-3
1968-69	11-3	
1970-71	29-6	
1971-72		25-12
1972-73	32-0	
1973-74		12-3
1974-75	0-20	
1975-76		18-12
1976-77	16-0	
1977-78		20-14
1978-79	24-7	
1979-80		15-3
1983-84		6-10
1984-85	19-0	
1985-86		16-3
1986-87	13-8	
1987-88		12-25
1988-89	28-14	
1989-90		14-12
1990-91		21-21
1991-92	28-15	
1992-93		12-20
1993-94	15-17	11-24
1994-95	19-13	21-27
1996-97	15-26	13-18
1997-98	18-10	15-31
1998-99	26-21	24-15
1999-2000	12-54	21-15
	25-22	
	23-31 (played at Twickenham)	
2000-01	18-21	17-53
2001-02	23-10	6-17
2002-03	34-20	9-16
		10-19
2003-04	27-17	5-31
		20-57
2004-05	9-10	9-39

WATERLOO

Season	Home	Away
1935-36	5-3	9-14
1936-37	9-5	8-23
1937-38	8-10	
1938-39	0-3	0-11
1945-46		5-18
1946-47	11-6	
1947-48		29-9
1948-49	6-3	
1949-50		23-6
1950-51	13-3	
1951-52		0-0
1952-53	9-3	
1953-54		3-6
1954-55		0-6
1956-57		5-11
1958-59		16-9
1959-60	38-3	
1960-61		8-3
1961-62	21-9	
1962-63		8-11
1963-64	16-8	
1964-65		17-3
1965-66	34-11	
1966-67		11-10
1967-68	24-13	
1968-69		8-18
1969-70	42-14	
1970-71	8-19	
1971-72	16-11	
1972-73		55-0
1973-74	33-7	
1975-76	15-0	
1976-77		3-36
1977-78	29-7	
1978-79	11-17	
1979-80	9-8	
1980-81		17-6
1981-82	20-6	
1982-83		7-17
1983-84	0-10	
1984-85		7-24
1985-86	16-9	
1986-87		6-9
1987-88	17-23	
1989-90		12-6
1993-94	22-3	
1995-96	69-5	69-3

WELLINGBOROUGH & KETTERING

Season	Home	Away
1933-34	20-0	

WELLINGBOROUGH OLD BOYS

Season	Home	Away
1942-43	15-6	

WELSH GUARD & REGIMENT

Season	Home	Away
1922-23	16-6	

WEST HARTLEPOOL

Season	Home	Away
1901-02	0-3	
1902-03	11-7	
1904-05	6-9	3-13
1905-06	16-8	0-6
1906-07	8-10	6-12
1982-83		3-27
1983-84	12-24	
1992-93	55-9	
1994-95	25-14	21-12
1996-97	46-20	57-17
1998-99	19-14	33-9

WEST HERTS

Season	Home	Away
1929-30	36-0	
1930-31	23-3	

WEST LONDON INSTITUTE

Season	Home	Away
1990-91	25-15	

WESTLEIGH		
Season	Home	Away
1974-75		7-3

WICKHAM PARK		
Season	Home	Away
1899-00	43-0	

WORCESTER		
Season	Home	Away
2004-05	6-17	19-21

WESTMINSTER BANK		
Season	Home	Away
1926-27	7-8	
1927-28	17-9	
1928-29	47-6	
1929-30	23-5	

WIDNES		
Season	Home	Away
1976-77	21-10	

WREXHAM		
Season	Home	Away
1979-80	23-9	

WINNINGTON PARK		
Season	Home	Away
1988-89		37-4

WESTON-SUPER-MARE		
Season	Home	Away
1935-36	9-6	
1937-38		6-35
1938-39		0-19
1980-81	10-6	
1982-83	32-0	

WOLVERHAMPTON		
Season	Home	Away
1895-96	35-0	
1896-97	11-3	
1897-98	28-0	

How the *Bystander* magazine depicted the Saints in 1928

The league seasons

Rugby Union in England took on a more structured format from 1987 onwards with the introduction of the Courage League. Opponents played each other once and this was supplemented by the domestic cup competition. It was not until the 1993/94 season that home and away league fixtures came into being. Prior to leagues, Saints had featured in the RFU Merit Tables (Midlands Division) which started in the 1975/76 season.

1987/88

Saints scores first
Courage League Two
PC = Pilkington Cup

September

19	Richmond	H	3-16

October

03	London Scottish	A	3-50

November

21	Bedford	A	16-17

December

12	London Irish	H	15-13

January

02	London Welsh	H	14-16
17	Blackheath	A	12-19
23	Plymouth Albion (PC)	A	7-14

February

07	Saracens	A	6-22

March

06	Liverpool St Helens	H	9-13
12	Rosslyn Park	H	0-22

April

16	Headingley	A	3-38

The teams placed in Division One (in the order they finished) were: Leicester, Wasps, Harlequins, Bath, Gloucester, Orrell, Moseley, Nottingham, Bristol, Waterloo, Coventry and Sale. The last two clubs were relegated.

1988/89

Courage League Two
PC = Pilkington Cup

September

10	London Scottish	A	3-3
24	Headingley	H	19-7

October

08	London Irish	A	10-18
22	Sale	H	15-12

November

05	Winnington Park (PC)	A	37-4
12	Saracens	H	4-32
19	Richmond	A	12-15
26	Bedford	H	42-3

January

14	Blackheath	H	15-7
28	Richmond (PC)	A	0-6

March

11	Coventry	A	10-22

April

08	Gosforth	H	13-12
22	London Welsh	A	22-0

1989/90

Courage League Two
PC = Pilkington Cup

September

09	Plymouth Albion	H	6-4
23	Headingley	A	3-15

October

14	London Irish	H	33-21
28	Sale	A	16-3

November

04	Northern (PC)	H	25-4
11	Waterloo	A	12-6
18	Richmond	H	12-6
25	Liverpool St Helens	A	13-13

January

13	Blackheath	A	10-9
27	Metropolitan Police (PC)	A	16-4

February

10	Wakefield (PC)	H	22-10
24	Leicester (PC)	H	23-7

March

10	Coventry	H	24-18
24	Gloucester (PC)	H	12-17
31	Gosforth	A	22-15

April

28	Rugby Lions	H	41-25

1990/91

Courage League One
PC = Pilkington Cup

September

22	Saracens	H	15-6

October

06	Liverpool St Helens	A	23-13
13	Bath	H	10-16
27	Orrell	A	0-60

November

10	Bristol	H	12-9
17	Harlequins	A	6-21
24	Harrogate (PC)	A	18-4

January

12	Leicester	H	18-28
26	Saracens (PC)	H	16-10

February

23	Moseley (PC)	H	10-6

March

09	Gloucester	H	6-7
22	Wasps	A	21-21

April

06	Orrell (PC)	H	18-10
13	Nottingham	H	22-15
20	Moseley	A	18-10
27	Rosslyn Park	A	0-48

May

04	Harlequins (PC final)		13-25

The league seasons

1991/92

Courage League One
PC = Pilkington Cup

November

16	Saracens	A	14-9
23	London Irish	H	12-12
30	Coventry (PC)	A	31-7

December

| 07 | Bath | A | 6-15 |
| 21 | Orrell | H | 12-3 |

January

| 04 | Bristol | A | 15-9 |
| 11 | Harlequins | H | 25-14 |

February

| 08 | Bath | H | 9-13 |
| 29 | Rugby Lions | H | 29-0 |

March

| 14 | Gloucester | A | 17-10 |
| 28 | Wasps | H | 28-15 |

April

07	Leicester	A	22-19
11	Nottingham	A	9-18
25	Rosslyn Park	H	20-12

1992/93

Courage League One
PC = Pilkington Cup

September

| 19 | Bristol | H | 16-6 |
| 26 | Saracens | H | 21-17 |

October

03	London Irish	A	3-12
10	Bath	H	11-8
31	Orrell	A	10-9

November

| 21 | Harlequins | A | 12-7 |
| 28 | Tabard (PC) | A | 50-13 |

January

| 09 | Leicester | H | 12-13 |
| 23 | Newcastle (PC) | H | 33-3 |

February

| 13 | Rugby Lions | A | 13-7 |
| 27 | Moseley (PC) | H | 37-15 |

March

| 13 | Gloucester | H | 16-21 |
| 27 | Wasps | A | 12-20 |

April

03	West Hartlepool	H	55-9
10	Leicester (PC)	A	6-28
24	London Scottish	A	34-21

1993/94

Courage League One
PC = Pilkington Cup

September

11	Leicester	H	19-10
18	Bath	A	9-37
25	London Irish	H	23-12

October

| 02 | Bristol | A | 31-22 |
| 09 | Harlequins | A | 7-15 |

November

| 13 | Orrell | H | 9-13 |
| 20 | Gloucester | A | 14-19 |

December

04	Wasps	H	15-17
11	Newcastle	A	28-8
18	Waterloo (PC)	H	22-3

January

08	Leicester	A	9-36
15	Bath	H	9-30
22	Gloucester (PC)	A	6-11
29	London Irish	A	16-13

February

| 12 | Bristol | H | 22-19 |

March

| 12 | Harlequins | H | 15-14 |
| 26 | Orrell | A | 6-27 |

April

09	Gloucester	H	19-3
23	Wasps	A	11-24
30	Newcastle	H	43-23

1994/95

Courage League One
PC = Pilkington Cup

September

10	Leicester	A	15-28
17	Bath	H	16-32
24	Sale	A	6-41

October

01	Bristol	H	15-18
08	Harlequins	H	16-23
15	Orrell	A	10-13
22	Gloucester	H	9-6
29	Wasps	A	21-27

November

| 05 | West Hartlepool | H | 25-14 |

December

| 17 | Moseley (PC) | A | 16-6 |

January

07	Leicester	H	18-20
14	Bath	A	5-26
28	Richmond (PC)	H	27-6

February

| 11 | Sale | H | 9-22 |
| 25 | Bath (PC) | A | 6-26 |

March

| 04 | Bristol | A | 24-13 |
| 25 | Harlequins | A | 9-10 |

April

08	Orrell	H	15-9
15	Gloucester	A	13-14
22	Wasps	H	19-13
29	West Hartlepool	A	21-12

The league seasons

1995/96

Courage League Two
PC = Pilkington Cup

September

09	London Irish	A	65-32
16	Moseley	H	50-7
23	Nottingham	A	43-7
30	Wakefield	H	23-9

October

07	Bedford	A	49-17
14	Blackheath	H	69-14
21	Newcastle	A	52-9
28	Waterloo	A	69-3

November

04	London Scottish	H	54-11
11	London Irish	H	52-24

December

23	Bath (PC)	A	3-12

January

06	Nottingham	H	35-5

February

24	Moseley	A	46-16

March

23	Bedford	H	48-0
30	Blackheath	A	24-10

April

06	Newcastle	H	26-5
13	Waterloo	H	69-5
20	Wakefield	A	34-21
27	London Scottish	A	50-17

1996/97

Courage League One
AW = Anglo Welsh League
PC = Pilkington Cup
EC = European Conference

August

31	West Hartlepool	H	46-20

September

07	London Irish	A	21-34
10	Treorchy (AW)	H	51-8
14	Bristol	H	29-21
21	Orrell	H	41-7
28	Harlequins	H	15-20

October

02	Newport (AW)	A	67-19
05	Sale	H	20-12
13	Toulon (EC)	A	38-29
16	Orrell (EC)	H	61-7
19	Connacht (EC)	A	31-11
26	Dunvant (EC)	H	48-32
29	Saracens	A	23-24

November

02	Padova (EC)	A	29-9
09	Bath	H	9-6
16	Narbonne (EC)	H	22-23
26	Caerphilly (AW)	H	107-5

December

08	Leicester	A	9-23
21	Preston Grasshoppers (PC)	A	40-11
28	Wasps	A	13-18

January

11	Leicester	H	22-19
19	Bath	A	14-52
25	Coventry (PC)	H	26-17

February

08	Saracens	H	17-10
22	Sale (PC)	H	9-32

March

04	Gloucester	A	6-19
09	Sale	A	15-31
29	Orrell	A	50-14

April

05	Bristol	A	11-20
12	London Irish	H	31-21
19	West Hartlepool	A	57-17
26	Wasps	H	15-26
30	Harlequins	A	16-36

May

03	Gloucester	H	25-27

1997/98

Allied Dunbar Premiership
EC = European Conference
TBC = Tetley Bitter Cup

August

23	NEC Harlequins	H	23-26

September

09	Connacht (EC)	A	13-43
13	Begles Bordeaux (EC)	H	25-13
20	Nice (EC)	H	66-7
27	Begles Bordeaux (EC)	A	16-23

October

04	Nice (EC)	A	26-10
08	Newcastle Falcons	A	12-37
11	Connacht (EC)	H	15-20
18	Leicester Tigers	H	25-6
26	Bristol Shoguns	A	15-22

November

08	Saracens	H	13-19

December

13	London Irish	A	51-10
21	Richmond	A	24-21
27	London Wasps	H	18-10
30	Bath Rugby	A	3-26

January

03	Bedford (TBC)	H	31-26
10	Sale Sharks	H	33-14
18	NEC Harlequins	A	30-5
24	Gloucester (TBC)	H	30-11
31	Newcastle Falcons	H	17-21

February

14	Gloucester	A	15-20
28	Newcastle (TBC)	H	17-7

March

07	Leicester Tigers	A	15-15
14	Bristol Shoguns	H	35-12
28	Saracens (TBC)	H	10-25

April

18	Richmond	H	38-47
22	London Irish	H	33-18
26	London Wasps	A	15-31

May

02	Bath Rugby	H	16-15
10	Sale Sharks	A	19-30
14	Saracens	A	20-43
17	Gloucester	H	22-24

The league seasons

1998/99

Allied Dunbar Premiership
TBC = Tetley Bitter Cup

September

06	Saracens	A	7-34
12	NEC Harlequins	H	25-6
19	Leicester Tigers	A	25-35

October

03	Sale Sharks	H	37-17
10	London Scottish	A	33-22
17	Bedford Blues	H	34-29
24	London Irish	A	26-10
31	Gloucester	H	22-8

November

07	London Wasps	H	26-24
15	Newcastle Falcons	A	35-45
21	Richmond	H	44-27

December

12	Bath Rugby	A	15-9
20	West Hartlepool	A	33-9

January

02	Sale Sharks	A	39-24
05	London Irish	H	8-32
09	Sale Sharks (TBC)	A	47-31
16	NEC Harlequins	A	24-17
23	West Hartlepool	H	19-14
30	London Irish (TBC)	H	6-21

February

06	Saracens	H	18-21

March

13	Leicester Tigers	H	15-22
27	Newcastle Falcons	H	57-16

April

13	London Wasps	A	24-15
17	London Scottish	H	44-13
24	Bedford Blues	A	42-31

May

01	Bath Rugby	H	40-17
08	Richmond	A	31-19
16	Gloucester	A	31-43

1999/2000

Allied Dunbar Premiership
HC = Heineken Cup
TBC = Tetley Bitter Cup

September

11	Leicester Tigers	H	46-24
25	Bath Rugby	A	13-33

October

02	NEW Harlequins	H	29-27
09	Saracens	H	8-32
17	Sale Sharks	A	13-9
30	Gloucester	H	9-25

November

05	Bristol Shoguns	A	29-19
13	London Irish	H	24-19
20	Neath (HC)	H	21-12
27	Grenoble (HC)	A	18-20

December

04	Bedford Blues	A	41-17
11	Edinburgh Rugby (HC)	H	32-8
17	Edinburgh Rugby (HC)	A	47-8
26	Newcastle Falcons	H	37-5
29	London Wasps	A	21-16

January

02	Nuneaton (TBC)	H	118-3
09	Grenoble (HC)	H	27-16
15	Neath (HC)	A	39-23
22	Bedford Blues	H	38-16
26	London Irish	A	44-20
29	Saracens (TBC)	A	34-32

February

12	Bristol Shoguns	H	19-23
26	London Welsh (TBC)	A	35-26

March

11	Gloucester	A	35-11
25	Sale Sharks	H	26-7

April

09	London Irish (TBC)		24-17
16	London Wasps (HC)		25-22
19	NEC Harlequins	A	17-29
22	Bath Rugby	H	13-17
29	Leicester Tigers	A	21-26

May

07	Llanelli (HC)		31-28
09	London Wasps	H	12-54
13	London Wasps (TBC final)		23-31
17	Saracens	A	24-29
21	Newcastle Falcons	A	32-23
27	Munster (HC final)		9-8

The league seasons

2000/01

Zurich Premiership
HC = Heineken Cup
TBC = Tetley Bitter Cup

August

| 20 | Newcastle Falcon s | A | 21-27 |
| 26 | London Irish | H | 27-10 |

September

02	Leicester Tigers	A	19-33
06	NEC Harlequins	H	27-20
09	Sale Sharks	A	23-34
16	Rotherham Titans	A	32-19
23	Bath Rugby	H	24-13

October

01	London Wasps	A	17-53
07	Biarritz (HC)	A	30-37
14	Edinburgh Rugby (HC)	H	22-23
21	Leinster (HC)	H	8-14
27	Leinster (HC)	A	31-40

November

04	Leeds Tykes (TBC)	H	73-35
11	Birmingham (TBC)	H	47-14
18	Newcastle Falcons	H	26-18
25	Bristol Shoguns	H	24-6

December

03	Saracens	A	30-18
09	NEC Harlequins (TBC)	A	6-11
16	Gloucester	H	34-15
23	NEC Harlequins	A	34-25
27	Gloucester	A	15-12
30	London Wasps	H	18-21

January

06	Bath Rugby	A	13-36
13	Biarritz (HC)	H	32-24
19	Edinburgh Rugby (HC)	A	15-18

February

| 10 | Rotherham Titans | H | 42-0 |
| 24 | Sale Sharks | H | 32-26 |

March

10	Leicester Tigers	H	9-12
17	London Irish	A	10-13
31	Saracens	H	25-14

April

| 16 | Bristol Shoguns | A | 16-46 |
| 28 | Saracens | H | 45-17 |

(championship quarter final)

May

| 05 | Leicester Tigers | A | 13-17 |

(championship semi final)

2001/02

Zurich Premiership
HC = Heineken Cup
PC = Powergen Cup

September

01	Gloucester	A	9-22
08	Bath Rugby	H	26-7
16	Leeds Tykes	A	26-6
23	Saracens	A	20-25
28	Cardiff (HC)	A	17-25

October

07	Glasgow Rugby (HC)	H	30-9
13	Leicester Tigers	H	11-21
20	Sale Sharks	A	14-34
27	Montferrand (HC)	H	15-21

November

03	Montferrand (HC)	A	17-50
09	NEC Harlequins	H	13-13
18	London Irish	A	12-48
25	Bristol Shoguns	H	20-23

December

02	Newcastle Falcons	A	28-13
15	Birmingham (PC)	H	32-19
08	London Wasps	H	23-10
20	London Irish	H	24-15

January

04	Glasgow Rugby (HC)	A	27-31
12	Cardiff (HC)	H	25-11
19	Saracens (PC)	A	30-28
26	NEC Harlequins	A	24-16

February

| 09 | Sale Sharks | H | 10-20 |
| 23 | Leicester Tigers | A | 6-17 |

March

08	Newcastle Falcons (PC)	H	36-7
16	Leeds Tykes	H	34-14
30	Bath Rugby	A	29-11

April

13	Gloucester	H	58-21
20	London Irish (PC final)		7-38
27	Saracens	H	52-27

May

04	London Wasps	A	6-17
08	Bristol Shoguns	A	37-27
12	Newcastle Falcons	H	24-19
19	London Irish	A	38-14

(championship quarter final)

June

| 01 | Bristol Shoguns | A | 24-32 |

(championship semi final)

The league seasons

2002/03

Zurich Premiership
HC = Heineken Cup
PC = Powergen Cup

August

30	Sale Sharks	A	21-24

September

07	Newcastle Falcons	H	31-13
15	Bristol Shoguns	A	36-28
21	Bath Rugby	H	24-3
28	Saracens	A	19-31

October

05	London Wasps	H	34-20
13	Ulster (HC)	H	32-9
19	Biarritz (HC)	A	20-23
27	London Irish	A	14-12

November

02	Gloucester	A	9-18
09	Leicester Tigers	H	3-16
17	Leeds Tykes	A	19-26
23	NEC Harlequins	H	35-7
30	Leicester Tigers	A	25-12

December

07	Cardiff (HC)	H	25-11
15	Cardiff (HC)	A	31-0
21	Orrell (PC)	A	55-44
28	Gloucester	H	13-16

January

04	London Irish	H	10-22
11	Biarritz (HC)	H	17-14
17	Ulster (HC)	A	13-16
25	Bath Rugby (PC)	A	30-29

February

02	London Wasps	A	9-16
08	Saracens	H	34-25

March

02	London Irish (PC)		38-9
15	Bath Rugby	A	27-10

April

05	Gloucester (PC final)		22-46
12	Toulouse (HC)	A	16-32
16	Bristol Shoguns	H	43-13
20	Newcastle Falcons	A	20-22
26	Sale Sharks	H	27-17

May

02	NEC Harlequins	A	31-19
10	Leeds Tykes	H	28-6
17	London Wasps	A	10-19

(championship semi final)

2003/04

Zurich Premiership
HC = Heineken Cup
PC = Powergen Cup

September

12	Sale Sharks	A	37-37
20	Bath Rugby	A	6-24
27	London Wasps	A	27-17

October

04	Rotherham Titans	A	42-13
11	London Irish	H	24-30
18	Newcastle Falcons	H	33-20
25	Leicester Tigers	A	32-15

November

01	Gloucester	H	30-17
08	NEC Harlequins	A	21-43
15	Bath Rugby (PC)	A	13-42
22	Leeds Tykes	H	48-24
29	Gloucester	A	20-28

December

05	Llanelli Scarlets (HC)	A	9-14
13	Agen (HC)	H	25-10
20	Leicester Tigers	H	14-0
28	Newcastle Falcons	A	19-23

January

04	London Irish	A	36-15
10	The Borders (HC)	H	20-3
16	The Borders (HC)	A	39-3
23	Agen (HC)	A	19-6

February

01	Llanelli Scarlets (HC)	H	9-18
07	Rotherham Titans	H	18-8
15	Saracens	A	22-18
21	Sale Sharks	H	51-12

March

27	Saracens	H	24-3

April

04	London Wasps	A	5-31
18	Bath Rugby	H	16-6

May

02	Leeds Tykes	A	31-15
08	NEC Harlequins	H	18-17
16	London Wasps	A	20-57

(championship semi final)

The league seasons

2004/05

Zurich Premiership
HC = Heineken Cup
PC = Powergen Cup

September
04	Bath Rugby	H	29-14
11	NEC Harlequins	A	45-13
18	Gloucester	H	12-18
25	Leicester Tigers	A	13-32

October
02	London Wasps	H	9-10
10	Saracens	A	12-23
16	Sale Sharks	H	6-23
24	Glasgow Rugby (HC)	A	13-9
30	Llanelli Scarlets (HC)	H	25-3

November
05	Leeds Tykes	A	21-26
13	London Irish	H	20-23
20	Worcester Warriors	H	6-17
28	Newcastle Falcons	A	16-27

December
04	Toulouse (HC)	H	23-21
11	Toulouse (HC)	A	12-25
18	Bedford Blues (PC)	H	41-8
27	London Irish	A	22-21

January
01	Leeds Tykes	H	18-9
09	Llanelli Scarlets (HC)	A	22-20
14	Glasgow Rugby (HC)	H	33-23
22	Leeds Tykes (PC)	H	19-24
28	Sale Sharks	A	24-37

February
05	Saracens	H	20-21
20	London Wasps	A	9-39
26	Leicester Tigers	H	26-11

March
12	Gloucester	A	26-18
26	NEC Harlequins	H	22-20

April
01	Toulouse (HC)	A	9-37
09	Bath Rugby	A	12-30
15	Newcastle Falcons	H	23-22
30	Worcester Warriors	A	19-21

Cheering the boys on week in week out:
Bernie the mascot

Cup competitions

English Knock Out Cup results:
(Saints scores first)
RFU KO Cup:

1971/72:	Moseley (1)	A	12-25
1972/73:	Moseley (1)	H	9-12
1973/74:	Leicester (1)	H	22-6
	Saracens (2)	A	15-4
	Orrell (qf)	A	0-19
1974/75:	Gosforth (1)	H	4-7

John Player Cup:

1975/76:	Bedford (1)	H	9-6
	London Scottish (2)	A	28-16
	Wakefield (qf)	A	6-12
1976/77:	Widnes (1)	H	21-10
	London Welsh (2)	A	11-17
1977/78:	Walsall (1)	A	16-8
	Wakefield (2)	H	21-4
	Leicester (qf)	A	11-20
1978/79:	Leicester (1)	A	3-29
1979/80:	Nottingham (1)	H	0-3
1980/81:	Sale (3)	H	13-20
1981/82:	Kettering (1)	H	31-0
	Walsall (2)	A	32-9
	Morley (3)	H	12-7
	Leicester (4)	H	10-23
1982/83:	Hinckley (1)	H	31-4
	West Hartlepool (2)	A	3-27
1983/84:	Rosslyn Park (3)	A	20-6
	London Scottish (4)	A	6-34
1984/85:	Nottingham (3)	A	3-15
1985/86:	Gosforth (3)	A	6-6

(went through on away rule)

	London Scottish (4)	H	6-11
1987/88:	Plymouth Albion (3)	A	7-14

Pilkington Cup:

1988/89:	Winnington Park (2)	A	37-4
	Richmond (4)	A	0-6
1989/90:	Northern (2)	H	25-4
	Metropolitan Police (3)	A	16-4
	Wakefield (4)	H	22-16
	Leicester (qf)	H	23-7
	Gloucester (sf)	H	12-17
1990/91:	Harrogate (3)	A	18-4
	Saracens (4)	H	16-10
	Moseley (qf)	H	10-6
	Orrell (sf)	H	18-10
	HARLEQUINS (final) Twickenham		**13-25**

(after extra time)

1991/92:	Coventry (3)	A	31-7
	Bath (4)	H	9-13
1992/93:	Tabard (3)	A	50-13
	Newcastle (4)	H	33-3
	Moseley (4)	H	37-15
	Leicester (qf)	A	6-28
1993/94:	Waterloo (4)	H	22-3
	Gloucester (5)	A	6-11
1994/95:	Moseley (4)	A	16-6
	Richmond (5)	H	27-6
	Bath (qf)	A	6-26
1995/96:	Bath (4)	A	3-12
1996/97:	Preston Grasshoppers (5)	A	40-11
	Coventry (6)	H	26-17
	Sale (qf)	H	9-22

Tetley Bitter Cup:

1997/98:	Bedford (4)	H	31-26
	Gloucester (5)	H	30-11
	Newcastle Falcons (qf)	H	17-7
	Saracens (sf)	H	10-25
1998/99:	Sale Sharks (4)	A	47-31
	London Irish (5)	H	6-21
1999/2000:	Nuneaton (4)	H	118-3
	Saracens (5)	A	34-32
	London Welsh (qf)	A	35-26
	London Irish (sf) Madjeski Stadium		24-17
	LONDON WASPS (final)		
	Twickenham		**23-31**
2000/01:	Leeds Tykes (4)	H	73-35
	Birmingham Solihull (5)	H	47-14
	NEC Harlequins (qf)	A	6-11

Powergen Cup:

2001/02:	Birmingham (6)	H	32-19
	Saracens (qf)	A	30-28
	Newcastle Falcons (sf)	H	38-7
	LONDON IRISH (final)		
	Twickenham		**7-38**
2002/03:	Orrell (6)	A	55-44

(after extra time)

	Bath Rugby (qf)	A	30-29
	London Irish (sf) Kassam Stadium		38-9
	GLOUCESTER (final)		
	Twickenham		**22-40**
2003/04:	Bath Rugby (6)	A	13-42
2004/05	Bedford Blues (6)	H	41-8
	Leeds Tykes (qf)	H	19-24

Cup virgins: Twickenham 1991 – for most Saints players it was the pinnacle of their career

Cup competitions

Steamy affair: European action from 1997 and the visit of Bordeaux, which resulted in a 25-13 win for Saints

Europe:
(Saints scores first):
European Conference:

1996/97:	Toulon (pool 3)	A	38-29		Montferrand Vulcans (5)	H	15-21
	Orrell (3)	H	61-7		Montferrand Vulcans (5)	A	17-50
	Connacht (3)	A	31-11		Glasgow Rugby (5)	A	27-31
	Dunvant (3)	H	48-32		Cardiff (5)	H	26-15
	Padova (3)	A	29-9	2002/03:	Ulster pool 6)	H	32-9
	Narbonne (qf)	H	22-23		Biarritz (6)	A	20-23
1997/98:	Connacht (pool 4)	A	13-43		Cardiff (6)	H	25-11
	Bordeaux-Begles (4)	H	25-13		Cardiff (6)	A	31-0
	Nice (4)	H	66-7		Biarritz (6)	H	17-14
	Connacht (4)	H	15-20		Ulster (6)	A	13-16

Heineken Cup:

					Toulouse (qf)	A	16-32
1999/2000:	Neath (pool 6)	H	21-12	2003/04:	Llanelli Scarlets (pool 4)	A	9-14
	Grenoble (6)	A	18-20		Agen (4)	H	25-10
	Neath (6)	A	39-23		The Borders (4)	H	20-3
	London Wasps (qf)	H	25-22		The Borders (4)	A	39-3
	Llanelli (sf) Madjeski Stadium		31-28		Agen (4)	A	19-6
	MUNSTER (final				Llanelli Scarlets (4)	H	9-18
	Twickenham		**9-8**	2004/05:	Glasgow	A	13-9
2000/01:	Biarritz (pool 1)	A	30-37		Llanelli Scarlets	H	25-3
	Edinburgh Rugby (1)	H	22-23		Toulouse	H	23-21
	Leinster (1)	H	8-14		Toulouse	A	12-25
	Leinster (1)	A	31-40		Llanelli Scarlets	A	22-20
	Biarritz (1)	H	32-24		Glasgow	H	33-23
	Edinburgh Rugby (1)	A	15-18		Toulouse (qf)	A	9-37
2001/02:	Cardiff (5)	A	17-25				

Anglo-Welsh League:

	Glasgow Rugby (5)	H	30-9
1996/97:	Treorchy Rhondda	H	51-8
	Newport	A	67-19
	Caerphilly	H	107-5

League tables

Courage League Division Two
1987/88

	P	W	D	L	F	A	Pts
Rosslyn P	11	8	2	1	155	83	37
Liverpool SH	11	8	1	2	154	97	36
Saracens	11	7	2	2	228	86	34
Headingley	11	6	2	3	202	104	31
Bedford	11	6	2	3	168	164	31
Richmond	11	6	0	5	140	156	29
L Scottish	11	4	1	6	141	158	24
London Irish	11	4	1	6	129	177	24
L Welsh	11	3	2	6	152	185	22
Gosforth	10	2	1	7	124	145	17
Blackheath	11	2	0	9	102	187	17
SAINTS	**10**	**1**	**0**	**9**	**81**	**221**	**13**

Courage League Division Two
1988/89

	P	W	D	L	F	A	Pts
Saracens	11	11	0	0	288	80	22
Bedford	11	6	2	3	141	187	14
SAINTS	**11**	**5**	**1**	**4**	**165**	**131**	**13**
Sale	11	5	2	4	195	152	12
Coventry	11	6	0	5	150	143	12
London Irish	11	5	2	4	194	222	12
Headingley	11	5	1	5	179	136	11
Blackheath	11	4	1	6	181	144	9
Richmond	11	4	1	6	112	216	9
Gosforth	11	4	0	7	176	246	8
L Scottish	11	3	1	7	146	160	7
L Welsh	11	1	1	9	125	235	3

Courage League Division Two
1989/1990

	P	W	D	L	F	A	Pts
SAINTS	**11**	**9**	**1**	**1**	**192**	**135**	**19**
Liverpool SH	11	8	2	1	154	106	18
Richmond	11	7	1	3	282	135	15
Coventry	11	6	1	4	206	185	13
London Irish	11	6	0	5	228	247	12
Rugby	11	5	0	6	238	172	10
Plymouth A	11	5	0	6	206	164	10
Headingley	11	5	0	6	161	226	10
Sale	11	4	0	7	153	182	8
Blackheath	11	3	2	6	141	205	8
Waterloo	11	3	0	8	147	193	6
Gosforth	11	1	1	9	108	266	3

Joyous scenes at Franklin's Gardens after the last game of the season against Rugby in 1989/90

Courage League Division One
1990/91

	P	W	D	L	F	A	Pts
Bath	12	11	0	1	280	104	22
Wasps	12	9	1	2	252	151	19
Harlequins	12	8	0	4	267	162	16
Leicester	12	8	0	4	244	140	16
Orrell	12	7	0	5	247	105	14
Gloucester	12	6	0	6	207	163	12
Rosslyn P	12	6	0	6	215	174	12
Nottingham	12	6	0	6	138	194	12
SAINTS	**12**	**5**	**1**	**6**	**149**	**254**	**11**
Saracens	12	5	0	7	151	228	10
Bristol	12	4	1	7	135	219	9
Moseley	12	1	1	10	113	244	3
Liverpool	12	0	0	12	88	349	0

Courage League Division One
1991/92

	P	W	D	L	F	A	Pts
Bath	12	10	1	1	277	126	20
Orrell	12	10	0	2	204	96	20
SAINTS	**12**	**9**	**1**	**2**	**209**	**136**	**19**
Gloucester	12	7	1	4	193	168	15
Saracens	12	7	1	4	176	165	15
Leicester	12	6	1	5	262	216	13
Wasps	12	6	0	6	177	180	12
Harlequins	12	5	1	6	213	207	11
London Irish	12	3	3	6	147	237	9
Bristol	12	4	0	8	192	174	8
Rugby	12	2	3	7	124	252	7
Nottingham	12	2	1	9	133	204	5
Rosslyn Pk	12	0	1	11	111	258	1

Courage League Division One
1992/93

	P	W	D	L	F	A	Pts
Bath	10	9	0	1	296	78	18
Wasps	10	9	0	1	168	102	18
Leicester	11	8	0	3	192	111	16
SAINTS	**10**	**6**	**0**	**4**	**126**	**120**	**12**
Bristol	10	6	0	4	133	140	12
Orrell	10	5	0	5	150	133	10
London Irish	11	5	0	6	165	214	10
Harlequins	10	4	1	5	157	148	9
Gloucester	10	4	0	6	126	137	8
London Scot	10	3	1	6	165	174	7
Saracens	10	3	0	7	115	151	6
W Hartlepool	10	2	0	8	101	166	4
Rugby	10	1	0	9	85	305	2

League tables

Courage League Division One 1993/94

	P	W	D	L	F	A	Pts
Bath	18	17	0	1	431	181	34
Leicester	18	14	0	4	425	210	38
Wasps	18	10	1	7	362	340	21
Bristol	18	10	0	8	331	276	20
SAINTS	**18**	**9**	**0**	**9**	**305**	**342**	**18**
Harlequins	18	8	0	10	333	287	16
Orrell	18	8	0	10	327	302	16
Gloucester	18	6	2	10	247	356	14
London Irish	18	4	0	14	217	391	8
Newcastle	18	2	1	15	190	483	5

Courage League Division One 1994/95

	P	W	D	L	F	A	Pts
Leicester	18	15	1	2	400	239	31
Bath	18	12	3	3	373	245	27
Wasps	18	13	0	5	469	313	26
Sale	18	7	3	9	327	343	16
Orrell	18	6	3	9	256	325	16
Bristol	18	7	0	11	301	353	14
Gloucester	18	6	1	11	269	336	13
Harlequins	18	6	1	11	275	348	13
W Hartlepool	18	6	1	11	312	412	13
SAINTS	**18**	**6**	**0**	**12**	**267**	**335**	**12**

Courage League Division Two 1995/96

	P	W	D	L	F	A	Pts
SAINTS	**18**	**18**	**0**	**0**	**867**	**203**	**36**
London Irish	18	15	0	3	584	405	30
London Scot	18	10	2	6	361	389	22
Wakefield	18	8	0	10	328	331	16
Waterloo	18	7	2	9	309	483	16
Moseley	18	7	0	11	327	447	14
Blackheath	18	6	1	11	341	469	13
Newcastle	18	5	1	12	348	405	11
Nottingham	18	5	1	12	333	433	11
Bedford	18	5	1	12	287	520	11

Courage League Division One 1996/97

	P	W	D	L	F	A	Pts
Wasps	22	18	1	3	685	406	37
Bath	22	15	1	6	863	411	31
Harlequins	22	15	0	7	745	416	30
Leicester	22	14	1	7	600	395	29
Sale	22	13	2	7	603	525	28
Saracens	22	12	1	9	568	449	25
Gloucester	22	11	1	10	476	589	23
SAINTS	**22**	**10**	**0**	**12**	**515**	**477**	**20**
Bristol	22	8	1	13	432	625	17
London Irish	22	6	0	16	502	747	12
W Hartlepool	22	3	0	19	382	795	6
Orrell	22	3	0	19	350	886	6

Allied Dunbar Premiership 1997/98

	P	W	D	L	F	A	Pts
Newcastle	22	19	0	3	645	387	38
Saracens	22	18	1	3	584	396	37
Bath	22	13	0	9	575	455	26
Leicester	22	12	2	8	569	449	26
Richmond	22	12	0	10	607	499	24
Sale	22	10	2	10	605	558	22
Gloucester	22	11	1	10	512	528	23
SAINTS	**22**	**9**	**1**	**12**	**493**	**472**	**19**
Wasps	22	8	1	13	4909	609	17
Harlequins	22	8	0	14	516	645	16
London Irish	22	6	0	16	457	673	12
Bristol	22	2	0	20	351	733	4

Allied Dunbar Premier One 19998/99

	P	W	D	L	F	A	Pts
Leicester	26	22	0	4	771	423	44
SAINTS	**26**	**19**	**0**	**7**	**754**	**556**	**38**
Saracens	26	16	1	9	748	583	33
Harlequins	26	16	1	9	690	653	33
Wasps	26	15	1	10	717	506	31
Bath	26	15	0	11	698	574	30
London Irish	26	15	0	11	703	607	30
Newcastle	26	14	0	12	719	639	28
Richmond	26	11	2	13	720	715	22
Gloucester	26	9	1	16	554	643	19
Sale	26	9	1	16	604	731	19
Kondon Scot	26	8	0	18	491	734	16
Bedford	26	6	0	20	541	840	12
W Hartlepool	26	3	1	22	501	1007	7

Championship celebrations of 1996 after a record-breaking season in Division Two

League tables

Allied Dunbar Premiership
1999/2000

	P	W	D	L	F	A	Pts
Leicester	22	18	1	3	687	425	51
Bath	22	15	2	5	690	425	43
Gloucester	22	15	0	7	628	490	40
Saracens	22	14	0	8	729	514	37
SAINTS	**22**	**13**	**0**	**9**	**551**	**480**	**35**
Bristol	22	12	1	9	632	602	34
Wasps	22	11	1	10	640	461	31
London Irish	22	9	1	12	613	616	25
Newcastle	22	6	2	14	377	630	19
Harlequins	22	7	0	15	441	687	18
Sale	22	7	0	15	381	633	18
Bedford	22	1	0	21	396	802	3

Zurich Premiership
2000/01

	P	W	D	L	F	A	Pts
Leicester	22	18	1	3	571	346	82
Wasps	22	16	0	6	663	428	74
Bath	22	14	0	8	680	430	70
SAINTS	**22**	**13**	**0**	**9**	**518**	**463**	**59**
Saracens	22	12	0	10	589	501	58
Newcastle	22	11	0	11	554	568	57
Gloucester	22	10	0	12	473	526	48
London Irish	22	10	1	11	476	576	45
Bristol	22	9	1	12	443	492	44
Sale	22	8	1	13	561	622	43
Harlequins	22	7	0	15	440	538	38
Rotherham	22	2	0	20	335	813	12

Zurich Premiership
2001/02

	P	W	D	L	F	A	Pts
Leicester	22	18	0	4	658	348	83
Sale	22	14	1	7	589	517	69
Gloucester	22	14	0	8	692	485	68
London Irish	22	11	3	8	574	465	57
SAINTS	**22**	**12**	**1**	**9**	**506**	**426**	**56**
Newcastle	22	12	1	9	490	458	56
Wasps	22	12	0	10	519	507	54
Bristol	22	9	1	12	591	632	50
Harlequins	22	5	3	14	434	507	35
Saracens	22	7	0	15	425	671	34
Bath	22	7	0	15	311	524	33
Leeds	22	6	0	16	406	654	28

Zurich Premiership
2002/03

	P	W	D	L	F	A	Pts
Gloucester	22	17	2	3	617	396	82
Wasps	22	13	2	7	553	460	67
SAINTS	**22**	**13**	**0**	**9**	**512**	**376**	**62**
Sale	22	12	2	8	556	470	62
Leeds	22	12	2	8	478	435	58
Leicester	22	12	0	10	448	396	55
Harlequins	22	9	0	13	461	560	44
Saracens	22	8	0	14	499	587	42
London Irish	22	8	1	13	432	485	40
Newcastle	22	8	0	14	388	545	40
Bath	22	7	2	13	385	490	36
Bristol	22	7	1	14	504	633	36

Zurich Premiership
2003/04

	P	W	D	L	F	A	Pts
Bath	22	18	0	4	508	311	79
Wasps	22	16	0	6	575	406	73
SAINTS	**22**	**15**	**1**	**6**	**574**	**416**	**70**
Gloucester	22	14	0	8	491	412	63
Leicester	22	11	3	8	537	430	55
Harlequins	22	10	2	10	502	449	54
Sale	22	9	3	10	510	472	53
London Irish	22	10	1	11	427	454	49
Newcastle	22	7	2	13	497	525	45
Saracens	22	8	1	13	397	543	39
Leeds	22	7	1	14	449	588	37
Rotherham	22	0	0	22	309	770	3

Zurich Premiership
2004/05

	P	W	D	L	F	A	Pts
Leicester	22	15	3	4	665	323	78
Wasps	22	15	1	6	561	442	72
Sale	22	13	0	9	513	442	60
Bath	22	12	2	8	407	355	58
Saracens	21	11	2	8	370	415	53
Gloucester	22	10	1	11	407	487	47
Newcastle	22	9	2	11	475	596	47
Leeds	22	9	0	13	390	431	43
Worcester	22	9	0	13	385	493	42
London Irish	22	8	0	14	378	421	40
SAINTS	**22**	**8**	**0**	**14**	**410**	**473**	**40**
Harlequins	22	6	1	15	416	459	38

Coach Wayne Smith looks across Franklin's Gardens, perhaps reflecting on what might have been during his time with the Saints

Captains

1880-81	F Barker	1924	A G Bull	1967	R B Taylor
1882	A Timms	1925	R Vaughan	1968-72	D L Powell
1883	T Racer	1926	A F Blakiston	1973-74	M J Roper
1884	E Eyles	1927	R Jones	1975-76	I D Wright
1885-86	C Stanley	1928	J B Merry	1977-78	J J Page
1887	T Stanley	1929-30	W H Weston	1978-79	P Johnson
1888	E S Dunkley	1931	E Coley	1979-80	P R Sweet
1889	C Stanley	1932	T Harris	1981-82	P McGuckian
1890	A E Orton	1933-34	W H Weston	1983	V Cannon
1891	C Stanley	1935	A D Matthews	1984	J A G D Raphael
1892-93	A E Orton	1936	R J Longland	1985-86	D R Woodrow
1894-95	C H Davis	1937	T Harris	1987	G J Poole
1896	K H Kingston	1938	W H Weston	1988	G Steele-Bodger
1897	C H Davis	1939-41	G S Sturtridge	1989-91	G Pearce
1898	K H Kingston	1943-46	A P Bell	1992-93	C J Olver
1899	H B Kingston	1947	R J Longland	1994-99	T A K Rodber
1900-01	W H Kingston	1948	R W Hamp	1999-2001	P Lam
1902	H T F Weston	1949	E R Knapp	2001-02	B Pountney
1903-04	H E Kingston	1950-54	D R White	2002-04	B Pountney &
1905	R West	1955	M J Berridge		J Leslie
1906	E C Palmer	1956-57	D R White	2004-05	C Krige &
1907	J H Miles	1958	R E G Jeeps		S Thompson
1908-13	E R Mobbs	1959-61	C R Jacobs	2005-06	S Thompson &
1914	E C Cook	1962-63	P J Taylor		B Reihana
1920-22	A G Bull	1964	A R Turnell		
1923	C P Tebbitt	1965-66	C R Jacobs		

A. P. Bell   E. R. Knapp   M. J. Berridge

Early post-war captains: Bell, Knapp and Berridge
Three modern-day captains: Leslie, Krige and Thompson

England (46)
In chronological order with date of their first cap
(while playing for Northampton) and number of
caps (while playing for Northampton) in brackets
* indicates won more caps with other clubs
c indicates current international

Henry Weston (1)	March 9, 1901
Edgar Mobbs (7)	January 9, 1909
Gilbert Bull (1)	January 17, 1914
Arthur Blakiston* (8)	March 20, 1920
Bob Webb (3)	February 27, 1926
Tom Harris (2)	March 16, 1929
Eric Coley (2)	April 1, 1929
Ray Longland (19)	March 19, 1932
Billy Weston (16)	February 11, 1933
John Dicks (8)	January 20, 1934
Don White (14)	January 18, 1947
Lewis Cannell* (1)	March 29, 1948
Mike Berridge (2)	January 15, 1949
John Hyde (2)	February 25, 1950
Trevor Smith (1)	January 20, 1951
Jeff Butterfield (28)	February 28, 1953
Phil Taylor (6)	January 22, 1955
Frank Sykes (4)	February 26, 1955
Ron Jacobs (29)	January 21, 1956
Dickie Jeeps (24)	January 21, 1956
Jim Hetherington (6)	February 1, 1958
Martin Underwood (4)	January 20, 1962
Roger Hosen* (5)	May 25, 1963
Andy Hancock (3)	February 27, 1965
David Powell (11)	January 15, 1966
Keith Savage (13)	January 15, 1966
Bob Taylor (16)	January 15, 1966
Trevor Wintle (5)	March 19, 1966
Peter Larter (24)	January 7, 1967
Jim Parsons (4)	January 20, 1968
Derek Prout (2)	January 20, 1968
Bryan West (4)	December 20, 1969
Chris Wardlow* (5)	January 16, 1971
Ian Wright (4)	January 16, 1971
Jacko Page* (1)	March 15, 1975
Gary Pearce (36)	February 3, 1979
John Olver (3)	November 3, 1990
Martin Bayfield (31)	July 20, 1991
Tim Rodber (44)	January 18, 1992
Ian Hunter (7)	October 17, 1992
Matt Dawson* (c)	December 16, 1995
Paul Grayson (32)	December 16, 1995
Nick Beal (15)	December 14, 1996
Ben Cohen (c)	February 5, 2000
Steve Thompson (c)	February 2, 2002
Robbie Morris (2)	February 22, 2003

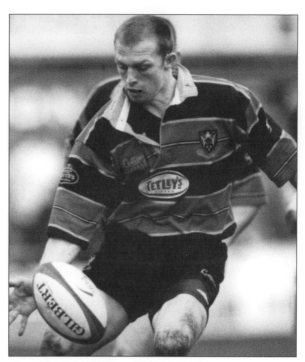

Most England caps – Matt Dawson

Newest cap – Robbie Morris

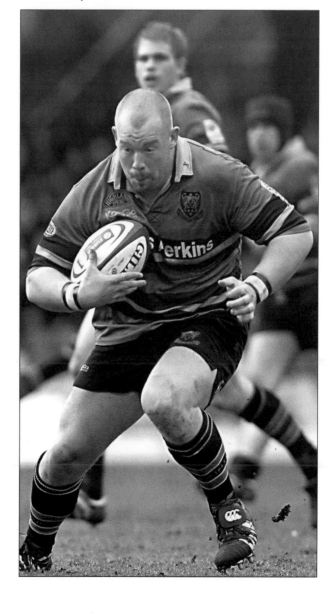

Internationals

Ireland (3)

Niall Bailey (1)	March 29, 1952
Jonathan Bell* (13)	November 18, 1995
Allen Clarke* (6)	November 18, 1995

Scotland (13)

Tommy Gray (3)	March 18, 1950
Rodger Arneil* (4)	January 15, 1972
Neil Edwards* (1)	January 15, 1994
Peter Walton* (6)	February 15, 1994
Michael Dods* (5)	November 18, 1995
Gregor Townsend* (20)	November 18, 1995
Mattie Stewart (34)	December 14, 1996
Budge Pountney (31)	November 21, 1998
Craig Moir (3)	March 18, 2000
Richard Metcalfe* (3)	April 2, 2000
Steve Brotherstone* (3)	November 4, 2000
John Leslie* (7)	March 17, 2001
Tom Smith* (c)	September 22, 2001

Wales (4)

Bobby Jones (3)	January 16, 1926
Wick Powell* (3)	January 19, 1935
Allan Bateman* (15)	June 5, 1999
Steve Williams* (8)	June 8, 2002

France (1)

Olivier Brouzet* (10)	November 4, 2000

Italy (1)

Luca Martin* (14)	November 11, 2000

Argentina (2)

Federico Mendez* (8)	November 7, 1998
Martin Scelzo* (3)	June 3, 2000

Samoa (1)

Pat Lam* (13)	September 22, 1998

British Lions Tourists
1955 (South Africa)
Jeff Butterfield, Dickie Jeeps, Frank Sykes
1959 (Australia, New Zealand)
Jeff Butterfield, Dickie Jeeps
1962 (South Africa)
Dickie Jeeps
1966 (New Zealand)
David Powell, Keith Savage
1968 (South Africa)
Peter Larter, Keith Savage, Bob Taylor, Bryan West
1993 (New Zealand)
Martin Bayfield, Ian Hunter
1997 (South Africa)
Nick Beal, Matt Dawson, Paul Grayson, Tim Rodber,
Gregor Townsend
2001 (Australia)
Ben Cohen, Matt Dawson
2005 (New Zealand)
Steve Thompson

Lions appearances
Jeff Butterfield (4), Dickie Jeeps (13), Keith Savage (4),
Bob Taylor (4), Peter Larter (1), Martin Bayfield (3),
Tim Rodber (2), Matt Dawson (5), Gregor Townsend (2),
Steve Thompson (2)

■ In 1899 and 1904 Blair Swannell was capped seven times
by a British touring side, an early forerunner of the Lions

Wick Powell (Wales)

Rodger Arneil (Scotland)